LEARNING MATHEMATICS

Learning Mathematics

The Cognitive Science Approach to Mathematics Education

Robert B. Davis

Ablex Publishing Corporation
New Jersey

Third printing 1990

© 1984 Robert B. Davis

First published in the United States of America 1984
by Ablex Publishing Corporation, 355 Chestnut Street,
Norwood, New Jersey 07648

Library of Congress Cataloging in Publication Data

Davis, Robert B. (Robert Benjamin), 1926-
    Learning Mathematics.

    Bibliography: p.
    Includes index.
    1. Mathematics—study and teaching. 2. Cognition in
children. I. Title
QA11.D365   1984   510'.7'1   84-2853
ISBN 0-89391-245-X

CONTENTS

ACKNOWLEDGEMENTS

Since 1957, the teachers and researchers associated with the Madison Project have been developing improved curricula to help students learn mathematics. They have also been collecting data on student performance, with particular emphasis on following the same students for as long as possible, preferably for at least five years, on the assumption that the most important results of education develop slowly and reveal themselves over reasonably long intervals of time. One always wonders: what will those students be like in two years? In five years? In ten years? One is not primarily interested in 'what will that student be like in two weeks?'

Beginning in 1974, and building on earlier work, some Madison Project teachers assumed responsibility for creating a new mathematics curriculum at University High School ('Uni'), the Laboratory School at the University of Illinois in Urbana, Illinois. From that time until the present, they have created curricula, taught courses and observed student performance at Uni, for students in grades seven through twelve. The student observations, reported especially in Davis, Jockusch and McKnight (1978), constitute what has come to be called the Long Term Study, because again the same students have been followed for five consecutive years, or even longer.

The observations of junior and senior high school students at Uni have been supplemented by observations of elementary school students at Booker T. Washington Elementary School, Champaign, Illinois, by community college students at Parkland Community College, by university students at the University of Illinois, by various categories of adult experts and by additional students elsewhere.

The original idea for this book was that it would be a report of the methods and results of the Long Term Study. This goal was modified for at least two reasons.

First, there is at present a tug-of-war going on in education, between a 'drill-and-practice' and 'back-to-basics' orientation that focuses primarily on memorizing mathematics as meaningless rote algorithms, vs. an approach based upon 'understanding' and 'making creative use' of mathematics. The outcome of this struggle − or competition − will be important for American education. The issues are complex, but many of them can be analyzed and evaluated.

Second, the moment we attempted to report on the Long Term Study it became apparent that this was only one part of what is going on nowadays in mathematics education. A new approach to the study of knowledge itself has developed from Piaget's observations of children, from computer scientists' development of 'intelligent' computer programs, and from research into human information-processing capabilities. Any attempt to separate the Long Term Study from other recent work seemed artificial and unjustified. We have been aware of work by Matz, Minsky, Papert, Greeno, Simon, Brown, Rissland, Karplus, Steffe, Shumway and others, and they have often been aware of our work. Hence it seemed wiser and more useful to take a broader look at this so-called *cognitive science* approach, and to try to use the results to help illuminate the controversy over 'rote learning' vs. 'understanding'. That decision determined the shape of the present book.

It is our hope that this volume will be of interest both to researchers in the area of cognitive studies, and also to teachers and those who are studying to become teachers.

Whatever part of this volume may prove valuable owes its worth to many contributors. The Long Term Study itself was carried out by Curtis C. McKnight, Elizabeth Jockusch, Stephen Young, Patrick McLoughlin, Katie Reynolds Hannibal, Jodie Douglas and the author, assisted in various ways by James Raths, Alan Purves, Hester Suggs, Mary Ann McClary, Janet Neathery, Patricia Bandy, Katie Schoeneweiss and Carol Erb. For financial assistance in the preparation of this manuscript I want to thank Dean Linda Wilson and The Research Board of the University of Illinois.

The *cognitive science theory* which provides the foundation for modern research of this type began largely as the creation of Jean Piaget, Marvin Minsky, Seymour Papert, Herbert Simon and Adriaan de Groot, with recognizable contributions from Kurt Lewin, George Miller and others.

The *data collection* method – using task-based interviews – was developed primarily by Piaget, Herbert Ginsburg, Jack Easley and Stanley Erlwanger, among others.

That the combination of this theory and this data collection method has moved forward to the point of addressing important problems in a useful way is due to a sizeable outpouring of excellent work by Marilyn Matz, Andrea di Sessa, John Seely Brown, Edwina Rissland, Robert Karplus, Karen Fuson, Jill Larkin, James Greeno and others.

The *teaching approach* used at University High School owes debts to many inspired teachers, including at least Beryl S. Cochran, Leonard

Sealey, David Page, Caleb Gattegno, Norman Levinson, Donald Cohen, Douglas McGregor, Earl Kelley, Nathaniel Cantor, Cynthia Parsons, George Polya, Katherine Kharas, Gordon Clem and W. Warwick Sawyer. Unknown to most of these, a somewhat similar approach was developed independently by R.L. Moore at the University of Texas.

Most of the data reported in this volume comes either from the Long Term Study, or from work of Robert Lawler, Stanley Erlwanger, John Clement, Peter Rosnick, Jack Lochhead, James Kaput, Jamesine Friend and Robert Karplus.

My own education in such matters owes much to Donald Michie.

Finally, without inspiration and argument from Ian Westbury this volume would never have been written.

1 'MATHEMATICS' AND 'MATHEMATICS EDUCATION'

Mathematics Today

In the United States today, mathematics has come to play a remarkably important role: the engineering of highways, the search for energy, the design for TV sets, the profitable operation of most businesses, astronauts flying spacecraft, the study of epidemics, the navigation of ships at sea – all depend upon mathematics. For an individual, career and financial prospects depend heavily upon how much mathematics that person has learned, and how complete a mastery he or she has achieved, with generally more rewarding and better paying careers being available mainly to those who have learned more mathematics. From a social point of view, modern science, technology, manufacture – even farming – depend increasingly upon mathematics.

Consequently, for both social and personal reasons, there has developed a growing interest in how one learns mathematics, how one thinks through the analysis of mathematical problems. Notice that there are two distinct subjects involved here: the study of mathematics itself, and the study of how one studies mathematics. This second subject is sometimes called 'mathematics education', or 'didactics of mathematics' or 'cognitive studies of mathematical performance'. Mathematics education, which is what this book deals with, is not the same as mathematics; but, on the other hand, the two subjects are not entirely different, either. Usually a person studying mathematics is at least partly interested in the question of 'how anyone would ever think of that in the first place', and whether they themselves are understanding the subject correctly. Clearly, this sort of concern represents a crossing of the line of demarcation; 'mathematics' very often includes some important aspects of 'mathematics education'.

Mathematics Education Today

At the present time, the study of mathematics education is experiencing a rapid change of direction. Some of the liveliest, most creative

1

researchers in the United States have turned to the question of how the human mind deals with mathematical ideas. Their research studies are using new methods, and their analysis of human mathematical thinking is itself beginning to take the shape of an important area of study.

The Problems of Mathematics Education

Mathematics might be said to deal with the basic patterns that human beings find in (or impose upon) their environments. What, then, does 'mathematics education' deal with? Presumably the way that human beings *think about, communicate about* or *learn to deal with* these basic patterns. But when we view mathematics in this way, it becomes clear that the information processing – the 'thinking' – that is involved in mathematics is not very different at all from the most basic kinds of thinking that human beings must do. Hence it is not surprising to find cognitive scientists turning often to the study of mathematical thought in order to learn about human thought in general – at the fundamental levels, 'thinking' about almost any complex area of knowledge is similar to thinking within almost any other complex area, and it makes little difference whether our concern is 'human information processing related to reading comprehension', or 'human information processing related to playing chess', or 'human information processing related to finding your way around New York City' or 'human information processing in mathematics'.

We could, consequently, defend the studies of mathematical thought as an important part of basic cognitive science, the general study of how human beings think. But mathematics education can also make a more specific contribution – namely, to improving teaching, learning and creative thought in mathematics – and in the present section we shall look briefly at this specific 'mathematical' role of mathematics education.

Mathematics education as a discipline could be said to date from around 1900, particularly in the work of David Eugene Smith and J.W.A. Young, at the University of Chicago and at Teachers College, Columbia University. Now this confronts us with something of a paradox; the study of mathematics itself dates back at least several thousand years, as we know from research on Ishango, not to mention Euclid and Archimedes,[1] and has been of considerable importance for centuries. How can the study of mathematics be so old, and the study of mathematical thinking be so new?

The answer is probably that mathematics education is in this respect somewhat like medicine — centuries ago there was very little sense of control, and more acceptance of fate, in both fields. If many infants died, that was what happened; only in recent years have we adopted the point of view that every single infant death must have a rational cause, that these causes must become known, and that this knowledge must be on so fundamental a level that appropriate interventions can be devised. The modern point of view has virtually eliminated polio, entirely eliminated smallpox, provided a measure of control for diabetes, and greatly reduced the impact of cardio-vascular diseases. Interestingly enough, though, strong traces of ancient fatalistic attitudes still survive into late twentieth-century medicine: we tend to regard the common cold as 'just one of those things', and many diseases of old age, such as arthritis and failing vision, are commonly accepted as essentially inevitable and incurable.

It has been known for centuries that some people acquire a powerful command of mathematics, but most people do not. This, too, used to be considered part of the natural scheme of things, further reinforced by individual life-style decisions and by the economic needs of society. We are less disposed to accept such things fatalistically nowadays. If a person *wants* to learn certain mathematics, we are less inclined to accept the verdict that he or she cannot do so. We want more specific information; we want to know *exactly what* obstacles impede this person's progress, *exactly what* they cannot seem to do, *exactly what* errors they are making and why they make them.

I do not want to overstate the case: at the present time we cannot help everyone to learn all the mathematics they may want to know, nor can we always pinpoint (much less eliminate) every specific obstacle that blocks a learner's path to knowledge. But in this respect, also, mathematics education parallels medicine, which cannot cure every cancer, nor even every respiratory infection, nor diagnose every pain — yet modern medicine is of tremendous value. Consider the difference between our grandparents' acceptance of the inevitability of heart attacks, as opposed to modern studies of (and use of) diet, exercise, cholesterol, stress tests, catheterization, coronary artery bypass operations, valve implants and electronic heart pacers. We cannot overcome every educational problem related to the teaching and learning of mathematics, much less turn every student into a twentieth-century Archimedes, but we are beginning to get a more precise and detailed description of how human beings think about mathematical problems, and this can move us towards far more control, and far less need for fatalistic acceptance of everyday obstacles to learning.

Recent Studies of Educational Effectiveness

Later in this book we shall look in detail at some studies of student knowledge that have been carried out by Clement, Lochhead and their colleagues, at the University of Massachusetts. Similar studies have been undertaken by Bert Green and colleagues at Johns Hopkins, by Andrea di Sessa and his colleagues at MIT, and by several other investigators elsewhere. These studies may point to an important direction for the future, for two reasons: in the first place, they all show that many university students have actually learned far less than everyone had assumed. Students who have completed five or more years of studying mathematics in high school and college may still have very wrong ideas about *variables* (or 'unknowns', 'literals', etc. – the ubiquitous x's and y's of algebra). This, despite the fact that these same students were thought to have learned about linear equations, systems of linear equations, quadratic equations, graphs of conic sections, and many other things *that depend upon a correct understanding of variables*. At first glance this may seem to be impossible: how can you learn something that depends fundamentally upon various things you don't know? Later in this book we shall see an answer: *different types of 'learning' are possible*. One type does depend upon certain skills, concepts and understandings. Another type does not. This is not entirely mysterious. A singer may sing German lieder without in fact possessing any real command of German as a language; the singing can be a matter of imitation. So in this example we see two different behaviors: the use of German as a language, where the words and phrases have meaning; and, second, the use of German as a set of sounds to be produced imitatively. This is probably a passable parallel to the two different mathematical behaviors, one of which builds on understanding, and the other of which does not. The implications of this unsuspected deficit in student knowledge are extremely far-reaching.

The Clement, Green, etc., studies are interesting also for a second reason; in several cases this work has been carried out in university departments of physics, in departments of mathematics or in departments of engineering. This represents an increased commitment by a few university departments to understanding the precise nature of student difficulties, and hopefully gaining the means of overcoming some of these difficulties. If this small beginning in fact represents a trend, the results for university education can be dramatic, and the implications for mathematics education no less so.

Note

1. One of the earliest records of sophisticated mathematics was found two decades ago in central Africa. Cf. Jean de Heinzelin, 'Ishango', *Scientific American* (June 1962), pp. 105-16.

Questions to Think About

1. Suppose you had a student who had never studied positive and negative numbers — that is to say, he or she does not know about $^-2$, or $^+3$, or the fact that $5 - 6 = ^-1$, and so on.

You want to introduce this student, for the first time, to the idea that

$$6 - 10 = ^-4$$

and

$$10 - 6 = ^+4$$

and

$$5 - 6 = ^-1$$

What would you do? (You may want to plan several days of preliminary activities if you think they will help.) Assume that the student is around 11 or 12 years old.

2. Suppose that you observe Marcia, a third-grade girl, solving the problem

$$\begin{array}{r} 7{,}002 \\ - 25 \\ \hline \end{array}$$

by writing

$$\begin{array}{r} 61 \\ \cancel{7}{,}002 \\ - 25 \\ \hline 7 \end{array}$$

$$\begin{array}{r} 5 \\ \not{6}\ 11 \\ \not{7},002 \\ -\ \ \ \ 25 \\ \hline 87 \end{array}$$

$$\begin{array}{r} 5 \\ \not{6}\ 11 \\ \not{7},002 \\ -\ \ \ \ 25 \\ \hline 5,087 \end{array}$$

(a) How would you try to help Marcia?

(b) How would you modify the school's instructional program so that future students would be more likely to avoid this error?

3. Bill is in grade 2 (seven years old) and has not yet met *fractions*. Which idea or ideas about fractions do you want Bill to learn first? What activities or learning experiences would you provide for Bill, so that he could learn these ideas?

4. Suppose you are teaching a third-grade class (about eight-year-olds). You are discussing the problem

$$\begin{array}{r} 64 \\ -\ 28 \\ \hline \end{array}$$

and you have explained that 'you can't take 8 from 4', when one of the third graders, a boy whom we'll call K., interrupts and says: 'Oh, yes, you can! Four minus eight is negative four

$$\begin{array}{r} 64 \\ -\ 28 \\ \hline {}^{-}4 \end{array}$$,

and sixty minus twenty is forty

$$\begin{array}{r} 64 \\ -\ 28 \\ \hline {}^{-}4 \\ 40 \\ \hline 36 \end{array}$$

What would you say to K., the third-grade boy who carried out this unusual computation?

5. What kinds of geometry should students learn about in grades 4, 5 and 6? Why? Which kinds of geometry would NOT seem appropriate?

6. From your own personal experiences, can you identify some situation, occurrence or problem that involved mathematical thinking — especially some difficulty, unpleasantness or uncertainty? If we had had available a well-developed theory of mathematics education, how might this have helped you, or helped your teacher to help you?

2 WHAT IS MATHEMATICS?

Before we look in depth at how people learn mathematics, and how people think about mathematics, we need to look briefly at what mathematics actually is, and how it is used. The necessity of doing this comes from the widespread misunderstanding of mathematics. Because mathematics has often been badly taught, many people misunderstand the true nature of the subject; and, in an unhappy circularity, because so many people misunderstand what mathematics is all about, the subject almost inevitably continues to be badly taught.

To most people, 'mathematics' means the arithmetic they studied in school, plus a little high school algebra, geometry or trigonometry. In the past, these subjects have commonly been taught by rote. The result is that people hold the erroneous view that mathematics is mainly a matter of learning a few rules and then following them precisely. This is hardly a correct view of what mathematics really is, or of how it is learned, or of how it is used in later life. It leads to a quite wrong notion of what it is that our students really need to learn.

Rote Mathematics vs. Meaningful Mathematics

Arithmetic, as we have said, is commonly learned by rote; the student is told what to do and how to do it, and that is about all that happens — that, plus a substantial amount of drill and practice.

Our main goal in this book is to study how people *think* about mathematics, and in later chapters we shall be looking at 'rote mathematics' vs. 'meaningful mathematics' from the point of view of differences in thought processes, but viewing matters in such a light is a complex task which requires certain advance preparations. Let us, for the moment, consider the distinction between 'rote mathematics' and 'meaningful mathematics' from a somewhat simpler point of view: The way students *learn* new ideas in mathematics.

As an illustration, it is not uncommon for students to be told to add

$$325$$
$$+\ 198$$

by the usual algorithm: five plus eight is thirteen, write the '3' and carry the '1' . . .

$$
\begin{array}{r}
1 \\
325 \\
+\ 198 \\
\hline
3
\end{array}
$$

. . . now, in the next column, add $1 + 2 + 9$ to get twelve, write the '2' and carry the '1'

$$
\begin{array}{r}
11 \\
325 \\
+\ 198 \\
\hline
23
\end{array}
$$

. . . and, finally, add $1 + 3 + 1$ to get five, and write '5':

$$
\begin{array}{r}
11 \\
325 \\
+\ 198 \\
\hline
523
\end{array}
$$

Suppose that this algorithm has been taught by rote. What has been left out? We would ordinarily say that *meaning* and *understanding* have been omitted. But that answer raises another question: what, then, do we mean by 'meaning' and 'understanding'? Later in this book, after we have studied mental representations of knowledge, we will speak of this in terms of *the creation of appropriate frames*, but our best answer in this chapter will be to consider a contrasting way of teaching the addition algorithm.

Around 1960, the Hungarian-born British educator Zoltan Dienes introduced a special set of blocks known as Multibase Arithmetic Blocks. (Despite the implied redundancy of the designation, we shall refer to these as 'MAB blocks'.) MAB blocks are available in a base ten set, in a base six set, a base five set, a base three set, and to other bases as well. We shall be concerned primarily with the base ten set (cf. Figure 2.1). The smallest block in this set is a cube, about (or exactly, depending on the company from which they are purchased) one centimeter along an edge. We shall call such blocks *units*. If you imagine ten units lined up in a row and glued together in that con-

Figure 2.1: Dienes' MAB blocks, base ten.

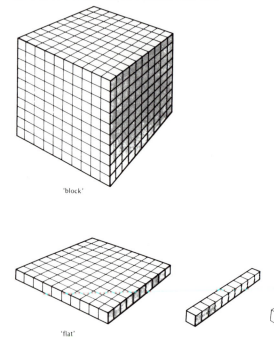

'block'

'flat'

'long'   'unit'

figuration, you have a *long*. (Following Dienes, we use the word 'long' as a noun in this context; doing so will simplify the language in some situations.) If you imagine ten longs laid side by side, then glued together, you have a *flat* ('flat', too, will be used as a noun). Finally, stack up ten flats, glue them together, and you have a *block*. (There are certain peculiarities in this language, but it works well in typical discussions with students. If this seems hard to believe, consider the way the word 'ball' is used in baseball.)

Different educators use MAB blocks in different ways. We present here an introduction to column addition developed by The Madison Project.

First Exercise. A child (or group of children) have, say, the array of MAB blocks shown in Figure 2.2. They draw pictures of the array they have (or, if the children are unable to draw pictures, they may use stickers with units, longs, etc., shown on them in order to depict the array).

Figure 2.2: The first array of Dienes' MAB blocks, representing one 'thousand', two 'hundreds', three 'tens' and eight 'ones'. The student begins with actual wooden blocks, then makes a record of the block display, either by drawing, or by using stickers that show units, longs, etc.

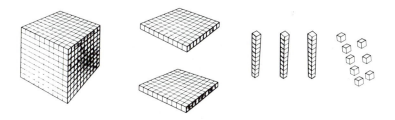

Figure 2.3: The second array of MAB blocks, also presented as tangible wooden blocks, then recorded by drawings or stickers.

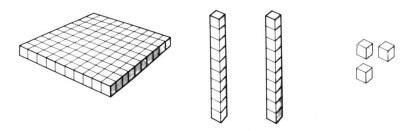

They are now given the array shown in Figure 2.3, and they draw it. Both of the original arrays are displayed on a large sheet of poster board, marked with column headings as in Figure 2.4, and the drawings are also made on large paper with corresponding columns (but without the headings, so as to avoid confusion in counting).

All of the blocks are now pushed together, keeping each kind of block in its appropriate column. The result is drawn (or depicted by using stickers). After completion of this task, the written record should look like Figure 2.5.

The important point is that:

(i) *an actual physical act has been carried out*;
(ii) *the drawing is a written record of what actually happened.*
In this sense, the drawing has a perfectly clear meaning: *it*

Figure 2.4: Actual wooden blocks are placed on poster board. (Column headings are merely pictures, printed on the poster board.)

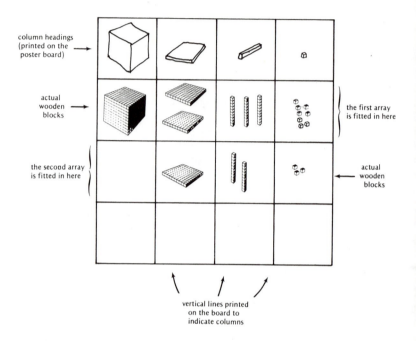

column headings (printed on the poster board) →

actual wooden → blocks

the second array is fitted in here

the first array is fitted in here

actual → wooden blocks

vertical lines printed on the board to indicate columns

is a written record of what we did. It is thus similar to the minutes of a meeting, or to the statistics that are kept after a baseball game has been played.

Second Exercise. After the first exercise has been mastered, the students are introduced to the Second Exercise. For this, we proceed exactly as in the First Exercise, with one important exception; we now proclaim the Rule: *thou shall not have ten*! Whenever you find yourself with ten pieces of the same shape, you must make a ten-for-one trade with the 'banker'. This trading is natural, because ten units look like, and feel like, one long; ten longs look like, and feel like, one flat; and so on.

The Thou-shall-not-have-ten rule introduces the usual arrangements for 'carrying', and — *after we have carried out a full transaction* — we end up with a written record such as the one shown in Figure 2.6.

Figure 2.5: Pictorial record of what happens can be kept on 'butcher paper', which is available on rolls.

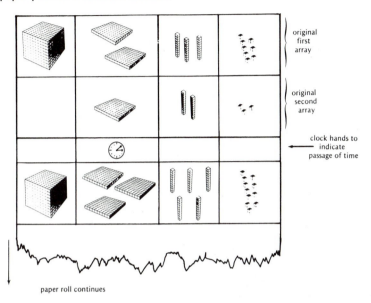

original
first
array

original
second
array

clock hands to
indicate
passage of time

paper roll continues

Subsequent Exercises

After the Second Exercise is mastered, subsequent exercises move the students gradually into the standard algorithm: by substituting tally marks for pictures, then numerals for tally marks, and then finally eliminating the intermediate steps.

Our immediate purpose is to indicate two quite different ways that one could teach children about column addition with 'carrying' for place-value numerals: in the first method, the child is told what to write, and where to write it. No reasons are given; the method is what one usually calls 'rote'. In the second method, certain operations with wooden blocks are carried out; a written record of these operations is kept, at first primarily a pictorial record, but this pictorial record is gradually made into a more abstract 'shorthand', and gradually becomes the standard algorithm. Thus, in one sense at least, a 'meaning' is provided: the algorithm is a recognizable written record of an actual occurrence. Consequently, a child can 'understand' this record the same way a child can understand his or her own essay on 'What I did over the summer vacation'. Both records deal with the student's actual past experiences.

Figure 2.6: Pictorial record of what has happened.

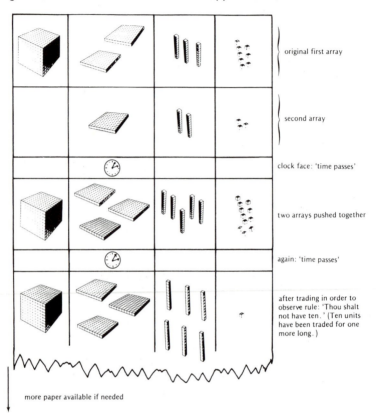

| | | | | original first array |
| second array |
| clock face: 'time passes' |
| two arrays pushed together |
| again: 'time passes' |
| after trading in order to observe rule: 'Thou shalt not have ten.' (Ten units have been traded for one more long.) |

more paper available if needed

The distinction between 'meaningful' mathematics and 'rote' mathematics is not so easy to draw as one might at first imagine, but it is one of the most fundamental aspects of learning mathematics and thinking about mathematical problems. It will be an important theme throughout this book, weaving its way through the fabric of everything we consider.

Creative Mathematics

'Rote' vs. 'meaningful' is one distinction; a related, but different, distinction could be called the *routine* vs. *creative* dimension. Just as the average person probably imagines that mathematics should normally be taught by rote, the average person probably also assumes that the typical use of mathematics is *routine*; that is to say, one does what one was taught to do, and does it the way that one was taught. This kind of routine use of mathematics undoubtedly does exist, but a quite different use of mathematics is becoming increasingly important – a kind of use that we shall call *creative*, where either the relevant mathematics was not taught to you in school, or else the present method of using it was not taught in school.

That 'creative' uses of mathematics are becoming more common should be clear, for many reasons:

(i) increasingly inexpensive digital computer components are making it possible to use machines for almost any operation that is routine and repetitious;

(ii) the fact that more new mathematics is created every year, and more new opportunities for using mathematics are created every year, means that each generation must expect to go beyond what previous generations knew and did.

Designing a more fuel-efficient automobile involves new calculations, not merely repetitions of old calculations – as one realizes in looking at the new shapes of recent fuel-efficient cars. A composer, using a computer to help him or her create a new piece of music, is not merely repeating the calculations of previous generations. Estimating the effect of a new tax bill on the national economy can require new considerations and new kinds of calculations.

But perhaps we are prepared to accept innovation in such exotic areas as computer-generated music and automotive engineering. However, the true arguments for creativity in mathematics bring matters much closer to home. *The average person, the average student, and the average teacher are inevitably involved with creative mathematics.* We consider now six reasons why a creative approach is necessary:

1. The Complexity of Mathematics

If there were only a few mathematical techniques that needed to be learned, one might consider the possibility of the rote teaching of routine methods. This is not the case. The number of mathematical techniques that may be needed is exceedingly large, far too large to be taught in their entirety. What one must do, instead, is to try to enable students to make new combinations of old methods, even to extend old methods. (In the ideal case, we would even like the student to be able to invent new methods, which is not so impossible as it may sound.)

We can teach the solution of quadratic equations, but there is a vast range of problems where students will have to rely upon ingenuity and originality in order to concoct appropriate methods of solution. The equation

$$e^{2t} - 5e^t + 6 = 0$$

may not be a kind the student has seen before, but by clever thought the student ought to be able to solve it; the same is true if we are interested in the value of an unknown t, determined by the system of equations

$$\begin{cases} 3e^X + (1 + t)y = 2 \\ e^X + ty = 0 \\ 2e^X + 3ty = {}^-2 \end{cases}$$

The resourceful, knowledgeable student can even solve the equation

$$\ln X^{1nx} - 9 \ln x + 14 = 0,$$

but the uncreative student may not be able to do so.

2. Students Do Invent Original Solutions

Learning to Add

Patrick Suppes, Guy Groen, Lauren Resnick and their colleagues in a series of studies,[1] have made precise measurements of the response times (so-called 'latencies') when students solve certain elementary arithmetic problems. By this means one can discriminate between different methods of solution, because some methods take longer than others. Consider an addition problem, such as 5 + 2. At least eight different methods might be distinguished:

(a) The 'Count-ALL' Method, With Concrete Counters. Count five fingers (or use some other concrete objects to count), count two fingers (or other objects), now count *all* of them together: 1, 2, 3, 4, 5, 6, 7. This is fairly time consuming, and indeed wastes time, because some of the work is unnecessary.

(b) Count On, From Two, With Concrete Counters. It is not really necessary to count *each* collection twice (as is done in Method a). Having counted two objects, merely count on for *five more*. This should take less time than Method a. In effect, one says: 3, 4, 5, 6, 7.

(c) Count On, From Five, With Concrete Objects. This method is the same as Method b, except that the collection of five objects is not recounted; 'counting on' from the five merely requires counting: 'six, seven'. Hence this method takes less time than either Method a or Method b (and, if one number is quite a bit larger than the other, this method can be substantially faster).

(d) The 'Choice' Method, With Concrete Objects. For two numbers A and B, this method involves first noticing which is larger, A or B. One then chooses the larger collection as the one that should *not* be counted twice. In other words: start with the larger of A or B, and count on from there.

The dramatic differences reported by Resnick and her colleagues do not, however, deal with counting using physical counters, but rather with the four corresponding methods — call them a^1, b^1, c^1 and d^1 — where the child does not bother with counting external physical objects, but (presumably) counts some kind of abstract counters in his or her mind. At this more abstract level, a remarkable thing occurs.

Resnick and Groen worked with four-year-olds, and themselves provided the instruction, so they knew what the children had been taught — specifically, they had been taught Method a, with concrete objects to count. Within weeks, however, most of the children had abandoned the use of external physical objects as counters, and found sums by some form of internal thought process. By precise measurement of response times, Resnick and Groen were able to determine which method — a^1, b^1, c^1 or d^1 — the children were using. What they found was that the majority of the children were using Method d^1, the most sophisticated and most efficient of the eight methods, *and a method which they had not been taught*! Indeed, a method very different from what the children had been taught. From a number of studies of this type, it is clear the *the vast majority of school children invent their own methods for solving mathematics problems.* Notice that this applies *even to problems that might be thought to be routine.*

Given these studies by Resnick, Groen and their colleagues, it seems to be the case that a completely routine approach to mathematics — 'doing exactly what you're told to do, and nothing more' — is very nearly nonexistent. We may (or may not) present mathematics to children this way, but this is not the way that the children learn it.

Peter's Method for Finding Per Cents

With older children, simple observation shows a great diversity of solution methods, extending quite beyond what is taught in school. Peter, a 17-year-old high school senior, was asked to make up a per cent problem, and to solve it. He made up this problem:

> Ten is what per cent of twelve?

Here is what Peter said aloud as he solved the problem:

> You've got one sixth left over ... so ... you need to figure out how to get 6 out of 100. Six times fifteen is ninety ... so you've got 15 and a little bit more. You've got 6 left over, so it's 16 ... ... You've got 4 left over, so it's two thirds, or point six six six and so on, so that's sixteen point six six six (forever). Now, you need the opposite [sic!] of that ... that subtracted from 100 — so you've got eight three point three three three three (forever) percent.

It seems next to certain that Peter was never *taught* this method of thinking about per cent. How could you teach a method like this?

3. The Need to Recognize Originality

In a third-grade class in Weston, Connecticut, the teacher was showing the class how to subtract when 'borrowing' or 're-grouping' was necessary; she had written

$$\begin{array}{r} 64 \\ -28 \\ \hline \end{array}$$

and she was saying 'Now, I can't take eight from four, so ...' when Kye, a third-grade boy, interrupted. Here is what Kye said and wrote:

Kye said	Kye wrote
Oh, yes, you can!	64
Eight from four is negative four	$\begin{array}{r} -28 \\ \hline {}^-4 \end{array}$

. . . and twenty from sixty	64
is forty . . .	− 28
	‾4
	40

. . . and negative four and	64
forty is thirty-six . . .	− 28
	‾4
	40
	36

The teacher had never seen this algorithm before. In fact, nobody in Weston, Connecticut had seen this algorithm before. Essentially, it was an original discovery by Kye Hedlund, a third-grade boy.

Kye thought his method made sense, and was even a rather good way to do subtraction problems. But suppose you had been Kye's teacher. What would you have done? And what effect would your action have had on Kye?

4. How to Make Classes Dull

One additional consequence of teaching mathematics as a collection of routine procedures to be learned by rote is to make class lessons extremely dull. This dullness is not inevitable. Treated for what it really is — an exploration of a rich world of possibilities and a persistent challenge — mathematics can be exciting, and mathematics classes can be fun.

5. Sometimes Originality Is the Very Thing We Need to Teach

In some mathematics subjects, originality is the very thing we are trying to teach. Hence, if we eliminate originality, we destroy our main goal.

That is clearly true if we are teaching the writing of poetry, the composing of music or the painting of pictures. It is often equally true within mathematics. Consider the case of geometry; in teaching Euclidean synthetic geometry we probably have three main goals:

(i)   to show how a mathematical system can be developed by starting with an explicit set of axioms, and by establishing additional statements through the use of explicit methods of formal logic;

(ii) to give students some analytical knowledge about the nature of one model of physical space;

(iii) to help students learn how to make original proofs of theorems.

All too often, tenth-grade geometry courses lose this last goal entirely because they treat mathematics as merely a routine process of following directions, instead of helping students to develop their individual analytical skills.

6. Mathematics In the Real World

Finally, if one watches to see where mathematics is used in the real world, one finds that these uses are by no means as routine as is often imagined. In World War II, US submarines were equipped with a new version of radar. Whether this increased, or decreased, their vulnerability to attack by enemy aircraft was, in fact, a mathematical question, which many submarine captains misinterpreted and solved incorrectly, leading them to make some wrong decisions. But this could hardly have been taught to them when they were in school; hence it became a question of how shrewdly they analyzed the new situation that they suddenly found themselves in.

Are there unsafe intersections in your community? If so, is this a *mathematical* problem?

If you have savings, how wisely are they invested? To what extent is this a mathematical problem? Are interest rates today similar to what they were twenty years ago? If not, many people need to have adjusted their thinking to the new situation; do you suppose that most of them have done so?

Finally, we reproduce a mathematics problem which one mathematician has described as his favorite problem from any mathematics textbook. Here is the problem — in its entirety it consists only of seven words:

A pile of coal catches on fire.

In what sense is this a mathematics problem?

Summary

For six reasons creativity is a proper part of learning mathematics: (i) mathematics is too complex and too vast to learn by rote; (ii) students do invent original solutions as a regular daily event; (iii) we need to be able to respond to surprising and original contributions that other people (including our students!) may make; (iv) learning mathematics by rote and routine is dull and unmotivating; learning it creatively is exciting and interesting (at least for many people); (v) sometimes our specific goal is to teach originality, as in learning to make original proofs of geometric theorems; (vi) in real-world uses of mathematics, creativity is often required.

Note

1. Cf. Suppes and Groen, 1967; Groen and Parkman, 1972; Groen and Poll, 1973; Woods, Resnick and Groen, 1975; Resnick, 1976.

Questions for Consideration

1. Can you solve the three 'non-routine' mathematics problems mentioned earlier in this chapter?

2. Try to go through Peter's solution of the per cent problem and explain every single step that he takes, and each remark that he makes.

3   THE ROLE OF THEORY IN SCIENCE

Anyone who looks carefully at education today will surely be struck by its complexity, and by the profound disagreements about methods and goals. Hence it is hardly surprising that educators concerned with improving education have sought to build a 'scientific' foundation for their work. Science, after all, has seemed to hold the promise of simplicity, agreement and objectivity — and, in many fields, *progress*.

Yet somehow most past attempts to deal 'scientifically' with education have failed. They have not provided the means for achieving a far more effective educational system; they have typically not led to important new ideas and new discoveries. Little that has been learned has seemed useful to teachers. As David Hawkins (1966) has said, it has been apparent that the practical (and intuitive) 'know-how' of the best practitioners has seemed to be more valuable than the theory of the best theorists.

To some people, this is seen as proof that education is not merely 'applied science'; there is something *more* to education than most 'scientific' studies have been able to reveal. This may well be the case.

There is, however, another possibility and one which underlies the present book: perhaps the attempts to use the methods of science have failed because science has been misunderstood.

In these attempts it had been assumed that science was primarily factual, that indeed it dealt almost solely in facts, that theory had no role in science. Careful observation of science reveals this to be false. It might be closer to the truth to say that 'facts' — at least interesting facts — are almost unable to exist *except in the presence of an appropriate theory*. Without an appropriate theory, one cannot even state what the 'facts' are.

Consider first the fictional account, often used for illustrative purposes (and it is good for no others), of the man who set out to study the hearing of fleas. He trained the fleas to jump in response to a certain loud sound, after which he conducted experiments in changing the loudness of the stimulus, varying its pitch, and so on. As one experiment — so the story goes — he surgically removed the legs of one flea. After this operation, he found that this particular flea no longer responded to the stimulus sound. 'Aha,' the man said, 'a flea hears by means of his legs. Remove the legs and the flea instantly becomes deaf!'

Clearly this is ridiculous nonsense, and was of course intended to be. But ask one question, and a serious point emerges: *why are we so sure this story is nonsense?*[1] The answer, obviously, is that we already have a set of concepts dealing with jumping, legs, sound, hearing, intentions vs. actions, capabilities vs. inabilities, and so on. According to these concepts the sound is heard by the flea, giving rise to an intent to jump. In order to carry out this intent the flea uses its legs to jump. 'Hearing' refers to receiving an audible signal and transmitting it to the brain; the fact that jumping does not occur cannot be accepted as proof that hearing has not occurred, especially since an alternative explanation lies right at hand: without legs, the flea *cannot* jump even if it has the intent of doing so.

This 'set of concepts dealing with jumping . . .' is, of course, what in science is referred to as a *theory*. We could say 'we already have the theory that it is jumping, and not hearing, which has been impaired'. Against this theory the competing theory of 'hearing with the legs' cannot immediately prevail.

The key point, of course, is that one *cannot even discuss the matter* without using *some* theory to explain the relatedness of the component parts. If you doubt this, try to tell the story in non-theoretical language: 'From one flea, six small linear appendages were surgically removed. After this, production of the stimulus sound was not followed by abrupt changes in the altitude of this flea . . .' Does this seem to be the same 'fact'? Or, for that matter, is this language actually theory-free, or is there still an underlying theory lurking in definition of words such as 'six', 'linear', 'removed', 'abrupt', 'changes', 'altitude', and so on? (Moreover, we have not yet reached the critical concepts of *hearing, deafness* or *jumping*.)

Consider, as a second (and more realistic) example, Torricelli's invention of the barometer. Popular legend has it that, in Italy in the early 1640s, the water table had receded so far that a very deep well had to be sunk in order to reach water. Though difficult and expensive, this was done. Then pumps were fitted to the pipes, and . . . disaster! . . . no water poured out of the spigot. It was clear to everyone that something must be wrong, probably with the pump itself. Better pumps were sought, designed, built and installed . . . then still better pumps, then better ones yet. But the result was always the same; no water emerged from the spigot.

Finally, in 1643, Evangelista Torricelli, a mathematician-scientist who had studied with Galileo, presented an alternative explanation: it was not, he said, the *pumps* that lifted the water. The pumps merely evacuated air, creating unequal pressures at the two ends of the column of water, after which atmospheric pressure at the lower end of the column pushed the water up. What really lifted the water was the *air* – or the *air pressure*! But this, of course, explained the difficulty; the pressure of the air is about 15 pounds per square inch, which is enough to support a column of water 34 feet high. That is the longest column of water, then, that can be lifted by atmospheric pressure. If your well goes more than 34 feet before hitting water, you will not be able to lift the water out by using atmospheric pressure – i.e., by pumping in the customary way.

There was, Torricelli said, nothing wrong with the pumps, and better pumps would not help.[2]

Now, in this case, what was the *fact*? Can it be said that there was *any* fact beyond those that were related to one theory or another? Well, there was the relatively trivial fact that no water came out of the pumps. But that fact, like the fact that a certain automobile refuses to start, does not lead anywhere. Unless you can say *why* there is no water, or *why* the car will not start, you are usually unable to do anything to change the situation. And in order to say why, you must interpret the 'facts' in terms of an appropriate theory.

Indeed, although we, today, are quite accustomed to the idea that we live at the bottom of an ocean of air, this idea was not universally accepted in Torricelli's day, and was not in those days something that easily entered into anyone's thought processes. In the 1640s many found it easier to think in terms of statements such as 'nature abhors a vacuum'. Of course, if pumping water was really based upon nature's abhorrence of a vacuum, it was difficult if not impossible to see why nature's abhorrence of vacuums disappeared when the length of the column of water reached 34 feet, and not everyone agreed with Torricelli.

Or consider this particularly interesting example: the relation of 'fact' to 'theory' played a critically important part in the discovery of oxygen. There was the fact that when a certain orange-colored powder was heated, a gaseous substance appeared. But this fact was largely meaningless until it could be related to an appropriate theory. Which theory should one use? Joseph Priestley related this 'fact' to first one theory, then another. In 1774 he thought that the gaseous substance was 'laughing gas', which he had encountered elsewhere. (Today we know this identification was wrong.) In 1775, after further tests, Priestley decided the gaseous substance was air from which some of the phlogiston had been removed. (Today we would say that Priestley's identification was again wrong, and so, in fact, was the entire phlogiston theory.) Also in 1775, the great French chemist Antoine Laurent Lavoisier reported heating this same power, and getting this same gas, but Lavoisier described the gas as 'air itself entire without alteration [except that] ... it comes out more pure, more respirable'.[3] (From the perspective of today's science, this is getting closer; in fact, there is very little wrong with it, yet it misses what we today would consider the essential truth.) By 1777 Lavoisier had invented a theory which dealt adequately with the experimental fact, and formed the basis for the modern theory used today − essentially, Lavoisier proclaimed that there should be *elements*, which could not be broken down into their components, and *compounds*, which were made when two or more elements were in some way 'welded' together. The orange powder, he decided, was probably a compound; heating it caused it to release one of the elements which it contained. Today we would say that the orange powder was red mercuric oxide (whoever named it had a poor eye for colors!), and that the gas was oxygen. Our view today is not substantially different from Lavioiser's in 1777 − except that nowadays elements *can* be 'decomposed', but that is another story entirely, a story that includes radioactivity, H-bombs and nuclear energy.

You can see the crucial role that theory plays if you try to describe in your own words what Priestley and Lavoisier did. In the late twentieth century, it is almost irresistible to use contemporary chemical concepts. The 'orange powder' we can hardly resist calling 'mercuric oxide', but to use that designation presupposes one of the most important theories in chemistry: that 'compounds' are made up of 'elements', and that in this particular case we are dealing with a compound, which is made up of the elements *oxygen* and *mercury*. Even more is presupposed: that oxygen and mercury combine in definite proportions, that at least two different proportions can occur, and that this compound has the ratio with the larger proportion of oxygen. Without all of those concepts, one cannot arrive at the name *mercuric oxide*.

Within this conceptualization − but not otherwise − we can say that Lavoisier and Priestley each heated mercuric oxide and obtained gaseous oxygen. Chemistry is not merely the study of orange powders; rather, it is concerned with developing a theory that explains the interrelationships among chemical substances and chemical processes. The theory of elements and compounds does this far better than any previous theory had done.

When we look carefully at science, we find that nearly every important 'fact' gets its importance from being describable within some appropriate theory.

Where Do Theories Come From?

Assuming that theories were not important is not the only error that was made in earlier attempts to develop a 'scientific' study of education. A second mistake was to assume that whatever theory might be useful would appear suddenly and automatically, springing forth full-grown from the data like Minerva from the brow of Zeus. In fact this is not at all what happens. At their beginnings, scientific theories must be created by proclamation. Lavoisier *proclaimed* that some chemical substances should be considered 'elements', unable to be built up from anything more primitive, whereas all other chemical substances must be 'compounds' built up by combining two or more elements in definite proportions. Fitting the various chemical substances of the world into this scheme must clearly have been a major task. If someone showed Lavoisier some specific substance, how could Lavoisier decide whether that substance should be classified as an 'element' or as a 'compound'? In most cases there was no immediate way to decide, and there was always a real possibility of error.

Or, to use an example closer to the interests of mathematics, consider Greek Euclidean synthetic geometry. The Greeks could have stared at hillsides, beaches, waves and mountains for an interminable time without developing Euclidean synthetic geometry, if they had thought only about shapes like mountains, pebbles, waves and trees. Such shapes are far too complex; looking at clouds can be fascinating, but just try to describe to someone what it is that you have seen!

The step that allowed the development of Greek geometry was the proclamation: Let there be points, lines, planes and space! This provided a conceptualization that made progress possible; in terms of these ideas one could define and study (after various additional proclamations) such matters as triangles, circles, parallelism, perpendicularity, congruence, conic sections, and all the familiar topics of Euclidean geometry.

If the 'scientific' study of education is to be helpful, careful explicit attention must be given to the basic conceptualization. This will not be handed to us *gratis*; it will have to be invented.

Where did the idea of 'points' and 'lines' come from? Presumably from the Greeks looking thoughtfully at mountains and beaches and so on, and choosing a simplification that seemed appropriate for the further discussion of such matters. Inasmuch as their choice has survived for two thousand years, and still provides the basis for modern science and technology, one can reasonably conclude that the Greeks chose wisely.

In the next chapter we shall look at some observations of human mathematical behavior, and present a conceptualization that has been developed for the purpose of discussing how people think about mathematical problems.

Notes

1. Actually, are we really sure that fleas do NOT hear with their legs?

2. Actually, the popular account of Torricelli's invention of the barometer is somewhat over-simplified. In this instance, as in nearly every scientific invention or discovery, the truth is considerably more complex. Cf., e.g., Kuhn (1977), p. 45 and elsewhere. For one thing, an earlier 'thought experiment' by Galileo contained the essential features of the answer, and this work by Galileo was known to Torricelli.

3. Kuhn, 1970, p. 54 (quoted from Conant, 1950).

Questions For You to Think About

1. Suppose you were Torricelli. Your contemporaries refuse to believe your explanation of the 'no water from the deep wells' problem. What could you do?

2. Some people claim that, in standard Euclidean geometry, the shortest line segment that you can draw has *exactly* the same number of points on it as the *longest* line segment you can draw. Do you believe this is true? If so, can you prove it? If not, can you disprove it?

3. Some people think of 'points' as rather like very, very tiny marbles or ball-bearings. Other people argue that points are much more abstract than that. Can you show some attribute of points that proves that they are very different from tiny marbles?

4 BASIC CONCEPTS

In this chapter we shall consider a collection of basic concepts that have been introduced by various researchers in order to facilitate the discussion of human information processing as it relates to the solution of mathematical problems. Notice that the nature of this task is such that we shall be dealing with a borderline situation that involves both human behavior and also the structure of, organization of and nature of knowledge itself. This borderline area is sometimes called *cognitive science*, sometimes called *artificial intelligence* and sometimes called *knowledge engineering*. In this chapter we focus on ideas from three sources:

(i) generalizations drawn from observations of student performance (or expert performance);

(ii) details of the way typical present-day digital computers process information;

(iii) concepts from the literature of cognitive science and artificial intelligence, especially the work of Papert, Minsky and their colleagues at MIT, Schank and his colleagues at Yale, and the Simon and Larkin group at Carnegie-Mellon University and the Greeno and Resnick group at Pittsburgh.

To some readers, any attempt to consider electronic computers and humans in the same discussion is evident folly, since the one is totally unlike the other. We certainly agree that many aspects of information processing in computers have a 'mechanical' nature that seems quite different from human thought. Yet considering human thought and computer information processing side by side can be extremely valuable, if only because computers operate in a highly explicit way that forces us into greater clarity in analyzing information processing. When you are programming a computer you are teaching a very stupid student. Effective pedagogy becomes a necessity.

Unit Steps

The simplest ordinary human acts are already quite complex. Taking one step forward in walking, or buttoning a button, or reading a single word are all, for most adults, 'simple' things to do. Yet each of these is itself complex, as one realizes if one watches a young child just learning to walk, or a slightly older child trying to 'sound out' a new word. Since our goal is to deal with school and college level mathematics, we do not want our analyses to begin in every case with the most elementary operations. For the students we will be observing, many such operations have been practiced for years and have become automatic. Our typical high school student, for example, knows that $6 + 1$ is seven, and does not ordinarily have to pause to think about it. In order to start at this level of 'automatic' processes, we shall select, for any particular student at any particular time, some level of processing and accept processes on this level as *unit steps*, which we shall not usually attempt to analyze in terms of anything smaller, simpler, or more basic.

Thus, if a ninth-grade student were factoring $x^2 - 5x + 6$ into $(x - 2)(x - 3)$, we *would* be interested in how or why the student wrote the parentheses, selected '2' and '3', and selected subtraction signs, but we *would not* attempt to analyze how the student knew that $3 \times 2 = 6$, or that $3 + 2 = 5$. We would accept these later decisions as 'unit steps', and not ordinarily attempt to analyze them into anything more primitive.

Of course, if we were observing a six- or seven-year-old child, we probably would *not* accept '$3 \times 2 = 6$' as the result of a single unit step; on the contrary, we would be very much interested in how the student decided that 'three times two' was 'six'. Consequently, the choice of accepting certain processes and procedures as unit steps depends upon which student we are considering, and at what point in his or her life. What requires thought today may be automatic tomorrow.

Procedures

The mathematical tasks which will interest us cannot usually be carried out by one single unit step. When several unit steps are carried out in a definite sequential order, this sequence is called a *procedure*. Procedures ordinarily have well-defined goals — they attempt to accomplish something.[1]

Two remarks about procedures are in order: first, our primary concern is not with the *action* that the student carried out, but rather with *something stored in memory* that caused the student to carry out this procedure. It may be helpful to consider an analogy; if we say that a certain recipe for sweet and sour pork is a good recipe, do we mean the recipe as it is printed in the cookbook, or do we mean the actions we took, this evening, in preparing a serving of sweet and sour pork? The recipe in the book is the more important of the two. If it is unsatisfactory, we must modify it, or find a new recipe. What we actually did today was a transient event; its success or failure may help us to make a judgement on the book's recipe, but inferences of this type must be made carefully. After all, we may have deviated from the book recipe, and if so, what we eat this evening may not be representative of what the book's recipe ought to produce.

Second, the phrase 'definite sequential order' does *not* imply inflexibility, because some steps in a procedure may be *decision* steps; perhaps we do one thing if today is warm, and some other thing if today is cool; or perhaps we look at some number and do one thing if this number is odd, and something else if it is even. Using the language of computer programming, we could say: we usually deal with 'branching programs' that involve 'conditional branching'.

Operating Memory and Storage Memory

Before considering human memory, we look briefly at the 'memory' of modern computers. By 'memory' in a digital computer we refer to some device, such as magnetic tape cassettes or magnetic core storage or floppy discs, where information can be stored in some coded form. One can insert information — usually called 'writing' — or one can read out information that was previously stored there — called 'retrieval'.

Computer memory can be thought of as consisting of a large number of separate 'slots' or 'pigeon-holes'. Each pigeon-hole can contain one small piece of information; following contemporary practice, we shall call each separate pigeon-hole a *register*; the contents of one register is sometimes called one *word*, but this does not have the same meaning as in ordinary English. It just means 'one small piece of information, stored in one register somewhere in the memory'.

Active Registers

A very small number of the registers — perhaps only two or three — are quite special. Active processes of various sorts can be carried out on any word written in these registers. We shall call these the *active registers*.

Passive Memory

A very large number of registers are arranged so that they can play only a more passive role. A word can be written into one of these registers, or a word can be read from one of them, but nothing else is possible. Access to this part of memory may, however, be subject to certain restrictions.

Operational Memory

A modest number of registers can be arranged as *operational memory* or *work space*. This part of the memory may contain all the information that is available for certain information processing activities.

There are differences from one computer to another, but in typical cases if someone wants to make use of certain information that has been stored in passive memory, he or she must first do two things:

(i) the desired information must be *located* wherever it is in passive memory (which may not be easy, because passive memory can often be a vast warehouse containing a huge amount of information);

(ii) having been located, the desired information must be *copied into* the 'operational memory' section of memory (this step is usually easy).

This two-part process is often called *retrieval*.

Human Memory

Is it reasonable to imagine that human memory resembles computer memory? In some respects the two are clearly quite different. But our present concern is with the division of memory into a vast 'passive memory' and a smaller 'work-space' portion of memory. Do humans resemble computers in this specific sense?

There is considerable evidence that they do. Consider, for example, all the male first names that you know — that is to say, all those that are coded and stored in your memory. 'John' is probably there, and 'William', and 'Harold', and 'Robert'. But can you write down the *complete* list? If you write a very long list today, you will almost certainly be able to think of some additional names tomorrow, and a few more will occur to you sometime next week. The division of memory into 'work space' and 'passive (warehouse) storage' provides an explanation. In passive memory you have a very large collection of male first names — indeed, it may well be impossible ever to retrieve the entire list, and be able to say that there are no unretrieved names still lurking in some cobwebby corner of passive memory — but limitations of one type or another prevent the transfer of more than a modest number of these names into working memory. These limitations may be limitations of available space within working memory, they may be limitations on the allowable rate of transferring information from passive memory to work space, or they may be limitations on how quickly one can search among the vast contents of passive memory. The result in any case is the same; one cannot transfer more than a reasonable number of names into working memory. But one has conscious access only to information that is in working memory (and perhaps only to *some* of that).

So — if we want to be aware of something, or able to think about it in a conscious way, we must first *find it* in passive memory, and then *copy it into working memory*.

A partial awareness of some such human thought process dates back to far earlier times than the appearance of electronic digital computers, as witness the prevalence of phrases such as 'I knew it; I just couldn't *think* of it!' and 'That *brings to mind* the time I landed in Entebbe. . .' Or even the phrase '*Try to recall* what it was like when. . .'

(Notice that one could get the same result by having an 'awareness location' and moving information into this location, or by leaving the information itself stationary, while shifting 'attention' from one memory register to another. It is like the difference between having a spotlight immovably fixed on center stage, and moving performers into the lighted area when their turn comes, as opposed to lining up performers, and aiming the spotlight at each performer in turn. Since the essential results are similar either way, we shall not bother to ask which of these is a better model of human thought processes.)

'To Retrieve' Means 'To Copy'

We speak of 'copying information from one memory location into another'. The use of the word *copying* is important; *we never destroy the original information merely by making a copy*. If you write your name and return address on an envelope, you have not *removed* this item from your memory so that you no longer know your own name and return address! Computer people speak of 'non-destructive read out', in order to emphasize this important arrangement. To put matters another way: do not let yourself slip into the habit of thinking of information as similar to cans of tomato soup! When you remove a can of tomato soup from a pantry shelf and take it to the stove, that can is no longer on the shelf. By contrast, when you copy information out of a memory register, *you* have the information, *and it is also still in the register*. Think of it as making a Xerox copy, without destroying the original.

Of course, one can *erase* the contents of a memory register, but only by a deliberate act of erasing. *Copying* never *erases the original*. (If you *write* into a memory space, that obliterates any previous contents of that space. In this regard, computers behave exactly like most modern hand-held calculators.)

This is all very different from the behavior of cans of tomato soup, where putting one can on the shelf increases the number there, and 'retrieving' a can from the shelf decreases that number. To combat tomato-soup thinking, we present one more metaphor: 'copying information from a register' is like taking a photograph of an oil painting; after you've made the copy, the original is still hanging in its usual place; but of course, if you paint over the original, you now have a new original, the earlier one being lost. (The earlier *message* need not be lost; you may still have one or more copies, located somewhere else.)

Sub-Procedures and Super-Procedures

Recall that a *procedure* is a sequence of instructions, usually stored in passive memory. A procedure was created to accomplish some specific result. There are two other aspects of procedures that deserve mention: (i) a procedure typically has some kind of name or label, so that it can be called out of passive memory when it is needed; (ii) a procedure typically includes certain 'slots' or 'variables' that can accept input data of various types.

Sometimes one procedure, P_1, having been retrieved, copied into work space, and told to begin operation, will arrive at a step where it needs to call upon some *other* procedure, say P_2. That is, P_1 causes P_2 to be located in memory, copied into the work space, provided with appropriate input information, and told to get to work. When P_2 has completed its work (successfully or not) it 'returns control to P_1' — that is, it passes any appropriate information to P_1, and causes P_1 to resume activity. In such a case, we say that P_1 is a *super-procedure* in this transaction, and P_2 is a *sub-procedure* in this transaction.

Transactions of this type are extremely common. Indeed, within human behavior it must be a rare occurrence to find a procedure that does *not* make use of sub-procedures. To write this sentence I presumably call upon previously-developed sub-procedures dealing with the meaning of words and sub-procedures dealing with spelling. 'Writing' sub-procedures must themselves have sub-procedures (one could speak of sub-sub-procedures, and sub-sub-sub-procedures, but we shall not usually do so) that deal with 'holding a pen', sub-procedures that deal with 'making the letter a', 'making the letter b', and so on. These 'letter' sub-procedures probably call upon their sub-procedures, dealing with 'making a short vertical stroke', 'making a long vertical stroke', and so on.[2]

Visually-moderated Sequences

A student asked to factor

$$x^2 - 20x + 96$$

might ponder for a moment, then write

$$x^2 - 20x + 96$$
$$(\quad)(\quad) \quad ,$$

then ponder, then write

$$x^2 - 20x + 96$$
$$(x\quad)(x\quad) \quad ,$$

then ponder some more, then continue writing

$$x^2 - 20x + 96$$
$$(x-\quad)(x-\quad)$$

and, finally, complete the task as

$$x^2 - 20x + 96$$
$$(x-12)(x-8)$$

Or, to consider a different example, a student asked to divide

$$21\overline{)6932}$$

might look carefully at what is written, ask himself 'How many times does 2 go into 6?', then write

$$\begin{array}{r} 3 \\ 21\overline{)6932} \end{array}\quad,$$

look at what he has written, then write

$$\begin{array}{r} 3 \\ 21\overline{)6932} \\ 63 \end{array}\quad,$$

again look at what is written, ponder, then write

$$\begin{array}{r} 3 \\ 21\overline{)6932} \\ \underline{63} \\ 6 \end{array}$$

and continue in this way: look, ponder, write, look, ponder, write, and so on.

This is a frequent kind of behavior in mathematics, and has led to the postulation of *visually-moderated sequences*. (We shall often call these 'VMS sequences', despite the implied redundancy, similar to 'MAB blocks'.) A VMS sequence can be thought of as a visual cue V_1, which elicits a procedure P_1 whose execution produces a new visual cue V_2, which elicits a procedure P_2,. . . and so on.

VMS sequences also occur frequently outside of mathematics. The reader may have had the experience of trying to drive to a remote location visited once or twice years earlier. Typically, one could not, at the outset, tell anyone how to get there. What one hopes for is, again, a VMS sequence: see some key landmark – an old water-wheel-powered mill, perhaps – and hope that one will remember what to do at that point – 'Oh, yes, turn right just after the old mill!' Then one drives on, again hoping for a visual reminder that will cue the retrieval of the next string of remembered directions.

Integrated Sequences

Of course, if one drives to this location often enough, the mental representation of how to get there becomes transformed. One no longer needs to receive reminders in the form of visual landmarks. On the contrary, one could sit in a windowless room that provided no relevant cues whatsoever, and retrieve from memory a complete set of directions for driving to that spot. At this stage, the old mill is no longer a visual cue needed to aid retrieval of a piece of information; on the contrary, one can 'drive' the route in one's imagination, retrieving a memorized representation of the old mill, and visualizing it at the correct point in the sequence, even if the actual mill itself is out of sight — 'out of sight, but *not* out of mind', as it were.

At this stage we speak of an *integrated sequence*. The visual cues are now represented in memory and retrievable when needed, and the separate short sequences have become 'welded' together. Whereas a VMS sequence has the form

$$V_1 \rightarrow P_1 \rightarrow V_2 \rightarrow P_2 \rightarrow \ldots,$$

where $V_1, V_2, V_3, \ldots$, and so on, must actually be seen as visual inputs, by contrast in an integrated sequence every V_1 and every P_1 is well represented in memory, and can be retrieved without requiring external visual inputs; further, the sequence

$$V_1 \longleftrightarrow P_1 \longleftrightarrow V_2 \longleftrightarrow P_2 \longleftrightarrow V_3 \longleftrightarrow \ldots$$

is 'welded' together and can be retrieved from memory as a single entity.

The process by which the bits and pieces of a VMS sequence are united into a single entity — an integrated sequence — must be one of the fundamental processes in learning mathematics. We shall call this process 'sequence integration' or 'welding'.

Achieving Noun Status

Another fundamental change occurs as a VMS sequence is repeated and becomes more familiar; it becomes itself an entity that can be talked about, scrutinized and analyzed. When a procedure is first being learned, one experiences it almost one step at a time; the overall patterns and continuity and flow of the entire activity are not perceived. But as the procedure is practiced, the procedure itself becomes an entity — it becomes a *thing*. It, itself, is an input or object of scrutiny. All of the full range of perception, analysis, pattern recognition and other information processing capabilities that can be used on any input data can be brought to bear on this particular procedure. Its similarities to some other procedure can be noted, and also its key points of difference. The procedure, formerly only a thing to be done — a verb — has now become an object of scrutiny and analysis; it is now, in this sense, a noun. This distinction occurs also outside of mathematics; one hears it when experienced professional athletes talk about their sport. Batting or pitching are things that can be analyzed in a detail that the lay person can find hard to believe.

Descriptors for Procedures

If we are to select an appropriate procedure we can hardly search blindly, or try prospective candidates in an entirely haphazard fashion. On the contrary, we need to have associated with each procedure a descriptive analysis that tells us what general kind of thing it is likely to be able to do, and which things it ought not to be asked to do. The *distributive law*

$$x (y + z) = xy + xz$$

has, for example, the distinctive property that it relates *addition* to *multiplication*. No other algebraic axiom does this. Having this description helps us know when the distributive law is likely to be a good bet.

Descriptors are perhaps less important when one is dealing with routine problems that are already familiar. Each step can be taken at the proper time and in the proper way. But for novel problems that one has never encountered before, having a good set of descriptors for various procedures is probably essential. Without them, one reaches blindly on the shelves of memory, seizing tools that probably will not prove useful for the task at hand.

These descriptors form what we shall call a *meta-language*; this is not a language for talking about the usual objects of mathematics (such as points or numbers), but rather a language for talking about how we can solve mathematical problems or perform mathematical tasks. Some researchers (e.g., Herbert Simon) speak of a 'planning space' where we can plan beforehand the way we will tackle some novel, non-routine problem. Thus we could say that resourceful problem solvers are typically people who have learned many useful procedures, have developed a good collection of descriptors that indicate which procedures are likely to be helpful in which situations, for whom these descriptors provide a usable *meta-language* that enables them to plan work beforehand, laying out their plans in a portion of active memory that we can call a 'planning space'. After plans have been laid out, one retrieves the appropriate procedures and actually carries out the work that has been planned. This process is sometimes conscious and explicit, and at other times more automatic and less accessible to conscious awareness.[3]

Knowledge Representation Structures in General

Procedures have some expected features. Another knowledge representation structure, known as a *frame* (which we shall meet presently), has a somewhat different kind of internal organization or structure. But sometimes it is useful to have a term that can refer to *any* kind of structure, without implied assumptions about any internal organization within that structure. For this we shall use the term *knowledge representation structure*, or *KRS*. Example: most people have considerable knowledge about the arrangement of rooms, doors, stairways, etc., in their own home. This knowledge has to be represented somehow in each person's mind — the evidence is clear, since portions of this knowledge are readily retrievable. We may not, however, be able to get much evidence to indicate *how* this knowledge is structured *within* the KRS. In such a case, the term 'knowledge representation structure' allows us to talk about the representation itself, without compelling us to commit ourselves to any assumptions about the internal structure of the KRS.

It may be useful to consider some different ways in which knowledge is organized. (i) In a usual telephone directory, people with phones are listed in alphabetical order by last names. This is very efficient provided you know the last name of the person whose phone number you want to find. It usually fails if, as is sometimes the case, you know only the person's first name, or if you cannot spell their last name. (Would you know how to spell 'Hjalmarson' or 'Cholmondeley' or 'Worcester' if you had only heard the names pronounced?) In larger cities, especially, the system can fail if a married woman is listed only under her husband's name. (Which one of all those Smiths is Ruth Smith?) (ii) Sometimes you have a phone number and want to know whose number it is. The usual phone book is not much help in this case; there do, however, exist phone books where the *numbers* are listed in order of increasing size. With such a book, finding the name when you know the number is easy. (iii) In some cities, the various suburbs have separate telephone directories, and in order to find someone's number you must know which suburb he lives in — but of course one may not know this. If the number of separate suburbs and separate directories is large, finding someone's number can be difficult. By contrast, in some cities one directory lists everyone, no matter which suburban town they may live in. This, clearly, is quite a different way to organize this same basic information.

Notice that the problems of organizing information, and finding the piece you want when you want it, exist as fundamental matters independently of how you code knowledge and where you store it, whether in books, in computers, or in somebody's mind.

Production Systems

Some knowledge can be represented as specific rules to be followed in specific situations, such as: 'If the engine is laboring, shift down into second gear' or 'If the room is too chilly, adjust the thermostat to a higher temperature setting'. Instructions of the form 'If P is the case, then do Q' are called *condition-action pairs*, where P is the *condition* and 'do Q' is the *action*. In some knowledge representation structures *every item is of this same form*, a knowledge-action pair. Such a KRS is called a *production system*. Production systems are controversial, inasmuch as they figure prominently in the work of some researchers, but other researchers reject them as not effective in laying out the relationships that exist within a body of knowledge, and not representative of how human beings think. They tend to break knowledge down into seemingly independent small pieces, which may distort the reality. But the existence of production systems shows us one more possibility for the organization of knowledge.

Active vs. Passive Representation Structures

The information in a telephone book can be helpful, but it, itself, is presented in a passive form. If you want to make use of this information, how you do so is up to you. This is an example of a *passive* knowledge representation structure.

By contrast, most of the information in a cookbook is presented in the form of recipes: do this, then do so-and-so, then do such-and-such. This is an example of an *active* knowledge representation structure.

Notice in particular that every procedure or other memorized algorithm or program constitutes an active knowledge representation structure.

It is worth pointing out that we are talking here about how knowledge is *represented* for storage, either by printing on paper, or by 'writing' it into the registers of a computer's memory, or by some other method. This has nothing to do with *where*, in memory, this information is stored. When not being used, both active KRSs and passive KRSs are stored in the passive portion of memory. This is the 'low-cost warehouse storage' part of a computer's memory, and anything not presently in use is stowed away here somewhere.

Retrieval vs. Real-time Synthesis

For the next discussion, please do NOT make a drawing. Try to visualize the figure in your head. Suppose I tell you that a certain geometric figure consists of two congruent squares, lying in the same plane, and sharing a common side. The common side is vertical. In the left-hand square a circle has been inscribed. In the right-hand square, an isosceles triangle has been inscribed so that it shares a common base with the square, and its vertex opposite this base lies at the center of the top side of the square. The vertical altitude of this triangle, which divides the right-hand square into two congruent rectangles, has been drawn in. Inside the isosceles triangle, a circle has been inscribed.

Now if, having made no drawing, you can visualize this diagram, you have certainly made some kind of representation structure in your mind. Did you *retrieve* it from memory, or did you *construct* it right now as you read this description? Surely you constructed it; while the component parts − triangles, circles, etc. − are common enough that they may have been stored in your memory, the entire diagram is sufficiently unusual (and useless!) that it can hardly have been stored in memory and retrieved. After all, if you store in memory every weird figure you ever see, how will you ever find one when you want it? You may have retrieved from memory 'square', 'side', 'circle', 'triangle', 'rectangle', and so on; these are basic shapes worth remembering. But surely you *put these pieces together* in order to make the total diagram. Since you made the knowledge representation structure while you were reading the description of the figure, we would say that you *constructed it in real time*.

In many situations one needs to remember that a knowledge representation structure, whose presence may be demonstrable by the knowledge a student displays overtly, can have either of two origins; it may have been retrieved from memory, or it may have been constructed at that very moment on an *ad hoc* basis.

Associations

We again describe an information-handling procedure used in computers, which can serve at least as a metaphor for some aspects of human thought.

Perhaps the best-known device for linking together information in computers is the 'association' or 'cross-reference' linkage. These associations can take several forms; we now mention four of these.

Simultaneous Loading. If a certain knowledge representation structure, S_1, is to be copied (or 'loaded') into work space there may be instructions in S_1 that direct that certain *other* representation structures — S_2 and S_3, say — must also be loaded into work space at this same time. Thus, whenever some cue causes the retrieval of S_1, it must happen that S_2 and S_3 will also be available in the work space.

Branching. At some step in a procedure P_1 there may be a command that requires the loading into work space of some other procedure P_2, and the activation of P_2 as a sub-procedure. This will often involve conditional branching; that is to say, the calling up of P_2 will occur if and only if the contents of certain specific registers have certain specific values.

Pointers. How are these smaller pieces of information assembled into larger 'chunks' of information? We have seen various mechanisms, such as simultaneous loading, etc. When we want to discuss such matters rather abstractly, we sometimes speak of *pointers*. A *pointer* is a reference, inserted at a definite step into some procedure P_1, that gives the address of some other information, I_1, that has been stored in memory. I_1 itself may or may not be a procedure.

Notice that 'pointers' give us a more general way of speaking of connections; if I_1 is itself a procedure, the pointer in P_1 may call up I_1 as a sub-procedure; the pointer may itself be conditional, so this includes conditional branching. Or I_1 may be the first item in a queue — a list of items to be considered one at a time; in such a case, after using I_1 we may move to the next item in the queue, which can be easily done by updating an appropriate address. By 'address' one means a designation that identifies a specific location in the computer's memory, and thus makes it possible to retrieve the contents of that specific memory location. In effect, the 'address' tells us which electronic pigeon-hole contains the information we are seeking.

Adjusting Parameters. We have presented both simultaneous loading and branching as 'all-or-nothing' processes. In fact, however, they can be handled in a different way. One can arrange things so that every KRS has a parameter that describes the 'urgency' of loading it into the small work-space memory, or a parameter that describes the 'urgency' of branching to it. At any moment, any procedure which is active can increment or decrement the 'urgency' rating of any other KRS. Whenever the value of the urgency rating of some KRS becomes large enough, that KRS can be loaded into the work-space, or control can branch to it.

Continuous vs. Discrete Models

The point just made, about adjusting parameters, raises a serious question. Thus far in this book we have mainly treated *every* aspect of information processing as an 'all-or-nothing' phenomenon. Either you *do* transfer control to Procedure P, or you *do not*. Either you *do* load Procedure Q into the work space, or you *do not*. Models with such alternatives might be called 'discrete'. By contrast, *all* decision processes (or many of them) can be made to depend upon the values of parameters, in the way described in the preceding section. Such models might be called 'continuous', because they allow small adjustments in the value of any parameter. There are a number of reasons for giving serious consideration to 'continuous' models of this type. In the first place, the physical composition of the human brain suggests some such mechanism; the signals transmitted by neurons seem more like increments or decrements than like complex 'messages' of any sort. Even if one thinks *only* of computers, the arguments in favor of 'continuous' models seem compelling. (See especially Pollack and Waltz, 1982.) A large amount of important work in this direction has been carried out (for example, see: Minsky (1980); Collins and Quillian (1972); Fahlman (1979); Ortony (1976)).

Continuous models certainly embody the 'feel' of many human examples; consider, for instance, the matter of hunger. This is not at all an 'all-or-nothing' matter. On the contrary, what matters is *how* hungry we feel, *how much* hunger sensation we are experiencing.

Indeed, the design of electronic computers themselves is moving somewhat in the direction of 'continuous' processing (cf., e.g., Sussman, 1982). Why, then, do we focus our attention on discrete 'all-or-nothing' models? *Because they are simpler, and because they represent knowledge in a more transparent form.* An auditory experience may involve the continuous phenomena of acoustic wave patterns, but it is only when we recognize the sounds as identifiable spoken *words* that the information becomes something that we can easily think about. Much the same can be said for the thought processes in your mind.

Critics

As we have mentioned earlier, third-grade children often subtract $7,002 - 25$ as follows:

$$
\begin{array}{r}
5 \\
\cancel{6}\ 11 \\
\cancel{7},002 \\
-\quad\quad 25 \\
\hline
5,087
\end{array}
$$

Children making this error usually see nothing wrong with their work, and believe that they have obtained the correct answer.

An experienced adult would probably reject the answer 5,087 immediately, perhaps on the grounds that 'if I have about seven thousand dollars, and if I spend twenty-five dollars, and if I then find that I have about five thousand dollars left, then I know something has gone wrong.'

Clearly, if an adult can reject the answer 5,087 by producing this kind of analysis, there must be some kind of knowledge representation structure in that adult's mind which made possible the creating of this line of argument. Any KRS that enables a person to create an analogy, an interpretation or a line of argument that can be used to decide whether some answer is correct or incorrect is called a *critic*. Here, one could say that the adult possessed a *size* critic that could be applied to the answer 5,087, and led to a rejection of that answer as obviously too small.

Bugs

Within computer science, a specific flaw in a procedure is called a *bug*. This term has come to be used also in analyzing student work in mathematics (cf. Brown and Burton, 1978). What is novel about such analyses is their *specificity* and *determinism*. As we shall see later in this book, student errors are not so random as people used to imagine. On the contrary, student errors turn out to be very regular and systematic, and it is often possible to predict exactly which wrong answer is most likely to be given by a particular student. Slips of the tongue, and other 'errors', provided Freud with some of his most valuable clues to human thought processes. In just this same way, systematic wrong answers given by a student will often provide valuable clues as to how that student is thinking about a certain class of mathematical problems.

The identification of specific 'bugs' will be an important theme in the rest of this book.

Correcting Procedures

Clearly, a procedure which a student has learned may be correct, or it may not be. Suppose the procedure has been found to contain a bug, or to be otherwise in need of modification. How can modifications be made?

At least four methods are possible within the present conceptual framework:

(i) A conditional transfer can be inserted into the procedure at some appropriate step, so that at this point a certain sub-procedure is activated. (ii) The buggy procedure itself can be modified. (iii) The buggy procedure can be left untouched, and a new, correct procedure can be added to memory, so that now both buggy and correct procedures coexist within memory. (iv) It may happen that a correct procedure already exists within memory, and the only bug consists of selecting procedure P_1 instead of procedure P_2. If this is the nature of the problem, a 'screening' or 'receptionist' procedure can be created and inserted so as to be activated *before* procedure P_1. This screening procedure will check the contents of various registers, and on the basis of this check will activate whichever of P_1 or P_2 is appropriate at that time.

State Variables

We have had to refer several times to procedures which may 'check the contents of certain memory registers', and thereafter respond differently depending upon the contents of these registers. Because this is a persistent need, we introduce some simpler language. The particular contents of the work-space portion of memory we shall say determines a *state* of the computer or student, and those key registers that are queried in order to find out what this state is we shall call *state variables*. All conditional transfers are thus determined by the value of the state variables at the time when a check is made.

Frames

Perhaps the most interesting and the most provocative phenomena in information processing relate to the ways in which certain complex and highly-interrelated bodies of information, often of an active type, can be represented in memory. To deal with such matters, it has been necessary to postulate a very special kind of knowledge representation structure, known as a *frame*.[4]

We consider first some of the evidence that led to the postulation of frames.

Reading Comprehension

Some important evidence comes from studies of reading comprehension.[5] For example, consider this paragraph.

> It was Paul's birthday. Jane and Alex went to get presents. 'Oh, look!' Jane said, 'I'll get him a kite.' 'No, don't,' Alex responded, 'He already has one. He'll make you take it back.'

What is interesting about this paragraph is this: suppose a typical literate adult in the United States reads this paragraph, and is then asked the following questions:

(1) Why are Jane and Alex buying presents?
(2) Where did Jane and Alex go?
(3) What did Alex refer to by the word 'it' in her last sentence?

Our typical US adult will easily answer all three questions, and will believe that the answers were contained in the printed paragraph.

To one who practices the careful study of information processing, both of these behaviors are surprising. The answers to the three questions are, in fact, *not* contained in the printed paragraph. Where, then, does our standard adult get this information? And how can he or she believe that it came from the paragraph?

In case the present reader also believes the answers are in the paragraph, let us look carefully at what really is there. To be sure, the first sentence tells us that it was Paul's birthday, but it does not offer this as the reason why Jane and Alex went to get presents. 'Well,' you may say, 'clearly the first sentence gives us the *reason* for what happens in the second sentence.' Can we then assume that the first sentence in any paragraph gives reasons for the actions described in the second sentence? Clearly not; suppose we had:

> It was raining hard and was very disagreeable outside. Jane and Alex went to get presents.

Would we say that Jane and Alex went to get presents *because* it was raining hard and was very disagreeable outside? Clearly, we would not. So it cannot be the juxtaposition of the sentences which establishes the causality.

Well, perhaps it's because we know that on *birthdays* one receives presents. Of course; but does the paragraph say 'on birthdays one typically receives presents'? Clearly it does not. So this key piece of information came from the reader's memory, and *not from the printed paragraph*.

Minsky, Schank and other researchers would explain this by saying: something early in the printed paragraph triggered the retrieval of the 'birthday' frame. This frame is a fairly large knowledge representation structure that includes a considerable body of information: a 'birthday' is the anniversary of the day someone was born, or of the day when some organization or entity was created. This day is typically celebrated by a party. There may be invited guests. There may be a cake. There may be candles on the cake. There may be one candle for each year the person has lived, or perhaps one more than that number. Guests may bring presents. There may be ice cream . . . and so on. Indeed, this 'birthday' frame even poses questions; it tells us what to look for in the story: whose birthday was it? How old was he or she? Was there a party? Were these children or adults? Was there a cake? Did they play games? . . . and so on.

It does even more than that: when we find answers, the frame accepts these answers. It does this by containing 'slots' or *variables*, and information from the current input data is entered into these slots. We say that 'the variables are evaluated' or that 'the variables are filled by appropriate replacements' or that 'the variables are instantiated'. But the frame poses a great many questions, and has slots ready to be filled with a great many answers. Frequently we cannot find answers for many of these questions. If not, the frame will often perform another remarkable service: it will fill in an answer itself. It does this by drawing on past experience, and fills in what has been a 'typical' answer in the past. We call this a *default evaluation*. Obviously, a default evaluation is, in effect, a reasonably shrewd guess; it may be right, or it may be wrong. But default evaluations have the advantage that they allow information processing to continue, even in the absence of some information.

Sometimes certain information is so critical that the frame refuses to make a default evaluation; in such cases, if input information is not available to fill a key slot, the frame may simply refuse to perform.

Hence, when we read the paragraph:

(i) a cue triggers the retrieval of the 'birthday' frame;

(ii) the birthday frame tells us questions that need to be answered; we search the printed paragraph for answers to these questions;

(iii) when an answer is found, it is entered into an appropriate slot (or *variable*) in the frame;

(iv) in most cases, if an answer is *not* found, the frame makes a *default evaluation* of that variable;

(v) after the key slots are filled, we say the frame has been *instantiated*; that is to say, key information from the input data (in this case, the printed paragraph) has been combined with information contained in the frame;

(vi) subsequent information processing – that is, 'thinking' – now makes use of the instantiated frame; it does *not* usually make use of the primitive input data itself; hence, whatever is remembered or argued or processed is a melding of input data and frame data. (People, however, are typically unaware of the role of the frame, and attribute all of this information to the input source alone.)

(vii) in case a key slot cannot be filled, either by input data or by default evaluation, the frame may refuse to perform. (Just how this works will become clearer in subsequent pages.)

A New View of 'Reading'

What has emerged from the work of Minsky, Schank and others is, in fact, a new view of what it means to 'read'. An earlier view might have described reading as a process of careful extraction of the information contained on the printed page.

The post-Minsky view is more like this: (i) a written sentence or paragraph cues the retrieval of one or more *frames* from memory; (ii) these frames then pose certain questions; (iii) the reader seeks answers to these questions, and inserts these answers into 'slots' (or 'variables') in the frame, thus bringing together *general* frame information and *specific information from this individual input*; (iv) where answers are not forthcoming from input data, the frame may make default evaluations; (v) if neither input data nor default evaluations are available to fill a key 'slot', the frame may refuse to function; (vi) an evaluation is made, to determine whether frame selection has been correct, and whether the variable slots have been filled correctly; (vii) from this point on, nearly all subsequent information processing will be based on data in this instantiated frame – and the 'primitive' data inputs will be ignored.

This view of what it means 'to read' is a radical departure from earlier views. Where earlier views would expect different readers to extract the same information from reading some particular paragraph, this new 'frame-oriented' view would expect differences, because different readers will have non-identical frames in their memories.

If a retrieved frame poses too few questions, the reader will not look for certain information, and, not looking, will not find it. In this case we will have someone who is a superficial reader.

If a retrieved frame is unable to make enough default evaluations, we will have a 'naïve' reader who is lacking in the knowledge born of experience.

If a reader exercises too little care in confirming the appropriateness of frame selection and variable instantiation, we have a person who surprises us by doing erratic and irrational things, someone who gets things 'all mixed up'.

In addition, mistakes or distortions in the frame itself are a major source of common errors in observable performance, as we shall see in subsequent chapters.

Variables

The idea of a 'variable' is important in mathematics education for two reasons: (i) within mathematics itself it is a key concept, and one that gives students more than a little trouble; (ii) the idea of a 'variable' is also important in cognitive science, and therefore in the model that we propose for the analysis of human information processing.

The idea is very simple, but not well known to the general public. Consider this example:

$$1 + 0 = 1$$
$$2 + 0 = 2$$
$$3 + 0 = 3$$

and we clearly could go on. There are infinitely many statements that are candidates for that list, such as

$$1066 + 0 = 1066 \quad,$$

and so on. A more parsimonious notation is urgently needed. Indeed, one has been created:

$$\square + 0 = \square, \tag{1}$$

where you may write whatever number you wish in the left-hand $\square$, provided you write *that same* number in the right-hand $\square$.

The notation $\square$, used in this way, is an example of a *variable*. Equation (1) could also be written as

$$X + 0 = X.$$

What, then, is a 'variable'? A variable would seem to be a place where you can write numbers, subject to certain rules. If numbers are involved, we speak of a *numerical variable*. But variables need not involve numbers. If a printed application form reads

Name: _____ ,

then *that* is a variable. So a variable can also be a place where you write a *name*. Indeed, a *variable* can be a place where you write *anything*.

In a computer, a *variable* is any space in any part of the memory that is used in this same way. Suppose 10-year-old Tim sits down at a computer terminal in school, and types in his student number and his password. The computer now 'knows' who Tim is, and may type back to him:

GOOD MORNING, TIM!

The computer had in its program a command something like this:

Type 'GOOD MORNING,' /NAME/ '!'

Elsewhere in memory the computer had a record of Tim's student number, and his secret password. Listed with these was his name, in a form something like:

NAME: TIM.

When the 'type' command was executed, the computer knew that

/NAME/

meant the contents of the memory position whose address is NAME.

The contents of that entry was, of course, the symbol string TIM.

Turning from computers back to humans, it is interesting to observe that people often make errors at precisely that point in a sentence, as when a politician says 'Good afternoon, friends. I'm pleased to be here in Cleveland.' — but he's really in Detroit! Evidently, he was constructing a sentence from instructions of the form, say, 'I'm pleased to be here in' /CITY/. However, when (in some complex way) the politician's mind tried to find /CITY/, it came up with the wrong answer.

Errors of this type can give us considerable information about the way the human mind works. Here is an actual example:

Peter [speaking at a time when the Atlanta Braves led the National League West by 10½ games]: 'The Braves could lose quite a lot, and still be ahead by a good number of runs. Oh, I mean "a good number of games!"'

When Peter's mind wanted to execute some command (roughly) similar to

Say 'a good number of' /COUNTERS/   (2)

it found 'runs' instead of 'games'. This error gives us valuable information; of course we do not know the precise internal mental language corresponding to the formula (2), above, but we do know that, however

/COUNTERS/

was represented, it led to 'runs' when 'games' was intended. What do 'runs' and 'games' have in common? Each is a counter for measuring how far you are ahead (or behind, as the Braves were a few weeks later) in a baseball competition. If the competition is a *game*, then the counter is a *run*. If, on the other hand, the competition is the *season*, then the counter is a *game*.

In a later chapter we shall develop the argument that a new idea is created in your mind by the process of finding an old idea that is almost good enough, making a Xerox copy of it, and modifying this copy until you have something that *is* good enough. Presumably Peter knew about *games* before he knew about 'the season', so presumably he had this idea (roughly) in his mind:

Name: GAME
Counter: RUN

Divisions: INNINGS
Divisional Stopping Rule: 3 OUTS
Final Stopping Rule: ONE TEAM LEADS AT END OF K$\underline{th}$ INN-
ING, WHERE K $\geqslant$ 9.

As he learned about the major leagues, the 'season' and the World
Series, he made a Xerox copy of this entry, and modified it something
like this:

Name: SEASON
Counter: GAME
Divisions: [blank]
Stopping Rule: ONE TEAM LEADS AFTER N GAMES, WHERE
N $\geqslant$ 162.

However, the search for

/COUNTER/

works in the human mind, it led Peter to the wrong KRS, so that he
retrieved 'runs' when he should have retrieved 'games'.

Finding the Correct Frame: 'Top-Down' vs. 'Bottom-Up'

In this section we shall consider one of the most important — and most
paradoxical — questions in human information processing. As with so
many of the key questions, it confronts us with the dilemma of which
came first, the chicken or the egg?

How should I integrate

$$\int \frac{\cos x}{\sin x} \, dx \qquad ? \tag{3}$$

Now, *if* I knew that I wanted to use

$$\int \frac{du}{u} = \ln |u| + C \ , \tag{4}$$

then I could try various ways to map the terms in (3) into terms in (4).
This would be 'top-down' processing, in the sense that a knowledge
representation structure (namely, the mental coding of (4)) has been
retrieved from memory and is now guiding the processing. Finding an
appropriate mapping can now be done by systematically exploring a
decision tree like the one shown in Figure 4.1. *But this depends upon
a previous decision to use (4).*

Figure 4.1: A decision tree for the integration problem (3), *if* we have already decided to use (4).

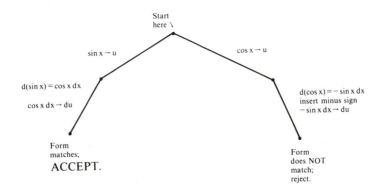

Figure 4.2: A portion of the decision tree for the integration problem (3), if we operate in 'bottom-up' mode by making *local* or *microscopic* decisions first. Many further alternatives exist, for example in the possible selection of other integration formulas. A typical human would NOT have the entire decision tree constructed in his mind, and would construct additional branches, probably in a non-systematic way, when they became necessary. This process, for most people, is subject to errors and omissions.

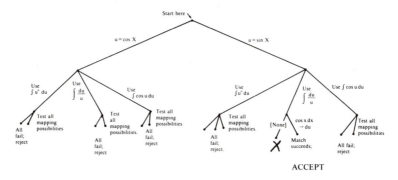

On the other hand, we could delay the 'macroscopic' decision to use (4) (or to use some other integration formula instead), and we could look at smaller, 'local', 'microscopic' cues, and try to make decisions on a more microscopic level. Since this approach might be considered 'closer to the data', it is often called *bottom-up*, or *input-driven*. In this approach we do *not* make any early commitment to which integration formula we shall ultimately use.

The decision tree for this approach looks something like Figure 4.2. In general, the matter is far more complex than Figures 4.1 and 4.2 suggest, because many other decisions may need to be made, and the actual search trees would be very large. In particular, as in examples (5), (6) and (7), one may never be able to match the original input string to any formula stored in memory, but may need to insert one or more transformations before any match becomes possible.

$$\int \frac{x^3 \quad \cos^2 x}{1 - \sin^2 x} \quad dx \tag{5}$$

$$\int \sqrt{\csc^2 x - 1} \quad ln \, (\sin x) \, dx \tag{6}$$

$$\int ln \, x^3 \quad dx \tag{7}$$

Since there is no *a priori* bound on the number of intermediate transformations that may be needed, there is no *a priori* bound on the size or complexity of the decision trees.

The question of 'top-down' *vs.* 'bottom-up' processing is not, of course, limited to *mathematical* thought. On the contrary, it is a basic question in all sophisticated information processing, whether in humans or by machines. Papert and Minsky (1972) present the elegant example

where a human easily reads 'the cat', despite the fact that the middle letter in each word is drawn exactly the same. If one assumes 'top-down' processing, so that we somehow *guess* that we should look for possible occurrences of the words 'the' and 'cat', then the decision tree to check this out is trivially simple. But . . . *how did we guess that these were the words to try*?

If, on the other hand, we assume bottom-up processing, then the decision tree has an extremely large number of branches, each of which in turn leads to a large number of branches. Searching such a tree hardly seems compatible with the apparent speed and ease of our reading those two words, even from carelessly-drawn lettering.

This ease of reading can be explained more easily if one assumes a 'continuous' model, with many information-processing activities occurring simultaneously. Alternatively, one can relegate this to the mysterious category of 'pattern matching' or 'pattern recognition'. This does not really explain what happens, but it does allow us to move ahead with the discussion of other issues that may be less paradoxical.

Control

It may simplify subsequent discussions if we introduce the idea of 'control'. A typical computer – a so-called 'von Neumann machine' – will examine only one command (or one 'step') at a time; as soon as this single step has been performed, the computer moves on to a new command. How is this new command chosen? Precise details vary, depending upon the computer, but one could imagine that each command names its own successor, telling the computer which (other) command should be performed next (this still allows conditional branching, because a command may say 'If P, then do Q').

If we use language akin to Robert's Rules of Order we could say that among all the (perhaps millions) of commands stored in memory, only one command 'has the floor' at any given moment. This is what we mean by *control*. If this single active command is contained in a procedure P_1, then we say that 'control is in P_1', since it is usually procedures, rather than individual commands, that we care about. If P_1 plays the role of a super-procedure, and calls upon a sub-procedure P_2, then what typically happens is something like this:

At first control is in P_1.

At this point, procedure P_1 communicates certain input data to sub-procedure P_2 (again, by writing it in certain 'slots'), then transfers control to procedure P_2. P_2 is thus active, performing one step at a time. Sooner or later, P_2 communicates certain data (we say P_2 *returns* certain data) to procedure P_1, then returns control to P_1.

P_1, of course, is not the active procedure. But, typically, P_1 is itself a sub-procedure, called upon earlier by some super-procedure P_0. When P_1 completes its assigned task, it will return certain information to procedure P_0, and will return control to P_0.

The one-step, one-action-at-a-time von Neumann machine hardly seems to provide a metaphor directly applicable to human thought. For one thing (Lindsay and Norman, 1977, p. 330), there is convincing evidence that separate processing is carried out for acoustic/aural inputs and for muscular movement actions. (Thus, the claims of many students that they can write term papers while listening to music may well be justified.) There are apparently other examples of independent processing for different sensory modalities.

But it is tempting to suppose that simultaneous processing goes very much further (cf., e.g., Sussman, 1982). Suppose we start with a von Neumann machine. 'Control', in this case, is easy to define. Although the computer may have a large memory, containing large amounts of data and a large collection of commands (or 'steps in a program'), *only one step in one program is active at this moment.* When this step has been carried out, some other step must be selected to become active. *The method by which this next active step is chosen is called 'control'.*

In typical computer programs this choice is made in a relatively simple way. One method is this: all of the steps in a single procedure are numbered. For the most part, they are executed (i.e., chosen to become active) in numerical order, as some bakeries call for the next customer to be served. There are two common exceptions: (i) if a program step involves an unconditional transfer, that program step itself determines which command will become active next; or, (ii) if a program step involves a *conditional transfer*, then some specified test is carried out, and which command becomes active next is determined by the outcome of that test.

In programs of this type it is easy to define *control* because only one command is active at one time, and because the presently-active command always chooses the next command to become active. In the preceding chapters we have often implicitly assumed those two attributes:

    (i) only one command is active at a time;
   (ii) the command which is active at this moment determines which command becomes active next.

We can call this arrangement *single processing with directed transfer of control*. The memory location where the active command is located will be called the *control register*.

A major alternative consists of an arrangement where several (perhaps many) control registers exist, and several (or many) of them are active at the same time. Within each individual control register an orderly sequence of commands flows through, just as in the case of single processing, so that many different procedures are being executed simultaneously. This arrangement becomes fundamentally different when one adds *control initiation by pattern recognition* — that is to say, each procedure has one or more pattern-recognizers attached to it. These pattern-recognizers continually scrutinize various aspects of the ongoing information processing; whenever a pattern-recognizer recognizes its distinctive 'trigger' pattern, it causes its attached procedure to enter one of the unoccupied control registers and to become active. We describe this as *pattern-initiated activation*.

The difference between these two control structure arrangements is of great importance and deserves serious thought. We illustrate the difference, at least roughly, with examples of human social behavior.

In the novel *Lord of the Flies*, by William Golding,[6] a group of boys on an island find a large conch shell, and use it for their version of Robert's Rules of Order. At group meetings, whoever holds the conch shell 'has the floor', and may speak. When others wish to speak, they hold up a hand. When the person holding the conch shell tosses the shell to someone else, the person catching it becomes the next speaker.

This arrangement parallels what we have called *single processing with directed transfer of control*, because (i) only one person has the floor at any given moment; and (ii) the person who has the floor, when he selects the person to whom he tosses the conch shell, determines the next person to have control.

Something resembling the alternative control arrangement may occur when, say, a group of urban dwellers get together to renovate their neighborhood. Anyone who sees some contribution he or she can make may volunteer to do so. Under this arrangement, anyone becomes active because he or she sees an appropriate opportunity, and many people may be active at the same time, so we have the two features of *pattern-initiated activation* and *simultaneous processing*.

Even with these features — pattern-initiated activation and simultaneous processing — it can be useful to postulate a single-step processor at the so-called 'highest level', charged with overseeing what might be called the 'final assembly'.

Fortunately, many important properties of models are not necessarily dependent upon the details of processing. One such matter is the question of assembling pieces from a large computation, or, more generally, 'keeping track of where you are' during any kind of information processing. The Sharp EL-5100, a hand-held calculator, will evaluate this input

$$3 + 2 \times (\ (1 + 5) \times (3 + 4) \ )$$

correctly, getting the answer 87, so even a mere calculator has — and needs — some capability of this sort.

Stacks: 'Keeping Track of Where You Are'

For the arithmetic problem just mentioned the operation tree is shown in Figure 4.3. Depending upon one's purpose, this tree can be processed either top-down or bottom-up, but in either case it is necessary to keep track of what has been done, what needs to be done, and where the partial results have been stored.

Figure 4.3: The 'operation tree' for the arithmetic problem $3 + 2 \times$ $(\ (1 + 5) \times (3 + 4) \ )$.

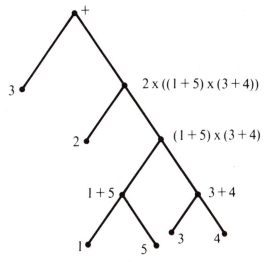

Preceding 'bottom-up', which is necessary for a straightforward arithmetic calculation, one computes $1 + 5$ and must store this answer, say in memory slot A. One computes $3 + 4$ and stores this in slot B. Now what do we do with these partial results? Oh, yes — hopefully we have a note reminding us to multiply these results. And, continuing, we work our way upwards through the operation tree, finally emerging at the top-level node with the answer 87.

Imagine that we write simple messages on scraps of paper — one simple message per scrap of paper — and put them in order:

add

3

multiply

2

multiply

add

4

3

add

5

1

This constitutes a so-called 'stack'. You can execute this operation by starting at the bottom of the stack, and proceeding upwards. To do this, you will need to work out some system for keeping track of partial results, and also for 'keeping track of where you are' in the calculation.

Experts frequently traverse this tree in the 'top-down' mode, and for some purposes this is essential although this is not the way to compute the numerical answer.

Preceeding top-down, we get a stack

add

3

x

multiply

2

y

multiply

z

w

add

1

5

add

3

4   ,

or some such thing. Of course, no one knows just how such stacks are handled by the human mind, but we all use them, very frequently.

As I leave the house I may have in mind:

Go home.
Pick up unfinished invitation list at home.
Work on invitation list while waiting.
Wait at dentist.
Drive Jeff to dentist.
Bring fresh vegetables home.
Go to farmers' market (cash required).
Go to bank and get cash.
Buy gasoline with credit card.

This stack may need to be executed from the bottom up — depending on how much cash I already have, and how much gasoline the car has. If so, one item is out of order. If I fail to correct this, I will not be able to execute the list as I have intended.

To make matters worse, in complicated problems we often encounter a need to modify these stacks — to add some further items or some further constraints, to change the order, and so on. Even a stack that had been in fairly good shape may develop contradictions after a considerable amount of editing and reshuffling.

Two important aspects of 'stacks' are of special importance for mathematics education. First, items in stacks may be in the wrong order, and finding a correct order is not always easy. Second, for humans the maximum length of stacks held in memory is rather small, and can be further reduced by fatigue, preoccupation, etc. Matz (1980) uses the possibility of items getting lost off the end of stacks to explain certain common errors. We shall pursue this explanation in later chapters.

Steps in Using Frames

'Frames' are of special importance, and merit further discussion. We have introduced frames primarily in relation to reading, but of course they are a kind of knowledge representation structure that can find application in any area of human information processing (or machine information processing). Hence the steps described above for the use of frames in reading are followed also in more general uses of frames.

The Input

In every case, we start with some specific *input* information. At the beginning, we call this 'primitive' or 'unprocessed' input. In the case of reading, the primitive input is a written or printed sentence or paragraph, but in more general cases it can be a spoken message, or sensory data of any sort. It need not come from the outside world at all; for example, a procedure which has just been carried out has left some kind of record in the student's memory, and this memory record may itself serve as input for some subsequent information processing. We all experience this general phenomenon when we find ourselves reflecting on something we did earlier that day, wondering what else we might have done, and so on.

Retrieval

As in the case of reading, this input must quickly cue the retrieval of a seemingly appropriate frame. But the simplicity of the phrase describing this process should not be allowed to blind us to the great complexity of this task. For one thing, an input offers us many cues; which cue or cues shall we select to guide us in frame retrieval? (We shall see in later sections that the choice of cues to attend to, vs. cues to ignore, is one of the most pronounced differences that distinguishes the problem-solving behavior of experts from that of novices.)

There is, as often in cognitive science, a 'which-came-first-the-chicken-or-the-egg' type of question: we can start with a list of cues, and search memory for one or more matching frames, or we can start with a list of tokens representing frames, and scrutinize the input, seeking a cue that will match one of our tokens. Either assumption leads to complications. If we hypothesize that one starts with a list of cues, how does one get from the 'primitive' input to a cue? Clearly, the primitive input must be compared against *something in order to recognize a cue*. What is that 'something'? The input could be compared against a list of 'cues-to-look-for'. But where does this list come from? Since we are proposing that we *start* with the input and only move in search of a frame *after* we have selected one or more key cues, then we cannot *begin* by ranging over all of the frames in memory. Searching memory, in this alternative, must come second, not first. There are ways out of this difficulty, but the matter is clearly complicated.

Well, suppose we propose the opposite order; let us postulate that we start with a list of available frames, and look for a cue in the input data that matches one of these frames (or, more precisely, matches a certain descriptor for one of these frames). This assumption confronts us with a different difficulty: one has in memory an extremely large number of frames. How can we start with so long a check list?

This, of course, is our 'top-down' vs. 'bottom-up' dilemma. There are many mysteries as to how the human mind solves this — and, of course, it often fails to.

A possible answer to this difficulty goes as follows: recall our division of memory into 'passive memory' vs. 'work space'. One could postulate an extension of this arrangement. Suppose there is 'passive memory' and 'work space', and also an intermediate memory we could call an *on-deck circle* (borrowing a phrase from baseball). When, for example, a student enters a mathematics classroom, certain knowledge representation structures (or else tokens that refer to these structures) are moved into this intermediate-readiness section that we have labeled the 'on-deck circle'. Now, when we study an input, looking for a match with some frame-retrieval-indicator, we do *not* work from the entire list of all the frames stored in memory. On the contrary, we work only from frames represented in the 'on-deck' listing.

But this extension need not be limited to *one* intermediate level of readiness. One could postulate n intermediate levels; using the symbolism $A \subset B$ to mean, in set theoretical language, that 'set A is a subset of set B', we can write:

$$WS \subset I_1 \subset I_2 \subset I_3 \subset \ldots \subset I_k \subset M.$$

By this we mean: the contents of the work space is (considered as a *set*) a subset of the 'most ready' level of KRSs, which is a subset of the 'next most ready' level, and so on, until finally the list representing the lowest level of readiness (among the intermediate levels) is a subset of the set M of all KRSs stored in memory.

This arrangement provides an information processing mechanism that appears to match certain observable aspects of behavior.

If you say to me only the word 'distance' there is considerable doubt as to what ideas this brings to mind. If, however, I am driving in my car from Urbana to Chicago, I will usually think of how far I have left to go, how far I can go before I need to refill my tank with gasoline, how far I have already driven or the total distance from Urbana to Chicago. Interpreted in terms of our postulated 'intermediate levels of readiness', this would become: because I am driving, and maintaining some vigilance over my degree of fatigue-vs.-alertness, and also over my remaining fuel supply, one or more KRSs representing these matters will be in 'work-space' memory, or in an intermediate level for a rather high degree of readiness. By contrast, various other distance-related KRSs will remain back in passive memory, as 'unlikely to be needed'.

Of course, if conversation in the car moves towards a future possible trip to Copenhagen, then KRSs dealing with air travel from Chicago to New York, across the Atlantic and in Europe will move into higher levels of readiness, or even into the work space, and now ideas such as 'polar routes' and 'choice of air lines' will appear, which was not the case when one thought only of driving the automobile.

If that same driver enters a mathematics class in point-set topology, then ideas about a metric d (P,Q) may move into a higher level of readiness and be triggered by the word 'distance'. If, instead, it is a calculus class, the formula

$$\overline{ds}^2 = \overline{dx}^2 + \overline{dy}^2$$

may move to higher readiness levels. If the present chapter in the calculus book deals with polar co-ordinates, the formula

$$\overline{ds}^2 = \overline{dr}^2 + r^2 \overline{d\theta}^2$$

may move to a higher readiness level. The word 'distance' will trigger different ideas in different situations.

One mechanism for doing this could involve the lists of tokens mentioned above — each token represents some KRS, and $I_1, I_2 \ldots$, I_n are all lists of tokens, with

$$I_1 \subset I_2 \subset \ldots \subset I_n$$

Other mechanisms would accomplish the same result, although their descriptions are different; one of these is to assume that every KRS in memory has one variable slot that contains a 'readiness parameter' that receives increments and decrements from time to time. A third, and particularly elegant, mechanism has been proposed by Minsky ('K-lines', 1980), that accounts for this behavior and much more.

Our main point, however, is that by *some* mechanism a cue must be selected from the input, and matched with a seemingly appropriate KRS. However this is done, it must be an exceedingly complex process. A student can fail at this stage for any of several reasons, including:

    (i) he does not possess the frame that is needed;
    (ii) the relevant frame in his memory is flawed or incomplete;

(iii) the retrieval mechanism does not locate the correct frame.

Terminating Search

Whenever any search is proving unproductive, there is always a question about what mechanism will terminate the search. This clearly applies if we are pursuing a fruitless search in an effort to match an input with some frame. If we get a match, fine! We have found what we were looking for. But suppose we've searched for some time, and we have *not* found a match. What do we do now?

This problem can be serious in searching a vast store of data in memory; it is even worse if the collection through which we are searching consists of items that are synthesized in real time. In this case, there may be no *a priori* bound on the size of this collection.

Transformations Prior to Retrieval

A further complication in retrieval is that we cannot expect 'obvious' matches between input and frame. Before a match can be found, some preliminary 'tactical' transformations of the input may be needed. For example, the input

$$e^{2t} - 5e^{t} + 6 = 0$$

cannot be matched to the 'quadratic equation' frame (and $ax^2 + bx + c = 0$) until we make the substitution

$$x \longleftrightarrow e^{t}$$
$$x^2 \longleftrightarrow e^{2t}$$

to get

$$x^2 - 5x + 6 = 0$$

Mapping Input Data Into Frame Variables

After a frame is selected, the specific data from this particular input must be extracted and used for the instantiation of the frame variables. This, too, can be a complicated process. To show how difficult it can be, consider this example. Kazuko Suzuki, when in grade 9, was asked to prove that, for any $\epsilon > 0$, there exists an integer N such that

$$\frac{1}{n} < \epsilon$$

provided $n > N$, by using the Archimedean postulate[7] (which says: if *a* and *b* are any positive numbers, then there exists an integer N such that

$aN > b$).

The Archimedean postulate can be put into words by saying: no matter how long a journey you want to make (b), and no matter how short your step is (a), you can go far enough if you take enough steps (namely, N of them).

Kazuko was, in effect, being asked to prove that

$$\text{Lim}_{n \to \infty} \frac{1}{n} = 0.$$

She had never seen this problem before, nor ever before seen the Archimedean postulate, so this was a new task for her, requiring originality and creativity. The key steps are, first, to transform

$$\frac{1}{n} < \epsilon$$

into its equivalent form

$$n > \frac{1}{\epsilon} \qquad , \qquad \text{(A)}$$

and, second, to show that inequality A is obtainable from the Archimedean postulate

$$a N > b \qquad \text{(B)}$$

by making a correct replacement of the variables. Kazuko solved this novel task easily and immediately — a performance far beyond what one would ordinarily expect from someone her age — by making this correspondence between 'input' variables and 'frame' variables:

Symbols in this example		Variables in the general Archimedean postulate
$\frac{1}{\epsilon}$	$\longleftrightarrow$	b
n	$\longleftrightarrow$	N
1	$\longleftrightarrow$	a

The main point of this instance, for our present purposes, is that mapping input data into frame variables should not be taken for granted. It is not always easy. Nor, it is important to remember, is it always a matter of *numerical* variables. Information of any sort whatsoever can be involved.

Default Evaluations

As in the previous discussion, if a frame variable requires an information input, and if no appropriate input can be obtained from the present 'primitive' input source, a frame will typically make a *default evaluation*: some information will be inserted in the writing slot, by drawing on past typical situations.

No Replacements for Key Variables

If no replacement for a variable can be made, either from input data or via default evaluations, and if the variable is critical for the frame to perform, then the frame will refuse to carry out its tasks, and will instead return control to the super-procedure that caused the frame to be activated. We shall see some consequences of this in later chapters.

Judging the Appropriateness of the Instantiated Frame

A frame has been selected and copied into work space. This frame may, or may not, provide a reasonable match for the primitive input data. Consequently a judgement needs to be made: is the choice of frame acceptable?

Further, data has been mapped into variable slots in the frame. This may, or may not, have been done correctly. Here, too, a judgement needs to be made.

It is easy to relate these decisions to Piaget's concepts of *assimilation* and *accommodation*. When the judgement is made that the instantiated frame is an acceptable match to the input data, we can say that 'assimilation' occurs. If this judgement is that the match is unacceptable, we have a precondition for 'accommodation' to take place, although more steps are needed before accommodation can be considered complete. (Maybe all that is needed is the retrieval of a new candidate frame.)

Reliance on the Instantiated Frame

Once an instantiated frame is judged acceptable, nearly all subsequent information processing *uses this instantiated frame as a data base. The original 'primitive' data is thereafter ignored.*

This produces results with which we are all familiar, such as different people arguing over what a paragraph says, or what person A told person B, and so on. Statements quite unsupported by the original data source are made, and the source is cited as authority. *People do not typically distinguish between the information contained in the primitive data source, and the information contained in the instantiated frame*. This information has been obtained by combining informa-tion from the actual input and from the frame, and so subsequent processing makes no distinction. People typically believe that *all* of the information came from the (usually external) primitive data input. Since, however, the frames in one person's memory will not necessarily be the same as those in someone else's, very substantial disagreements become possible. Indeed, they are to be expected.

Frame Modification

In this process, modifications of the frame may be made. Consider-able evidence (some of which we shall see in subsequent chapters) suggests that, when modifications are made, the new (modified) frame is added to the permanent memory store in addition to the previous version, *but the previous version is not deleted.*

Writing an Episodic Record into Memory

If there has been some input stimulus, and if we have selected a frame and probably done other information processing then 'something has happened'. This information processing is itself an event that has occurred. Some record of it may be retained in memory. In a subse-quent chapter we shall look at some evidence suggesting what this record may be.

Reflection and Meta-language

Furthermore, after an input-retrieval activity of this type, a thoughtful student will often reflect on what has occurred. What worked? What failed? How would one handle such a situation differently in the future? The results of such reflection may modify the meta-language descriptors for the frame or frames in question, or may contribute to modifications of the frame itself.

Goals and Subgoals

The shifting of control from one procedure to another is obviously a matter of considerable importance. When we wish to describe this shifting around, we sometimes analyze the information processing activity into *goals* and *subgoals*.

Consider this illustrative story:

Suppose it is a holiday. You and your family decide to go to the beach. You look for a map of routes to the beach, but cannot find the map, so you set out anyway. Unfortunately, too many other families have had the same idea; the road is so crowded that you realize you cannot get to the beach in a reasonable time. You consider, decide that the purpose was to enjoy a family outing, so you stop instead at an amusement park.

By way of illustration, we can analyze this somewhat fanciful episode either in terms of procedures and control, or in terms of goals and subgoals.

Procedures and Control

A procedure is activated: *Go-to-the-beach*. This procedure calls upon a sub-procedure − *find-map* − and transfers control to *find-map*. The procedure *find-map* is unable to perform, and returns control to the procedure *Go-to-the-beach*, which decides to proceed on the basis of default evaluations (guesses, and possibly defective recollections of previous trips). On the way there, the traffic delay provides a new piece of primitive input data, which triggers retrieval of an *Impossible-traffic-situation* frame (or something roughly equivalent to this). This frame carries out a computation of estimated time of arrival at the beach (this computation may involve sub-procedures), and finds this to be unsatisfactory. The *'traffic'* frame returns this unhappy conclusion to the *Go-to-the-beach* frame, and also returns control to the *'beach'* frame. The *'beach'* frame recognizes that it cannot achieve its assigned goal, and returns control to the super-procedure which had activated it, namely, the *Let's-enjoy-a-family-outing* procedure, together with the fact that the *'beach'* procedure cannot succeed.

Or, to analyze this story in terms of goals and subgoals we could say: The highest level goal in this story is to 'Enjoy a family outing'. This has potentially many subgoals, two of which appear in the story. The first, 'Go to the beach' has its own subgoals, including 'Find map' and 'Evaluate progress'. When the evaluation returns a negative prognosis, the 'beach' goal is abandoned, and an alternative subgoal is selected (cf. Figure 4.4).

Summary

Our purpose in this chapter has been to introduce language − borrowed from work with computers, and from other sources − to facilitate

Figure 4.4: The 'family outing' episode can be analyzed either in terms of super-procedures and sub-procedures, or else in terms of 'higher-level goals' and 'subgoals'. In either case, the hierarchy is similar to what is shown here.

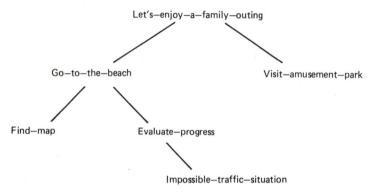

the discussion of human information processing in general and, in particular, discussions of how people think about mathematical matters. For readers familiar with this literature, this will seem trivial or even superficial. For readers to whom most of this is new, it may seem exceedingly complex. In fact, it can provide an entirely new way of looking at the performance, sometimes inspired and sometimes erroneous, of students or of experts.

Notes

1. Without intending to do so, I have just used a sentence that may lead us into error. (Because we have all believed certain personal, unexamined, 'naïve' theories about knowledge, it is unhappily easy to make unwarranted and inadvertent assumptions.) We typically *do* think of procedures (or any actions) as having some purpose. There is growing evidence that this is not always the case. As one instance, Lawler (1982) describes how his son, Robbie, while exploring the possibilities of using the LOGO computer language to draw pictures on a TV screen, developed a certain method for organizing his explorations. Essentially the method involved trying the number one, then two, then three, and so on, in a certain systematic fashion. Later, Robbie used this in an entirely different situation (namely, when he was cutting some loops of paper with scissors). Did Robbie have

a clear 'purpose' to his systematic procedure? Or was it merely something he *did*, that he subsequently repeated — as many students take
the same seat in class on different days, even when there is no external
requirement for doing so? (One might call this the one-trial learning of
a *habit*.) The distinction is important for a precise theory of learning —
at what point does a procedure acquire a 'purpose'? Lawler writes:

> I believe that Robbie learned a heuristic that was specific with
> respect to activity but vague with respect to purpose.

Of course, as Robbie continues to follow this 'habit', he is likely to
notice some of the things it does accomplish, and some of the things
that it fails to accomplish. In this sense, the *purpose* of the procedure
becomes clearer. This information, too, must be coded and recorded
for later use.

2. Seymour Papert, of MIT, has developed an interesting language
for programming computers, known as *LOGO*. The LOGO language
serves the dual role of allowing young children to program computers,
and also providing a useful metaphor as an abstract model of certain
aspects of human thought.

The 'procedures' that we speak of are well represented in LOGO.
For example, there is a procedure for guiding a wheeled vehicle around
on the floor:

```
TO POLY          :side        :angle
10 FORWARD       :side
20 RIGHT         :angle
30 POLY          :side        :angle
END
```

The symbols ':side' and ':angle' are variables or slots for input data.
The variable :side tells the procedure how *long* each side should be,
and the variable :angle tells the procedure the angle through which
to turn the wheeled vehicle.

In particular, if you tell the computer

```
POLY   10   90   ,
```

the computer will cause the wheeled vehicle to trace out a square on
the floor; as a second example, the command

```
POLY   1   1
```

will cause the wheeled vehicle to trace out a circle (or a polygon that is indistinguishable from a circle). Cf. Papert (1980).

Suppose, now that you modify POLY by inserting an appropriate rule for stopping when the polygon is complete. Using this modified version, which we might call PPOLY, you could write this procedure

```
TO EIGHT
10 PPOLY      1        1
20 RIGHT      180
30 PPOLY      1        1
END
```

What will the procedure EIGHT accomplish? (Note that the procedure EIGHT calls upon PPOLY as a sub-procedure.)

Of course we do not mean to imply that the human mind contains commands that are identical to those of LOGO. The usefulness of LOGO as a metaphor is considerably more abstract than that. But on some general level, there must be some kind of parallel to the way one procedure can build upon 'more primitive' sub-procedures, because a large portion of knowledge is built up in this way, and the structure of knowledge itself must somehow be dealt with by any animal or machine that seeks to embody this knowledge.

3. An alternative, and possibly better, way of thinking about 'descriptors' is presented in Chapter 5. In the present chapter we start with a procedure (or other knowledge representation structure), and attach to it 'descriptors' that tell us something about how it works or when to use it.

Observation of students suggests that the creation of these descriptors may often occur during periods of reflective thought *after* a problem has been solved, or during periods when progress has halted and one is 'stuck', with no idea of what to do next.

Chapter 5 takes a different view, and focuses on the need to replace a long procedure (or other knowledge representation structure) with something very much shorter, a mere sketch or outline of the original procedure. Ideally, this outline would contain all the information about the procedure that is needed in order to think about how it relates to other knowledge representation structures, or to plan its use, but would omit 'internal' knowledge needed at the moment of implementation. Starting with some original procedure, the mind can create a shortened version. But, perhaps, then it can go on to create a still *shorter version*. And, after that, another that is shorter yet.

Are some of these very short versions the same thing as descriptors?

4. The *idea* of a 'frame' is of the greatest importance and value; by contrast, the *name* given to this idea is something between a nuisance and a disaster. Marvin Minsky, who spelled out the idea with exceptional clarity in an early study (Minsky, 1975), chose the name 'frame'. Unfortunately, this word has a very large number of other meanings, so that considerable confusion often results. Other researchers have used the word *schema*, or the word *script*, but both of these choices also involve confusion with alternative meanings. Avoiding confusion may be somewhat easier if one remembers that Minsky's *frame* is always a special kind of knowledge representation structure, stored in memory and retrievable from memory.

5. For further discussion of evidence leading to frames, cf. Davis, Jockusch and McKnight (1978) and also Davis (1982).

6. William Golding, *Lord of the Flies* (Capricorn Books, New York, 1955).

7. This classroom episode was videotaped, and the videotape is available from The Study Group for Mathematical Behavior, Inc., PO Box 2095 – Station A, Champaign, Illinois 61820; for a more complete description of the episode see Davis, Jockusch and McKnight, 1978, pp. 90-1.

Questions for Consideration

1. If you read the sequence 'glove', 'tie', 'shirt', 'handkerchief', 'shoe' and 'sock', you probably think of *sock* as a cloth covering worn over a foot, inside a shoe. But if you read the sequence 'kick', 'slap', 'hit', 'bite', 'poke' and 'sock', you probably think of *sock* quite differently. This phenomenon – different responses to the same stimulus in different settings – is called *mental set*. How could you explain 'mental set' in terms of the idea of *passive memory* and *work space*?

2. In this chapter we have described a somewhat complicated geometric figure built out of squares, circles, triangles, and so on. We have talked about the *knowledge representation structure* that is built up in a person's mind to represent this figure. But do we know that *any* representation of this figure exists in the mind of some specific reader? *How might you prove that some representation does exist*?

3. We have mentioned that adults typically possess a *size* critic that causes them to reject 5,087 as an answer for 7,002 − 25. Actual

observation shows that almost no third-grade child possesses (or uses) this critic. How would you explain this difference between adults and third-graders?

4. Observations have shown that many students, learning to plot points in rectangular Cartesian co-ordinates, make the following errors: asked to plot (3, 4), they erroneously mark (2, 3). Asked to plot (9, 5), they erroneously mark (8, 4). Asked to plot (¯3, ¯2), they erroneously plot (¯2, ¯1).

(a) What error are they probably making in the way they think about these questions?
(b) If you wanted them to discover their error, what point (a, b) would you ask them to plot next?

5. It has been observed that, when a procedure has been found to be defective, and has been 'corrected' in some way, there is often a period of time during which performance is unreliable. The corrected procedure may be activated and may perform properly, but there is a possibility that the old, uncorrected procedure will be activated instead, so that the performance will display precisely that 'bug' which the learner is trying to eliminate.

How would you explain this?

6. From your own experience either in mathematics or outside of mathematics, try to recall a procedure which you learned in an incorrect form. How did you learn that it was incorrect? How did you correct it?

7. An armed forces manual on proper maintenance procedures for a certain piece of equipment read as follows:

Locate the linkage pin, W. Remove pin W and examine it carefully. If it is bent, replace it.

What do you suppose happened? How would you explain this in terms of frame retrieval?

8. Make sure you understand Kazuko Suzuki's proof that

$$\lim_{n \to \infty} \frac{1}{n} = 0.$$

5   WHAT NEEDS TO BE EXPLAINED?

In the preceding chapter we introduced many of the basic concepts that can be used in describing how human beings think about mathematics. However, in studying any subject it is important to keep sight of the goal, which usually means keeping in mind *the problem (or problems) which one is seeking to solve*. What problems is mathematics education seeking to solve?

Well, obviously one problem is to understand why so many people make so many errors, as in the very common erroneous use of the distributive law that rewrites

$$2\,(x + y)$$

as

$$2x + y$$

In a later chapter we shall see how Matz explains this error by relating it to a *control error* in her model of mathematical thinking (Matz, 1980). There are many errors of this kind, and some of them are very persistent.

Indeed, that persistence is itself a matter that needs explaining. When, in a later chapter, we look more deeply at studies by Clement and his colleagues, we will be forcibly struck by how persistent some errors can be. A student may *want* to learn, may see that a particular information-processing act is *wrong* in a certain context, and yet *may continue to make this same error*, time and time again! That behavior clearly needs to be explained.

There is also the difficulty that many people have in *learning certain key concepts*. Many students, for example, never seem to learn to be comfortable with *fractions*. Among other examples, it is well known that many calculus students never seem to understand the concept of *limit of an infinite sequence*. Why are these ideas so difficult for so many people? That needs to be explained.

Further, many students seem to be uncreative, uninventive, not resourceful in their attempts to deal with mathematics. Why not? This, too, needs to be explained.

Of course, everything that we have just stated negatively could also be stated positively: how do we process information so that we can perform tasks correctly? How do we identify errors and correct them? How do we store concepts in our minds? How do we deal flexibly and powerfully with novel situations?

Expert Performance

Ordinarily, when we try to teach students how to do something, we (who are creating the curriculum) do know how to do it. That is, we know how 'experts' do it. Or at least we think we know. However, in the case of mathematics, it has only recently been realized that, in most instances, we do *not* know how the experts do it. Many recent studies have dealt with precisely this question: how *do* the experts do it?[1] So this has become an important task for mathematics education: *find out how the experts do mathematics*.

Mind

We are confronting a large area of mathematical thinking, and it may simplify our task if we try to divide this large area into three separate pieces: first, phenomena that are caused by the way the mind works (as best we can tell from an imperfect model); second, strategies for using the mind effectively; and, finally, phenomena related to the organization of mathematical knowledge itself and the organization of mathematical tasks. In this section we focus on difficulties − or opportunities − caused by the way the mind itself seems to work.

Vast Memory and Small Work Space

We have seen that the human memory is very large, and that we cannot search through all of our memory. For example, you cannot write down all the male first names that you know − no matter how many you write, there is always the likelihood that sooner or later you will think of another one that you had omitted from your list. You know it; it was stored *somewhere* in your memory; but on your earlier search attempts you had somehow failed to find it. From the point of view of the vast amount of information that we want to learn, having a tremendously large storehouse is a blessing; but when we want to search in our memory to find something, its vastness is itself a major difficulty. *You cannot search through your entire memory.*

If, then, you are seeking some particular item, how on earth can you hope to locate it in this fantastically large warehouse? That is one of the main problems that students face every day – indeed, every hour if not every minute – and one of the main processes that mathematics education seeks to understand.

But if our warehouse of passive memory is uncomfortably large, our 'workbench' of active memory (or *work space*) is uncomfortably small. In order to deal with complicated tasks, we need to keep many things in mind, all at once. But consider the phrase 'we need to keep many things in mind all at once'. That does not refer to our vast passive memory warehouse; it clearly refers to our active memory work space. And on this workbench, space is very tight! This is clearly true for computers, and seems to be equally true for humans. When we locate in memory an entry which we need, in order to make use of it we must 'load' it (i.e., copy it) into active memory. But the entry we need may be something rather large; there may not be enough space in workbench memory to permit loading. In such a case we must erase part of the contents of the workspace memory. (Erasing part of what is written on a chalk board, in order to create space to write something else, is a very precise parallel.)

What happens if we still need all of the 'old' contents of the workspace memory? Yet we do still need to load this new item. But there is not enough space. . . Crisis!

Present-day computers solve this problem by 'swapping' back and forth. That which is most urgently needed is moved into work-space memory, while something slightly less urgently needed is moved into passive 'warehouse' storage. But even the less-urgently-needed material *is* needed, and must soon be swapped back in. To carry out one such swap in a modern computer may take about 50 to 60 microseconds.[2]

There is abundant evidence that something of the sort happens in the human mind. We have all experienced occasions where the need to think about one matter seems to make us forget – at least temporarily – something else.

Partitioning Work-space Memory

We can improve the postulated model of human information processing somewhat if we postulate a partitioning of work-space memory into three or more smaller memory areas. One, called *control memory*, keeps track of where we are in the task we are carrying out, which things we have done, which things we still need to work on and where these items are located.

A second part, which might be called *abstract* or *token memory*, contains, not the large whole items we need, but very abbreviated versions of them, possibly merely *token descriptors*.

A third part, *whole-text memory*, could then contain the entire memory entry for a few items most urgently needed at this instant. Swapping becomes most critical for this whole-text memory, because the entries themselves are so large. By contrast, the individual entries in token memory are much smaller, so that this area can typically contain a complete 'outline' for the performance of the entire task. If these tokens or abstract representations contain enough of the key information about the corresponding full texts that they represent, then a large part of the problem-solving or planning activity can take place in the token memory, resulting in a great saving of space on the workbench. Once this planning has been carried out, the details can be dealt with in whole-text memory, where considerable swapping in and out will probably be necessary.

Workbench memory could be partitioned even further, to allow for several levels of 'abbreviated' versions of memory entries. Figure 5.1 shows, schematically, a small control memory (A); a small 'token' memory (where each relevant entry in warehouse memory is represented by some highly abbreviated token) (B); then – on a slightly more expanded scale – an abstract representation memory where each relevant item is represented by a brief 'outline' of *some* key features (C); and, finally, a 'whole-text' section of work-space memory, large enough to accommodate only a few items in their whole-text form (D). Other whole-text items are off to the right somewhere in the vast warehouse memory (E). If some specific item has been identified as relevant to the present task, that specific item will be represented by a token in B, connected (by pointers, or otherwise) to an 'outline' or 'sketch' version in C, and to the whole-text (complete) version, which may be located either in D, or somewhere in the remote vastness of E.

Of course, one of the main ways to deal with the crowded workbench memory is to augment it by adding some external memory: as we think, we can also write part of our work on paper! Especially if the written notations are arranged shrewdly on the paper, this can effectively enlarge workbench memory in a significant way, as nearly everyone knows who has ever done much mathematics.

Figure 5.1: Workbench memory partitioned into control memory, very abbreviated token memory, abstract representation memory and whole-text memory. Indicated on the right is the vast 'passive' warehouse memory.

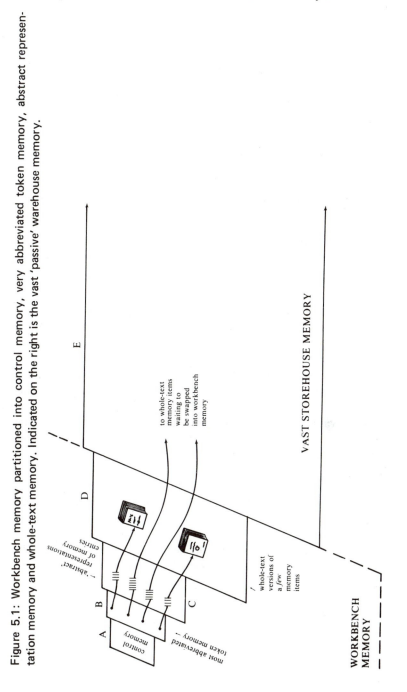

'Chunking'

We have seen, earlier, the general argument that information, whether stored in a computer or in the human mind, must *not* be stored in tiny pieces. On the contrary, it must be arranged in sizeable chunks of some sort.[3] (The word 'chunk' is from Miller, 1956.) VMS sequences, integrated sequences and frames are examples of chunks. (Our most general name for *any* kind of chunk is *knowledge representation structure*, or KRS.)

As we look, in subsequent chapters, at examples of human behavior in dealing with mathematics, 'chunks' will be one of the things we shall need to keep in mind. Where do chunks help us perform better? Where — and how — does the form of 'chunking' constrain our behavior, even cause us to make mistakes?

Representations

In speaking of 'chunks' we are, as it were, looking at a package from the outside, as someone carrying heavy books might be mainly aware of their weight. But one can open a book and read it. Similarly, we can focus our attention not on the size of the chunks, but on the specific information contained inside. To emphasize this point of view we speak of 'representations' rather than 'chunks'. What does the chunk represent, and in what way does it do it?

Representations are fundamental to mathematical thought. In later sections we shall see that whether a problem is hard or easy often depends primarily on two matters:

(i) how you *represent* the problem;
(ii) how you represent relevant knowledge that you have learned in the past.

Hence, a major question for mathematics education is to explore the *representations* which beginners, or experts, build in their own minds.

Abstract Representations

As we saw in Figure 5.1, in working with a work-space memory that is often uncomfortably small, it is helpful to use shortened, abbreviated 'sketches' in place of whole-text memory items, which can be too large to fit into the workbench memory. The nature of the abbreviation process is clearly critical. If we have successfully preserved every piece of information that is essential, and if we have it coded in some readily usable form, then our abstract representation can be very helpful. Conversely, if the abbreviated representation has omitted key information, or coded it in a form that is difficult to use, then our shortened representation may prove unhelpful.

In later chapters, especially in looking at some elegant studies by Stephen Young, we shall see the importance of these 'abbreviated' or 'abstract' representations in determining the effectiveness — or lack of effectiveness — of various attempts to think about mathematics.

Recall that the need for short 'abbreviated' representations has been inferred from our abstract model, and particularly from the current design of large digital computers. Since our ultimate concern will be with human thought processes, it may be worthwhile to broaden our perspective, and to look at the question of mental representation from the point of view of a psychologist who deals with humans, not computers.

William Brewer, reviewing earlier work by Ebbinghaus, Collins and Quillian, and Tulving (and proposing some modifications), distinguishes three types of information stored in human memory:

> . . . [the contents of] human memory must be analyzed into three basic types: personal memory, generic memory, and skills. . . .
>
> In order to make the distinction between the three types of memory clear, consider the following example: An undergraduate goes to the psychology building for a psychology experiment. He finds his way to the correct room, hesitates a minute, knocks on the door, and goes inside. He sees the experimenter and a memory drum in a small bare room. After some preliminary instructions, he is given a number of trials on a long paired-associate list. One of the items on the list is the pair DAX-FRIGID. After the experiment is over he breathes a sigh of relief and leaves the experimental room. This one event can be used to illustrate the three types of memory:
>
> *Personal memory.* If, the next day, the undergraduate were asked, 'Do you remember the psychology experiment you were in yesterday?' he might say something like: 'Sure, I remember walking down to the room from the elevator. I remember feeling nervous as I stood there in front of the door. I remember opening

the door and seeing the experimenter standing behind the table. I remember being surprised she was a woman. She had a white laboratory coat on, etc.' If he were asked, 'Was anything going through your mind while you were telling me all this?' the undergraduate might say something like 'Yes, I was seeing in my mind's eye much of what I told you. I could see the door, the expression on the experimenter's face when I opened the door, etc.' It is this type of memory that will be called personal memory in this paper.

Generic memory. If some months later, the undergraduate were asked, 'Do you remember that you were in a verbal-learning experiment several months ago?' he might say, 'Yes.' If asked, 'Was anything going through your mind while you were giving me this answer?' he might say, 'No, I just knew that I had been in the experiment. There were four experiments required for the course – two were filling out social psychology questionnaires, one was a perception experiment, and the other one was the verbal-learning experiment.' This is an example of the type of memory that will be called generic memory.

Skill. If, some days later, the undergraduate were asked, 'When I give you a nonsense syllable you tell me what word followed. DAX?', he will probably say 'FRIGID.' If asked, 'Was anything going through your mind when you gave the answer?' he might say, 'No, I had practiced the list so many times I just knew what the response was.' This is an example of rote memory, one type of skill.

This example was intended to provide an intuitive understanding of the distinction between the three types of memory... [We now give] a general description of each type...

Personal memory. A personal memory is a recollection of a particular episode in the past of an individual. Personal memory is (always?) experienced in terms of some type of mental imagery – predominantly visual. It usually also includes non-imaginal information. The image is experienced as the representation of a particular time and location. The personal memory episode is accompanied by a propositional attitude that 'this occurred in the past' and is accompanied by a belief that the remembered episode was personally experienced by the individual. A personal memory is also frequently accompanied by a belief that it is a veridical record of the past episode. Personal memory statements frequently fit the linguistic frame: 'I remember X.' Thus, in the above example: 'I remember the expression on the experimenter's face.'

Generic memory. A generic memory is the recall of some item of general knowledge. Generic memory is not experienced as having occurred at a particular time and location and is not accompanied by a belief that the information was personally experienced by the individual. Generic memory statements frequently fit the linguistic frame: 'I remember *that* X.' Thus, in the earlier example: 'I remember that I was in a verbal learning experiment.' *Semantic memory* is the subclass of generic memory which involves the memory for abstract propositional information — for example: 'good is the opposite of bad' or 'the speed of light is a constant'. The operation of semantic memory does not typically carry along with it an experience of mental imagery. Thus when asked, 'What is the opposite of good?' the correct answer is given without report of any mental imagery. *Perceptual memory* is the subclass of generic memory which involves the memory for perceptual information — for example: a map of the United States or the Statue of Liberty. The operation of generic perceptual memory does typically involve mental imagery. Thus, if asked, 'Is Oklahoma to the south of Kansas?' or 'Which hand of the Statue of Liberty holds the torch?', most individuals will report a 'generic' mental image. These generic images are not typically experienced as involving a particular time and location. The similarities and differences between a generic perceptual memory and a personal memory can be examined by the following exercise. Recall the center of our university campus (i.e., form a mental map); now recall your most recent walk across that campus. The first is a generic perceptual memory; the second is a personal memory.

Skill. A skill is the ability to perform a given sequence of motor or cognitive actions. A practiced skill is typically not accompanied by mental imagery. There are a number of subtypes of skill that need to be distinguished. *Motor skills* refer to the ability to carry out a sequence of motor actions. This type of memory underlies the ability to ride a bike or hit a tennis ball. *Rote skills* refer to the ability to repeat a sequence of linguistic objects. This type of memory underlies the ability to repeat the alphabet or give one's social security number. *Cognitive skills* refer to the ability to carry out some sequence of cognitive operations. This type of memory underlies the ability to take the square root of a number or to make the verb agree in number with the subject in a spoken sentence. Many statements involving skills fit the linguistic frame: 'I remember *how* to do X.' Thus, 'I remember how to ride a bike, how to say the alphabet, how to take a square root.'[4]

Brewer, of course, does not deal explicitly with our distinction between a 'whole-text' representation, where an item is large and contains much detail, *vs.* a short 'abstract' representation for this same item, shorn of most of the details. None the less, he seems to be discussing a behavior that corresponds to our information-processing phenomenon: somehow, a detailed 'personal' (or *episodic*) item ('I remember feeling nervous as I stood there in front of the door. I remember opening the door and seeing the experimenter standing behind the table . . .') gives rise to a much shorter memory entry ('. . . I knew I had been in the experiment . . .'). This shorter entry, in Brewer's account, seems also to have different associations, of a 'broad context' nature, and not of 'internal details', as when the hypothetical subject says: 'There were four experiments required for the course – two were filling out social psychology questionnaires, one was a perception experiment, and the other one was the verbal-learning experiment.'

Somehow, this shorter entry has been created. Internal detail has been reduced or eliminated, broad context associations have been added.

Has the longer version been destroyed? Evidence from hypnosis and psychoanalysis suggests not; it is still there in memory, somewhere.

Why, then, can the student no longer access it? Presumably because it is off *somewhere* in the truly vast warehouse of permanent memory. It is important to remember that no one can search through everything he or she has stored in permanent memory. It is like arriving in New York City and looking for your friend's sister-in-law, if you don't know her married name, nor her address, nor her phone number, nor her place of employment. *Whenever you want to search permanent long-term memory, you MUST have a clue or cue to guide you to the correct part of memory*. Without a guide, you will inevitably be lost.

A knowledgeable mathematics student has a vast amount of information stored in memory. The question of how he or she finds the correct piece of information for the present task – whatever that may be – is known as the *memory search* problem. This, clearly, is a matter that mathematics education needs to study.

Pattern Recognition

What sorts of guides exist, to lead us to the appropriate entry in memory?

One kind that has to be included is *pattern recognition*. This phenomenon is something of an over-simplification, if not an excuse; it would often be preferable to know explicitly what cues were being used, but frequently one does not know. You can probably recognize the letter in the line below

I

and you probably recognize it as the letter 'I'. How did you recognize it? Most people feel they 'just see it and know what it is'. A similar phenomenon often occurs within mathematics, especially to more experienced students or experts. They quickly identify an input, correctly, but are quite unable to explain *how* they know — they 'just know'.

Combining Cues

Another phenomenon involves several partial cues, no one of which would guide you to the desired memory entry. Taken together, however, the combination of cues may do so.

There is a certain single word that is frequently paired with each of the following words:

line   birthday   surprise

What is that word? If you find it, can you say what cues guided you to the correct entry in your memory? Almost certainly you cannot. (For the 'correct' answer, see note 5 at the end of this chapter.)

Is this use of multiple cues different from 'pattern recognition'? Any answer at this point would be more nonsense than reason.

Perhaps the sense of searching the vast reaches of one's memory becomes clearer with the following example.

A simple substitution cypher is a code created by making a one-to-one mapping of the alphabet into itself. Thus, if the cypher letter 'A', say, really means 'W', then:

'A' *always* means 'W', in every occurrence;
no *other* cypher letter ever means 'W'.

The symbol string

ABAMPAMP

is the cypher representation of a word that you know. What is that word?

You can clearly see the pattern

$$. . .AMPAMP \quad ,$$

which suggests words like

ringing
bringing
singing

and so on. Can you find the word — which assuredly *is* stored in your memory — that matches the ABAMPAMP pattern exactly? Caution: your memory is a vast place. Do not become permanently lost!

Does it help, if I tell you that the word appears in this present chapter?

And . . . *if* you find the word, can you say how you were led to it?

Summary

A physicist works both ends against the middle. On the one hand, he has a postulated model that involves atoms, electrons, atomic nuclei, quantum transition rules, resonant frequencies, and so on. On the other hand he has phenomena observed in the real world: heating a gas in a closed container increases the pressure; water, when enough heat is added, will boil away; the sky is blue. He wishes to bring the two ends together, to show how the resonance frequency of orbital electrons explains why light is scattered the way that it is, and why, consequently, we see the sky as blue. In general, he wants to show how the observed physical phenomena correspond to the possibilities indicated by the model.

Our goal in this volume is very similar to this. We, too, have a postulated model, with a vast permanent memory where one gets lost unless one is somehow guided to the correct memory items; where the 'workbench' or work space is too small to accommodate everything that we need to assemble there; where — since we can never put real cats or real pyramids or real physical motions inside our minds — we are compelled to create some kind of *representation* for a cat or for a pyramid or for some physical movement; where information cannot be left lying around in very tiny bits and pieces, but must somehow be bundled up into larger packages or 'chunks' in some way.

And, on the other hand, we have a very large collection of obser-

vations of students and experts working to solve mathematical problems, to learn some new mathematical concepts, or to carry out some
other mathematical task. Often they do very clever things. Often, too,
they make various errors.

*Our goal is to match up phenomena that we observe with attributes
of the model that 'explain' why this behaviour took place.*

Of course, the abstract models in physics and chemistry are among
the best developed and most useful that humans have ever created.
Models for human information processing are far more recent, and far
less well developed. None the less, these models are nowadays good
enough so that making correspondences between attributes of the
model and observations of actual human behavior is possible and
useful. In Chapters 1 through 5 we have focused attention mainly on
the model. In the following chapters we shall focus mainly on human
behavior, *and on the task of making correspondences between the
model and the observed behavior.*

Notes

1. See, for example, Larkin, McDermott, Simon and Simon (1980);
also, Clement (1982).

2. To look in more detail at swapping on a modern computer, cf. a
CDC PLATO system. Memory entries are arranged as 'Lessons', and
each Lesson is sub-divided into *units*. A Lesson is originally written in
TUTOR. This TUTOR code is ordinarily stored in disk memory (our
'passive warehouse memory'). When a Lesson is needed, the TUTOR
code is loaded into the *condensor*, which recodes the information in
binary form. This binary version is stored in ECS (Extended Core
Storage), a high-speed memory, and at the same time another copy of
the binary version is stored in AMS (Auxiliary Mass Storage). The reason for two identical copies is that ECS is so busy, and so crowded,
that copies there will frequently need to be erased. After this has
occurred, a 'Xerox' copy of the AMS record can be re-entered into
ECS.

When a lesson is needed for immediate processing, PLATO first
looks for the lesson in ECS. If a copy is there, that *unit* of the lesson
which is needed is copied (via the usual Xerox copying, or *non-destructive read-out*) into the computer's mainframe central memory
(CM). Note that an entire lesson (typical length: 2,000 to 4,000 words)
is considered too long for loading into CM, which is the main 'active

processing' part of memory, so only a *part* of a lesson (namely, one *unit*, which is 500 words long at most) is loaded into CM. Transferring a unit from ECS into CM takes about 50 microseconds, or 0.000050 seconds. This unit will then remain in CM for a maximum of one 'time-slice', namely, 20 milliseconds, or .02 seconds. After that, some other unit must be moved into CM, replacing the previous one.

If, when PLATO goes looking for the needed lesson in ECS, it does not find it there, PLATO then retrieves (by 'Xeroxing') a copy from AMS, and moves it into ECS.

Information can be transferred from AMS to ECS at the rate of 10 million words per second (each 'word' is 60 bits long). A lesson of 2,000 words can thus be transferred from AMS to ECS in 20 milli-seconds, or .02 seconds.

Active processing can occur only in CM. Information transfer into CM must originate in ECS, and out of CM must go to ECS. ECS, how-ever, communicates with all other memories (CM, AMS and disk).

All of these transfers take place so quickly that a PLATO user is unaware of them, but lessons and units are in fact being shifted around within the machine at a fairly fantastic speed. None the less, they are where they should be every time you need one.

3. For further arguments supporting the inevitability of chunking, see Davis (1982).

4. From Brewer (1982).

5. This example is taken from Bernard J. Baars and Diane N. Kramer, 'Conscious and Unconscious Components of Intentional Control' (paper delivered at the Fourth Annual Meeting of the Cognitive Science Society, Ann Arbor, Michigan, 4-6 August 1982). 'Party' is the word that Baars and Kramer give as the 'correct' answer.

6 DATA COLLECTION

Task-based Interviews

A few years ago the most important forms of data collection in mathematics education were probably standardized multiple-choice achievement tests and so-called 'curriculum-specific' tests. These methods are, unfortunately, somewhat akin to peeping through a keyhole in order to find out what is going on in a room. They provide a certain kind of data, but they omit much more; they do not give a broad comprehensive picture of what is taking place. In particular, they usually fail to reveal the thought processes that were used by the students, and it is precisely these thought processes that are the main concern for student and teacher alike.[1]

For the cognitive science studies with which this book is concerned, a different method of data collection has come to occupy the center stage: *the task-based interview.*

The basic idea is very simple. A student is seated at a table, paper and pens are provided, and the student is asked to solve some specific mathematics problem. One or more adults are present collecting data.

Exactly how the session is conducted can vary considerably. For one thing, there can be more or less adult participation. At the extreme of minimal adult participation, the problem might be posed, after which the student might be left to work on it with no interference from the observers. Usually the student will have been asked, beforehand, to talk aloud, explaining in as much detail as possible what he or she is doing, why they have decided to do it, and so on. The whole session nowadays is nearly always audiotaped, and quite often it is videotaped.

At the end of the session, then, the researchers will have:

an audiotape or videotape of the session;
the paper on which the student has written;
various written notes made by the observers during the session.

Immediately after the session, the observer(s) may jot down additional notes before they forget them.

All of this material is then subject to later analysis. (In our own

87

work we find that a single 20-minute session may require 50 person-hours of analysis after the session is over.)

But to return to the matter of variations: we have described a session with minimal adult interference during the problem solving. More often, however, one of the adults (usually referred to as the 'interviewer') will interrupt the student from time to time. These interruptions may be in order to pose a further question, in order to provide a hint, or in order to correct an error or misunderstanding. They may also be intended to provide more motivation or perhaps some encouragement. Typical questions might be: 'How did you decide to multiply instead of add?' 'Would you use that same method if this number here were negative?' 'Is there any other way to solve that problem?' 'What are you trying to do right now?'

The interviewer may also pose a new problem, after seeing what the student does with the first problem.

We have spoken of some of these sessions as lying on the 'non-interventionist' extreme: no questions asked by an interviewer. But in fact this is not truly the *extreme*; probably the real 'non-interventionist extreme' occurs when *no adult even poses the original problem*. That is to say, the student spontaneously displays mathematical behavior, as in this example:

> Paul is eight years old. He climbs up and stands on a chair and says to his sister (who is 10 years old, and considerably taller than Paul): Now I'm bigger than you are! [pause – then Paul adds softly] ... but I'm not really, though. . .

Here is a second example with Paul, when he was five years old. Paul was traveling in a car that had just made a normal stop at a 'stop' sign. At precisely this moment, a squeal of tires could be heard as some distant automobile, somewhere out of sight, made a sudden stop. With nothing more than this sound as a stimulus, Paul volunteered the following remark:

> The cars have to stop, because if they didn't, BANG! [accompanied by gesture of left fist crashing into right palm]

Why this is a piece of *mathematical* behavior, and an exceedingly interesting one, will be dealt with in later chapters. The present point is that it belongs to the *spontaneous* category of interview/observation studies. There was no adult participation other than being physically present and therefore available as an audience.

Task-based interviews vary along other dimensions. Students — or *subjects*, because pre-school children and adult experts are sometimes studied — may be asked to verbalize their thoughts as much as possible as they work at the task, or such verbalizing may take place immediately after the mathematical task has been solved (or abandoned, if no solution is achieved). The *depth* of probing can vary a great deal. Further, the subject may be participating in his or her first interview of this type, or — as in the case of the Long Term Study[2] from which much of our present data is drawn — the student may have participated in such interviews for the past five years. The interviewer may be the student's regular teacher, or may (at the opposite extreme) be a complete stranger.

The equipment available may also vary. Hardly ever less than pen and paper[3] will be available (except in the case of some spontaneous student-initiated episodes which may occur in playgrounds and elsewhere), and there may also be rulers, compasses, textbooks, hand-held calculators, graph paper, computer terminals or manipulatable materials such as geoboards, Dienes' MAB blocks or Cuisenaire rods, and so on.

There is also considerable variation in whether an interview is required to adhere rigidly to a pre-planned format, or whether it is adjusted flexibly to student responses. There have even been experiments in using a computer to serve as interviewer,[4] but this does not seem to have been used very successfully thus far.

Several difficulties encountered in task-based interviews deserve mention.

First, interviewers are often teachers or former teachers. Their habitual orientation is to help students, and their traditional goal is to see students succeed. Hence, they often have difficulty in remaining a neutral observer, for whom the goal is to reveal the student's thought processes as clearly and unmistakably as possible, with the minimum amount of contamination or influence from the observer's thoughts. If a student seems to need help, it can be very hard to remain a neutral bystander.

Second, as a corollary to the preceding remark, it is important that questions be phrased so as to offer no extraneous cues or clues, and that the interviewer's inflections, gestures, etc., give no indication of desired responses.

Third, there is the observer's need to establish rapport with the student. There is a continuing set of trade-offs between building rapport and obtaining deeper insights or better data about the student's thought processes. Persistence is one aspect of this trade-off; sometimes more persistence may elicit a clearer picture of the student's thought processes, but at some cost to rapport.

Fourth, there is − perhaps surprisingly! − a question of who is leading whom. We have seen interviewer reports where the interviewer sought to probe into what meanings, if any, the various mathematical symbols had for the student. But the student declined to follow that path, and insisted in dealing with the problem as a rote algorithm to be performed by following explicit instructions, without thinking about it. The interviewer thus faced a dilemma: he did want to explore meanings; yet, he also wanted to reveal the *student's* thinking, not his own. If he were too quick to conclude that the student really did not deal with meanings, and if he therefore too quickly abandoned his questioning into meanings, he could draw a false conclusion. Perhaps the student did have meanings for the symbols that could have been revealed by a more persistent line of questioning.

But there is also the other horn of the dilemma: if the interviewer is *too persistent* in pursuing meanings, he may turn the student into a kind of intellectual mirror, reflecting back the interviewer's ideas, but not revealing the student's ideas. Perhaps, for the student, the matter is entirely one of carrying out a meaningless prescribed algorithm. Sometimes, in reports, interviewers confess that they felt that the student was leading them along a path of the student's choosing. Perhaps not entirely a bad thing − but it often leaves the interviewer wondering if he has missed a chance to probe more deeply, and in other directions.

Finally, there are ethical questions. Clearly, the students must not be exploited. While the interviewer may have to avoid teaching during an interview (depending upon the goal of the study, 'teaching' may or may not be allowable within the interview proper), there is a possibility − even a need − to perform some remedial teaching *after* an interview, so that some of the diagnostic knowledge acquired by the researcher can be turned to the advantage of the student who helped to create it. The interviewer must sometimes deal with a subtler version of this problem. For some children, an indecisive response from an adult indicates that an answer is acceptable; whenever they have been wrong they have heard about it immediately and forcefully. So ... in the absence of loud rejection, they construe that an answer has been accepted. When an interviewer wants to allow a child to develop his or her own ideas (whether right or wrong), the interviewer must avoid signaling 'right' or 'wrong' at each step in the work. This can be a problem if the student construes silence (or noncommittal responses) to mean 'correct'. Our own practice is to try to talk this situation over candidly with our students.

Analysis of Student Answers

Another data source is found in studying the patterns of wrong answers given by students. One gets a rather clear idea of the error being made by a student who has written

1082	972	536
− 369	− 281	− 294
1327	711	362

The answers can be obtained from homework, tests, computer-assisted instruction sessions or any convenient source.

Films of Classroom Lessons

Another data source has been the filming or videotaping of actual classroom lessons, allowing leisurely subsequent analysis of student errors, teacher-student interactions, student contributions, student questions, and so on. Films and videotape have a potential which has hardly been tapped yet.

'Results'

What kind of results have been obtained from the Long Term Study? Essentially, five kinds of results:

(1) an accumulation of *direct data*. This takes the form of 16 mm sound films (that show, for example, a group of seventh graders working with topics in calculus), transcriptions of audiotapes of task-based interviews, and audiotapes and videotapes of interviews;

(2) the development of a matching between the conceptualizations discussed in this book, and observed instances of human behavior;

(3) the emergence of some 'laws' which are, in some cases, of striking regularity, suggestive of the laws of physics;

(4) a large body of general descriptive data on student performance;

(5) individual case studies on students followed for every school
day for five years, or in some cases even longer.

Methodology

The work of the Long Term Study will undoubtedly strike some
readers as a methodological novelty, and in some cases perhaps a
distasteful one. No part of the study is statistical, because – given
the questions we sought to answer, and the opportunities we had
for seeking answers – no part of the study seemed appropriately
statistical. It has been our belief that the *goals* of a study – and not
any *a priori* commitment to orthodoxy – should determine the methods
employed. We have sought to know more about four matters:

(1) How do students think about mathematical problems?
(2) Where, and why, do they seem to encounter special difficulties?
(3) What seems to help?
(4) What are the natural parameters for learning mathematics – for
example, how old should a student be before undertaking the
study of calculus?

But perhaps, even more than our questions, it has been our philo-
sophy that has determined the methods of this study. We do not see
'mathematics' as a collection of algorithms, to be memorized by rote
and practiced. Nor do we see mathematics as something to be 'taught'
to students, with control in the hands of the teacher (which is not to
deny the *importance* of the teacher, but merely to redefine the teacher's
proper *role*). Instead, we see 'mathematics' as a collection of ideas
and methods which a student builds up in his or her own head. In
recent years this has come to be called the 'constructivist' approach
to the study of the learning of mathematics, an approach that has
developed through work of Piaget, Papert, Lawler, Easley, Ginsburg,
Thompson, Steffe, Duckworth, Erlwanger, and others.[5]

Concerning methodology, the remarks of Clifford Geertz, in the
American Scholar (1980) are of special importance.

... many social scientists have turned away from a laws-and-instances
ideal of explanation toward a cases-and-interpretations one ...

... analogies drawn from the humanities are coming to play the kind of role in sociological understanding that analogies drawn from the crafts and technology have long played in physical understanding.

. . . Something is happening to the way we think about the way we think.

. . . freed from having to become taxonomically upstanding . . . individuals thinking of themselves as social (or behavioral or human or cultural) scientists have become free to shape their work in terms of its necessities rather than [in terms of] received ideas as to what they ought or ought not to be doing.

. . . Inquiry is directed toward cases or sets of cases, and toward the particular features that mark them off; but its aims are so far-reaching as those of mechanics or physiology: to distinguish the materials of human experience.

. . . As theory, scientific or otherwise, moves mainly by analogy, a 'seeing-as' comprehension of the less intelligible by the more (the earth is a magnet, the heart is a pump, light is a wave, the brain is a computer, and space is a balloon), when its course shifts, the conceits in which it expresses itself shift with it.

. . . If the result is not to be elaborate chatter or the higher nonsense, a critical consciousness will have to be developed . . .

. . . If [social scientists] are going to develop systems of analysis in which such conceptions as following a rule, constructing a representation, expressing an attitude, or forming an intention are going to play central roles — rather than such conceptions as isolating a cause, determining a variable, measuring a force, or defining a function — they are going to need all the help they can get from people who are more at home among such notions than they are. It is not interdisciplinary brotherhood that is needed, nor even less highbrow eclecticism. It is recognition on all sides that the lines grouping scholars together into intellectual communities, or (what is the same thing) sorting them out into different ones, are these days running at some highly eccentric angles.

There are . . . many social scientists at work today for whom the anatomization of thought is wanted, not the manipulation of behavior.[6]

Notes

1. A particularly interesting discussion of standardized tests and

student thought processes is contained in V.A. Krutetskii, *The Psychology of Mathematical Abilities in Schoolchildren*, Jeremy Kilpatrick and Izaak Wirszup (eds.); translated by Joan Teller (University of Chicago Press, Chicago, Ill., 1976). See also Robert B. Davis, Thomas A. Romberg, Sidney Rachlin and Mary Grace Kantowski, *An Analysis of Mathematics Education in the Union of Soviet Socialist Republics* (ERIC Clearinghouse for Science, Mathematics, and Environmental Education, Ohio State University, Columbus, Ohio, 1979).

2. *The Long Term Study*. Since 1972, a study of mathematics teaching and learning has been underway at the Computer-Based Education Research Laboratory and at the Curriculum Laboratory, both units of the University of Illinois, Urbana/Champaign. But this was not, in fact, the actual beginning, which had occurred in Syracuse, New York in 1958, and had also involved work in Weston, Connecticut and in Webster Groves, Missouri. The present book reports primarily on data collected in Illinois, but makes use of some data from New York, Connecticut and Missouri.

The Illinois program — which we refer to as the Long Term Study — had four components:

(1) The design and implementation of a curriculum in mathematics for academically-gifted students in grades 7 through 12. A feature of this program was the inclusion of topics in calculus as early as grade 7, with the final two years devoted entirely to calculus. (Another feature, dictated by the school where the work was done, was that the normal six years of grades 7-12 were compressed into five calendar years. Thus, these students began the 'serious' study of calculus when they were about 15 years old.)

(2) The design and implementation of a computer-based curriculum (delivered by the PLATO computer system, which was invented at the University of Illinois) in mathematics for grades 3 through 7. Each student received one half hour of CAI lesson material every school day. This curriculum combined arithmetic, algebra and geometry, including some co-ordinate geometry. This curriculum was designed for, and taught to, the full range of elementary school students, *not* just gifted students.

(3) Observational studies of the mathematics students in the two curricula just mentioned. A particular effort was made to follow these students for as long as possible. Since some students entered the CAI program at around age 10, and later moved into the secondary school program, we have been able to follow some students for

at least seven consecutive years of pre-college mathematics. In some cases even more has been possible: a few of these '7-year' students entered the University of Illinois after graduation from high school, and it has consequently been possible to follow them even after grade 12. Beyond even that, some students who had been in the Connecticut, New York or Missouri studies appeared in the Illinois study, making still longer periods of observation possible. The longest period of observation on any student has been 15 years (two such students), the mode has been five years (42 students).

(4) Observational studies on students who were NOT in the curricula listed above. The purpose of these observations was to obtain data on the full demographic range of students, on students in different curricula (and in different schools), on students of different ages and on topics not included in the two special curricula. Students in this category include students in elementary schools, junior and senior high school and community college, plus university students and students in adult education courses. In some cases, the problem-solving performance of adult experts was observed and analyzed.

Lest there be misunderstandings, please notice that students in the Long Term Study are NOT all 'gifted students', nor are they all in the same curriculum, nor even in the same school system.

The main elementary school in the study is Booker T. Washington School in Champaign, Illinois, but there are also five other elementary schools, in four different school districts. The main secondary school is University High School in Urbana, Illinois, but, again, there are also several others. The curriculum studied by the University High School students, and the observational studies of how the students solve problems, are published in:

Robert B. Davis, 'An Economically-Feasible Approach to Mathematics for Gifted Children', *Journal of Children's Mathematical Behavior*, Supplement Number 1 (Summer 1976), pp. 103-58.

Robert B. Davis, 'Mathematics for Gifted Children — The Ninth-Grade Program', *Journal of Children's Mathematical Behavior*, Supplement No. 1 (Summer 1976), pp. 176-215.

Katie Reynolds Hannibal, 'Observer Report on the Madison Project's Seventh Grade Class', *Journal of Children's Mathematical Behavior*, Supplement No. 1 (Summer 1976), pp. 159-75.

Robert B. Davis and Jody Douglas, 'Environment, Habit, Self-

Concept, and Approach Pathology', *Journal of Children's Mathematical Behavior*, Supplement No. 1 (Summer 1976), pp. 229-65.

Robert B. Davis, Elizabeth Jockusch and Curtis C. McKnight, 'Cognitive Processes in Learning Algebra', *Journal of Children's Mathematical Behavior*, vol. 2, no. 1 (Spring 1978), pp. 10-320.

Robert B. Davis and Curtis C. McKnight, 'Modeling the Processes of Mathematical Thinking', *Journal of Children's Mathematical Behavior*, vol. 2, no. 2 (Spring 1979), pp. 91-113.

Robert B. Davis, Curtis C. McKnight, Philip Parker and Douglas Elrick, 'Analysis of Student Answers to Signed Number Arithmetic Problems', *Journal of Children's Mathematical Behavior*, vol. 2, no. 2 (Spring 1979), pp. 114-30.

Robert B. Davis and Curtis McKnight, 'The Influence of Semantic Content on Algorithmic Behavior', *The Journal of Mathematical Behavior*, vol. 3, no. 1 (Autumn 1980), pp. 39-87.

In addition, reproductions of actual student work appear in *Journal of Children's Mathematical Behavior*, Supplement No. 1 (Summer 1976); also vol. 2, no. 2 (Spring 1979); and *Journal of Mathematical Behavior*, vol. 3, no. 1 (Autumn 1980). Also, some actual classroom lessons have been recorded on 16mm sound film, or on videotape.

The investigators who have worked on this project have been: Robert B. Davis, Director; Curtis C. McKnight, Stanley H. Erlwanger; Katie Reynolds Hannibal, Stephen Young, Patrick McLoughlin and Jody Douglas. Important consultant assistance has been received from Seymour Papert, Robert Karplus, Edwina Michner Rissland, Sharon Dugdale and Herbert Lin.

3. In the Long Term Study, we have preferred giving *pens* to students, instead of pencils, because we want to be able to reconstruct the student's line of reasoning after the interview has ended, and if the student erases, some desirable data may get lost.

4. Cf. Kay Andert, Robert B. Davis, Derek Kumar and Curtis C. McKnight, 'Assessing Student Knowledge by Task-Based Interviews and Other Methods' (unpublished research report, Curriculum Laboratory, University of Illinois, Urbana, Ill., 1981).

5. Cf., e.g., Davis (1982); Thompson (1982).

6. Clifford Geertz, 1980. Reproduced by permission.

7 PROCEDURES/THE REGULARITY OF STUDENT ERRORS

Any plan to develop a 'reasonable' explanation for mathematical behavior must start at a grave disadvantage if there are no systematic *patterns* in that behavior. Fortunately, things are not so disorderly as they may seem. On the contrary, there is a large amount of regularity in how students deal with mathematics, and this regularity underlies every aspect of the present book. In this chapter we shall look at some of the persistent patterns in student errors, and shall see how the concept of *information-processing procedure* can be used to explain why these particular errors occur.

The Regularity of Errors

A number of studies of mathematical errors made by students show that there is a great deal of regularity in these errors.[1] Indeed, there are two kinds of regularity. When one looks at errors made by many different students, certain errors are extremely common. For example, if someone gives a wrong answer for

$$4 \times 4 =$$

that wrong answer will probably be 8; or if someone gives a wrong answer to

$$2^3 =$$

that wrong answer will probably be 6; finally, if someone gives a wrong answer to $6 \div \frac{1}{2} =$, that wrong answer will probably be 3. This kind of regularity — certain 'standard' wrong answers given by many different people — should certainly be explained by any adequate theory of human mathematical thought, and we shall turn our attention to it later in this book.

But there is a second, quite different kind of regularity that appears when we examine the wrong answers given by *one single person*, in response to a sequence of questions. For example, when Erlwanger[2] asked Benny, a twelve-year-old boy in grade 6, to write $\frac{2}{10}$ as a decimal, Benny wrote 1.2; asked to write $\frac{5}{10}$ as a decimal, Benny wrote 1.5;

asked to write $\frac{2 \cdot 7}{1 \cdot 5}$ as a decimal, Benny wrote 4.2. Although this method is wrong, Benny uses it *consistently*. (Exactly how Benny's method works — if it is not immediately obvious — will be considered presently. What may make it seem confusing is that it involves two cases that must be distinguished from one another.)

Let us ask, first, a more general question: is it reasonable that an individual should be consistent in his or her errors? Yes, of course, at least where the most important errors are concerned, because these errors are errors in *method* or *process*, and should appear whenever this faulty process is used. A student who learns to subtract by the following defective method (which is common)

$$
\begin{array}{r}
53 \\
- 28 \\
\hline
35
\end{array}
$$

will presumably use this method consistently, so that the problems

$$
\begin{array}{ccc}
92 & 31 & 76 \\
- 17 & - 14 & - 28 \\
\hline
\end{array}
$$

would presumably be answered 85, 23 and 52. Observation of students, as in Erlwanger's study, shows that this is exactly what happens.

There is such a phenomenon as the seemingly random error, but this is quite a different matter. Since, for random errors, the student's *method* is not wrong, it should be possible, with sufficient care, to reduce the number of random errors. But to correct faulty procedures is a different kind of task; the student needs to become aware of the nature of the error, and must somehow correct the 'bug' in his method.

Super-procedure Failures

Erlwanger's studies of errors made by students contain much that is interesting. For one thing, it is worth noticing that in nearly every student error reported by Erlwanger, the malfunction occurs, as it were at the same location in the cognitive machinery. *In nearly every case, a super-procedure selects the wrong sub-procedure.* The sub-procedures themselves, however, function correctly (although one sub-procedure turned out to be a bit odd).

Converting Fractions to Decimals

We have already seen how Benny, asked to write $\frac{2}{10}$ as a decimal, would write 1.2. What super-procedures and sub-procedures were involved here?

Step 1. Super-procedure P_1 is activated by the visual stimulus $\frac{2}{10}$, and the auditory stimulus of the interviewer's words.

Step 2. Super procedure P_1 calls up sub-procedure p_1, which accepts 2 and 10 as inputs, and outputs 12. Sub-procedure p_1 is some form of ordinary addition. [Note that sub-procedure p_1 is working correctly, although of course P_1 should not have called for p_1.]

Step 3. Super-procedure P_1 calls up sub-procedure p_2, which inserts a decimal point after the first digit in the input of P_1 if there are two or more digits in the output, and otherwise inserts a decimal point to the left of the first digit. Thus $\frac{5}{10} \longrightarrow 15 \longrightarrow 1.5, \frac{4}{6} \longrightarrow 10 \longrightarrow 1.0,$ $\frac{429}{100} \longrightarrow 529 \longrightarrow 5.29, \frac{3}{2} \longrightarrow 5 \longrightarrow .5$ and $\frac{2}{3} \longrightarrow 5 \longrightarrow .5$.

The sub-procedure p_2 is an unusual one. It is an exception to the rule that nearly all procedures used by a student were correct for some earlier task, as performed in some earlier context; their erroneousness, thus, usually lies only in being used where they ought not to have been used. Sub-procedure p_2, however, seems to have no correct role in ordinary mathematics. It is one of the extremely rare procedures that seems to have been invented by a student for no recognizable legitimate reason. But even it performed consistently.

Adding Decimals

In the course of his interviews with Benny, Erlwanger[3] asked Benny to add

$$.3 + .4 =$$

By way of answer, Benny wrote

$$.3 + .4 = .07 \quad .$$

For problems of this type he used this method consistently. What procedures are involved?

Step 1. A super-procedure Q_1 responds to the visual input .3 + .4 =, and the interviewer's spoken instructions, and calls up a sub-procedure q_1.

Step 2. Sub-procedure q_1 inputs 3 and 4, and outputs 7.

Step 3. Super-procedure Q_1 calls up sub-procedure q_2.

Step 4. Sub-procedure q_2 counts the number of digits to the right of the decimal point in '.3', counts the number of digits to the right of the decimal point in '.4', adds the result $(1 + 1 = 2)$, and locates the decimal point in the output of Q_1 so that there are two digits to the right of the decimal point

.07 .

Clearly, both sub-procedures are important ones, with legitimate roles to play. Procedure q_2, however, should not have been called into action in this situation.

Binary Reversions

Two related, and interesting, phenomena were reported by David Page.[4] First, there are some 'standard wrong answers':

Problem	Standard Wrong Answer
4 X 4	8
2^3	6
6 ÷ ½	3

Page pointed out that, in every case, the student was *giving a correct answer* — but a correct answer *to a different question*. The student had not answered the original question, Q_1, say.

Page proposed, and tested, a remediation procedure. He recommended that the teacher figure out the question, Q_2, that the student *had* answered; the teacher should then ask question Q_2. Page predicted that, in nearly every case, the student would not answer question Q_2, but would immediately correct the answer to question Q_1. Page's prediction is easily confirmed. The following actual dialogue is quite typical:

Teacher: How much is seven times seven?
Student (in grade seven): Fourteen.
Teacher: How much is seven plus seven?
Student: Oh! It should be forty-nine!

The frequency of dialogues on exactly this pattern suggests that there is some kind of echoic 'second hearing' or (in the language of TV sports reporting) 'instant replay capability'. Somehow the student was able to reply the first question, and his answer to it, and to observe the contrast with the second question. It reveals something interesting about the student's control structure, and about the student's understanding of the teacher's goals, that the student does NOT bother answering the second question, assuming (correctly) that what was really wanted was a correct answer to the original question.

One might try to represent the control structure that would be naïvely expected of a student as in Figure 7.1, where the act of answering the first question, Q_1, discharges any hold that Q_1 has on the student's attention; the student then turns his or her attention to the next question, Q_2.

Figure 7.1: This diagram represents the control structure that might be naïvely expected when a student is asked a sequence of questions.

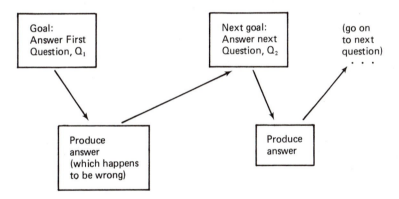

In fact, however, this is not what occurs. The student never bothers to answer question Q_2; instead, his behavior clearly shows that Q_1 still maintains a hold on his attention, and Q_2 is in fact interpreted as nothing more than diagnostic feedback concerning his response to Q_1. This is diagrammed in Figure 7.2. There are, however, two more aspects of this phenomenon that are interesting:

(i) In nearly every case, the question that *is* answered is one that was studied in school *before* the question that was answered incorrectly; e.g. $7 + 7 = 14$ was studied before $7 \times 7 = 49$

Figure 7.2: This diagram represents a control structure closer to that which is revealed when a student omits answering Q_2, changes answer to Q_1.

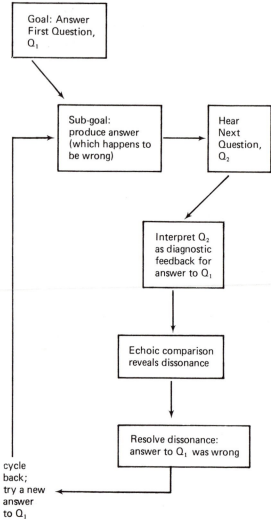

was. Thus, a question is asked about a recent (and seemingly insecure) piece of learning; this question is (erroneously) *replaced* by a question dealing with earlier (and presumably more securely-learned) material, as when 4×4 is answered *as if it had been 4 + 4*. (Because of the going back to an earlier idea, these errors are called *binary reversions*.)

(ii) In nearly every case, the visual cue that should trigger Q_2 is very similar to the visual one that should trigger Q_1. For example:

Visual Cue for *intended* Question Q_1	Visual Cue for 'replacement' Question Q_2
4×4	$4 + 4$
2^3	2×3 or $(2)(3)$ or $2 \cdot 3$
$6 \div \frac{1}{2}$	$6 \times \frac{1}{2}$
	or $6 \div 2$
	or $\dfrac{6}{2}$

Sometimes it is not only *visual* cues that are similar. Tape recordings of students reading their own equations as they write them show many students reading '2^3' as 'two three', and reading x^2 as '*x* two'. In the last example above, 'six divided by one half' sounds rather like 'six divided by halves'.

Does the conceptualization of Chapters 4 and 5 provide any way to discuss how an information processing failure can produce this commonly-observed result? In fact, it does. The primitive input data ('7 X 7', say) must be matched up with a retrieved frame. Now, there is a well-developed frame for 7 + 7, but only the beginnings of a frame for 7 X 7. Apparently, some aspect of 'familiarity' weights the outcome in favor of the more familiar frame. Also, apparently, those students who make this error are not doing a careful enough job of verifying that frame selection and instantiation have proceeded correctly. When question Q_2 is asked, however, the contrast between Q_1 and Q_2 triggers a new re-evaluation, which returns a negative judgement on the original answer, and so a new attempt is made to answer the original question, but this time with the correct frame in place. (Earlier research in the Piagetian tradition would often speak of 'assimilation paradigms'. Using this language, we could say that, in the student's first attempt to answer, he or she used 7 + 7 (or 'the addition frame') as the *assimilation paradigm* for the actual primitive data input, '7 X 7'. This was (ultimately) found to be in error, and so a second attempt was made, this time using the multiplication frame as an assimilation paradigm for the input data (so that this time the instantiated frame is actually a correct representation of the input data.) [Alternative explanations are possible; we consider one in the next chapter.]

Page's recommended remediation — ask the question that the student *did* answer — is so frequently effective that there must be some interesting phenomenon of perception, control or short-term memory[5] lurking here, and perhaps also an interesting matter of student attributions of purpose to the teacher's remarks.

Other Studies of Observed Regularities

Erlwanger is by no means alone in observing consistent patterns, both in individual students and in studies looking for patterns common to many students. The Long Term Study found many commonly-made errors; so did Clement, Rosnick and Lochhead at the University of Massachusetts; so did Jamesine Friend (1979), using data from students in Nicaragua. All of this work will be considered in more detail in later chapters.

An ingenious alternative explanation for certain observed regularities has been proposed by Matz (1980), by John Seely Brown, and by Kurt Van Lehn (1982). Put briefly, the idea is that one can distinguish two levels of mental procedures. One, that we might call the 'surface level', consists of procedures that carry out familiar operations of arithmetic and algebra — e.g., factoring a quadratic trinomial, subtracting one number from another, etc. A second level — call it 'higher' or 'deeper' according to your taste — makes modifications on, or link-ups between, the first level procedures. These second-level procedures are by no means infallible; on the contrary, they produce many first-level procedures that are erroneous — *but the second-level procedures DO operate in a systematic and consistent fashion*. Errors such as the 'simplifications'

$$\sqrt{a^2 + b^2} \longrightarrow a + b$$

$$(\sqrt{a} + \sqrt{b})^2 \longrightarrow a + b$$

$$\sin 2x \longrightarrow 2 \sin x$$

are readily explained in this way. We shall look at some examples of this work in later chapters. For complete details, see Matz (1980) and Van Lehn (1982).

Summary

Student behavior is obviously diverse and varied, in mathematics no less than in other areas. None the less, at least two kinds of consistency are observable. In some things, a student will be consistent in his/her own behavior, using a flawed procedure, but using it in a systematic and continuing way. A possibly more surprising kind of pattern is also observable in many cases: there are certain errors that are commonly made by many *different* people. Some of these errors, also, can be remarkably persistent.

Clearly, 'systematic' errors require a different sort of remediation than 'random' or 'careless' errors do.

This chapter has dealt with errors. We are, however, equally concerned with correct, 'orthodox' performance, and also with unorthodox performance of great insight and ingenuity.

Notes

1. Among the best-known studies showing the regularity of student errors are:

Stanley H. Erlwanger, 'Benny's Conception of Rules and Answers in IPI Mathematics', *Journal of Children's Mathematical Behavior*, vol. 1, no. 2 (Autumn 1973), pp. 7-26.
Jamesine E. Friend, 'Column Addition Skills', *Journal of Children's Mathematical Behavior*, vol. 2, no. 2 (Spring 1979), pp. 29-57.
Peter Rosnick and John Clement, 'Learning Without Understanding: The Effect of Tutoring Strategies in Algebra Misconceptions', *Journal of Mathematical Behavior*, vol. 3, no. 1 (Autumn 1980), pp. 3-27.
John Seely Brown and Richard R. Burton, 'Diagnostic Models for Procedural Bugs in Basic Mathematical Skills', *Cognitive Science*, vol. 2, no. 2 (April-June 1978), pp. 155-92.

2. Erlwanger, 'Benny', pp. 8-9.
3. Ibid., pp. 9-10.
4. David Page, now at the Chicago Circle campus of the University of Illinois, was one of the most important contributors to the 'new mathematics' curriculum improvement movement of the 1950s and 1960s. His research was regularly reported in lectures and seminars, but – as in the case of far too much of the 'new math' activity –

almost none of it has been reported or analyzed in books and professional journals. For one of the rare exceptions, see Hayden (1981).
(Hayden separates the mathematics curriculum movement into two
parts, one called 'new math', the other called a continuation of progressive education. He assigns Page to the second category.)

Another important exception is a careful study by Christine Keitel
(1981). For a world-wide perspective, see Howson, Keitel and Kilpatrick
(1981).

5. Cf. Lindsay and Norman (1977), Chapter 8.

For You to Think About

1. Suppose Henry answered

$$\begin{array}{r} 37 \\ +\ 24 \\ \hline \end{array}$$

by writing 51. What answer would you *expect* Henry to give to the
problem

$$\begin{array}{r} 7{,}963 \\ +\ \ \ \ 528 \\ \hline \end{array} \quad ?$$

2. Patricia answered this question

$$5{,}279 + 481 =$$

by writing 9,018, answered the question $256 + 12 =$ by writing 376
and answered the question $95 + 21 =$ by writing 17. What answer would
you expect Patricia to give for $3{,}986 + 295 = $? What is Patricia doing
wrong? What would you do to help her eliminate this error? How
would you change the curriculum in Patricia's school so that future
students will not make this error?

8 A FEW COMMONLY-SHARED FRAMES

You Are Consistent With Yourself

We saw earlier that some of the most valuable clues to the nature of human information processing can be found by studying errors. The feasibility of such an approach is greatly increased by the fact that there are consistent patterns in errors. These patterns are of two types. One individual will usually show considerable consistency from one problem to another, and from one day to another, which often enables a teacher to identify the specific flaws (or 'bugs') in that individual's procedures, and thus help the student recognize the systematic error and eliminate it. For most purposes this is the more important kind of consistency.

Different People Doing Similar Things

There is, however, a second kind of consistency — not within the life of one person, but observable across different people. That is to say, there are certain errors that *many different people* make at certain points in their educational growth. In this chapter we shall look primarily at this second kind of consistency, in order to obtain evidence for certain knowledge representation structures that seem to be developed by many different people. This, too, is an important area of study; it should not, however, be allowed to obscure the fact that most of the ideas in your mind are uniquely yours, not fully shared by any other human being. Or, in our present formulation, we would say: you hold in memory a truly vast collection of knowledge representation structures, or 'frames'. This collection grows continually, as you learn new things. Growth takes place by new, more complex, frames being built up on a foundation of previously-built frames. How could your collection of frames be identical with someone else's? Another person has had different experiences, and they went into these experiences with different collections of frames to build on.

But mathematics, and especially elementary arithmetic, is to some extent an exception. From one nation to another, from one culture to another, from one time to another, elementary arithmetic retains an almost identical form; it is even the basis for attempts to communicate with intelligent life in outer space. When one object is put near two others, there is a very large commonality in what can be perceived, abstracted and generalized, and relatively little room for fundamental variations, so in beginning arithmetic we have one of our best opportunities to find frames that may exist in nearly identical forms in the minds of different people.

We now look for evidence for a few specific frames which most people seem to develop.

Some General Principles of Human Information Processing

Before turning to our main discussion of frame identification, it will be well to consider some commonly-used general principles of human information processing.

Discriminations Are Only as Fine as Necessary

Imagine yourself needing to discriminate reliably between the printed words

$$ГОРЯЧО$$

and

$$ХОЛОДНО$$

which, in Russian, mean 'hot' and 'cold'. If your only purpose is to turn on taps to get water of the desired temperature, you could remember that one word ends in what looks like the first two letters of 'HOT', and that is the one that does *not* mean 'hot'. The *other* word means 'hot'. Such a system might or might not suffice to permit you to make the distinction correctly, but it will serve to illustrate a general principle, used by Feigenbaum (1963) and others: *information processing systems will come to make essential discriminations but may not develop discrimination finer than necessary*. We shall ourselves make use of this principle when, in a later section, we begin our search for specific frames.

As a second example, if you need to discriminate the nonsense syllable DAX from the nonsense syllable JIR, you need only consider, say, the first letters of each. No better criterion for successful discrimination is required. Of course, if you are subsequently confronted with three possible inputs – DAX, JIR and JUK, say – your discrimination procedure will fail, and JIR will look to you exactly like JUK, *until you refine your discrimination procedure* (which, of course, you do). (In the case of the Russian words, the search for a terminal 'HO' will make a very large number of Russian words look the same, in that they all fail the test.) We shall refer to this as *Feigenbaum's Law of Minimal Necessary Discrimination*.

The Permanence of Productions

J.R. Anderson, in his ACT theory of human information processing, represents procedural knowledge as a collection of so-called *productions*. (We have seen earlier that a 'production' is a step or command of the form

> If A is true, then do B.)

Hence ACT computer simulations are cast in the form of *production* systems.[1] To each production there is associated a numerical value called its *strength*. ACT represents factual knowledge by a set of propositions, arranged in a propositional network. (There is more structure to ACT than we have indicated here, but this much will suffice for present purposes.)

ACT 'learns' by *adding new productions* to its collection, or by *adding new propositions*, or in certain other ways, *but not by deletion*. 'Old ideas' remain, although the system may refer to them less and less frequently. *Representations are not actually deleted from memory*.

We shall use this principle, also, in our search for identifiable frames.

Note that this implies that contradictory information, and 'competing' alternative procedures, will come to coexist in our memories – as, quite clearly, they actually do. We shall refer to this as *Anderson's Law of Non-deletion*.

The Highest-level Programs Must Run

A present-day computer program may grind to a halt because it lacks a needed piece of input data, or because of a programming error, or for other reasons. A terminal screen can remain blank, or a computer can return no answer at all. In such ways, computer programs may fail to run successfully.

Something similar can happen to human beings: we may be unable to solve a problem, or to answer a test question, or to complete a planned project. But we are not thereby reduced to a catatonic trance. In most cases we alter our plans, settle for lesser goals, compromise, or switch to a different project. John Seely Brown and Kurt Van Lehn (1980) have made use of this principle as a general law of human information processing: *the top-level programs must run*. If, for example, a high-level goal calls for a program which in turn calls for certain input information that is not available, the whole system does not halt. Some accommodation is made. Perhaps default values are used to fill the otherwise empty slots, or alternative sources of input information are employed, or a change is made in the lower-level programs that are called into action. This may, of course, lead to error; we may have made assumptions in the absence of the best possible data, or may have employed methods that were not our first choice. Still, things may work out. At least, the whole operation has not crashed to a sudden halt.

We shall call this the *Brown-Matz-Van Lehn Law*.

The Postulation of Certain Specific, Explicit, Commonly-shared Frames

A New Look at the Evidence

Physics, of course, is exciting not merely because one can postulate a structure of atoms, orbital electrons, atomic nuclei, and so on, but because observations can be made that permit an increasingly detailed description of these (basically hypothetical) entities — and also because the whole theory has important points of contact with the real world, including many important applications. Can a postulated theory of mathematical thought share these advantages?

The main purpose of this chapter is to combine certain empirical results, certain assumptions about *frames*, and certain general laws of human information processing to show that certain common error patterns *would be predicted if one assumed that most students acquire four specific frames, which we can identify explicitly. Furthermore, postulating these frames would be consistent with the general laws of human information processing.*

Frames are presumably *personal* constructs; yours are different from mine or from anyone else's. In our present search, therefore, we are engaged in a somewhat peculiar undertaking: we are looking for *commonly-shared frames*, frames that exist in more or less the same form in the minds of different individuals. Presumably, since frames are created as the result of experience, everyone has many frames that are his or her own private personal possessions, not necessarily shared with anyone else. In teaching, these personal frames are often of great importance; a teacher wants to correct the wrong ideas of this particular individual student. (Frames, of course, are not restricted to *wrong* ideas, but the present chapter focuses on errors, for reasons mentioned earlier.) But − even if most frames are private and idiosyncratic, based on one person's experience − the frames we are presently concerned with appear to exist, in about the same form, within the minds of a very large number of students. This fact, also, requires some explanation.

The Primary-grade Undifferentiated Binary-operation Frame

How can many different individuals come to develop virtually identical frames? Surely because parts of their experience are also commonly shared, and because there are some underlying principles that govern human information processing in general.

In the earliest school grades, when the child is five or six years old (or so), it is common to teach 'addition facts' such as $1 + 1 = 2, 2 + 2 = 4, 2 + 1 = 3, 3 + 2 = 5$, and so on. This, typically, is the *only* arithmetic operation that is taught. Hence one has, in effect, a situation where the inputs 3 and 5 should lead to a response, or output, of 8. There is no need to attend to the operation sign +. The child need not − and, in fact, *cannot* − ask *which* operation is being requested; the child cannot discriminate among binary operations *because he or she knows only one.*

When, in later grades, the child meets 4×4, there is one wrong answer which is exceedingly common, occurring far more often than any other error: 4×4 is said to be 8. This error, reported by many observers,[2] is a nearly inevitable response if one assumes:

(1) Because of the extensive drill in addition facts in the beginning school years, a very permanent and stable representation of addition facts − essentially what we are calling a *frame* − is created in the mind of the typical child.[3]

(2) Whatever system of naming procedures, sub-procedures, data addresses, etc., may be employed, *nowhere in this naming procedure will there be any discrimination to separate one binary operation from any others* (because at this stage in the child's experience, no such discrimination is needed).

(3) Whatever may in the future be *added* to the collection of procedures and representations in the child's mind, *nothing will be deleted*. In particular, the *primary-grade undifferentiated binary-operation frame*, which accepts as inputs the non-negative integers *a* and *b* and, ignoring any operation signs, returns a + b, *will not be deleted.*

Consequently, in later life, 4 × 4 will inevitably have some tendency to cue the retrieval of the *undifferentiated binary-operation frame* and return 8 (instead of the correct answer, 16) — at least until some modification has been made in the method for calling-up frames, so as to avoid this error.[4]

Consider, again, the common piece of teacher-student dialogue reported by David Page:

Teacher: How much is four times four?
Student: Eight.
Teacher: How much is four plus four?
Student: Oh! It should be sixteen.

As we have noted earlier, this dialogue occurs very frequently, essentially in the exact form Page has observed. Note the sequential order: (1) the teacher asks a question; (2) the student mistakenly answers a *different* question; (3) the teacher, following Page's recommendation for effective pedagogy in such cases, identified the question the student had in mind and *asks* THAT *question*; (4) the student does *not* answer the question just asked, but instead *revises* the answer to the *first* question.

How is this sequence to be explained? It, too, becomes nearly inevitable if (as suggested in note 4) one postulates that, as subsequent experience shows the need to attend to the operation sign and to distinguish addition from subtraction, or from multiplication, or from division, etc., one creates this distinction by creating a *binary-operation selection frame* that operates as a 'receptionist' or screening mechanism for inputs of the type 3 + 5. This *binary-operation selection frame* (BOSF) has the task of attending to the sign and calling up the appropriate calculational frame.

But, in Page's sequence, what has gone wrong? The BOSF has been by-passed, and the *undifferentiated frame* (which in fact always *adds*) has been retrieved instead. Given Anderson's 'conservation of old frames' postulate, this is entirely possible.

Ah, but how does the teacher's *second* question straighten things out? The combined effect of the teacher's two questions increases the demand for the 'receptionist' to sort things out correctly. If one also assumes — and many observations suggest one should — some kind of 'instant replay' mechanism (somewhat similar to the 'instant replays' used in TV sports reporting), the increased selection demand finally causes the 'receptionist' BOSF to be retrieved, and the 'replay' capability immediately turns on a warning light — an improperly-screened problem has slipped through, and been routed incorrectly! Hence the student's immediate reaction is to correct this previous error, instead of answering the second question itself.

The Primary-grade Addition Frame

Especially interesting is the *primary-grade addition frame* — especially interesting because it explains a less-well-known and quite surprising phenomenon, discovered by Jamesine Friend (1979) from an analysis of errors made by 2,873 students in grades 1 through 6 in Managua, Nicaragua.

It had been known for some time as an empirical fact that 'nonrectangular' addition problems such as

```
            3              3
551       204            53
+37       +12          +734
───       ───          ────
```

were generally more difficult than 'rectangular' problems such as

```
          822
61        323
35        914
+22      +510
───      ────
```

(The words 'rectangular' and 'nonrectangular' here refer to the array of digits in the addends.) By careful study of the proportion of wrong answers, Friend found that in actual fact nonrectangular problems are *not* more difficult than rectangular problems, *except for the case where the left-most column contains a single entry, and where there is no 'carry' to be added into this left-most column. It is this latter class of problems, and only these, that are more difficult.*

Friend also studied common error patterns in the situation where there is an isolated digit in the left-most column. She found three.

The first is 'borrowing' a digit from another column and making it do double duty, in order to have a second input for the *primary-grade addition frame*, as in

```
63
+ 2
──
85
```

(where the '2' has been added to the '3', as it should have been, *but has also been added to the '6'*, as it should not have been), or in the example

$$
\begin{array}{r}
561 \\
+\ 31 \\
\hline
892
\end{array}
$$

(where, similarly, the '3' has been used twice, once in $6 + 3 = 9$, and then again in $5 + 3 = 8$).

The second involves using the isolated digit as an addend to the column to the right, as in

$$
\begin{array}{r}
63 \\
+2 \\
\hline
11
\end{array}
\qquad
\begin{array}{r}
3 \\
204 \\
+12 \\
\hline
39
\end{array}
$$

Finally, the third common error reported by Friend consists of ignoring the isolated digit, as in the examples

$$
\begin{array}{r}
63 \\
+2 \\
\hline
5
\end{array}
\qquad
\begin{array}{r}
551 \\
+37 \\
\hline
88
\end{array}
\qquad
\begin{array}{r}
213 \\
21 \\
+40 \\
\hline
74
\end{array}
$$

Interpreted in traditional ways, this is truly a surprising result; of the three problems:

$$
\text{(A)}\ \begin{array}{r} 766 \\ +15 \\ \hline \end{array}
\qquad
\text{(B)}\ \begin{array}{r} 786 \\ +15 \\ \hline \end{array}
\qquad
\text{(C)}\ \begin{array}{r} 781 \\ +232 \\ \hline \end{array}
$$

traditional analysis would argue that (A) should be the easiest, since (B) involves an extra 'carry' and (C) involves an extra addition. Yet, as Friend's careful analysis revealed, problem (A) is the most difficult!

What we see, here, is the *primary-grade addition frame* revealing itself. This frame requires two inputs, and if the straightforward rules of column addition do not provide the two inputs the frame demands, the Brown-Matz-Van Lehn Law requires that some adjustment be made in order that processing can continue. Hence, the 'column-by-column' super-procedure is modified so that the *primary-grade addition frame* can be provided with the two inputs that it requires (which is what happens in the case of either of the first two errors that Friend reports), or so that the *primary-grade addition frame will not be called on unless both of the two inputs are available* (as in the case of the third error that Friend reports).

The Primary-grade Symmetric Subtraction Frame

The third specific frame that we postulate is the *primary-grade symmetric subtraction frame*, which is typically learned around grade one or two. Like the addition frame, it requires two inputs, and — again like the addition frame — it is symmetric in these two inputs. Given the inputs 8 and 5, this frame returns the answer 3. The frame does not distinguish between $8 - 5$ and $5 - 8$, again for the reason that such a distinction is unnecessary; at this stage the student has learned *only* to 'take the smaller from the larger'. (This pattern can be seen clearly in many word problems, which often contain phrases such as 'the difference between Bill's age and Mary's age is 2 years', without specifying who is older.)

Thus two errors should be expected: the error of claiming that $5 - 8 = 3$, and the 'isolated digit' error discovered by Friend. Both errors occur, quite commonly. The '$5 - 8 = 3$' error is reported, among other places, in Davis, McKnight, Parker and Elrick (1979), using data from students working on the PLATO CAI system. The 'isolated digit' error is reported in Friend (1979) and revealed with unmistakable clarity in interview protocols. Take, for example, this protocol from an interview with a third-grader (translated from the original Spanish):

> Interviewer: . . .Remember, you are going to explain to me step by step everything you do to find the answer. [Interviewer dictates the exercise $78 - 6$, which the child writes correctly.]
> Child: Now I say 8 minus 6 . . . 8 minus 6 . . . uh, 2. [Writes the 2.] Since I don't have another — what's it called? — another subtrahend, then here I have . . . we pretend the 6 is here [lightly sketching a 6 in the space under the 7], but it's invisible. So I say 7 minus 6 gives 1. [Writes the 1.]
> Interviewer: And what answer did you get?
> Child: Twelve. [Friend, 1979, p. 35]

Here we see the dramatic way our hypothetical mechanism can reveal itself in actual human behavior!

The Label or Unit Frame

Clement and his co-workers have made an extensive and careful study of the following phenomenon:

The subject is asked to write an equation, using the variables S and P, to represent the statement 'In a certain college, there are six times as many students as there are professors'. Subjects are asked to use S for the number of students, and P for the number of professors.

What happens, typically, is a very large proportion of incorrect equations – specifically, many students write the equation

$$6S = P$$

(Cf. Kaput and Clement, 1979; Rosnick and Clement, 1980). To give some specific results, in a group of 160 first-year engineering students, 63 per cent solved the problem correctly (writing 6P = S), 37 per cent gave wrong answers, and two-thirds of the wrong answers (i.e., 25 per cent of all students) took the form 6S = P.

By itself, this may not seem very surprising (although somewhat disappointing, given that these were *engineering* students). After all, there would seem to be two immediate explanations: perhaps the students are merely copying the word-order of the problem statement; or, alternatively, what other error would anyone expect? If you don't write 6P = S, the obvious alternative is to write 6S = P.

Careful subsequent studies by Clement and his collaborators have proved that these easy explanations are in fact wrong and that something much more interesting is involved here.

For one thing, they have varied word order, and the phenomenon is not effected. So the 'merely copying word order' explanation is wrong.

They have also varied semantic content, as in the task:

Write an equation using the variables C and S to represent the statement: 'At Mindy's restaurant for every four people who order cheesecake, five people order strudel'. Let C represent the number of cheesecakes ordered, and let S represent the number of strudels ordered.

In this new version, semantic content provides less guidance: after all, we know that colleges have more students than professors. True to this expectation, only 27 per cent of the engineering students answered the *cheesecake* problem correctly, 73 per cent answered incorrectly, and again two-thirds of the wrong answers showed the reversal error: 4C = 5S.

Students with non-engineering majors do substantially worse; Lochhead (1980) even reports data on college *faculty* members.

One might still be skeptical, but once again interview data settles the matter decisively. Before looking at this data, let us be clear on the 'frame' explanation.

Two relevant frames are learned in pre-college mathematics. One deals with equations that involve *numbers*, the other deals with *labels* or *units*. If x and y represent numbers, students learn that the equation

$$2x = y$$

says that (if x and y are positive), y is larger than x, and in fact the number x must be doubled to equal y. This state of affairs becomes represented by a *numerical-variables equation frame*, which may come to be labeled by a retrieval cue related to the word 'number', or something of the sort.

But there is also an alternative frame, that we might call a *units or label frame*, created for dealing with situations such as

$$12 \text{ inches} = 1 \text{ foot}.$$

This *units frame* relates to the *numerical variables frame* somewhat the way that a contravariant vector relates to a covariant vector: if I is the *number* of inches and F the *number* of feet, then

$$I = 12F,$$

with the coefficient vector (1, 12). But if i stands for the *unit* 'inch', and f for the *unit* 'foot', then

$$12i = f,$$

with the coefficient vector (12, 1).

Thus, once again, we find that the 'wrong' answers have been produced by the functioning of a frame that does have legitimate uses, but *not in the case at hand*.

Consider, now, some of the evidence. First, Rosnick and Clement (1980) report that students making the reversal error *describe the situation differently* from those who write the correct equation, with error-making students saying 'students', whereas those who write the correct equations say 'the number of students'. (As Rosnick and Clement point out, this involves a metaphoric extension of the meaning of the 'equals' sign, but precisely this metaphoric extension is required elsewhere in mathematical thinking, cf. Pimm (1980) and Kieran (1980). Once again one is struck by the orderliness of the underlying information processing.)

But one might still retain doubts. The interview protocols dispel these doubts decisively. Consider the case of Dawn:

Dawn, for example, initially reversed the *students* and *professors* problem. During a session lasting more than 20 minutes, she was alternately 'taught' and then interviewed. Several teaching strategies were used, including the use of tables, the focus on variable as number, the techniques of plugging in numbers to test an equation, and others. Throughout, she made comments like '6P = S, that's weird. I can't think of it that way.' She claimed that the interviewer was 'shaking all her foundations'. Eventually, however, she agreed that 6P = S was correct and was able to translate her learning to the *oil and vinegar* problem which follows. But then, she spontaneously redefined the problem to fit her preconceived notion, as seen in the following transcript segment: [*The oil and vinegar problem asks for an equation which represents the fact that there is 3 times as much oil as vinegar in a salad dressing.*]

1. Dawn: [Draws a table showing 3, 6 and 9 under O, and 1, 2 and 3 under V.] My first impulse would be to write three times; three times O equals V.
2. Interviewer: Mmmm. . .
3. Dawn: So then, because that's wrong, I would change it to 3V = O because I know it's the other way around . . . So then I'm gonna plug that in. And that's right. [writes 3V = O.]
4. Interviewer: Well, why don't you . . . I . . . I'll . . .
5. Dawn: I know that's right [3V = O] because I make oil and vinegar dresssing. And if you had a . . . If you had a cup – I'm rationalizing this – If you had a . . .
6. Interviewer: Okay.
7. Dawn: A . . . If you had a cup of oil and vinegar [draws cup] you'd put this much oil in and that much . . . I mean this much vinegar and that much oil or else it would be really greasy . . . [Dawn drew the pictures indicated in Figure 8.1. She pointed to the cup on the left when indicating vinegar.]
8. Interviewer: So you're saying that what this equation is saying is you're putting in more vinegar than oil? [indicates equation 3V = O.]

Figure 8.1: Dawn's picture, which contradicts her actual experience. [From P. Rosnick and J. Clement 'Learning Without Understanding: The Effect of Tutoring Strategies on Algebra Misconceptions', *Journal of Mathematical Behavior*, vol. 3 (1980). Reprinted by permission.]

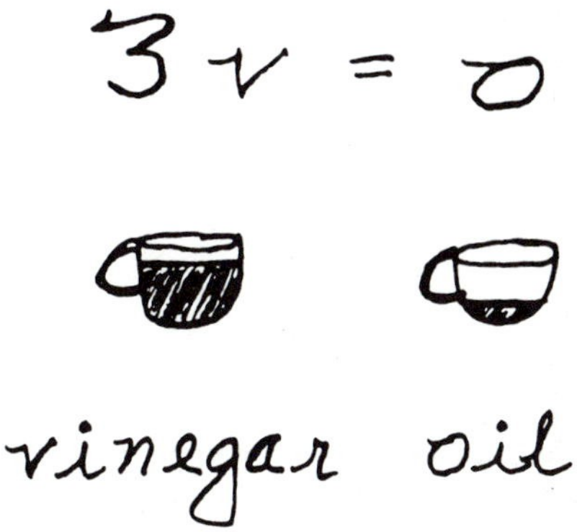

$$3V = O$$

vinegar   oil

9. Dawn: Hh-huh. [Rosnick and Clement, 1980]

As Rosnick and Clement remark:

> What is striking about this example is that when Dawn first wrote 3V = O she knew that there was more oil than vinegar. However, on re-examining the equation, her reversal misconception apparently took over, causing her to lose sight of the original relationship. (Rosnick and Clement, 1980.)

Or consider the case of Don:

Don, another precalculus student, had a similar experience. He, too, struggled through 30 minutes of work on the *students and professors* problem, where the interviewer tried several teaching strategies. One technique that ... [Don] ... found helpful was graphing, and he applied this technique to the *goats and cows* problem, which reads as follows:

> 'Write an equation using the variables G and C to express the fact that on a certain farm there are five times as many goats as cows. Let G stand for the number of goats and C for the number of cows.'

The graph in Figure 8.2 was appropriate, indicating that there were five

Figure 8.2: Don's first (correct) graph, showing the (temporary) effect of tutoring. [From Rosnick and Clement (1980). Reprinted by permission.]

times as many goats as cows. Don . . . then wrote the correct equation $1G = 5C$, while referring to his graph. However, he read it as follows: 'One goat equals 5 cows.' In analyzing the equation further he said that '5 goats = 25 cows', having derived this from the equation by multiplying both sides by five. A complete shift had occurred. The interviewer then asked if [Don's] . . . equation was consistent with the graph. The following ensued:

1. Don: If you had 1 goat, you'd have to have 5 cows. If you had 5 goats, you'd have to have 25 cows.
2. Interviewer: And does this equation express that?
3. Don: Yup.
4. Interviewer: . . . does this graph express that?
5. Don: Mmmm. . . [6 second pause] . . . Nope . . . The goats and cows should be on the other side . . . so it should be the number of goats on the bottom, I mean number of cows . . .
6. Interviewer: Uh-huh.
7. [Don now crosses out the original labeling at the axes and relabels the vertical axes 'goats' instead of 'cows' and the horizontal axis 'cows' instead of 'goats'. As a result of this change his graph becomes incorrect.] [See Figure 8.3.]

8. Don: So that should be . . . That should be the cows here, and that should be goats on this si-. . . on the . . . and this should be the cows here . . . and then it'd be all right.
9. Interviewer: Feel comfortable with that?
10. Don: Yup.

Figure 8.3: The graph after Don changed it, in a reversion to his earlier incorrect idea. [From Rosnick and Clement (1980). Reprinted by permission.]

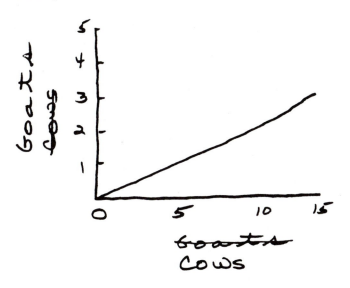

As Rosnick and Clement conclude, Don has totally lost sight of the original problem. Both he and Dawn learned to write the correct equation but then subsequently reversed the meaning of the original problem, enabling them to revert to their earlier way of writing variables.

One of the most striking characteristics of frames is this resistance to change or eradication. One final protocol demonstrates this convincingly:

Peter, a calculus and physics student, also learned to write the correct equation for the *China* problem, which states that there are eight times as many people in China as there are in England. He, unlike Don and Dawn, was able to stay conscious of the original meaning of the problem. However, after 45 minutes, it became apparent that though his behavior had changed; i.e. he was able to write the correct equation, he still tenaciously retained his original misconceptions about variables and equations, as the following section of transcript illustrates. Peter refers to the correct equation for the *China* problem, 8E = C, to help him understand analogous problems.

1. Peter: I mean I feel confident here now.
2. Interviewer: Okay. Um...
3. Peter: What's that ... I love that example where ... Well, the one with China, all right ... [I'll just] do that one again ... So you have the ratio China ... to ... uh ... England was equal to eight over one ... so, that's ...
4. Interviewer: Mmmm...
5. Peter: You know ... that's how ... I should know that! ... ... is that China is gonna equal eight E. Just in a pure algebraical sense. But I don't think of it that way. I think there's 8 little ... One Chinese person for eight little ... You know what I mean?
6. Interviewer: So what does the C mean there? [Points to the equation 8E = C.]
7. Peter: C means the English person ... uh, England itself.
8. Interviewer: Uh-huh.
9. Peter: The number of people in England ... naw, that's wrong ...uh, yeah. The number of people in England, I'd say.
10. Interviewer: And what does the E mean?
11. Peter: The number of people in China.

As Rosnick and Clement point out: 'Peter's misconceptions are so resilient that he is willing to associate the letter E with China and the letter C with England rather than change his internal conceptualization.' [Rosnick and Clement, 1980.]

The Rosnick-Clement phenomenon is surely one of the most interesting ever reported in mathematics education. Here we have people of some sophistication, many of them engineering students who have spent hundreds of hours studying variables, functions, graphs, linear equations, quadratic equations, systems of simultaneous linear equations, and so on — yet they *very* often retrieve an incorrect frame for such a simple matter as 6P = S, and having retrieved this frame, they are reluctant (or totally unable) to reject it in favor of a correct retrieval of the *numerical variables frame*. Even more strikingly, instructional programs that 'teach' them the correct behavior – that lead (temporarily) to correct performance – *are not able to eliminate the label frame* (and perhaps they should not, since the label frame does have its uses), *nor are they able to end the incorrect retrievals of the label frame* (and this they ought to do).

In some of the more traditional views of learning, this situation would be hard to understand. Within the analysis of the present chapter, however, it is not even surprising. Consider the following:

(1) The creation of two separate frames, the *label frame* and the *numerical variables frame*, is entirely reasonable. Each is needed at various points in the curriculum.

(2) So, once again, the initial error is one of *retrieving the wrong frame*, with a subsequent error in *not recognizing the retrieval error*. Given Anderson's 'conserving old frames' postulate, there is no great mystery about both frames being available for retrieval.

(3) Why the retrieval error is not detected more readily is more surprising, but is probably partly explained by (or at least related to) the willingness of the subjects to reconcile discrepancies by making adjustments elsewhere, as in using C for 'the number of people in England', and E for 'the number of people in China'.

It seems next to certain that students making this 'reversal' error *are not in the habit of checking formulas by making one or two quick numerical replacements for the numerical variables.* (This is entirely consistent with observations in the Long Term Study. Neither in Urbana nor in Amherst are students commonly disposed to make quick numerical checks on equations.)

(4) How does it happen that an instructional program can *temporarily* produce a correct performance? That is easily explained: the instruction leads to the synthesis of a new frame for the correct performance (or at least leads towards the partial synthesis of such a frame), but of course the old *label frame* is still there, ready to be retrieved at any time.

(5) So we see that the real essence of the phenomena lies in faulty retrieval. If, as in note 4, we postulate the existence of preliminary screening frames (PSFs), which play a role in selecting which operational frames to retrieve, then the Clement-Rosnick phenomenon is really a matter of PSF malfunctioning. This is entirely credible; no subject revealed any awareness that there was a conscious choice to be made, with *two well-defined alternative candidates* and *a very real possibility of error.* Interviews with some mathematicians have revealed

that some of them are well aware of the alternatives and the possible error and always perform a quick mental check on such equations, after writing them, to be sure they have selected correctly.

(6) This, in turn, suggests a revised instructional program: make sure that students are aware of *both* possible candidates, are aware of the likelihood of an incorrect choice, and form the habit of checking to see if they have in fact chosen correctly.

What this process is doing is not building up operational frames − they are alive and well − but is instead attempting to strengthen the *selection* frame, the PSF.

Which Specific Frames?

In this chapter thus far we have presented evidence in favor of the existence of several commonly-shared arithmetic-related frames.

For four frames we believe the evidence is rather strong: the *primary-grade undifferentiated binary-operation frame* (which ignores operation signs and always adds), the *primary-grade addition frame* (which, among other things, demands two inputs), the *primary-grade symmetric subtraction frame* (which does not distinguish $3 - 5$ from $5 - 3$) and the *label frame* (which produces the Clement-Kaput, or Clement-Rosnick, phenomenon). We have not considered the *symmetric division frame*, but the evidence for it closely parallels the evidence for symmetric subtraction, as in the exceedingly common error $6 \div \frac{1}{2} = 3$, and many other division difficulties.

All of the preceding frames would be constructed in accordance with the general rules, such as the Feigenbaum minimal-discrimination rule, and would operate in accordance with general rules, such as the Brown-Matz-Van Lehn Law. Each reveals itself forcefully and dramatically in easily-recognizable pieces of observable behavior.

If the *label frame* operates as we suggest, by implication there should be the alternative choice of the *numerical variables frame*; but if our criterion is that frames must reveal themselves by their ability to explain the *wrong* answers they produce, we can cite no such evidence in support of the *numerical variables frame*. (None the less, I would assume its existence.)

Perhaps more speculative is the *binary-operation selection frame* (cf. note 4) or, more generally, the *preliminary screening frames* (PSFs). We postulate that these are interposed between input data and the retrieval of the 'operational frames' that add, write equations, etc. PSFs are presumably created in response to the need to avoid retrieval errors, much as a large office might employ a receptionist to route visitors to appropriate destinations.

Simon and others[5] have commented on the difficulty in inserting warnings (or critics) *within* procedures; the PSFs provide an alternative mechanism that does not violate Anderson's 'accretion' or 'conservation' law. We would assume that any large experience of incorrect retrievals within some specific class of inputs would lead to the creation of a PSF, whose retrieval *ought* to be triggered by the recognition of any input belonging to that specific class. Evidently, however, PSFs can in some cases be bypassed.

Characteristics of Frames

The explicitly-identifiable information representation structures that we have been postulating, and seeking to relate to explicit observable behaviors, have a number of properties in common, including at least the following:

(1) *They serve as 'assimilation schemas' for organizing input data.* This, of course, is why they have been postulated by so many different writers, including Minsky, Simon, Schank, Papert and others. (Indeed, the process of 'recognizing' something — an incredibly perceptive word, 're-cognizing'! — is presumably the process of matching up input information with an appropriate previously-created representation structure.)

(2) Every representation structure (RS) that we have looked at has been identified by errors that reveal something of its inner workings. (Presumably one can identify RSs that are *not* producing errors, but their description always seems less certain, because errors are so revealing of *internal* functioning, whereas correct responses can be directly attributed to the features of the *external* situation.)

(3) Every representation structure we have discussed had a legitimate origin in 'correct' earlier learning — that is to say, each did *correctly* organize some earlier experience, and used in this earlier context it produced *correct* behavior.[6]

(4) Each RS demands certain input information and will not function correctly unless all of this input information is provided. (This, of course, seems to contradict one of the virtues ordinarily attributed to

'frames', namely, their ability to make default evaluations for missing input data. There are several possible reasons for this discrepancy, including the fact that we are dealing here with relatively simple frames, learned in a rigidly-stereotyped fashion in a rigidly-stereotyped environment. Children have far less experience, and much less varied experience, with 'addition' than they do with 'animal' or 'family' or 'room'. In school they seem to have had little experience with default evaluations for missing input data for the frames in question. Then too, in school, children are admonished not to 'guess'. Furthermore, processes like addition are already so sparse and abstract that, if much more is left out, nothing useful will remain!)

(5) *Frames are persistent.* Indeed, it is precisely this property that makes them recognizable as internal information-processing entities that can be explicitly matched with certain observable outward behavior. They continue to operate in the same precise way, in situations where they are appropriate and in situations where they are not.

This persistence is observable in several senses: (1) as just mentioned, identical functioning in a variety of situations; (2) the fact that frames seem to have a hold on the people using them, so that Dawn, for example, faced with an alternative to a cherished frame, says 'that's weird!' and claims that the interviewer, who is showing her a correct solution, is 'shaking all her foundations'; (3) so strong is this hold that subjects are led to bizarre distortions in order to avoid challenges to the content of the frame: Dawn, who has actually made vinegar and oil dressing, is moved to draw pictures of a large amount of vinegar mixed with a little oil, quite contrary to her actual experience, but necessary to protect her *label frame* from logical challenges, and Peter is willing to associate the letter E with China and the letter C with England rather than modify the *label frame* that he has retrieved; (4) mis-matches, as in the previous examples, are typically resolved by modifying the input data, or modifying the mapping-into-the-frame, in preference to modifying the frame itself; (5) instruction often avails little against frames; (6) finally, even if instruction produces a change in performance, *this change is often not permanent* — before long, the original frame reasserts itself, and behavior *reverts back* to what it was before the instruction. (This reversion-to-earlier-behavior phenomenon is well known within Piagetian psychology, although the theoretical Piagetian explanation for it is somewhat different, being stated in terms of 'developmental stages' and 'readiness for transition to another stage', whereas we explain it by the continued presence of earlier frames.)

(6) *The creation and operation of frames follows orderly rules.* One such rule is the *rule of initial over-generalization*, as when a young child says 'Daddy, I seed a butterfly!' The child's perception of a standard rule for forming past tenses has been correct, but the child has not yet learned the limitations of this rule and uses it more often than is proper (cf. Davis, 1971-2). Another rule, used by Feigenbaum and others, is that *discriminations are not made where they are not presently needed*, a rule which explains the formation of the *undifferentiated binary-operation frame.* Yet another rule, stated by John Seely Brown, Kurt Van Lehn and Marilyn Matz, is the rule that processing will tend to continue, and when an obstacle is encountered, modifications will be made (especially in the super-procedure to sub-procedure interface) to enable processing to continue (as in the modification of the column-by-column super-procedure for addition in order to continue past the obstacle of missing input data for the primary addition frame). Finally, the Rosnick and Clement protocols illustrate a rule reported by Davis and McKnight (1980) that contradictory semantic information is very frequently *not* influential in modifying algorithmic behavior.

(7) Frame retrieval may be cued by brief, explicit, specific cues (students often make remarks such as: 'I could have done it if you'd told me it was a quadratic equation!'), and presumably also by general situational similarity (as in Minsky, 1980). A particularly telling study is presented by Hinsley, Hayes and Simon (1977): for some subjects, merely the phrase 'A river steamer . . .' was sufficient to trigger retrieval of an appropriate schema.

(8) For successful problem solvers, much of the necessary information is contained in the retrieved schema and is *not present at all in the actual problem statement.* (One actual problem begins: 'A rope with a ring in one end is looped over two pegs in a horizontal line. The free end, after being passed through the ring, has a weight suspended from it, so that the rope hangs taut.' Many students cannot draw a correct diagram. Those who can are clearly drawing on information that is not explicitly presented in the problem statement. We shall consider this problem in the next chapter.)

A Possible 'Recipe' Frame

Karplus, in some elegant (and not-yet published) studies of ratio and proportion, reports protocols such as the following:

In a story presented to the student, there is a boy, John, who is making lemonade with 3 teaspoonfuls of (sweet) sugar and 9 teaspoonfuls of (sour) lemon; a girl, Mary, is also making lemonade, but using 5 teaspoonfuls of (sweet) sugar and 13 teaspoonfuls of (sour) lemon. Appropriate illustrative pictures accompany the story. The interviewer asks: 'Whose lemonade will be sweeter?'

1. Student: Let me see. Mary's would be sweeter.
2. Interviewer: Mary's would be sweeter? Um-hum [thoughtful tone invites further explanation . . .]
3. Student: Because Mary's has two less lemons in contrast with this [pointing to pictures] , with John's.
4. Interviewer: Actually, she has *4 more*.
5. Student: She *does*? [tone of great surprise]
6. Interviewer: [explaining his preceding remark] Well, she has 13 compared to 9.
7. Student: Yeah, but in relation to the *sugars*.
8. Interviewer: Could you explain to me how you figured that she has 2 less in relation to sugar?
9. Student: Well, O.K. . . . . . There's 3 and 9.
10. Interviewer: Uh-huh.
11. Student: And 3 goes into 9 3 times, and then you go 5 and 13. . .
12. Interviewer: Yes. . .
13. Student: 15 goes into 5 3 times [sic!] . So it's really too much . . .
14. Interviewer: Uh-huh. So it's 2 less. And so if Mary wanted to make it come out the same sweetness as John's . . .
15. Student: It would have to be 15.
16. Interviewer: She'd have to use 15. So, I see she has 2 less. O.K.[7]

The student's comparison of the table

	Sugar	Lemon
John	3	9
Mary	5	13

with a different table which is *nowhere in evidence except in her own imagination* is stunning! The alternative table, namely,

	Sugar	Lemon
John	3	9
Mary	5	15

is so real to her that she at first rejects the interviewer's 'common-sense' numbers − *which ARE the numbers that are actually in evidence* − in favor of her 'ideal' table.

This, and other evidence in various Karplus interviews, suggests strongly that many students have a 'recipe' frame, which allows them great facility in doubling recipes, halving recipes, etc.

A 'Cities' Frame

If you have seen the movie *Woodstock*, a documentary reporting on the famous 1969 music festival at Bethel, NY, you may recall that the members of the audience (and everyone else) were overwhelmed by the unanticipatedly huge number of people who turned up. Trying to make the number real to themselves, many people kept saying it, in various ways. Perhaps 500,000 people turned up (rumor, at the time, said two million). To make this more intelligible, people repeatedly shouted things like 'We are now the second largest city in New York State!' (Since the city of Buffalo was reported on 1 April 1970 to have a population of 462,768, this claim may have been true!) But of course the music festival was not a city; it was a very large crowd of people outdoors in a large field listening to Joan Baez, Jimi Hendrix and Ten Years After. The value of describing the festival as 'the second largest city in New York State' was that it gave a relatively well-defined unit of comparison − the *city*. Of course, if Americans typically have a frame for 'the city as an abstract social unit' − and probably they do − this frame is nothing like so universal and uniform as a frame for, say, addition. But if you know a few US cities of reasonable size, describing the open-field congregation at Bethel as 'the second largest city in New York State' is a highly meaningful way of putting it.

Conclusion

Several specific information-representation structures can be explicitly identified and described, as a result of observable behavior which they produce. Just as ideas such as 'atomic nuclei' and 'layers of electrons' provided a structural underpinning for macroscopic chemical behavior (such as valence) and physical behavior (such as Rutherford scattering), so the postulation of internal information-representation and information-processing structures can provide a mechanism for the analysis of human mathematical thought. The matching up of specific postulated internal structures with corresponding specific outward behaviors is now beginning to be possible.

I do not mean to suggest that most frames are consciously held, in the same form, by large numbers of people, nor do I mean to suggest that the total number of frames is small. Presumably, each of us has in memory an exceedingly large number of frames. Indeed, within the Rosnick and Clement paper there is also a strong suggestion of what could be called a 'geometric area frame'; Karplus has evidence of a 'recipe frame'; and almost any explanation of mathematical behavior will turn up evidence for other frames. A 'linear representation of quantity frame' seems nearly universal, presumably due to rulers, thermometers, etc., although this frame is elaborately developed in some people's minds, and more primitive in others', especially with regard to matters such as interpolation, etc. If there is a 'city' frame, there is also probably a 'nation' frame, a 'school' frame, a 'classroom' frame, and many others, which − among other things − serve as 'units' for numbers of people. (E.g., 'thirty people' are 'as many as all the kids in my class', and 'three hundred people' might be 'as many as all the kids in my school'.)

Our purpose here has been different. We have not been seeking to catalog *all* frames − presumably an impossible task! Rather our goal has been to seek evidence for the existence and nature of a *few* frames, in order to show at least some contact between the postulated theory of frames and observations of actual human behavior.

Remark

In the preceding pages, we have spoken occasionally of 'knowledge representation structures' (or KRSs), sometimes of 'procedures', sometimes of 'frames' and sometimes of 'productions' and 'production systems'. The reader may ask which one or ones do we really mean? For example, Anderson says *productions* are not destroyed. Does this mean, also, that *frames* are not destroyed? Does it mean that *procedures* are not destroyed?

The reader is clearly entitled to feel some uncertainty. In the hope of helping, we offer the following remarks:

(1) The *source* of the confusion lies partly in the fact that there does not, at present, exist one single conceptualization of human information processing that is accepted by every researcher. On the contrary, different researchers use different conceptualizations that do not

correspond with one another in simple ways. The MIT group, working with Papert, Minsky and others, tend to emphasize *frames*. Lawler (1981) speaks of *microworlds*, and Schank speaks of *scripts*. The group at Carnegie-Mellon University, with Simon, Newell, Anderson, etc., use almost exclusively *production systems*. Both frames and production systems attempt to represent knowledge, including 'active' knowledge that can accomplish something, such as solving an algebra word problem, or interpreting certain kinds of pictures, or moving blocks in response to English-language commands. But a production system is a computer program written in a particular way. A computer program written in some other format would not be a production system. A 'frame' might be a computer program of some different sort, or perhaps an arrangement of ideas in a person's mind (and not a computer program at all); hence one cannot ask which parts of this frame correspond to which parts of that production system. These questions may make no more sense than to ask which parts of this automobile correspond to which parts of this cherry tree.

(2) The *effect* of the confusion may not be so catastrophic as one might initially surmise; the history of electricity shows early confusions and disagreements as to what 'electricity' actually was; the basic entity ended up with a negative value because of initial errors in conceptualizing the 'flow' of electricity; there was confusion over a particle vs. the wave nature of electrons, and so on. None the less, extremely rapid progress has been made, and these uncertainties were inevitable and not especially harmful. Indeed, areas of uncertainty often helped to raise valuable questions, and the study of these questions often contributed to the rapid progress.

(3) Some *temporary resolution* can be achieved rather easily, if a reader restates results in language that he or she finds acceptable; I personally would say, for example:

> Some knowledge representation structures persist more or less permanently, and these earlier forms subsequently compete with later 'revised' or 'corrected' versions with which they simultaneously co-exist. [One version of the Anderson Law of Non-deletion.] Of course this leaves some open questions: e.g. how common is this 'competition among alternative versions'? But even without precise answers to such questions, one can see the Non-deletion Law at work in various specific instances of behavior.

Indeed, as a teacher I find much of this analysis into 'frames' and 'procedures' very helpful — it often enables me to understand more clearly the cognitive tasks which my students face, and helps to reveal where they are experiencing difficulties. The areas of uncertainty are not as limiting as one might at first fear.[8]

Notes

1. Two remarks may be helpful. First, our typical concern in this book is with *how human beings think*. Hence, any reference to computer information processing may tend to seem like an intrusion. We do not mean it to be so. For most of the book, references to computer information processing are intended merely as metaphors of a happily precise kind to facilitate discussions of human information processing. Anderson's ACT is a rare exception. For Anderson, Simon and other researchers at Carnegie-Mellon University, actual running computer programs are seen as simulations of human information processing, compelling the researcher to achieve high levels of precision and completeness. Anything left vague will necessarily be omitted from a simulation, so completeness and specificity become crucial.

The second comment, addressed only to those readers who are familiar with production systems, is that Anderson's ACT is not a traditional 'pure' production system; certain additional structure has been inserted, as for instance the numerical 'strength' assigned to each production, and also the propositional network representation of propositional knowledge.

2. A film showing sixth-and-seventh-grade children making this error is available from the Study Group for Mathematical Behavior. This film is entitled *Guessing Functions*.

3. The mental reproduction of addition facts is usually assumed to be essentially passive, rather like a log table printed on the pages of a book. Evidence that this may not be the case, that, on the contrary, addition facts are represented *dynamically* by calculation procedures (as logarithms are represented in hand-held calculators), has been reported by Suppes, Groen and others (cf., Suppes and Groen, 1967; Groen and Parkman, 1972). (Cf. also Woods, Resnick and Groen, 1975; Resnick, 1976; Groen and Resnick, 1977.)

4. One might conjecture that some preliminary screening procedure is interposed, so that *first* a problem such as 3 + 5 cues retrieval of a *binary-operation selection frame*, and thereafter this frame cues the retrieval of the *addition frame*.

5. From comments by Herbert Simon, on the complex information

processing aspects of mathematical thought, made at a Greeno symposium at the University of Pittsburgh.

6. We have seen one exception to this rule. In Chapter 6, Benny's sub-procedure p_2, which inserted decimal points in Benny's procedure for converting fractions to decimals, could not be recognized as useful in any plausible context. Where and why Benny had learned it remains a mystery. But this is a very rare exception in our data. Nearly always, the procedures students have learned were, once upon a time, good for *something*.

7. Robert Karplus, unpublished interview protocols. Reproduced by permission.

8. One interesting and valuable discussion is presented in Charniak (1981).

9 A NOT-COMMONLY-SHARED FRAME

In the preceding chapter we considered some frames, such as the *primary-grade addition frame*, for which there is considerable evidence to support the claim that many people synthesize this frame early in their educational careers. In this chapter we look at an example that suggests, in compelling fashion, a knowledge-representation capability that is NOT commonly shared.

Reading Word Problems

A few years ago, an earlier view interpreted reading as a straightforward process of getting all of the information out of a sentence or paragraph in an accurate form. The 'frame retrieval' view sees this process quite differently; cues in the written text trigger the retrieval of some frame or frames. The frame then directs some further specific data collection, so that the most important of the unfilled slots in the frame can be filled in from the input data.

To see how great is the difference between these two views, consider the following, which is an actual textbook problem:

A rope with a ring in one end is looped over two pegs in a horizontal line. The free end, after being passed through the ring, has a weight suspended from it, so that the rope hangs taut. If the rope slips freely over the pegs and through the ring, the weight will descend as far as possible. Assume that the length of the rope is at least four times as great as the distance between the pegs, and that the configuration of the rope is symmetric with respect to the line of the vertical part of the rope. (The symmetry assumption can be justified on the grounds that the rope and weight will take a rest position that minimizes the potential energy of the system. See Problem 25, Article 8-6.) Find the angle formed at the bottom of the loop.[1]

This problem, in this same written form, was presented to individual students from a calculus class, with an interviewer watching (and possibly asking questions) as each student attempted to solve the problem.

To the surprise of the teacher, in this eleventh-grade calculus class (high school juniors), out of 20 students only three were able to make a diagram. Without a diagram, of course, no further progress could be made.

Figure 9.1: Most students stood the two pencils vertically, in order to show the position of the two pegs in the 'hanging weight' problem. This, of course, is incorrect.

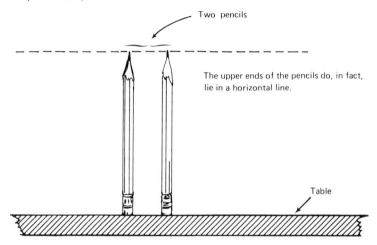

Two pencils

The upper ends of the pencils do, in fact, lie in a horizontal line.

Table

Students who could not make a diagram were handed two pencils to use as 'pegs' in order to demonstrate how the pegs in the problem were supposed to be arranged. This, of course, was the key obstacle. Except for the three students with correct pictures, all of whom went on to complete the solution of the entire problem, no students could arrange the pencils correctly. The most common wrong answer was to stand the pencils up vertically, each resting on the table top, as in Figure 9.1. Both pencils were the same length, so their higher ends were at the same height above the table top, and might, in this sense, be said to be in a horizontal line (though this would hardly be considered a good description). But, of course, with this configuration it was impossible to complete the arrangement of rope, ring, loop and weight.

Only after observing the students' difficulties did the teacher notice how confusing the words in the problem actually were. Immediately after seeing the problem the first time, the teacher had drawn a correct diagram, as in Figure 9.2c, and had considered this effortless and automatic; at that time he saw no possible difficulty in the language of the problem.

After observing the students' confusion, the teacher reread the problem, changed his view entirely, and began to wonder how anyone ever got the correct diagram. If the words of the problem have any literal meaning at all (which is arguable), it seemed to the teacher that it must mean construing each peg to be represented as a line segment, and to place the pegs so that these two line segments were disjoint and were subsets of the same horizontal line, more or less as in Figure 9.3.

From the point of view of 'getting information out of the para-

Figure 9.2a: A perspective view of the intended configuration.

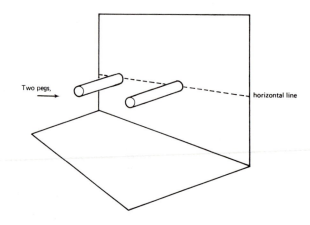

Figure 9.2b: View from the front (more useful for the appropriate mathematical analysis).

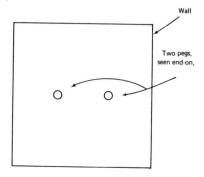

Figure 9.2c: The figure as drawn effortlessly by the teacher, who at first saw no possibility of any trouble in making a correct diagram.

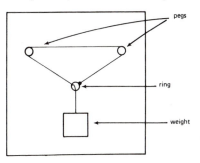

graph with 100% fidelity' this whole problem defies understanding. Some of the necessary correct information is not written in the paragraph in the first place, and some wrong information that *is* written in the paragraph would make it impossible to draw a correct picture if one took it literally.

Figure 9.3: Two pegs, lined up rather like two cars in a railroad train — this is possibly the closest to a literal interpretation of the problem statement (but, of course, it is incorrect).

Of course, from the point of view of frames, that is not the way the matter looks at all. Frame theory never contemplates 'extracting all the information from the paragraph' in any case; instead, it deals with cues for frame selection and retrieval. The three students who drew correct diagrams (and the teacher) immediately retrieved — or constructed! — a frame corresponding to Figure 9.2c, and had no further difficulty. (Notice that their figure did NOT satisfy a literal interpretation of the words in the problem. This did not bother them — in fact, the teacher and all three successful students were initially unaware of the discrepancy. But of course as soon as they accepted an instantiated frame, *they discarded the 'primitive' input* — i.e. the words of the problem. Working from their correct diagram, they had no further difficulties.)

Frame interpretations of reading challenge many traditional ideas. Besides the 'ignoring wrong clues' aspect that we have just seen, frame theory raises questions about where 'common-sense' knowledge comes from. *Where did the correct representation come from?* Not, as we have seen, from a faithful interpreting of the written words. But, surprisingly, it also did not come from 'practical everyday experience'!

Peter, the boy in the class who had had perhaps the most experience with belts, straps and ropes – from extensive camping and climbing experience – drew an 'incorrect' diagram, as in Figure 9.4. When the interviewer challenged this drawing, Peter made several actual arrangements with various ropes and straps, and demonstrated that in the real world of actual physical objects, the configuration of Figure 9.4 can be satisfactorily stable.

Figure 9.4: A physically-realizable configuration, both drawn and constructed by Peter, which differs from the stable configuration of the idealized theory.

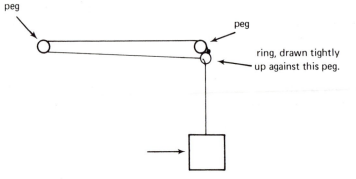

Notice, then, that two traditional theories are false in this case; (i) truth does not come from careful literal interpretation of the words in the book; and (ii), truth in the required form may not come from everyday practical experience. (As a result of our participation in the Long Term Study, we ourselves have come to believe that this case is actually typical; both traditional theories are false in general.)

Science and mathematics do not deal with reality, but rather with certain abstract, idealized models of reality. The match is usually so good that, for example, space ships can rendezvous successfully, we can land a man on the moon and bring him safely back to earth, and the vast Boeing 747 can actually take off, fly and land in safety. We have almost learned to take such successes for granted.

But the match is never perfect, and especially in certain cases it is not really very good. One such case includes many of the highly over-simplified models taught to beginning students. A real rope is not weightless; it has stiffness, and friction whenever it touches something. It is subject to compression and tension distortions, and to stretching in several dimensions. It will *not* 'slip freely over pegs', nor will it slip freely through a metal ring. Cloth belts on some women's dresses illustrate what can really happen in certain cases, where metal ring buckles work only because the simplified laws of this problem do not always govern the real world.

When a student is learning science, he is learning a certain mythology that by no means always matches commonplace experience. Nor can statements always be interpreted strictly. What is happening is that the student is building up a certain quite sophisticated cognitive representation structure; this structure can be very powerful, and certainly very valuable. Modern science depends upon it.

But truth defined by a literal use of words, truth defined by commonplace everyday experience and truth defined by this elaborate cognitive representation system are often three quite different things.

Constructed, or Retrieved?

Several questions should be raised. First, is the correct 'ring-and-peg-and weight' diagram itself a *frame*? Surely not! Probably none of the students had ever seen such a configuration before. That physical arrangement of ring and rope and weight is *far too specific*. If we postulate 'frames' of such fastidious specificity, we must either confront an impossible numerousness of 'frames', or else face the likelihood that no input data will ever match any assimilation pattern that is retrievable from memory.

What alternative is there? Well, we can assume that the *representation* for this physical configuration *was constructed* at the moment when it was needed. (This must be a very common kind of situation.) None the less, there would still be a frame involved – a frame for the construction of abstract 'sketch' diagrams from textbook statements of problems. Notice that all of the successful students, and the teacher, made the diagram so quickly and easily that they did not perceive any possibility of trouble at this point.

There are, in fact, quite a few orderly 'rules' for how one should make such a diagram. For example:

(i) use line segments, dots, circles, etc., to make a kind of 'stick-figure' sketch;

(ii) show *only* the key features; every unnecessary line is a possible source of confusion;

(iii) do NOT use perspective, which may distort some of the key angles, distances, etc.;

(iv) try to make key features appear True Shape (in the usual technical meaning of this phrase, as it is used in descriptive geometry);

(v) do not pay too much attention to most details;

and so on.

The most reasonable assumption would seem to be that the teacher, and the three successful students, each possessed a frame of this type. Note that it would thus be an 'active' frame, as opposed to some of the 'passive' frames that function more like, say, telephone directories.

Note

1. This is problem 39, on p. 294, of the textbook: George B. Thomas, Jr. and Ross L. Finney, *Calculus and Analytic Geometry* (5th edn) (Addison-Wesley, Reading, Mass., 1979). Reprinted by permission.

This problem is interesting for at least three reasons:

(i) it confronts students with an interesting reading problem;

(ii) it confronts students with the contrast (even conflict) between Newtonian physics applied to 'ideal' ropes, pegs, rings, etc., vs. the observable behavior of actual ropes, pegs and so on;

(iii) it confronts students with a choice between using a *principle* to solve a problem, vs. using a *formula*. The necessary principle is stated twice in the problem itself ('minimize the potential energy!') yet most students attempt, unsuccessfully, to use a formula.

10 TO PUT IT SIMPLY . . .

Papert, Minsky, Matz, Lawler, Simon and others who write about human thought processes in mathematics are careful writers, dealing with a complex and subtle area of investigation. In most of the preceding chapters I have tried to follow their example, which I find an admirable one. But one result of such care can sometimes be complications that leave the reader confused. Let me, in this chapter, set aside a certain measure of prudence, shout 'Damn the torpedoes! I will speak plainly! — Or, at least, intuitively . . .' and try to paint a simpler picture, omitting cautions as to where consensus grows thin and conjecture takes over. I think the result may be useful.

How Ideas Grow — First Version

Big ideas are built up out of little ideas, but not out of *very* little ideas. (They may, however, be built up out of very simple ideas that one first learned many years ago.) For mathematical topics, we can take the smallest ideas of interest to be 'units' or 'steps'; for the most part this is too small a size to concern us. When someone writes

$$\sin^2 \theta = 1 - \cos^2 \theta \quad ,$$

we do *not*, typically, ask how he distinguishes 's' from 'z', nor 'n' from 'm'. All of that lies years back in his past. At one time, ages ago, it was a struggle. Now he just reads 'cos' or 'sin' without thinking about it.

So we lump all these old achievements together, take them for granted, and if they appear in our discussion at all we'll call them 'units' or 'steps'.

The smallest piece we usually care about is a *piece of procedure*, as when a student is asked to find the square-root of 1398, marks off the digits in pairs, and writes

$$\sqrt{\overset{3}{13,98}}$$

but does not know what to do next. He used a 'piece of a procedure', and when he came to the end, there was no reference telling him where to go next.

For a beginning student, there may well be quite a few of these 'pieces of procedure'. Impressionistically, we can represent each piece of procedure as a line segment, and get a picture similar to Figure 10.1a.

Figure 10.1: 'Pieces of procedure' are represented as line segments. At first (a) they are separated, not linked up. With more practice or experience, they become joined together to form a complete algorithm (b). Still later (c) they acquire more effective means of retrieval; more, and more diverse, stimuli lead to retrieval of the appropriate string.

a)   (earlier, less mature version)

But of course if our student is to progress, he must get some of these short pieces of procedure joined together to make something more effective (for example, the complete square-root algorithm). Impressionistically, we have a picture like Figure 10.1b.

b)

But another change needs to occur. The whole sequence must be more readily retrievable from a greater diversity of cues. In one part of our study, we have asked students to write a number in the box so that the open sentence

$$\Box \times \Box = 2 \tag{1}$$

becomes a true statement, subject to the restriction that whatever number you write in the first box, you must then write that same number in the second box, also. A sizeable proportion of university students in non-math areas said they could not do this, explaining 'I don't think we had that in my high school' (or words to that effect). When we asked them about 'the square-root of 2', or used the notation

$$\sqrt{2} \quad ,$$

the results were somewhat better. For this group, equation (1) was not an adequate retrieval cue; the other two cues worked slightly better.

So we need to picture more different cues that can retrieve this procedure. Impressionistically, we might draw something like Figure 10.1c.

c)

stimuli

Still more changes are needed. If our procedure dealt with solving linear equations, we want to add a branch that tells us how to solve quadratic equations, and how to tell which equations are linear and which are quadratic. Impressionistically, we can think of something like Figure 10.2a. But still more ought to be added. If the procedure deals with equations, we want to insert pointers that head us towards the proof of the quadratic formula, the possibility of reducing other equations to quadratic, the graphs of parabolas, etc. Impressionistically (especially when we add determinants and matrices for systems of linear equations, factoring for higher degree equations, etc.) we can draw something like Figure 10.2b.

Frames?

The question arises, are any of these representations the kind of thing we think of as *frames*? Well, maybe so . . .

How could you tell? Well, (i) frames are more complete; (ii) they access more information; (iii) they can deal with a greater variety of task; (iv) they can be entered at more different points; (v) hopefully, they have more descriptors attached to them, so students can talk about them more easily; (vi) they contain *variables* (or 'slots'), and they seek information to permit the entering of correct data into these slots; (vii) they contain 'default evaluation procedures' that write best-guess information into slots that would otherwise remain vacant.

How Ideas Grow – Second Version

The second version is the same as the first version, with one exception,

Figure 10.2: With the acquisition of more knowledge, more elaborate representations are needed. Figure 10.2a shows branching to provide responses to more different situations; Figure 10.2b shows that still more retrieval cues are now available, some leading to alternative entry points into the frame; still more branching has been created; pointers lead to related topics; and 'tags' bearing descriptor labels have become attached, making possible advance planning by using meta-language and heuristics. (The tags advise us what this apparatus can do, and when to use it.) For purposes of illustration we have supposed that this frame deals with solving equations, so pointers point to items dealing with factoring, graphs, complex numbers, etc.

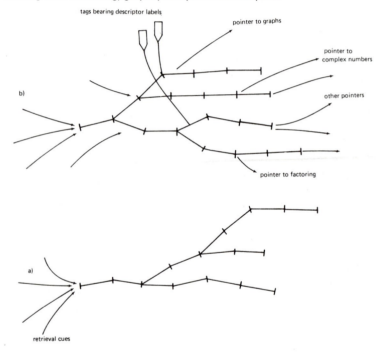

which may be important.

The 'one exception' deals with frames. Consider some of the frames that have been discussed in the literature;[1] these include:

(i) a 'birthday' frame, that contains information about all aspects of birthdays;

(ii) a 'supermarket' frame, that contains information about all

aspects of supermarkets;
(iii) a 'museum' frame;
(iv) a 'trip' or 'journey' frame;
(v) a 'meetings-I-have-attended' frame;
(vi) an 'elephant' frame (that records information about elephants).

From this kind of list one might say that typical frames discussed in the general cognitive science literature (*not* related particularly to mathematics) tend to be broader, and to deal more with actual episodes experienced in the past, than would be the case with most of the frames we have indicated in the First Version. Should we then plan to provide more episodes as foundations for mathematical frames? The idea is not fanciful; Papert has written of how, for him personally, some early experiences with gears helped to provide a foundation for many subsequent mathematical ideas.[2]

Furthermore (as we shall see in a later chapter) one important aspect of some of the 'new mathematics' innovations of the 1950s and 1960s was a teaching strategy that bases the introduction of each new concept upon a special kind of experiential episode called a *paradigmatic experience*. In effect, this is an experience intended to lay down the foundation for a relevant frame. Paradigmatic experiences are more complete than typical 'mathematics lessons' are, and probably involve students more deeply and more creatively. We shall consider paradigmatic experiences in more detail in Chapter 21.

Summary

Informal formulations are sometimes more informative than formal ones are. In this chapter we have tried to restate our main line of argument in an informal and intuitive way.

Notes

1. Recall, of course, that some writers speak of 'scripts', or 'schemata' or 'stereotypes'. These are all, roughly, frames. (Cf., e.g., Schank and Kolodner (1979), 'Episodic Memory'.) Pollack and Waltz (1982) have suggested that the word 'frame' has been overworked. We may be guilty of this (along with many others), but of course there is a reason: some kind of 'chunk' very much like a frame seems to be an absolute

necessity in order to construct sensible explanations of complex information processing. (A few researchers disagree with this judgement.)

2. Papert (1982).

11 THE O'HARE AIRPORT SOLUTION

In earlier chapters we have considered the question of how your attention is directed from one piece of knowledge to an appropriate 'next' thing that ought to be thought about. We considered the alternatives of 'sending' vs. 'volunteering'. There is a third mechanism, proposed by Schank and Kolodner (1979), that offers an elegant solution to this problem, as we now explain.

'Sending' vs. 'Volunteering'

As we work through complex problems our attention must shift from one line of thought to another. Thinking of the information processing control arrangements in our minds, when our attention shifts from A to B, was it 'sent' by A, or was it 'attracted' to B?

Or to put this in the language of procedures, does procedure A contain an instruction that says 'Go to Procedure B and do it!', or does Procedure B clamor for attention, does it 'volunteer' and shout 'Hey! Let *me* do that! I'm the expert on that kind of thing!'?

If we postulate that control is *sent* to the next task, then we must have a fantastic number of conditional transfer commands inserted in every procedure. Every critic must be represented this way, so every addition procedure must contain lines saying: 'Check the *sizes*; if they seem unreasonable, go to Procedure SIZE-ERROR.' This must be inserted not just in *one* procedure, but in every procedure involving addition — and also in every procedure involving subtraction or multiplication, or division or square-root extraction, and so on.

But then there has to be a critic for parity (i.e. whether an integer is *even* or *odd*), and *it* has to be inserted into every arithmetic algorithmic procedure. Is there also a critic for positive-negative checks? Any such arrangement seems wildly improbable, although not on that account actually impossible.

The advantage of 'sending' is that we know how to do it in computers, and probably (at least roughly) in humans. 'Paired associate' learning would seem to be mainly a matter of 'sending': one item causes you to think of the other. In computers, you insert an instruction known as a *transfer*, or an instruction known as a conditional transfer. You know where your attention (or the computer's) is now, and where you are now tells you where to go next.

The disadvantage of 'sending' is that it would seem to require an awesomely vast collection of transfers and conditional transfers. The typical program might well consist mainly of transfers. (Of course, perhaps this is the way things really are, but it hardly seems likely.)

The mechanism of 'competitive volunteering' might avoid this huge proliferation of transfers. Given a collection of active registers, any one of which can be an active center for one strand of simultaneous processing, we no longer have to go to the procedure or the memory location — they can bring themselves to our attention. They themselves can decide when to become active.

They can, that is, if one postulates that each procedure becomes activated when it recognizes a certain pattern in input data (or in information being processed at any appropriate level). Each procedure must then have its own attached *pattern recognizer* that can discriminate between certain patterns when the procedure should volunteer, vs. all other patterns when it will not volunteer. This pattern-recognizer then acts as a 'trigger' to activate the procedure.

The main disadvantage with postulating such an arrangement is the question of how the pattern-recognizers themselves work. (One would also need some additional apparatus to settle priority disputes, as in the case of two procedures attempting to occupy the same *active processing register* (like two reporters dashing for the same telephone).)[1] Minsky has pointed out that one common error in artificial intelligence is to take every task that really requires 'intelligence', and to assign them all to one small black box that might be labeled 'Little Miracle Intelligence Box'. Everything outside of the box, and nothing inside of it, is thereafter carefully explained.

Texas and Africa

B., a mathematics teacher, was talking with a mathematics educator who lived in Oklahoma, and told him of some relevant work being done in Texas. B. thought the Texas and Oklahoma researchers might get together. Then, recalling that Texas is rather large, B. wondered if he had just said something silly. He suddenly recalled hearing that there are places in Texas that are nearer to Chicago than they are to certain other places in Texas. That instantly reminded him that he had also heard that there are places in Africa that are closer to Alaska than they are to certain other places in Africa.

How might these associations have occurred?

'Sending'. One could imagine that when the Texas story was heard, a pointer was inserted, saying: 'Refer also to Africa-Alaska-Africa comparison.' There are at least two things wrong with this assumption. First, in order to realize that such a pointer ought to be inserted, some mechanism has to look at this story, compare it with the Africa-Alaska story, and recognize that both stories have an identical abstract skeletal structure. *In short, our 'pattern-matcher' is needed here, also, and in a distinctly sophisticated version.*

The second difficulty is that B. heard the Texas-Chicago story years before he heard the Africa-Alaska story. When the Texas-Chicago story was coded and stored in memory, there *was* no Africa-Alaska story to list as a reference! Are we to postulate that whenever new data is acquired, every existing memory entry must be updated with a reference to the new data whenever they share a pattern, character, scene or what-have-you in common? (Although, however, in the years of observing one particularly thoughtful student, P., it has sometimes seemed that he had a grand scheme like this that he actively pursued during his periods of ruminative thoughtfulness.)

This second objection is a fundamental one. The twenty-third time that a pattern appears, one may conceivably be prepared to recognize it. But how do you ever get started? The *first* time that a pattern appears it is NOT a pattern, since 'pattern' is defined in terms of aspects that are common to several instances. (On its first appearance, what was the 'pattern' of the Texas-Chicago story? That it dealt with a state whose name began with 'T'? That it dealt with the largest state in the United States (which, at the time, it did)? Or what?)

The Chicago-Atlanta Solution

If every airport in the USA had frequent flights to every other airport, every airport would be *very* busy. This air traffic jam is avoided by the use of regional centers. Living in Urbana, Illinois, if I want to fly somewhere, *first* I fly to Chicago or St Louis. *Then* I fly where I want to go (or near to where I want to go — the corresponding fan-out from a regional center may be in effect at the other end of the trip, as well). My friends who live in the south typically fly to Atlanta or to St Louis.

This reduces the number of daily flights in the USA to a level that is almost sustainable.

The Cognitive Equivalent of Chicago

There is an elegant way to apply the O'Hare Airport solution to the problem of cognitive associations and transfers of control, that has been used by Minsky, by Schank and by others (see especially Schank and Kolodner, 1979).

The key idea is the main collection of *frames*. These frames in fact function like the airports in Chicago and Atlanta. They operate so as to create a surprisingly orderly flow of traffic, while providing that connections do ultimately get made − even between Urbana, Illinois and Hyannis, Massachusetts, or Arcata, California, or Princeton, New Jersey.

The system works like this.

When the 'Texas-Chicago' story first appears, it involves *inequalities in distances*. It calls for the retrieval of the basic *distances* frame, which includes distance measurement, the triangle inequality, the definition of the 'distance from a point to a set', and so on. (Perhaps this is really a kind of mega-frame, and we are dealing with only a small sub-frame contained within it.) In the course of the Texas-Chicago story, a copy of the basic distance frame has its slots filled with relevant information and becomes an *instantiated* frame.

Now − what is stored in memory?

After hearing the Texas-Chicago story, B. still has in mind the original basic distance frame. (We never destroy our collection of basic frames,[2] we do all our processing using Xerox copies.)

But, as a result of hearing the story,[3] he now also has in memory:[4]

(i) the instantiated frame, its variables filled with 'Texas', 'Chicago', etc.

(ii) a record of *uses* of the basic frame, that refers us to the place in memory where the *instantiated frame* is stored.

Notice that this solves several of the basic problems:

(i) How is 'pattern' *defined* the first time it appears?
Answer: *By the portion of the basic frame that was used.* (Since the *distance* frame was used to compare the distance from point A to set Y, as against the distance from A to point A', *this* is the pattern. The fact that 'T' is the initial letter of 'Texas' is NOT part of the pattern. Cf. Figure 11.1)

Figure 11.1: Both the Texas-Chicago story and the Africa-Alaska story make use of the same basic geometric fact. If X and Y are sets, and if A and A' are points, it is possible (as shown here) for the distance d(A, A') between the points A and A', and the distance d(A, Y) between the point A and the set Y to satisfy the inequality

$$d(A, Y) < d(A, A').$$

This basic geometric fact may be a basic cognitive frame, stored in memory, or reconstructed from a sketch that is stored in memory.

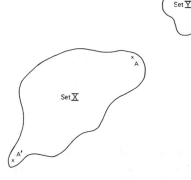

(ii) How can the Texas-Chicago story send us to the Africa-Alaska story, which did not exist when the Texas-Chicago story was entered into memory?

Answer: It doesn't — at least not directly. We go, as it were, by way of O'Hare Airport.

What happens in this: when *either* of these stories arises — or even when B. wonders how close a city in Oklahoma is to a city in Texas — what is retrieved is the *basic distance frame*. This is an 'open' frame — its slots are not filled with specific data from any single event. It is there to help us 'make sense' out of this new input data.

But — *whenever the basic 'open' distance frame is retreived, it shows us a list of previous uses, and where the results are stored in memory.* If any of these sound helpful or interesting, we know where to go to find them (in the form of instantiated frames). It does not matter which use comes first on the list of previous users. The open frame itself has always been there.[5] (Cf. Figure 11.2.)

Figure 11.2: A memory record procedure proposed by Schank and Kolodner, applied here to the 'Texas-Chicago' story.

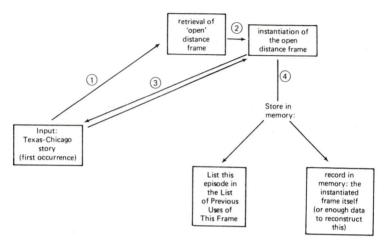

A Cautionary Note

All of this seems like an elegant solution, and a great triumph. Probably it is both. But we have not necessarily escaped from Minsky's Magic Black Box. B. obviously had a collection of frames that was adequate to these tasks.

Where did these frames come from?

Notes

1. There is, as a matter of fact, neurophysiological data that indicates that the nervous system is eager to go ahead and do a great many things, and that a major task of the 'higher' brain regions is to *prevent* this spontaneous activity from lower levels of the nervous system from becoming overwhelming. If a large (and carefully selected) portion of the brain of a cat is surgically removed — producing a so-called 'high-decerebrate cat' — the result is a living animal in many ways like an ordinary intact cat. Of course it can no longer 'think' — all of its sophisticated higher mental processes have been terminated.

How would such a cat behave? Would it lie motionless? Run around? Or what?

High-decerebrate cats have been studied by Graham Brown,

C.C. Boylls and others (cf. Boylls, 1982; Lundberg and Phillips, 1973). In fact, if the cat's body is supported in approximately a normal walking position, the cat's legs go through the normal motion of walking (whether or not they are actually touching the floor). If the cat is immersed in water, the motion becomes a swimming motion. If the cat's head is tilted upward, the leg motion shifts to one appropriate to descending an incline; if the head is tilted downward, the motion becomes one of climbing. (If you think of the position of a cat going up or down stairs, or a steep incline, you can see why this matching of head position to posture makes sense.) If the cat's head is turned left or right, the leg motion switches to one of walking in an appropriate circle. Hence it is clear that these motions do not normally occur because the higher brain centers 'think' about the matter and order up such behavior. *They occur if the higher centers do not forbid them.* It is rather as if the thoughtful part of the brain has the task of controlling a large collection of over-eager 'assistants' (Boylls, 1976).

2. Well, hardly ever. We do *add* to the collection. And since any frame may send you an *instantiated version* of itself, there is an effect of modification whenever a frame is used.

3. More accurately, as a result of *thinking about it*.

4. See Schank and Kolodner (1979), 'Episodic Memory'.

5. Well, obviously the basic frame has *not* 'always been there' — it was created at some earlier time.

12 ASSEMBLY

We intend to use the word 'assembly' as a technical term, to describe how a new knowledge representation structure is built up using bits and pieces of previously synthesized knowledge representation structures.

A 'collage' is an artistic production made by pasting old pieces of newspapers, or magazines or fabric onto a surface, perhaps also attaching small physical objects and painting the result in some places (if necessary), so as to obtain a result that can be hung on the wall like any painting, that probably sounds repugnant to those who have never seen one, but that can − when artistically composed − be a strikingly attractive piece of art.

If we were to try to encompass the main theme of this chapter in one paragraph, it would go as follows.

How is a piece of knowledge represented in the mind? By a 'chunk' made up out of bits and pieces that were lying around and available as building material − with a little bit of added construction or adjustment where necessary. *A single 'piece of knowledge' in the mind is, in fact, the cognitive equivalent of a collage.* That is what a frame, or any other knowledge representation structure, really is.

In the rest of the chapter we try to restate this thesis with more precision and more detail.

'When Paul is eighteen. . .'

Consider, first, a recorded episode with Alex, a five-year-old girl. (Alex's brother, Paul, was three years old at the time.)

> Alex: When Paul is six, I'll be eight; when Paul is nine, I'll be eleven; when Paul is twelve, I'll be fourteen; when Paul is fifteen, I'll be seventeen; when Paul is eighteen, I'll be twenty.
> Interviewer: My word! How on earth did you figure all that out?
> Alex: It's easy. You just go 'three-FOUR-five' [saying the 'four' very loudly, and clapping hands at the same time, so that result was very strongly rhythmical, and had a soft-LOUD-soft pattern], you go six-SEVEN [clap] -eight', you go 'nine-TEN [clap!] -eleven',. . .

154

This spontaneous behavior by a five-year-old girl deserves careful analysis, both for what Alex did do, and what she did not do. She did give correct answers. It was correct to claim that 'when Paul is eighteen, I'll be twenty'. That is no small achievement (and those who base judgements entirely on correctness or incorrectness of answers, without consideration of thought processes, would presumably have to accept this as all the evidence and discussion that is needed). However, Alex had learned to *count* in kindergarten — the records do not show just how high she could count at the time of this episode — but she had never learned the word 'addition', nor had she learned 'addition facts' such as $5 + 2 = 7$, nor had she learned the notation '+'. In the sense of formal school learning, she had not learned the *concept* of addition, although in outside-of-school experiences she had certainly 'added to' collections of concrete objects, had 'shared collections fairly with other children', etc. She had had many experiences that should have enabled her to synthesize a large collection of frames that can be the foundation for the later construction of the frames of formal mathematics. But these early foundation frames — call them *pre-mathematical frames* — are not themselves what people usually think of as 'mathematics'.[1] They are, however, the basic building material from which mathematical frames are constructed.[2]

Notice what she did. She took three behaviors she already knew,

(i) counting;
(ii) clapping her hands;
(iii) pronouncing words in a rhythmic pattern;

and put them together to accomplish something she had never done before.

We postulate that this is one of the basic methods for constructing a new frame. (Indeed, it may well be the ONLY method, but the basis for making such a claim at present seems inadequate.)

How did Alex know that her delicious confection would actually get the job done? Probably in any sophisticated sense she did not know. But she probably had checked it against a few cases (which is strongly suggested by the precise wording whereby she proclaimed her result to the world, announcing five separate instances with gleeful facility). She *could* figure out that if Paul is three right now, then a year from now he will be four. Thus she could generate legitimate test cases, and when applied to these test cases, her method could be seen to be successful.

Of course there are vastly interesting aspects of this example on which one can only speculate, and other aspects where one can only wonder.

How did Alex ever come to think of such a question? Here is a speculation, offered as nothing more than that: there may have been two antecedents that prepared for the episode in question:

(1) She may have been thinking about how she and Paul would grow up in relation to one another. We do not know that she did so, but we do know that, in general, brothers and sisters are *very* much interested in competitive aspects of growth: Who will be taller, stronger, richer? Who will be able to drive a car first? (and how old will the other one be when that happens?) Who will live longer? What grade will the other be in, when I start junior high? Who will learn to ride a bicycle first – and how long before the other catches up?

(2) It is known that Alex, like many young girls, played many games and did many 'dances' that involved counting and rhythm. In some of these, counting and rhythm determine how the parts fit together (as they do, for example, in singing rounds, or in choreographed versions of 'follow-the-leader').

If that was true, then Alex may have had in mind, at roughly the same time, both 'the problem' and 'the method for solving it'. By serendipity she brought them together. All she had to do was take a rhythm/counting frame, try fitting Paul's age into one of the slots . . . . . . and observe that *her* age appeared as one of the outputs!

Of course, if all of that happened – it is all mere speculation – there is still another step: Alex had to see the possibility that this happy result might occur again, and she had to generate her 'test cases' to see if the method would work reliably in the future. Seeing something potentially useful, and checking out that potential, has to be one of the most basic cognitive acts, known to humans, cats, dogs, and even the rats that quickly learn to run a maze in order to reach food.

Evolution

We do not propose to rest our case on evolution, but it *is* interesting to speculate, as Herbert Simon and others have done, on the role evolution has presumably played. To borrow a remark from Simon, if we prove a mathematical theorem, or win a game of chess, we feel we have done something 'intelligent'. But if we go into the back yard and work on our vegetable garden, we feel we have done something gratifying but intellectually undemanding. However, consider! Computers can nowadays prove theorems (not all that well, but . . .), and computers can play chess (again, not all that well, but quite respectably!). By contrast, we have had no success building a general purpose household robot that can dust the living room, make dinner and work in the vegetable garden.

How is it possible that a computer can (almost) match our thinking when we are being very clever fellows, but cannot come close to equalling our performance at pedestrian chores?

'Evolution', Simon answers. Evolution had millions of years to produce animals that can walk, run, jump, find their way around obstacles, interpret visual information about those obstacles, and so on. We are all so good at this that we accept this FANTASTIC ability as if it were commonplace – which, in the sense of frequency of occurrence, it actually is. It also actually is a marvel, a capability to be wondered at – and not easily built into a computer.

By contrast, no survival pressure led evolution to a million-year program of evolving chess players or experts in the theory of finite groups. What little skill we have in such matters is mainly of our own doing. We are self-taught, and really not very good at it. The computing machines can offer us some lively competition.

But a human being is one animal. While there are recognizably different parts of the brain, it is reasonable to suppose consistency of operation over most of the brain and over most kinds of information processing. Exceptions, one would expect, would be the exception.[3]

Now, in matters of physical movement, how do we arrange things? There are so many degrees of freedom – each toe and finger can move, and in intricate ways, for example – that the task of *planning* how to move your hand and arm in order to drink a cup of coffee would be formidable. When computers are used to control highly flexible multi-jointed robot arms in this way, the task of planning *is* formidable – usually resulting in failure.

You and I don't do it by planning – at least, not in the sense of confronting *all* the possible decisions. Instead, in order to carry out some *new* movement we make use of one or more *old*, *previously-established* movements, concatenating them, and revising them, until we have a new movement that will do the job (Greene, 1982).

We make an information-processing collage – using earlier movements (and the mental frames that control these movements) as our building blocks.[4]

It seems reasonable to expect we will use the same method to build up a new idea in the abstract cognitive area.

And, of course, this is exactly what Alex did. Put together some old frames, adjust them a bit if necessary, and if it works remember it!

It seems next to certain that if Alex had *not* invented her age-relationship-calculator, and if instead some adult had invented it and tried to 'teach' it to her, the effort would have failed.

Piaget's Formulation

The monumental studies by Jean Piaget postulate two basic learning mechanisms, *assimilation* and *accommodation*. Piaget's *assimilation* clearly corresponds to what we have called *frame retrieval* and *frame instantiation*. Piaget's *accommodation* corresponds to the synthesis of new knowledge representation structures, the theme of the present chapter.

The Importance of Very Simple Frames

The more carefully one examines instances of mathematical thought — or, as Gentner (1982), Quinn (1982) and others have demonstrated, the more carefully one examines *any* area of 'knowledge' — the clearer it becomes that even the most sophisticated thought about the most abstruse matters consists of a putting together of *very* simple ideas.

In her interviews analyzing marriage, Quinn (1982) finds extensive use of the idea of *marriage as a container*, as in these examples:

'We didn't know what we were getting into. . .'
'I didn't know what the boundaries were.'
'. . . when somebody outside the marriage says they love you. . .'
'When you no longer care enough to make the effort, maybe it's time to bail out.'

She also reports studies of news stories that show the use of *weight* and *mass* as a way to talk about — or to *think* about — abstract matters:

'Since he was a convicted felon, his testimony carried little weight with the jurors.'
'The burdens of office could be seen to weigh heavily on the

President's shoulders.'

'It is too soon to say how much weight the electorate will attach to this.'

'[a public figure] was frequently dismissed as a light-weight.'

'Higher interest rates weighed heavily on the stock market all week.'

Now the distinction between 'inside' and 'outside' is known to every normal two-year-old. Milk inside a cup, milk not inside a cup; being inside a play pen, or outside of it. And differences in weight are familiar to every child who has tried to lift or move various objects in his or her environment. Yet these very simple ideas, learned in the first few years of life, form the basis for even highly sophisticated thought about very abstract matters.

Jean Lave (1982) reports a very telling example. In her study of arithmetic procedures in everyday situations, she and her co-workers observe arithmetical performance during supermarket shopping, during the preparation of meals and in other everyday settings. One remarkable aspect of her study is the success of problem solving *in situ*, vs. success on a paper-and pencil test:

> In the course of our research, shoppers took an extensive paper-and-pencil arithmetic test, covering integer, decimal, and fraction arithmetic, using addition, subtraction, multiplication and division operations. The sample of shoppers was constructed so as to vary in amount of schooling and in time since schooling was completed. Problem-solving success averaged 59% on the arithmetic test, compared with a startling 100% — error-free — arithmetic in the supermarket, and this in spite of the fact that a number of problems on the test were constructed to have exactly the same arithmetic properties as problems grocery shoppers successfully solved in the supermarket. (Lave, 1982)

The example referred to above is this: the setting is a kitchen, during meal preparation. The subject is an adult male, on a diet which involves careful allocation of food amounts. For one food item, cottage cheese, he has $\frac{2}{3}$ of a cupful remaining in his weekly allowance, and today he is supposed to eat $\frac{3}{4}$ of what is left. That is to say, he should eat $\frac{3}{4}$ of $\frac{2}{3}$ of a cup, or actually one half cup of this item. The man does not compute this, and possibly could not have done so. However, the food in question could be shaped, and the man arranged it in a circular disc, similar to dough for a small pizza. By visual judgement, using symmetry, he sketched a vertical diameter, and a horizontal diameter. He separated the food into four equal portions, and ate three of them.

As Lave points out, at a concrete level the *language of mathematics* is often itself a 'recipe' for finding the solution. The phrase 'Take three fourths of . . .' not only states the problem, *it tells you how to solve it*!

The point, of course, is that everyone possesses a large and powerful repertoire of frames for dealing with physical movement, motion around obstacles, 'sharing', giving and receiving, and so on. Sophisticated mathematics is a 'collage' of these operations. (We shall see more evidence of this in the next chapter.) The successful mathematician has built on these early-childhood 'pre-mathematical' frames, and synthesized the abstract frames appropriate to what we recognize as mathematical thought. Not everyone has done this. *But we all have the pre-mathematical frames, and if we can bring them to bear on a mathematical problem, we can probably solve it. Hence good instruction should build on this capability, at least to help students get started.*

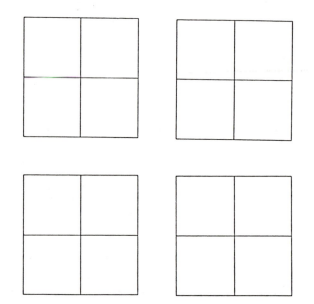

Figure 12.1: An eighth-grade girl was given a picture of four squares, each divided into four smaller squares. She was told that the squares represent candy bars, and was asked to share the candy equally among three people (Kieran, Nelson and Smith, in press). One person's share was to be shaded in.

Thomas Kieran and his colleagues (Kieran, Nelson and Smith, in press) report an interesting case. An eighth-grade girl was asked to solve some problems involving fractions. Had you asked her to express ⅓ as a base four number, she probably could not have done so; yet in fact she solved this problem, because she was working in a context that allowed her to use the powerful frames of 'common-sense experience', and to bring these frames to bear on the problem in question.

The problem was this.

Three persons are to share four chocolate bars equally. Shade in one person's share. [This problem statement included Figure 12.1.]

To begin, the girl shaded one complete bar, as in Figure 12.2. Friends 'B' and 'C' should similarly receive one complete bar each. But now the problem becomes more difficult. The remaining bar must be shared equally by the three people, and the task is complicated by the existence of scoring that divides it into fourths, not thirds.

But the girl solved this, *by merely continuing the same method she had used already*. After all, with the intact chocolate bars one had four equal items, and wished to take one-third of them. Here is how she proceeded: focusing on the fourth bar, she 'took one-third of it' by taking one-fourth (which we indicate by shading Figure 12.3), but this (though unexpected) was no error; it was merely the first step in her method of taking one-third. Imagine sharing two more quarters with friends 'B' and 'C', as in Figure 12.4. At this point all three recipients have received equal shares. One quarter-sized piece (lower right in Figure 12.4) remains undistributed.

In the next round of sharing, the girl cycles through her same method again! She draws lines to divide the undistributed quarter-size square into four equal parts, as in Figure 12.5, takes one, and allocates one each to 'B' and 'C'.

She did not continue the process indefinitely, but her method is so clear that one easily sees two possibilities: either continue until the undistributed piece is so small that nobody cares about it, or else imagine the process going on forever, in which case there is no undistributed remainder. In this second case, we can use the fact that

$$1 + x + x^2 + x^3 + \ldots = \frac{1}{1-x},$$

provided $|x| < |$, to calculate as follows:

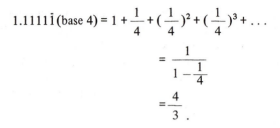

$$1.1111\bar{1}\,(\text{base 4}) = 1 + \frac{1}{4} + (\frac{1}{4})^2 + (\frac{1}{4})^3 + \dots$$

$$= \frac{1}{1 - \frac{1}{4}}$$

$$= \frac{4}{3}\,.$$

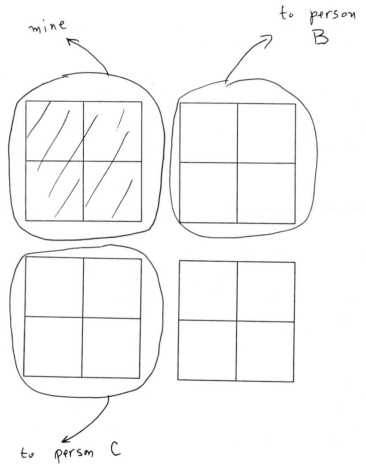

Figure 12.2: She began by shading in one complete bar. Person A ('myself') gets the shaded bar. The shares of B and C are indicated by arrows. (Her original nomenclature has been modified in the interest of greater clarity.)

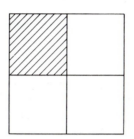

Figure 12.3: After three whole candy bars had been shared among A, B and C, there remained the task of sharing the fourth bar. Continuing her method of getting one third by taking fourths (a method dictated by the divisions in the problem), she shaded in one fourth to be hers.

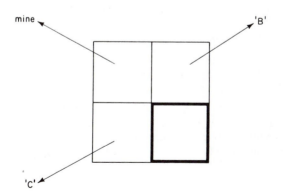

Figure 12.4: The pattern repeats: after three-quarter sections have been distributed (to 'me', to Person B and to Person C), there remains the task of sharing the quarter-section in the lower right-hand corner.

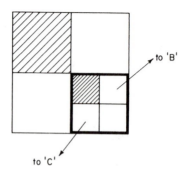

Figure 12.5: To divide up the remaining quarter-section there was no need to continue to use division into fourths, since no divisions were indicated within this small square. None the less, the girl continued the same method. She herself inserted dividing lines to make fourths, and continued her same method of division.

All of the essential ideas in this calculation are present in the unexpected procedure devised by this eighth-grade girl! Only notation needs to be added.

This is not to say that the girl's 'common-sense' frames are identical with the frames of mathematics — *but they clearly provide a more-than-merely-adequate foundation on which the relevant mathematical frames can be built.* It is a general truth that most people can solve mathematical problems if they can bring to bear their 'common-sense' frames.

In the present chapter we are concerned with observations of human behavior, and with a postulated theory that gives meaning to these observations. Pedagogical considerations will be dealt with in later chapters. We might anticipate, however, to the extent of pointing out that the pedagogical task with this girl would include the need to make contact with her ingenious 'common-sense' approach, and to help her express it in a more formal notational version. New questions would arise — such as the concept of limit of an infinite sequence — if this were done.

Papert's Gears

Seymour Papert, a world-famous mathematician who is one of the creators of modern artificial intelligence, reports that, as a very young

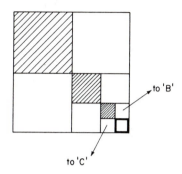

Figure 12.6: Although the girl did not continue her process further, one easily sees how it could be done. At every step, one quarter-section remains unallocated, and must be subdivided in the next step.

child he played with some special arrangements of gears. As a result, he writes, 'I became adept at turning wheels in my head and at making chains of cause and effect . . . I believe that working with [gears] . . . did more for my mathematical development than anything I was taught in elementary school' (Papert, 1980, p. vi).

As he moved through the school curriculum, Papert found himself relating a multitude of new concepts to his earlier ideas about gears, or to ideas that were built upon ideas built upon ideas built upon gears. He writes: '. . . I began to formulate what I still consider the fundamental fact about learning: *Anything is easy if you can assimilate it to your collection of [mental] models*' (Papert, 1980, p. vii, italics added). This is one more piece of expert testimony on behalf of the importance of pre-mathematical frames, and the process of *assembly* — the building of frames that are cognitive collages, built from remnants of earlier frames, which were built from remnants of earlier frames, which were built from . . . .

Complex Ideas Built on the Foundation of Simpler Ideas

Few things are more characteristic of mathematics than the way ideas are built on a foundation of other ideas, which are built on a foundation of other ideas, and so on — rather like a cognitive equivalent of the seven levels of Rome. We consider one case, drawn from the standard school mathematics curriculum. From an information-processing point of view, it will be useful to describe this in terms of 'super-procedures' and 'sub-procedures'.

What gives the idea of 'procedure' its power is, primarily, that once a procedure has been synthesized in a student's mind, that procedure can be given a *name*, and new procedures can be synthesized which use this name as if it were a command in the student's internal cognitive 'programming language'. (This arrangement is very familiar to readers who have used the programming language LOGO.)

We can illustrate this general process by observing how *algebraic addition*, ordinarily learned in grade 7 or 8, builds upon the earlier concept of *arithmetic addition* (learned in grade 1) and *arithmetic subtraction* (learned perhaps in grade 2).

In algebra, if *a* and *b* are numbers, then

$$a + b$$

involves *addition*, as indicated by the addition sign, +, between the *a* and the *b*. It does *not* matter what the numbers *a* and *b* are – the expression

$$a + b$$

involves *addition*. Looking ahead to the confusion that can appear, let us call this, more specifically, *algebraic addition*. This is (essentially) the *only* meaning that the word 'addition' has, from the beginning of algebra on, for all the rest of one's mathematical life.

Unfortunately, 'algebraic addition', while reigning supreme over nearly all of mathematics, does NOT reign supreme in elementary schools. In elementary school arithmetic, 'addition' does NOT mean 'algebraic addition'. The elementary school meaning of 'addition' might be thought of in terms of a machine with a hopper and a spigot – some sort of coffee-grinder or cement-mixer kind of machine – where you throw, say, '5' and '2' into the hopper, as in Figure 12.7, the machine grinds away, and finally a '7' comes out of the spigot (as in Figure 12.8). For clarity, let's call this 'elementary school addition' or 'arithmetic addition'.

There is another elementary school machine, which we shall call 'elementary school subtraction' or 'arithmetic subtraction'. With this machine, if you throw '5' and '2' into the hopper, what comes out of the spigot is a '3' (see Figure 12.9).

Now let's look at how 'algebraic addition' is related to 'arithmetic addition' and also to 'arithmetic subtraction'. The trouble arises in cases like

$$^+5 + {}^-2 =$$

Figure 12.7: A child learns an operation that accepts, as inputs, 5 and 2 . . .

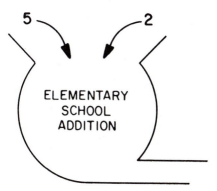

Figure 12.8: . . . and outputs 7. In the early grades, this operation is known as 'addition'.

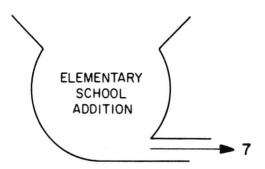

where we are asked to *add* 'positive five' and 'negative two'. From an algebraic point of view, *this IS addition.* But which elementary school machine do we use? We use elementary school *subtraction*!

Figure 12.10 shows a diagram (roughly, a so-called 'flow chart') for the procedure we have called *algebraic addition.* The point is that *everything in Figure 12.10, taken together as shown, constitutes alegbraic addition.* Thus we see that *elementary school addition* and also *elementary school subtraction* are part of algebraic addition. This

Figure 12.9: A different operation accepts, as inputs, 5 and 2, and outputs 3. In the primary grades, this operation is known as 'subtraction'.

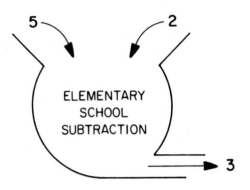

illustrates the entirely typical way that a later, more complex procedure builds upon earlier procedures.

In this specific instance, beginning students do not usually understand how these four concepts — arithmetic addition, arithmetic subtraction, algebraic addition and algebraic subtraction — relate to one another. Not knowing the correct relationships (as in Figure 12.10) children often assume the following *incorrect* relationships:

| 'arithmetic addition' | is the same as | 'algebraic addition' |
| 'arithmetic subtraction' | is the same as | 'algebraic subtraction' |

The reader can see the possible confusion by solving these problems:

1. Add
   (a) $^+3 + {}^+5 =$
   (b) $^+3 + {}^-2 =$
   (c) $^-2 + {}^-7 =$
   (d) $^+2 + {}^-7 =$

2. Subtract
   (a) $^+7 - {}^+2 =$
   (b) $^+7 - {}^-2 =$

These examples will prove instructive at several points in our discussion, but for our immediate purpose it shows how a super-procedure — in this case, algebraic addition — can call for, or make use of, earlier procedures. In this case, the earlier procedures are 'elementary school addition' and 'elementary school subtraction'.

The super-procedure known as 'algebraic addition' calls upon the sub-procedures 'arithmetic addition' and 'arithmetic subtraction'.

Figure 12.10: The entire process indicated below is 'algebraic addition'. Note that this process may use 'elementary school subtraction', as in $^+7 + {}^-2$. This is often a source of confusion: did we *add*, or did we *subtract*? In algebraic language, we have added. (Actual thought processes may differ from the formal description indicated here, but will resemble it logically.)

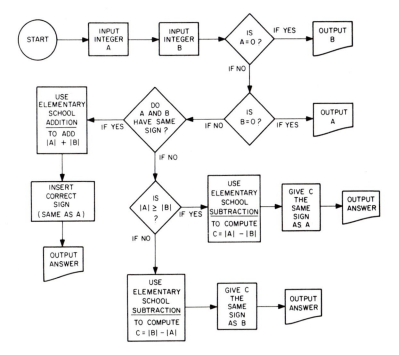

Successful mathematics students are not usually consciously aware of this arrangement, but this has to be close to the actual information processing.

It is interesting to note that when an effort is made to 'put the rules into words' — that is to say, to give a school-level description in natural language — the description given is nearly always wrong. The most common version of one rule goes as follows:

'To add numbers of unlike sign, subtract the smaller from the larger, and use the sign of the larger.'

If this rule were to be followed literally, the result would *always* be incorrect:

$$^+3 + {}^-5 \rightarrow +3 - {}^-5 \rightarrow +8$$
$$^+5 + {}^+2 \rightarrow {}^+5 - {}^-2 \rightarrow {}^+7$$

A fascinating aspect of this situation is that, while teachers and students alike proclaim unrestrained obeisance to the verbally-stated rule, they do in fact get correct answers in their calculations — which they would *not* do if they actually followed the rule. This is one piece of evidence, among a great many, indicating that mathematical ideas are NOT coded in the mind in the form of natural-language statments. We shall consider this question more deeply in the next chapter.

Kinds of Assembly

Let us agree to call this constructing of cognitive collages by the name *assembly*. Is there more than one kind of assembly?

Superficially, at least, the answer would seem to be 'yes'. (We avoid the question of whether, at a deeper level, the various kinds are fundamentally similar; it seems likely that they are.)

Alex concocted her age-predication method by the serendipitous experience of happening to do something, and discovering an interesting result.

More often, students try a 'Great Wall of China' approach, attempting to lay one small cognitive brick alongside another, in the hope that a structure will emerge that can be seen from the moon. This is a course of action recommended — or enforced — by most school programs. The observations of the Long Term Study do not support this approach — students who persist in dealing with very small independent items do NOT typically develop the larger concepts — or information representation structures — that are so essential in mathematics.

Far more effective is the strategy of trying to identify key ideas or key features. Consider the following episode, involving a teacher at the Laboratory School:

I needed to go from the school to the Undergraduate Library. I knew I wanted to go mainly south, and a little bit to the west — roughly toward the Law School or the College of Education. So I went south on the street I was on, and every now and then walked between some buildings to get further to the west. The result was a complicated path. I could never remember it, and probably could not have retraced it even the very next day.

Coming back from the Library I merely stepped outdoors and headed straight north, probably because that was the easiest thing to do. [Note that this was a mirror image of his original strategy: start where you are, and head south. Make corrections at a later point in the journey.]

Suddenly, as I came into a clear area, I saw the Student Union directly in front of me. I realized, for the first time, that the Undergraduate Library is directly south of the Student Union. I immediately had a simple, clear map in mind, one that I will probably never forget!

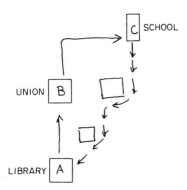

Figure 12.11: The southbound irregular route *to* the Undergraduate Library made its way between buildings, 'searching' for the library. It was complicated, and could not be remembered. By contrast, the return trip involved only three key elements, A, B and C. It was easily remembered, and from the point where he observed this simpler pattern, the teacher was able to keep track of the configuration correctly.

There are many protocols in the Long Term Study that parallel this episode, but deal with mathematical content — for example, many cases where one of the more successful students, or one of the teachers, will break down a complicated proof in Euclidean geometry into three main components — in effect, identifying two or three key subgoals — and thereafter deal with it far more easily. It is noteworthy that only teachers and outstanding students seem to do this. The less successful

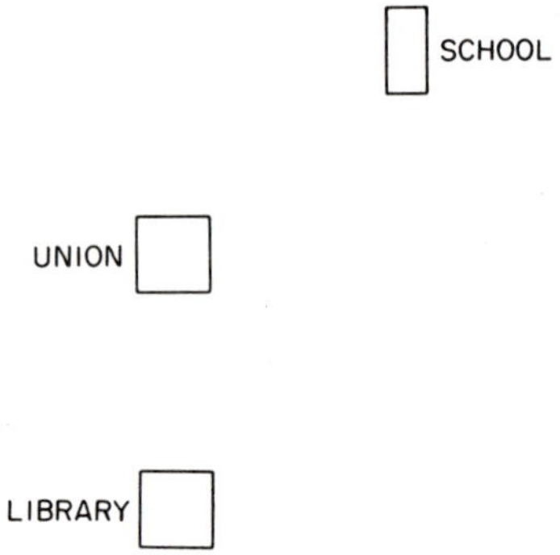

Figure 12.12: The simplified map which the teacher retained in memory.

students persist in using the 'one small brick at a time' approach and — to switch metaphors — they never see the forest, but only individual trees. It is very difficult to 'understand' a long proof in geometry if equal emphasis is placed on each of, say, twenty or thirty steps. The matter becomes manageable only when it can be seen in terms of perhaps three main subgoals. This fact — which is not restricted to geometry, nor even to mathematics — has to be telling us something important about how information is organized in the human mind. It is powerful evidence to support some kind of structure with a small number of 'top-level' nodes accessing a larger number of 'detail' or 'lower-level' nodes, as in Figure 12.13.

Finally, in any discussion of how new frames are created, one should not forget the mechanism proposed by Schank and Kolodner (1979), which we have discussed in the preceding chapter. They postulate that one mechanism for dealing with a novel situation involves these ingredients:

(1) Some initial interpretive frame is retrieved, based on some cues in the input data.
(2) We possess a collection of basic information processing frames, such as the 'distance' frame in our previous discussion in Chapter 11. (We likened these key frames to the airports at Chicago and Atlanta.)
(3) The initial frame recognizes that (in the Chapter 11 example) the input data deals with *distances*, so it sends us to (i.e. 'causes the retrieval of') this distance frame (or some other appropriate

Figure 12.13: There is a large weight of evidence supporting the general view that information in the human mind must be organized in some form so that a small number of 'top-level' nodes (A, B, C) access a larger number of lower-level nodes (D_1, D_2, ..., D_n). In *planning*, one deals primarily with higher-level nodes; in *implementing* a plan, the lower-level nodes become important.

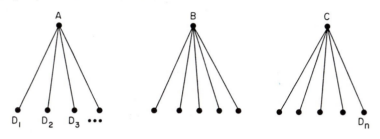

frame) in the 'O'Hare' collection.

(4) When we retrieve the basic distance frame we automatically see *a list of previous uses of this frame*. This allows us to consider whether any of these are similar to our present task.

(5) If so, we easily select pieces of this previous 'solution'.

But, of course, this is also a recipe for building a new frame. *The entire sequence that we have just gone through can be 'welded together' into a single cognitive entity.*

The Case Against 'Xeroxing'

In our earliest discussions of information transfer it was important to make clear how *non-destructive read-out* works. This is familiar in nearly any work with computers, or even hand-held calculators. When you get information from any memory register (or any other representation or location), *you leave the original there, still intact and in place*. This is NOT like taking a can of soup off the shelf. Instead, it resembles the process of making a Xerox copy, or taking a photograph of a painting in a museum.

To make this point clear, we used the metaphors of 'cans of soup', 'Xerox copies' and 'photographs'.

Unfortunately — as Gentner (1982) points out —whenever you use a metaphor you buy into its relevant features, and also into its irrelevant (or misleading) features. That happens in this instance. A Xerox copy is a faithful reproduction of the original, a successful cloning.

If that were in fact the case in|cognitive processes, how would the detailed recollections in *episodic memory* give rise to the abstract, 'featureless' generalities of *semantic memory*? A true copy is a true copy.

What occurs cognitively is clearly NOT the making of a true copy of an entire knowledge representation structure, but rather the creation of a partial copy, more like an outline, an 'executive summary', or a reporter's notes. Some relevant information is brought together, on a selective basis. A tree structure such as those suggested in Figure 12.13 makes this a relatively straightforward process. When we create an 'executive summary' for *planning* purposes, we focus on the top level nodes. We also include information about relationships to *other* representation structures or trees. We do NOT include the details, or lower level nodes (although these will be needed at a later stage when we try to implement our plan). These 'abstract summaries' become the basis for entries in semantic memory, and probably also for the *descriptors* that are so important in planning.

(Within the AI literature this kind of planning is commonplace; it runs into difficulties, however, when the details under one node are in conflict with the details under some other node. Cf., e.g. Charniak (1981) or Stefik (1981).)

Hence, in the future, it may be better NOT to think of 'Xerox copies' but instead of 'reporter's notes', whenever we collect information somewhere, for use somewhere else.

If There ARE No Existential Frames . . .

What happens if you try to learn a sophisticated mathematical idea, *and you do not possess any relevant simple frames on which to build*? This is a case that one can observe, especially where infinite processes are involved; many instances are included in the Long Term Study.

Some of our most dramatic episodes involve infinite sets of points. *There is nothing in a young child's experience that creates a pre-mathematical frame for the mathematical concept of a 'point'.* A point has no size, no length, no height, no width. A 'point' is really a *location*. No physical object in the real world can behave like a point. Students can learn this, and can come to realize that thinking of a point as a *very tiny* physical object is an almost certain road to disaster, but they do not know this at the very beginning. Hence they try to deal with this mathematical idea as they have dealt with all earlier mathematical ideas — by building a collage out of pre-mathematical frames dealing with objects, motion, frames, and so on.

Students think of points as tiny specks of pepper, or very small ball bearings, or extremely tiny raisins — or, to use an example we encountered, bees. No picture of this type can be made to correspond correctly to the actual mathematical situation.

Consider this remarkable fact: Let $\overline{AB}$ be a long line segment. Let $\overline{CD}$ be a short line segment. There are *exactly the same number of points on segment $\overline{CD}$ as there are on segment $\overline{AB}$.*

Recall that 'number' for infinite collections is determined by one-to-one correspondences. Thus, to prove the outrageous statement in the preceding paragraph, we must prove that there exists a one-to-one correspondence between the set of points on $\overline{AB}$ and the set of points on $\overline{CD}$.

We can do this easily, as Figure 12.14 indicates. Any point R on segment $\overline{CD}$ corresponds to exactly one point Q on segment $\overline{AB}$, if we use a line through point P to establish the correspondence. Similarly, any point Q on segment $\overline{AB}$ corresponds to exactly one point on segment $\overline{CD}$. Thus the correspondence is one-to-one, and there are exactly as many points on $\overline{CD}$ as there are on $\overline{AB}$.

Naïve students frequently try to make sense out of this remarkable result by 'squeezing' the points on $\overline{CD}$ more tightly together. But of course this attempt to save a 'tiny raisins' (or whatever) metaphor fails. One can also prove that the density of points on $\overline{CD}$ is identical to the density of points on $\overline{AB}$. Or, to express this in more dramatic form, a small modification of this proof shows the following: let point S be the mid-point of segment $\overline{AB}$. Then it is reasonable to speak of segment $\overline{AS}$ as the 'left half' of $\overline{AB}$, and of segment $\overline{SB}$ as 'the right half'. One easily proves that the left half, $\overline{AS}$, contains exactly as many points as the right half, $\overline{SB}$, and also — and at the same time! — *contains exactly as many points as the entire segment, $\overline{AB}$.* There is clearly no possibility of explaining *this* situation by 'compressing' some of the points more tightly together!

So, any metaphor borrowed from physical objects MUST fail when applied to *points*. Points are *not* physical objects, and clearly do not behave like them.

The case of the bees is amusing, and relates to the set of points (x,y) interior to the unit circle,

$$G = \left\{ (x,y) \mid x^2 + y^2 < 1 \right\} \quad ,$$

Figure 12.14: Every point (such as Q) on AB corresponds to exactly one point R on CD, and conversely. It is easy to prove that this is a one-to-one correspondence. Hence there are exactly the same number of points on AB as on CD. This could not happen if the points were physical objects, such as very tiny ball bearings. But, of course, points are NOT physical objects, they are idealized entities.

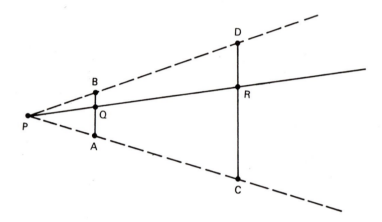

or the set of points (x,y,z) interior to the unit circle,

$$H = \left\{ (x,y,z) \mid x^2 + y^2 + z^2 < 1 \right\} .$$

Compare set H with bees (as one student did). Studies of bees show that they group into a large ball for protection against extreme cold. When the outer layer of bees become very cold, the bees shift positions; the cold bees move into the interior of the ball, and a new group of bees take their turn in the outside layer. Now, for $x^2 + y^2 + z^2 < 1$, which points (x,y,z) lie on the 'outside'? Answer: none of them! Every point is protected by *other* points nearer to the boundary — and these *other* points are themselves protected by still other points still nearer to the boundary — and . . . the process continues forever!

If such a configuration as

$$\left\{ (x,y,z) \mid x^2 + y^2 + z^2 < 1 \right\}$$

could exist as a physical entity, and if it were visible, and if points were opaque like tiny bright yellow marbles, what would you see if you looked at it? Anwer: flat black. No light would come from the unit sphere. Although there were before your eyes, a thoroughly dense packing of infinitely many points (uncountably many!), and even if every point could reflect light and was opaque, *you could not see ANY points*! Every point would be shielded from view by some other point that blocked their line of sight — and you couldn't see the 'blocking' points, either, because the view to them would be blocked by even nearer points . . . and so on! No light could be reflected, nor could any light be transmitted through the set. Hence, though made up entirely of bright yellow 'points', the interior of the unit cube would appear as the darkest and deepest and dullest of blacks.

When no experiential 'pre-mathematical' frames provide building materials, creating a correct mathematical frame can be a demanding task. In the case of points, we have had the best results by emphasizing that a 'point' should be thought of as 'a location', and never as some kind of tiny physical object.[5]

Summary, Thus Far

What have we said thus far in this chapter? The process of evolution has left each of us endowed with extraordinarily powerful mechanisms for representing the physical environment, and for manipulating and using these representations. As Herbert Simon says, evolution has created a mobile intelligence capable of operating a bulldozer or an automobile better than any computer can. On abstract matters, such as mathematics, we are not so richly endowed.

However, *to a very large extent we overcome this deficiency by applying to abstract areas the very same mechanisms that we use in dealing with the space and the objects around us.* We treat advanced mathematics as if it were nothing more than an elaboration of 'in', 'next', 'together with', and so on — as if it were milk held in a container, or milk spilled from a container, or a simple row of children's wooden blocks, whose order or spacing can be altered.

In part, we do this by constructing cognitive 'collages', metaphors based on simple ideas that children learn early in life. We call this process *assembly* — the making of cognitive collages. In their elaborated forms these collages embrace categorical algebra and non-standard analysis and all the rest of modern mathematics.

In one sense, this means that one of our most powerful tools for 'knowing' something is the *metaphor*. If we want to think about, say, *marriage* we are faced with a complex and incorporeal elusiveness. How do we get a grasp on it? [Even in asking this question I have been unable to avoid suggesting the answer – when I used the words 'get' and 'grasp'!] The answer is: *we map it into a more concrete representation.*

The point is that, *in order to 'think about' abstract matters, we make use of our cognitive collages.* But this means that, since we *use* these collages, built up from primitive origins, in order to *do* our thinking, *these collages themselves must play a major role in shaping our thinking.*

What does it mean to 'recognize' something? What, really, is Piaget's *accommodation*? The process is one of creating a new collage, a new synthesis of *existing* cognitive materials, and mapping the 'new' input data into this fabricated representation. When someone (unconsciously) makes use of a metaphor, the choice of metaphor will shape his or her thinking. As Lakoff (1982) writes: '. . . metaphors are essentially conceptual in nature, rather than linguistic.'

When we 'know' something, we know it metaphorically.

In the past, it was often assumed that metaphors were devices for *communication* – we employed a metaphor in order to convey an idea to someone else. Recent studies by Gentner, Lakoff and others make it clear that this is not the true role of metaphors. We use a metaphor *in order to represent some piece of knowledge within our own mind.* Quite apart from sharing any ideas with anyone else, *we use metaphors within our own minds in order to be able to think.*

Notes

1. It is interesting to compare what Alex did against a sophisticated adult definition of the task, which might be thought to involve at least these steps:

    (i) make an intuitive identification of possible variables and possible relations between them;
    (ii) use instances to determine the pattern of this relation;
    (iii) express this more precisely;
    (iv) confirm the correctness of this formulation.

2. This situation brings to mind Carl Sagan's poetic remark that you and I are made of the remnants of stars – stars are destroyed, scattering matter over vast regions of space. Some of this matter forms planets, including the earth. We are composed of matter from the earth – hence, we are made from the stuff of stars.

In this sense, we could say that mathematical frames are made of the stuff of pre-mathematical frames.

3. Hans Moravec, of Carnegie-Mellon University, works on the design of robots that can move around. There is a world of difference between such robots, and those presently seen on assembly lines. As Moravec says, stationary assembly-line robots 'have a standard sequence. Almost nothing unexpected ever happens. For a mobile robot, almost everything is unexpected.'

Moravec goes on to argue that mobility will force robots to acquire more characteristics that we think of as 'human'. In the process of evolution, Moravec says, 'mobility inevitably led to intelligence'.

A robot that moves around must be able to build up, in its memory, a representation of the physical environment. In order to avoid obstacles, a mobile robot must have priorities, and must interpret clues, which are not necessarily conclusive, and not necessarily even consistent. Moravec goes on to say: 'If it [a mobile robot] gets a hint there's a dropoff nearby, it gets cautious. With several hints it shows [what looks like] fear and backs up. That's very much like having emotions.' (From a *Wall Street Journal* report: Bulkeley, 1982.)

4. A few years ago a dance called the Twist was popular, and most people found the hip and knee motion difficult to get right. A friend discovered that anyone could get the motion correct if they thought of standing *beside* a chair — not in front of it — and preparing to sit down in it. In this way they made use of a sub-procedure that they already knew, merely adapting it to a new goal. Hence they avoided the need to create a new synthesis of elementary motions.

5. To be sure, only *part* of the difficulty here stemmed from the nature of 'points'. Effective instruction would have to deal also with certain troublesome aspects of *infinite sets*.

13 USING PRE-MATHEMATICAL FRAMES

If 'to know' is to use metaphors — or collages — dating back in part to the ideas of early childhood, what does it mean to 'know' mathematics? In this chapter we consider one small piece of this very large question, with the intent of emphasizing how even sophisticated mathematical ideas are made up of the pieces of ideas we learned when we were very young.

The Function

In the calculus course, the students came upon this function

$$y = \frac{1 - x}{1 + x} \tag{1}$$

or, if your prefer to write it in f(x) notation,

$$f(x) = \frac{1 - x}{1 + x} \tag{2}$$

The students were asked to work with equation (1), and to solve it for x. The result, of course, is

$$x = \frac{1 - y}{1 + y} \tag{3}$$

We could express this same fact by asking for a computation of the inverse function, $f^{-1}(x)$, which would lead to

$$f^{-1}(x) = \frac{1 - x}{1 + x} \tag{4}$$

Now this is surely a very weird situation! The function f(x) is its own inverse![1]

At first glance it might seem that such a situation could not exist. One very strong tenth-grade student in the Study immediately thought of some fairly obvious examples, including:

$$g(x) = -x \tag{5}$$

$$h(x) = \frac{1}{x} \quad . \tag{6}$$

In each case it is clear that if you use the operation twice, you get back to where you started,

$$\forall_x \, g\,(g(x)) = x$$
$$\forall_x \, h\,(h(x)) = x \quad .$$

Of course, there is a really trivial example:

$$p\,(x) = x \quad . \tag{7}$$

To rule out cases such as (7), we could say: we are interested in functions $f(x)$ such that it is *not* true that $f(x) = x$ for all x, but it *is* true that $f\,(f(x)) = x$ for all x; that is to say, using the transformation once does NOT leave everything unchanged, but using it twice does.

The goal in the calculus class was to get a clearer understanding of functions that have this weird property. Of course, *our* present goal in this chapter is to see how even sophisticated ideas are built on a framework of *very, very simple* ideas — the kind of things we learn when we are two or three years old.

The bones of some of this very basic structure can already be seen sticking out in a few places. The formulation

'. . . using the transformation once does NOT leave
everything unchanged, but using it twice does' (8)

clearly appeals to:

how many times something happens
things being left unchanged
things being changed
once
twice

which are all things well known to very young children.

Much more is involved by implication, including:

'before' vs. 'after'
everything
doing something or using something
an act
a transformation

which is probably based upon things like moving a block, spilling some milk, breaking a glass, and so on; underlying nearly all of this is the act of moving something.

All of that may not add up to a very convincing demonstration of our thesis — but we are not done!

We'd still like to have a clearer idea of what these weird functions are like. Notice that

$$f(x) = \frac{1 - x}{1 + x} \tag{2}$$

seems, at first glance, a *most* unlikely candidate! Of course, multiplying by negative one (as in e.g. (5)) has this property of cycling back on the second application. So does taking multiplicative inverses. But how on earth can the function in (2) behave this way. We take some number x, mess it all up by subtracting and dividing and adding in a complicated way, and yet, if we stir things up in exactly this way a second time . . . they unstir themselves, and return to their original condition! Incredible!

One attempt to understand this strange property goes like this:

Take some function, say r(x) = 2x.
Now use r(x) repeatedly, starting with any convenient number
   (let's choose 7).

Starting with 7, and using r(x) repeatedly, we have:

$$7 \to 14 \to 28 \tag{9}$$

and it seems clear we'll never get back to 7 this way. In particular, $28 \neq 7$, so we did not cycle back on the second application. So r(x) is NOT one of these odd functions.

Try $s(x) = x^2$, starting (say) with 5:

$$5 \to 25 \to 625, \tag{10}$$

and $625 \neq 5$, so s(x) isn't one, either.

But now let's try f(x), as given in equation (2). Suppose we start with the number 3, and apply f repeatedly:

$$3 \to -\tfrac{1}{2} \to 3 \to -\tfrac{1}{2} \to 3 \to \ldots$$

and so on, forever. Indeed, f(x) *does* cycle back! Unbelievable!
Just like a light switch or a ball point pen: once, it's out; twice, it's retracted; one more time, and it's out; and so on.

The representations (9) and (10) are clearly built on very simple ideas of the type we are considering.

But probably we still don't understand these functions very well. What gives them this property?

Students in the Long Term Study gave four further answers, each of which clearly depends upon *very basic ideas*.

First Answer

When you write

$$y = \frac{1 - x}{1 + x} \ , \tag{1}$$

it is hard to see what is involved. But (1) can be rewritten as

$$xy + x + y - 1 = 0. \tag{1'}$$

Clearly, x and y enter into formula (1') in identical ways. Hence, it makes no difference whether you solve for y or solve for x. The same 'rule', applied to either one, must yield the other.

Very young children have an excellent idea of what it means for two children to be involved in identical ways.

Second Answer

Another student refined the preceding answer by saying that we are dealing with relations that can be written in the form

$$F(x,y) = 0$$

where, for all x, and all y,

$$F(x,y) = F(y,x).$$

But the idea of switching around two blocks, or putting Billy's dish at Mary's place, and Mary's dish at Billy's, is well known to young children.

Third Answer

Perhaps this is not really an 'answer', in the sense that the other three are, but it *is* an interesting way of thinking about the problem. Imagine that a function is a 'machine', with an *input hopper* and an *output spigot*, as in Figure 13.1. Then the property that $f(f(x)) = x$ can be expressed by a 'cartoon strip' representation, as in Figure 13.2.

There is an even more dramatic way of thinking about Figure 13.1. If we feed 3 into the hopper, $-\frac{1}{2}$ comes out of the spigot. Now, we can

Figure 13.1: The mathematical concept of 'function' can be thought of as a 'machine' with an input hopper and an output spigot. [Cf. Davis, Young and McLoughlin, 1982.]

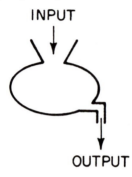

Figure 13.2: The 'machine' idea allows us to think of $f(f(x)) = x$ in terms of a cartoon-strip representation.

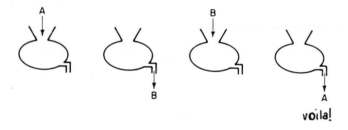

use Figure 13.1 to help us think about the *inverse function*: if we force $-\frac{1}{2}$ up the spigot, 3 will pop out of the hopper. This is the normal way of thinking about an inverse function: we 'run the machine backwards', interchanging the roles of input and output.

So, if we force $-\frac{1}{2}$ into the spigot, 3 pops out of the hopper. That's normal.

But, if we throw $-\frac{1}{2}$ into the hopper, because of the strangeness of this machine, *3 comes out of the spigot.*

No matter which way we run $-\frac{1}{2}$ through this machine, the output will be 3. Force it up the spigot, or toss it into the hopper – it makes no difference! Either way the machine will turn $-\frac{1}{2}$ into 3.

Fourth Answer

As Hans Moravec said, mobility created the evolutionary pressure towards greater intelligence. A mobile being, to use its mobility to full effect, must have in its memory an excellent representation of physical space, and a powerful processing capability to modify this representation as various changes occur. Observe your cat moving about your house, and see how many evidences she gives of understanding three dimensional space! (For example, she can find an alternative route if her usual route is blocked.)

Hence there will be special value in making use of this incredibly powerful capability that we have for dealing with space. Can we apply it here?

Yes, very nicely. With the usual conventions, y = f(x) would be shown graphically (on Cartesian co-ordinates) as in Figure 13.3, where we show that an input of α must yield an output of β,

Figure 13.3: The point P shows an input of α producing an output of β.

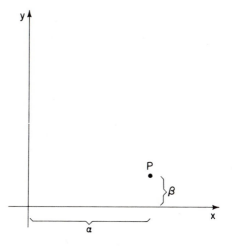

$$f(\alpha) = \beta \quad .$$

But now, if we throw β into the hopper, we will get α coming out of the spigot, which means graphically that point Q must also be on the graph, as shown in Figure 13.4. Together, we easily construct two

Figure 13.4: Point Q shows that an input of β yields an output of α.

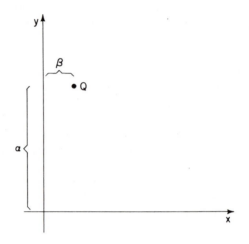

Figure 13.5: When both results are shown on the same axes, we see that, if (α, β) belongs to the graph, then so does (β, α), its mirror image across the 45° line y = x. Hence the graph must be symmetric across this line.

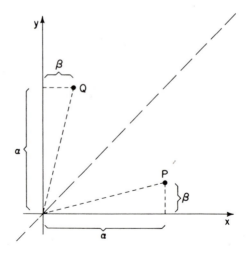

congruent triangles, as in Figure 13.5, and see that a necessary and sufficent condition for these strange functions is that their graphs be symmetric about the 45° line y = x.

The actual graph of

$$y = \frac{1 - x}{1 + x}$$

is shown in Figure 13.6, and clearly displays the required symmetry.

Figure 13.6: Here is the graph of

$$y = \frac{1 - x}{1 + x} ._,$$

showing the predicted symmetry about the line y = x.

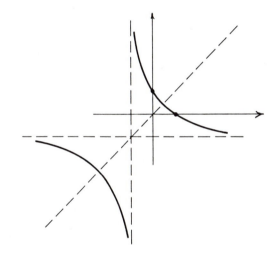

Finding your way around the house — the basic possession of mental maps of two- and three-dimensional space — is well within the capability of three or four year olds. (In our own protocols we have young children demonstrating a clear knowledge of bilateral symmetry, as (for example) when they use it in the process of exploring the keyboard of an electric typewriter. Young children's drawings also show clear attempts to depict such symmetry.)

So — in more ways than one would care to count — these sophisticated ideas come back, again and again and again, to foundations in very simple ideas. Our cognitive collages are built up from the pre-mathematical frames learned in early childhood.

Note

1. Notice that we are talking about 'inverse function' in the sense of inverse mapping. We are NOT talking about the multiplicative inverse, or 'reciprocal,

$$\frac{1}{f(x)}$$

14 NEITHER WORDS NOR PICTURES

We have argued that knowledge stored in our memories is not coded in ordinary English words and sentences, nor in any other natural language. The time has come to consider this claim.

Three positions could be asserted:

(I) Knowledge is stored in human memory in the form of ordinary English words and statements.

(II) Knowledge is stored in human memory in the form of pictures.

(III) Knowledge is stored in human memory in a form which is neither words and statements, nor pictures.

Clearly, these need not be mutually contradictory, nor mutually exclusive. It is quite possible that more than a single form of coding is employed.

We want to argue that coding mechanism II − pictures − is *not* used, although something close to it certainly is. (Indeed, many mathematics students would be better off if they could learn to make *more* use of quasi-pictorial representations.) Coding mechanism I − words and statements − *may* be used to a modest extent (we all know some quotations, or poems or slogans from memory, *verbatim*), but does not have the dominant role that one might naïvely suppose. The main mechanism for mathematics, and probably for many other things, is coding mechanism III, which is *not* verbal and is *not* pictorial.

Consider, first, the case of 'mental pictures'. This is admittedly subtle, and we shall not treat it extensively, although in one form or another it is important for mathematics education. As Holyoak (1982) points out, 'Most people will attest to their awareness of percept-like mental experiences' − that is to say, I feel *sure* that I can see my wife's face 'in my mind's eye' − I can *visualize* it. I can also 'see' the graph of $B^2x^2 + A^2y^2 = A^2B^2$. But what, precisely, is stored in my memory:

(1) A 'photographic' record?
(2) Some other kind of analogue record?
(3) Some systematic coding that represents the 'picture' faithfully?
(4) Some sketchier 'diagrammatic' representation, coded in some way?

(5) A propositional description?
(6) A direct recording of sensory data?
(7) None of the above?

To quote Holyoak (1982) further: 'The role of imagery in mental life has for centuries been a recurrent topic of debate. Over the past decade the controversy has become especially heated, fueled by resurgent scientific interest in human cognition.' All of that is surely true. To make matters worse, it is not easy to get the debate focused on the precise issue.

One aspect of the memory record deals with what we can retrieve from memory, and how our mind can process the retrieved record. When − as in our case it probably should be − the concern is mainly with the processing of pictorial data, the argument can be settled somewhat more easily. To assign the task to a photograph-like memory record would be to leave the problem entirely unsolved! The great complexity, as computer-vision researchers have amply demonstrated, occurs at the stage of getting correct information from a picture. Hence, if what our memory handed us were just such a picture, we would need to postulate some homunculus crouching in the attic of our brain, carefully scrutinizing the retrieved picture. But, as with the Orphan Annie Ovaltine shaker,[1] in *his* mind there would have to be a truly infinitesimal little man, crouching and scrutinizing this same picture, as served up by *his* memory. And so on. Nothing is solved.

But perhaps that is not the real question. Holyoak (1982), quoting Block (1981), writes:

> The debate between the 'pictorialists' (who claim images have depictive properties) and the 'descriptionalists' (who claim images are essentially propositional descriptions) is not about whether images *are* pictures, but about whether they are *like* pictures in relevant respects. The debate largely centers, in fact, on the question of what respects should be taken as relevant.

But, in fact, the debate, even in the book which Block edited, does *not* restrict itself to this question.

Fortunately, within mathematics education the matter may be simpler. We *are* concerned with how one's mind can extract information from 'pictures', whether mental or otherwise, and with how our mind can process this information, so our interest is shifted towards the interpretational machinery, which must be one of the cognitive triumphs of the human mind. Because we can picture our environment — because we can create a mental representation of the *geometry* of our home, of our back yard, of a tomato plant — we can move around our house, avoiding chairs even if someone has moved them, avoiding a freshly painted area, opening and closing doors, working in our garden, picking a tomato, or recognizing insects on the tomato plant. At present, no computer comes close to matching our performance in such matters — because we have a better representation for the geometry of space, and more powerful ways to work with, or modify, that representation.

For mathematics education, there are at least two facts about pictorial representation:

(1) Many students could improve their performance considerably if they would make more use of picture-like representations.[2] (We shall consider this further in the next chapter.)

(2) The 'pictures' of mathematics often have their own kind of weirdness.

As Kristina Hooper points out,[3] the 'pictures' of mathematics must often be deliberately incomplete, in important ways, in order to create a geometric equivalent of an important property of algebra (or of natural language). In algebra, we can write, if n is a **positive integer**

$$(a + b)^n = a^n + \binom{n}{n-1} a^{n-1}b + \binom{n}{n-2} a^{n-2} b^2$$
$$+ \ldots + n\,a\,b^{n-1} + b^n \ ,$$

and I have written *all* of the cases I meant to write. The notation does *not* tell me what the value of *n* is, and by 'keeping its options open' it is more powerful, it achieves generality.

But if I want to draw an inscribed rectangular approximation to the area under the curve y = f(x), in order to discuss upper and lower sum approximations to the definite integral, I must draw a most unusual kind of picture. It must contain flaws, and these defects are its strengths. My picture must have a vague inconclusiveness about it. I cannot, for example, draw exactly seven inscribed rectangles, for if I did, I would be showing you that the lower sum involved exactly seven rectangles, and *in general* this is false. A satisfactory picture must be more like Figure 14.1, which does *not* allow you to count the number of inscribed rectangles. Much more could be said about the use of 'non-deterministic' pictorial representations within mathematics, especially the need to give students more help in dealing with such pictures than they usually receive at present, but we do not pursue the matter here.

Figure 14.1: A good mathematical picture must have a vague inconclusiveness about it, in order to indicate a proper degree of generality. In this picture, there are n − 1 inscribed rectangles under the curve, and no specific value for n is shown.

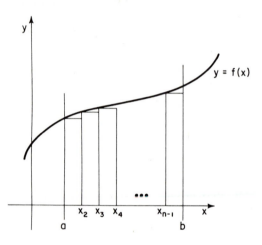

Words and Statements

The argument that knowledge in the mind is *not* coded solely in terms of words and statements is easier to make. We shall consider five kinds of evidence.

There May Be No Word

Perhaps the most obvious case is that where you do not know any relevant word. Consider 'those orange plastic cones used to divert traffic'.[4] Can you visualize a man leaning from a low platform attached to the back of a slowly-moving truck, and picking up these cones because they are no longer needed, the paint on the lane-marker lines having dried? Having driven behind such a truck, I can visualize this.

Is it credible that my mental information processing is based upon the phrase 'those orange plastic cones used to divert traffic'?

Can you visualize one of them lying on its side, having been knocked over by some passing automobile? Is your mental processing using that eight-word phrase?

Non-verbatim Restatement

Or, as further evidence, consider this. The phrase I recalled from Bobrow's article (which I had read several years ago) was: 'those orange plastic cones used to direct traffic'. When I consulted Bobrow's text just now, in order to quote it correctly, I found this had *not* been his actual phrase. Bobrow had written 'those small orange cones used to divert traffic'. [Notice that I ultimately opted for a compromise between what he had actually written, and what I had remembered. I do not think of those cones as 'small'. Unfortunately, I do not know whether they are really made of plastic.] If *words* had been the basis of my memory record, why should the word 'divert' metamorphose into 'direct'? why should the word 'small' disappear, and the word 'plastic' be added? The record in a dictionary *is* based on words, and whenever I re-open my dictionary it has just the same words, in just the same places, as the last time I had opened it.

By contrast, if the human mind uses some semantic tokens which are NOT words, and uses a two-way translation process

input words → semantic tokens → output words

then it is nearly inevitable that words will be changed. Recall will not be *verbatim*.

And one of the clearest facts of human behavior is that ordinary meaningful recall is NOT *verbatim*! People may be able to report some mysterious code recognition phrase *verbatim* − 'It's always nice to hear the clock strike twelve' − at least in spy movies, but if you ask your secretary to do something, and if she passes on the request to someone else, she will use different words than you used. Furthermore, an hour later she can still state the request, but she will *not* be able to repeat your exact words, even if you ask her to do so. The *words* are not what she stored in memory.

If one accepts the fact that memory records in such cases are *not* English words − a point I personally would insist on − this situation gives writers a problem. To describe an idea *I must use words*. But I do not want you to imagine that I believe that what you have in your memory are *words* and *statements*. I believe you have some kind of semantic tokens that capture *your experiences*, and capture the *meanings* (or at least part of the meanings).

But, clearly, I cannot write this sentence, or any other sentence, by using your mental tokens. For that matter, I cannot even use *my own* mental tokens, because I don't know what they are, either. So, although I *use* words, I do not mean to imply their use as the foundation for memory records, nor for information processing in your mind or mine.

Brain-damaged Patients

Even more impressive evidence comes from neurophysiological studies of patients with brain lesions. Brain lesions can often be localized with very great precision during surgery, and their effect can be determined with equally great precision by careful testing of the patient's behavior. Sometimes, of course, the behavioral effect is very broad — for example, the patient may be totally unable to read in any recognizable sense, or may be totally unable to write. But sometimes the behavioral effect is sharply defined; the patient makes errors, but only of a highly specific kind. Saffran, Schwartz and Marin (1976) report a patient who, attempting to take dictation and hearing the word 'hours', responded by writing *time*; hearing the word 'lilac', a patient wrote *orchid*. A male patient, reported by Peuser (1978), again taking dictation, was told 'Himmel' and wrote *Nacht*; told 'Onkel' and wrote *Grossvater*; upon hearing 'schmecken', he wrote *prüft*; when 'gestern' was dictated, he wrote it as *morgen*. Marshall and Newcombe (1966) report a male patient who, asked to write 'cousin', wrote *nephil*; asked to write 'parrot', he wrote *canisty* (presumably for 'canary'). Both the tasks of dictation and of oral reading are commonly used in identifying the precise areas of behavior that are impaired. In both cases, the substitution of synonyms, or of words related in *meaning* but not in sound nor in spelling, commonly occurs. This can only be explained by postulating 'translation' mechanisms of the following types:

written-word input → semantic token → spoken-word output
spoken-word input → semantic token → written-word output.

Marshall (1982) goes into more detail. He postulates a model that might be represented diagrammatically as in Figure 14.2. Different patients show the effects of lesions at different points. Patients who suffer lesions that destroy signals from the 'Visual Word Representations' component into the 'Lexical or Semantic' component are able to look at written text and say the words aloud, but they have no knowledge

Figure 14.2: Diagram representing Marshall's postulated model for reading (Marshall, 1982).

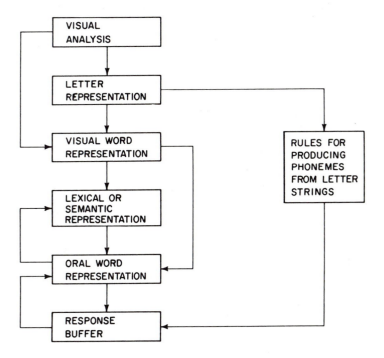

whatsoever of what the words and sentences mean. This disorder would be indicated on Marshall's diagram by severing the connections marked by A's in Figure 14.3.

If the connection from 'Oral Word Representation' into 'Lexical or Semantic Representation' is intact, some meanings can be found, but they are determined only by the *sound* of the word when pronounced. One patient with this disorder, presented with the printed word

    bristle ,

said that it was the name of a seaport city in England, at the boundaries of Somerset and Gloucestershire [Bristol, England]. Presented with the printed word

    listen ,

he said it was the name of a heavyweight boxer [Sonny Liston]. In

Figure 14.3: If lesions sever the connections indicated at A———A (in two places), the patient can look at printed text and pronounce the words aloud, but does not know what the words and sentences mean (Marshall, 1982).

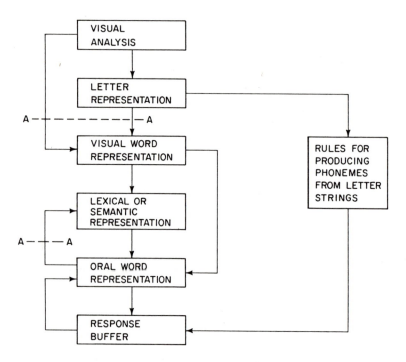

Figure 14.4, the path these signals were taking is indicated by the heavy line. The lesion is at B———B.

Another patient had lesions at C———C, as shown in Figure 14.5. Shown the printed word *bivouac*, he read it as 'camping'. Other errors included:

shown the printed word	pronounced as
soccer	'football'
ill	'sick'
gnome	'pixie'
large	'big'

These conversions seem to establish a process of translating into some system of non-verbal semantic tokens, then back again:

Figure 14.4: The written word 'bristle' was interpreted as a city in England. The signal path is shown in a heavy line, moving, in sequence, through links numbered 1, 2, 3, . . . , 7. The lesion is at B———B.

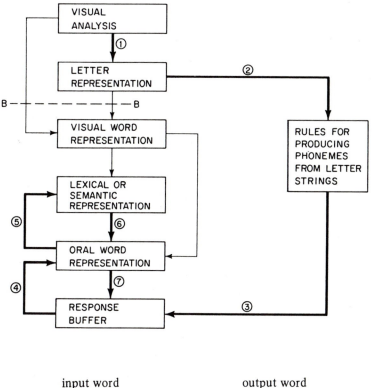

input word   output word
ill   → semantic token →   'sick'

There is no visual nor phonemic resemblance between *ill* and 'sick' that could explain *seeing* the printed word *ill* and believing that it was the word 'sick'. Only translation into, and back out of, mental semantic tokens could explain such errors.

Gestures

While the evidence already presented would seem to be decisive, there are also other kinds of evidence, to make the case even stronger. One particularly interesting episode appears in videotaped conversations in a study of gestures by David McNeill (1982). The videotape shows two mathematicians (at the University of Chicago) talking about mathematics.

Figure 14.5: With lesions interrupting two links, as shown by C———C, the patient saw the printed word *ill* and read it as 'sick', because of translation into semantic tokens, then re-translation into words.

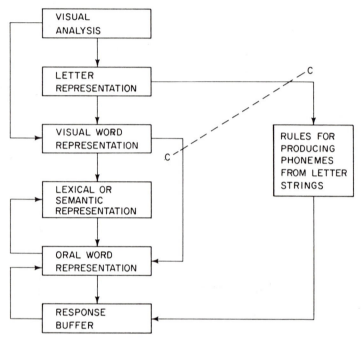

Call them **A** (who appears to be explaining something, or arguing for some interpretation), and **B** (who is primarily the listener).

1. A: [says] ... 'the inverse limit' [simultaneous with a gesture of twisting his right hand in a clockwise direction, the way one drives in a screw with a screwdriver].

[Later:]

2. A: [says] '... the direct limit' [simultaneous gesture of moving right hand outwards, away from the body, towards the front and to the right, somewhat as you might gesture to a host that you don't want any more food or drink].

[Later:]

3. A: [repeat of both the *words and the gesture* as in 1, above.]

[Later:]

4. A: [repeat of both the *words and the gesture* of 2, above.]

Thoughtful analysis suggests considerable importance in the four phrase-and-gesture occurrences above; but the next occurrence is the really exciting part:

    5. A: [says] '. . . the inverse limit' — but, simultaneously, his right hand makes the gesture for *the direct limit*. For the first time, words and gesture *do not agree*.
    6. B: [correcting A] '[you mean] the direct limit'
    7. A: [now correcting himself] '[I meant] the direct limit'.
    [makes the gesture for direct limit]

Remarkable! When, in utterance 5, words and gesture did not match, the *words* were wrong. The *gesture was correct*!

Observing the reliability of gesture, and the fallibility of words, it seems very likely that mathematical ideas are stored in memory in non-verbal form, and, furthermore, the mental semantic tokens, whatever they are, *are closer to gestures than they are to words*. Add this to the earlier evidence that mathematical ideas are ultimately based on frames, dealing with 'move', 'put', 'take', 'give', 'rearrange', 'turn', 'hard-to-move', 'easy-to-move', 'before', 'after', 'unchanged', 'changed', and so on, that we all learn before we are three or four years old!

Failures of Natural Language

Davis and Greenstein (1969) reports the case of Jennifer, a fourth-grade girl, who, asked to divide

$$6\sqrt{3606}$$

wrote

$$6\sqrt{3606} \quad \overset{6\ 1}{} \ .$$

The interviewer asked Jennifer to solve

$$6\sqrt{366} \quad ,$$

and, unsurprisingly, Jennifer again got the answer 61. The interviewer asked Jennifer if it seemed reasonable that both problems should have the same answer.

    Jennifer: Yes. They're both the same. Adding zero doesn't change it. 'Zero' means 'nothing'.

Both the statements 'adding zero doesn't change it' and 'zero means nothing' may well be quotes from Jennifer's teacher, and could have been well intentioned, but flawed by poor phrasing. Whatever their genesis, they now led Jennifer astray.

There is another interesting aspect of the 'Jennifer' interview, in light of Marshall's postulated model. Seeking to pinpoint Jennifer's difficulties, the interviewer went on to write, on paper,

6   60   600 ,

without pronouncing them. He asked Jennifer which was the largest.

Jennifer: They're all equal. Adding zero doesn't change it.

The interviewer then wrote

1   10 ,

again without pronouncing them, and asked which was larger.

Jennifer: They're both equal . . . [hesitation; then a sudden 'double-take'] Oh! That's *ONE*, and that's *TEN*!

If we consider Jennifer's behavior in terms of Marshall's model (and this is slightly dangerous, because, at least among dyslexics, numbers do not always get treated in quite the same way that non-numerical words do), it seems clear that her Oral Representation area could communicate with her Lexical or Semantic area, but that the Visual area did not necessarily do so, at least not easily and quickly.

This explanation does not really inspire confidence. A more likely explanation is that when Jennifer saw a notation that she identified as 'an arithmetic problem', she quickly retrieved some 'arithmetic' frames, *and these frames focused on algorithms while ignoring meanings.* (In a later chapter we shall see how typical this would be! Most students Jennifer's age do exactly the same thing!) As long as she considered herself in an 'arithmetic' situation, Jennifer relied on these 'algorithm-first, meaning-never!' frames. When, for whatever reason (and the interviewer must have seemed to be behaving atypically), Jennifer considered the possibility of taking a 'non-arithmetic' view of the matter, she corrected her previous errors and behaved sensibly. Notice that this explanation is consistent with Lave's data on error-free performance in supermarkets and kitchens. Doubtlessly, in a supermarket Jennifer would never confuse '1' with '10', nor '6' with '60' or '600'. Ginsburg also reports far superior arithmetical performance in non-school settings (Ginsburg, 1977).

Students being led astray by natural language statements is common enough. The Long Term Study has many examples, such as the student who wrote

$$2x - x,$$

read it as 'two x, take away x', and 'simplified' it to read

$$2x - x = 2.$$

Even for experts, however, natural language does not do an adequate job in describing mathematics. We have already seen the hanging weight problem, where teachers and successful students made correct drawings despite the fact that the problem-statement could not be consistent with a correct drawing — and none of them noticed the contradiction! For them there *was* no contradiction; they were not working from a literal interpretation of the sentence, which would have failed. Instead, they used some cues in the problem statement to enable them to create an abstract instantiated problem representation, *after which their mental information processing worked from this representation.* The words of the problem statement were ignored.

The same phenomenon occurred in the situation where, in older curricula, ninth-grade algebra students got correct answers when 'adding numbers of unlike sign', *despite the fact that the verbal rule which they professed to follow would lead to incorrect answers.* ['To add numbers of unlike sign, subtract the smaller from the larger and use the sign of the larger.']

Even beyond all that, try to use natural language to present any of the following

(i) $\quad \begin{cases} f(n) \overset{\mathbf{def.}}{\equiv} n \times f(n-1) \\ f(1) \overset{\mathbf{def.}}{\equiv} 1 \end{cases}$

(ii) $\quad \displaystyle\int_0^\infty e^{-x^2} \, dx$

(iii) $\quad \displaystyle\lim_{x \to 0} \frac{\sin x}{x}$

(iv) $\quad \displaystyle\lim_{h \to 0} \log \left(1 + \frac{h}{x}\right)^{1/h}$

In dealing with any of these, the retrieval of appropriate mathematical frames — and not the following of a natural language sentence (or paragraph) — is essential if one is to succeed.

Students Who Rely on Natural Language

We cannot leave this topic without remarking that we have observed students who placed their full reliance on natural language statements. They would carefully underline verbal statements such as definitions, would try to memorize them *verbatim*, and without exception experienced great difficulty in learning mathematics. Most of them fared very badly.

What is required in the learning of mathematics is not the *verbatim* repeating of verbal statements, but the synthesis of appropriate mental frames to represent the concepts and procedures of mathematics. In the next chapter we examine this question in more detail, looking especially at alternative representations, and their effect on problem-solving ability.

Notes

1. The Orphan Annie Ovaltine Shaker showed a picture of Orphan Annie, who was holding an Ovaltine Shaker, which (of course) showed a picture of Orphan Annie, who was holding an Ovaltine Shaker, which *should* have showed. .. .. .but my eyes were never good enough to be sure how far it went.
2. For Soviet views on the importance of visualization, see Keitel (1982).
3. Kristina Hooper, personal communication. Hooper's research in the area of mathematical imagery is of the first importance, and should be better known. Cf., for example, Hooper (1981, 1982).
4. We borrow this example from Bobrow and Collins (1975), p. 8.

15 REPRESENTATIONS

Any mathematical concept, or technique, or strategy – or anything else mathematical that involves either information or some means of processing information – if it is to be present in my mind at all, must be *represented* in some way. An exception may exist for some processing capabilities that are, as computer people say, 'hard wired in'. But such exceptions are surely the exception, and not the rule. In earlier chapters we have considered some aspects of these representations, but in those chapters we were looking at representations, as it were, 'from the outside'. We asked, for example, whether some particular representation might be too large to load into the active part of memory, which is relatively small. We were also interested in generalities about representation structures: how they might be created; in what ways one might be a copy, or a partial copy, of another; how they might be coded; and so on.

But there is another way to look at representations. Each representation is an important entity in its own right. A representation is, in some senses, an *idea*, and a single idea is an important matter indeed. (I would argue, however, against carrying the equating of 'an idea' with 'a representation' too far. The idea of 'idea' is by no means well-defined. If you speak of 'my *idea* of the United States', I suspect you are referring to a very large collection of frames, any one of which has far greater specificity than the general phrase suggests.)

Our earlier discussion might be likened to a general discussion of books – again, mainly as seen from the outside. How much they weigh, how much library shelf space they require, how much they cost, and so on. In this chapter we want, as it were, to select one or two books, open them up and actually read them.

That is to say, we want to look at a few specific representations, appreciating some of their uniqueness. We shall do this in the context of looking at three mathematical situations: (1) the idea of limit of an *infinite sequence*; (2) a problem involving a small circle that rolls around a larger circle without slipping; (3) a problem involving the fitting together of two pyramids. (The last two problems are adapted from questions on ETS tests where the answer keyed as 'correct' was not in fact correct. They are thus interesting as problems that were solved in the same wrong way by a group of experts, yet solved correctly by one or more beginning students. There is consequently real interest in the question: did those students have a better *representation* for the problem than the adult experts had?)

Representations and Problem Solving

In general, a problem may be quite easy if you have an effective representation for the problem itself, and effective representations for the relevant areas of knowledge. If not, the problem may be difficult or indeed impossible.

Even with our present intention of looking as closely as possible at the internal information in a representation, we (obviously) cannot see all that one might wish. Many aspects of the representation may remain inscrutable, at least for the present. But some aspects may be revealed. If we ask someone to name the states of the United States, and they start 'Alabama, Arkansas, Alaska, Arizona. . .' we can infer that they are retrieving names by a method that makes use of alphabetical order (or something equivalent to that, such as sequence of voting at a national political convention). If they start 'Maine, New Hampshire, Vermont, Massachusetts,. . .', we can infer that their retrieval is related to geographic location or visualization on a map.

Some aspects of representations are so conscious and explicit that we can identify them easily. Others are harder to get at, and leave more room for the skeptical to disagree.

Consider these examples:

1. Suppose the task was to obtain a decimal approximation for

$$\frac{1}{\sqrt{2}} \qquad (1)$$

by doing the arithmetic 'in your head' (i.e. without recourse to writing). Suppose also that you know that $\sqrt{2}$ is approximately 1.414.

If you try to work from the problem representation given in (1), this would be a very difficult task, probably too hard for most people.

But if you switch to an alternative representation

$$\frac{1}{\sqrt{2}} = \frac{1}{\sqrt{2}} \cdot \frac{\sqrt{2}}{\sqrt{2}} = \frac{\sqrt{2}}{2} \quad , \qquad (2)$$

then you need only divide 1.414 by 2, getting .707, which you probably *can* do in your head. And, although the transformations in (2), above, look clumsy when written on paper, many students can do this calculation in their head.

2. Some people can answer very quickly that

$$8^3$$

is actually 512. Multiplying

8 × 8 × 8

in your head is probably not the way to deal with this. But with an alternative representation, one sees at once that this is also

1,024 ÷ 2 ,

from which the result is easy. [The alternative representation follows from a transformation that can be done quickly in your head, but looks clumsy when written on paper:

$$\left(2^3\right)^3 = 2^9 = 2^{10} \div 2 \quad ;$$

one then uses the well-known fact that

$$2^{10} = 1,024 \quad .]$$

3. A more famous example is this one: some people can evaluate

$$\int_0^\infty e^{-x^2} \, dx$$

quickly in their head, getting the answer $\frac{1}{2}\sqrt{\pi}$. How is this possible?

Again, the re-statement of the problem looks clumsy on paper, but can be done easily in your head if you're good at this sort of thing:

Let

$$I = \int_0^\infty e^{-x^2} \, dx.$$

$$I^2 = \int_0^\infty e^{-x^2} \, dx \int_0^\infty e^{-y^2} \, dy$$

$$= \int_0^\infty \int_0^\infty e^{-(x^2 + y^2)} \, dx \, dy$$

$$= \int_0^{\pi/2} \int_0^\infty e^{-r^2} \, r \, dr \, d\theta$$

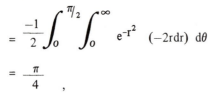

$$= \frac{-1}{2} \int_0^{\pi/2} \int_0^\infty e^{-r^2} \; (-2r\,dr) \; d\theta$$

$$= \frac{\pi}{4} \quad ,$$

so $I = \frac{1}{2} \sqrt{\pi}$. (This really *is* easy in your head if you've developed enough expertise in integrating and *that* fact certainly tells us something about mental representations!)

4. A very famous example: the British mathematician Hardy once arrived to visit Ramanujan, and as he came in he remarked that the license plate on the taxi he had just used was a very uninteresting number. Ramanujan, 'to whom every integer was a personal friend' (as someone once said), expressed skepticism, and asked what the number was. Hardy told him it was 1729, whereupon Ramanujan immediately responded that that was surely *not* an 'uninteresting' number! On the contrary, it was the smallest positive integer that could be expressed as the sum of two cubes in two different ways. That two different ways exist is in fact true, as you can see from this calculation:

$$1729 = 1728 + 1 = 12^3 + 1^3$$
$$1729 = 1000 + 729 = 10^3 + 9^3 \; .$$

To know that 1729 is the *smallest* number is a little more complex.

How Ramanujan represented 1729, or any other integer, in his mind is, unfortunately, unknown. Indeed, he was able to see, almost instantly, many mathematical results of almost unbelievable complexity.

5. Finally, an example closer to home. The participants were K., a 16-year-old girl who was by far the best solver of mathematical problems to appear in the Long Term Study, and S., a mathematics teacher at University High School who did not consider himself a strong problem solver. K., the student, had just participated in a contest-type test, and had been unable to solve one problem that had asked for the smallest positive integer N such that, in congruence notation from number theory,

$$N \equiv 1 \; (\text{mod } 2)$$
$$N \equiv 2 \; (\text{mod } 3)$$
$$N \equiv 3 \; (\text{mod } 4)$$
$$N \equiv 4 \; (\text{mod } 5)$$
$$N \equiv 5 \; (\text{mod } 6) \; .$$

S., the teacher, solved the problem immediately, as soon as K. stated it. Yet S. felt certain that K. was a far better problem solver than he was. How, then, had he beaten her on this problem?

S. finally explained it to himself when he realized — as he had not done immediately — that he had been working, earlier that day, on some algebra problems where the polynomial $P(x)$, divided by the polynomial $Q(x)$, left a remainder of 1.

This was in some sense still in his mind, and when K. told him the contest problem, S. immediately created a modified problem:

$$M \equiv 1 \ (\text{mod } 2)$$
$$M \equiv 1 \ (\text{mod } 3)$$
$$M \equiv 1 \ (\text{mod } 4)$$
$$M \equiv 1 \ (\text{mod } 5)$$
$$M \equiv 1 \ (\text{mod } 6) \ .$$

That is, if M is divided by 2, or by 3, or by 4, or by 5, or by 6, the remainder in every case will be *one*. But that says that M is *one* larger than the least common multiple of 2, 3, 4, 5 and 6,

$$M = \text{LCM} \ (2, 3, 4, 5, 6) + 1$$

$$= 60 + 1 = 61.$$

Now, the 'N' problem is exactly the same — more or less, that is. Instead of leaving remainders of 1, the divisions in the 'N' problem leave remainders of negative one, so that

$$N = \text{LCM} \ (2, 3, 4, 5, 6) - 1$$

$$= 60 - 1 = 59.$$

In short, as he realized after considerable introspection, S. had had in his memory a good representation structure for the 'M' problem; unconsciously — much like five-year-old Alex — he had mapped the new problem onto this representation (very much as Gentner describes the mapping process), saw that it could fit with one small adjustment — and had the desired result right there! S. had done this unconsciously, but had been able to reconstruct some of the process by determined introspection afterwards.

This episode, in fact, started a protracted search for representations that had the property of making certain specific problems *very* easy, and this quest has yielded some of the most interesting results in the Long Term Study.[1]

The Limit of an Infinite Sequence

A standard ϵ, N definition of the limit of an infinite sequence goes as follows:

Definition I

Consider the sequence

$$u_1, u_2, u_3, \ldots \quad .$$

The number L is the *limit* of this sequence, written

$$\lim_{n \to \infty} u_n = L,$$

if, for any $\epsilon > 0$, there exists an integer N such that

$$|u_n - L| < \epsilon$$

if $n > N$.

This is an elegant definition, that could be called the fruit of 2,000 years of effort by some very clever people. In eliminating Newton's language of *motion* ['as n *goes to* infinity'], and replacing it by *existence*, it put calculus on an acceptably precise basis. One surely wants every student to learn Definition I, above.

The question, however, is whether Definition I *tells* the student what a 'limit' is. Does Definition I allow a student to synthesize an adequate frame to represent the concept of 'limit of an infinite sequence'? Students at University High School meet this topic at approximately 16 years of age. Observations of Uni students, and also other older students elsewhere, suggest VERY STRONGLY that Definition I does *not* induce the creation of adequate frames, whatever the chronological age of the student. Probably an appropriate frame can *only* be synthesized from experience with some suitable collection of examples and counterexamples, and may also require more intuitive formulation.

As one part of the Long Term Study, students were asked to write out the clearest intuitive definition that they could, and also to write out the most diverse collection of examples that they could think of. This activity extended over a period of ten class sessions, and the instructions (which must have seemed vague at the beginning) were gradually clarified – indeed, by this same process of seeing examples, as a result of class discussions.

There was a theoretical reason for posing this task. We had become convinced that, in concepts of this sort, the mental representation of the concept depends in a central way on:

(i) the ability to recall or to invent *candidate exemplars*, things that may be examples or may turn out to be counterexamples;

(ii) The capability of *making judgements on examplar condidates* ('Yes, that has Property *X*' or 'No, that does not have Property *X*').

It is also very helpful if one can produce 'positive' instances when that is desired, and 'negative' instances when that is what is desired.

This theoretical position is so important that we digress from mathematics for a moment in order to make our meaning clearer with some non-mathematical examples.

Suppose you are asked 'Can a mammal live in the ocean.' [i.e. 'Do there exist mammals that live in the ocean?'] We postulate the following mechanism for answering the question: (i) think of some specific mammal; (ii) ask whether it lives in the ocean.

If the answer is yes, then the answer to the original question is yes. If the answer is no, then you need to think of another example. Continue this process until you either: (i) find a positive instance, or, (ii) conclude that there *are* none (in which case the answer to the question is 'no'), or (iii) conclude that you are not presently able to decide.

We have come to call this the *Exemplar/Judgement Hypothesis*.

What is at stake here is very fundamental. Many AI computer programs store information in memory in the form of *statements*. This has seemed to us to be incompatible with many familiar kinds of human behavior.

Some AI programs speak of storing statements such as:

All elephants are gray.

But this does not match how you and I think of elephants. If you tell me you have just seen a white elephant, I can immediately bring to mind several sensible explanations. Perhaps it was a plastic ornament shaped like an elephant; that could be white. Perhaps there are albino elephants — I *have* seen humans with an unearthly pink-and-white coloration. Perhaps the elephant had some disease — I have seen humans with jaundice. Perhaps the elephant was covered with mold. Perhaps someone painted the elephant. The elephant may be covered with baby powder or dust. Perhaps some elephants have experienced radiation damage to their genes.

Then, too, color is *not* a property of an elephant, nor of any other object. It is a joint property of several things, including the frequencies of light illuminating the object, the object itself, the media through which the reflected light must pass in order to reach my eyes, certain complex properties of eye fatigue and contrast, and probably other things as well. (Even, in fact, the relative velocities of object and observer.) So if you say the elephant looked white, I have no trouble believing you.

But if the knowledge in my mind is stored in the form of statements like

All elephants are gray,

then I am going to have trouble when you tell me that the one you just saw was white.

If knowledge is *not* stored in the form of statements (and we had also rejected this earlier for different reasons), then how is it stored?

The Exemplar/Judgement Hypothesis provides an alternative. Much knowledge is stored in the form of:

(i) an ability to bring to mind possible examples or instances;
(ii) an ability to consider a specific instance, and pronounce judgement on it: either 'Yes, it does have Property X' or 'No, it does not have Property X'.[2]

Try some questions out on yourself or your friends, for example questions such as:

Does any state in the United States of America have a name that begins with the letter R?

Did Beethoven write any symphony that consists of five movements?

Are there any animals which, in their normal mature states, have an odd number of legs?

Did you answer these by retrieving a statement, or a sequence of statements, which led directly to the answer by something akin to formal implication? Or did you check exemplars that you were able to bring to mind? Do you believe that you have, stored away in your memory and awaiting only retrieval, the statement

'No state in the United States of America has a name that begins with B'?

Do you believe you also have a statement, stored in memory, that says:

'No state's name begins with E'?

How *many* such statements do you have, stored in your memory? How about:

'No state has a name that is 200 letters long'?

or, for that matter,

'No state has a name that is 1,000 letters long'?

Any such scheme could involve a fantastically large number of statements, just to tell us about things that don't happen or don't even exist.

To Return to Mathematics...

Getting back to our basic theme, we were interested in how students developed the concept of 'limit of a sequence'. Consequently, students were asked to write out the clearest possible *intuitive* definition of 'limit of a sequence', in their own informal language, and to write examples of *as many different kinds* of series as they could. Because of the Exemplar/Judgement Hypothesis, we expected

(a) most student definitions would contain serious flaws;
(b) but a student's definition would probably handle more or less successfully those examples that that student had written down.[3]

In fact, this was the case. Here are some sample student responses:

Student A: 'The limit is what the numbers get nearer to.'
Examples of sequences:

$$1, \frac{1}{2}, \frac{1}{3}, \frac{1}{4}, \frac{1}{5}, \ldots$$
$$.9, .99, .999, \ldots$$

Student B: 'The smallest number that's not bigger.'
Examples:

$$\frac{1}{2}, \frac{2}{3}, \frac{3}{4}, \frac{4}{5}, \ldots$$

.9, .99, .999, .9999, ...

Student C: 'What you'd get if you went all the way out in the sequence.'
Examples:

.9, .99, .999, ...

Classroom Discussion

During the class sessions devoted to this topic, definitions were read aloud anonymously (by the teacher), and students were asked whether the definition was satisfactory or not. Classroom discussion would then consist of either citing examples to show why the definition failed, or else attempting to correct the weaknesses in the definition by revising it. In addition, the ϵ, N definition was used to prove some simple theorems (e.g. the limit of a sum is the sum of the limits).

Early in the discussion, the teacher proposed the sequence

$$1, 1, 1, 1, \ldots \tag{1}$$

The class felt, virtually unanimously, that sequence (1) must diverge, because 'the numbers aren't getting nearer to anything'. At this stage, the teacher could not shake student commitment to this conclusion.

Considering the definition of Student A ('what the numbers get nearer to'), the teacher asked why 1066 was not an acceptable limit for the sequence

$$.9, .99, .999, \ldots \quad . \tag{2}$$

The students agreed that it was, and the teacher pointed out that, to be acceptable, a definition must have the property that *if a limit exists, it is unique*. Hence it became clear that student A's definition was not satisfactory. [Notice that here the exemplar/judgement strategy was applied to candidates for the *limit*, and not to examples of *sequences*.]

Student B's definition fails the moment we consider a sequence such as

$$1, \frac{1}{2}, \frac{1}{3}, \frac{1}{4}, \frac{1}{5}, \ldots \quad . \tag{3}$$

Some students attempted to repair this definition by revising it to deal separately with sequences such as (3), where one said 'the largest number that's not too small', and sequences such as

$$.9, .99, .999, \ldots \tag{2}$$

where one used the original version. This attempt failed when the teacher suggested the sequence

$$1, -\frac{1}{2}, \frac{1}{3}, -\frac{1}{4}, \frac{1}{5}, -\frac{1}{6}, \ldots \quad . \tag{4}$$

Consideration of examples helped the students to get a better idea of what was involved, but neither the examples, nor Definition I, led most students to anything closer to a correct understanding. [A few did get a correct understanding, and very quickly. These were *exactly* the same students who achieved similar success on virtually every mathematical topic. Perhaps the most tantalizing mystery of the Long Term Study is: *how are these few students different? Why do they ALWAYS succeed, and always make it look EASY?* Interestingly enough, this small group includes the two *youngest* students (plus three others, and a few borderline cases). Among the top seven, two were female; one of those girls was at the *very* top.]

Perhaps the most-nearly-correct definition was this one:

'The limit is what the numbers are almost equal to.'

But of course that won't really work, either.

Definition II

By now it should come as no surprise that we wanted a definition that would make more use of a human's great ability to deal with *space* or geometry. Consequently we used a graphical definition as in Figure 15.1. The number ϵ was interpreted as a 'tolerance' or 'allowable error'. The use of *tolerances* was considered in the labeling of laboratory chemicals, in the specifications for resistors, etc.

A somewhat mythical example was used, concerning an assembly line to produce piston rings. The manufacturer would sign an agreement to guarantee to stay within pre-specified tolerances, but he needed to produce some trial piston rings before the agreement took effect. The tighter the tolerance, the more trial rings he had to produce in the process of getting ready. He insisted upon knowing the tolerance *before* he determined how many early attempts he might need to discard (and the

Figure 15.1: The positive integer N allows us to dismiss a finite number of terms at the beginning of the sequence, but from N onwards all terms must be larger than L − ε, and smaller than L + ε.

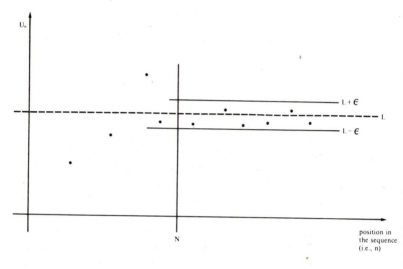

reason why temporal order was important was considered). N was described as the 'cut point', and only after that many possible discards (i.e., for $n > N$) did the agreement apply.

Definition III

For the task of proving that, if

$$\lim A_n = L_a, \text{ and } \lim B_n = L_b,$$

then the sequence

$$A_1 + B_1, A_2 + B_2, A_3 + B_3, \ldots$$

necessarily had a limit, and it was $L_a + L_b$, it was necessary to use a third definition, which was really a restatement of Definition I in more graphic terms. To say that a sequence converged was, according to Definition III, to say the following: there is a kind of 'bank teller' or 'ticket seller' at a window. If you give him a positive number (our old friend ϵ), he will give you two things: an *integer* N, and a *guarantee* that, for $n > N$, U_n will differ from some number L by less than ϵ.

Definition IV

It should also come as no surprise that we seek a definition that uses
informal language to cue the retrieval of appropriate frames, because
we have already indicated that we consider this to be a main function of
natural language. Hence:

> Definition IV. L is the limit of a sequence if every term in the
> sequence equals L.
> Of course, when I say 'equal' I don't mean *equal* – you have to
> grant me some allowable error.
> And when I say 'every term', I don't mean *every* term, I mean
> 'except for a few at the beginning that I'm going to throw away'.
> And remember, you've got to tell me the tolerance *before* I
> decide how many to throw away.

Result

A classroom sequence such as this is not readily amenable to careful
testing. Testing itself changes the situation. We cannot claim that the
classroom consideration of examples and counterexamples, plus
working with this sequence of definitions, produced a profound understanding in every student – although some students did arrive at an
impressive level of comprehension. In general, the combination would
have to be considered reasonably successful, but there is no presently-
feasible way to translate this into quantitative terms. Although one
could quote some numbers, their meaning would not be clear. (Nearly
all students have done very well in their subsequent studies at major
universities.)

Inferences

It was not, in any event, our purpose to prepare a treatise on pedagogical method. The point was that the concept of *limit of a sequence*
can be *represented* in different ways. Probably the last three definitions
all work better, in helping students build up their own frame representations, than Definition I does.

This does not mean we would omit Definition I. It is far too important for that. It does mean that we would supplement Definition I
with other experiences, designed to help students build up an adequate
frame to represent this very important topic.[4]

Notice that, once again, *geometric visualization* seems to be helpful
(Definition II); reduction to simple concrete acts ('giving the ticket-

seller a small positive tolerance' and 'receiving two things. . .' in Definition III) seems helpful; and *informal, intuitive language* seems helpful.

It is also important to contrast the informal phrases used by the students – which frequently led them astray – vs. the informal language of the teacher (Definition IV). This is probably an instance of a phenomenon studied by Gentner: *when you map input data into a frame, certain aspects of the frame can mislead you*. If you map the emerging 'atom' frame into the *solar system* frame (as a learner surely does), you must *not* assume that each orbiting electron attracts each of the others (as the planets do). If you think in terms of $U_1, U_2, U_3, \ldots$ 'getting closer to the limit 1', you must not allow this language to cause you to deny the convergence of

$$1, 1, 1, 1, \ldots \quad .$$

The students, especially early in the study, seemed almost to use a single example of a sequence as if *it* were the zero-th approximation frame. (Of course, perhaps it is!) But each single example had non-general properties that led the students astray when they attempted to use it in this way.

The Little Circle and the Big Circle

In a recent ETS test, one question dealt with a small circle that rolls, without slipping, around the outside of a larger circle. (Think of them, if you wish, as gears.) The radius of the large circle is three times the size of the radius of the small circle.

Now – to avoid confusion over words like 'rotate' and 'revolve', which generated a lively collection of letters to the editor in the *New York Times* – consider this. We have a TV camera that we focus on a close-up of the smaller wheel, and follow it as it makes its journey – just as TV cameras follow the Shuttle as it lands after returning from orbit. At all times we see this small gear – ah, circle – as it rotates before our very eyes.

The small circle starts in a definite position. It moves around the larger circle, stopping on the first occasion when its center has returned to the point it occupied at the moment just before it started.

All the while, we see the small circle turn. (We never see it move in translation, because the center of the little circle always lies at the very center of our TV screen, thanks to some very alert camera work by the TV crew.)

How many times do we see the small circle revolve on our TV screen?

The Expert Answer

The experts apparently reasoned essentially as follows: if the radius of the larger circle is three times as great, then the perimeter is three times as great. 'Rolling without slipping' means that the arc-lengths are equal. Since the arc-length s is the product of radius times central angle, the angle for the little circle must be three times as great as the angle for the larger circle. But the angle on the large circle must increase by 2π; therefore, the angle for the small circle must increase by $3 \times 2\pi = 6\pi$, and the small circle revolves (or 'turns', or 'rotates') three times.

This answer is wrong.

Teacher Protocols

We have protocols (transcriptions of audiotaped remarks) as two teachers, independently, worked on the problem. Their responses were sufficiently similar to allow us to discuss them as a single case.

Both saw the possible 'solution' given above, but had already heard that it was wrong. Hence they rejected it, although without some warning they would probably not have.

Both then went through a period of spatial disorientation, trying to keep their mind on the small circle, and having trouble comparing it against some non-moving notion of 'north' or 'south' or whatever. They realized that they needed some non-rotating frame of reference, but at first had some difficulty in finding one.

When each finally drew a picture on paper, the situation immediately became clear, so that an observer was left to wonder that the problem had ever seemed difficult (cf. Figure 15.2). One rule for such pictures is to focus on some 'general' position which is NOT the same as the initial starting position.

In Figure 15.2, C is the center of the small circle in the starting position. A moment after the motion starts, the center has moved to C′. Because of non-slipping, arc BA′ on the small circle has the same arc-length as arc AB on the large circle. Therefore angle BC′A′ is three times the size of angle AOB.

But, the moment we have available to us a non-rotating reference line, PC′, that *translates* so as always to pass through the center of the smaller circles, we see easily that angle BC′A′ is NOT the angle through which the small circle has rotated. Instead, angle PC′A′ is.

The rest of the solution is now routine: angle COB is congruent to

Figure 15.2: As soon as the picture is drawn on paper, the true situation becomes clear.

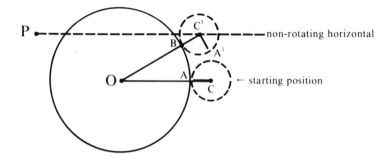

angle OC'P (alternate interior angles of a transversal cutting two parallel lines), and since

$$\angle P C' A' = \angle P C' O + \angle B C' A',$$

we see that angle PC'A' is four times the size of angle AOB. This always holds, so when AOB becomes one complete rotation (2π radian), angle PC'A' must become four complete rotations (8π radian).

The small circle revolves — or rotates — or turns — exactly *four* times.

A number of students, taking the test, found this answer, and were confident that they were correct. They were.

The Wrong Representation

Notice that the wrong representation comes close to being right. If a bicycle wheel that has a perimeter of 87 inches rolls without slipping along a flat sidewalk, and covers a distance of 3 × 87 = 261 inches, then the wheel will have rotated exactly three times. Presumably some cognitive representation of this phenomenon was retrieved, or constructed, by the experts, so that they all agreed — on the wrong answer.

This problem representation is sufficiently consistent within itself that it does not suggest any grounds for doubt. (Indeed, some of the letter writers to the *Times* never did recognize this as an incorrect representation of the problem, and instead tried to reconcile the different answers by taking refuge in alternative meanings of the words. In fact, it makes no difference which words you choose — 'rotation', 'revolution', or whatever. What is involved here is a well-defined physical situation, represented by many readers (and the experts) by an inappropriate cognitive representation, which led them to the wrong answer – three.)

The Pyramid Problem

The pyramid problem appeared on the Preliminary Scholastic Aptitude Test for 1980. Here, too, the answer keyed as 'correct' – that is to say, agreed upon by the experts – was in fact wrong.

We are to construct two pyramids. Every line segment we will use has length L (they are all equal in length). Every face we will use – with one important exception! – is an equilateral triangle (every side has length L). The one exception is a square of side L. We now construct our two pyramids, one having this square base. If we now glue these two pyramids together by gluing together two congruent faces, how many faces will the resulting solid have?

The ETS answer was 7, on the grounds that there had been 9 (4 on one pyramid, 5 on the other), and 2 had disappeared as a result of gluing.

One student said it was obvious that the correct answer was actually 5, because in two separate cases what had been two distinct faces would become single faces after gluing.

The question, of course, is whether a certain pair of two faces lie in the same plane or not. Do they?

All the experts to whom ETS had shown the problem considered it obvious that the faces did NOT lie in the same plane. If you think hard about the pyramids, you will probably agree. The angles don't work right – the faces will *not* lie in the same plane.

But in fact the student is correct.

Young (1982) set himself the task of proving what might be called a 'cognitive existence theorem' – of showing that

(i) there does exist a representation in which the correct answer *is* immediately obvious;

(ii) this representation is one which a student might reasonably build up from everyday experiences (if, of course, one has had the right 'everyday experience' – which clearly, most people had not).

Here is Young's representation:

1. Most of us think about the pyramids with each pyramid sitting on a face, in a stable position. The physical stability itself guarantees

that pyramids will usually be in this position when we see them.

2. If we think of the pyramids in this stable position, it seems unlikely that any exposed faces of one pyramid will be coplanar with any exposed faces of the other pyramid.

3. Indeed, one student gave this 'proof' that they are not coplanar: 'The key faces of the 5-sided pyramid are, in a sense, "parallel". The square base makes them move along, not getting closer to one another, nor further apart [as you move horizontally].

'But for the all-triangle pyramid, the faces come together in a point. Therefore, the pairs of faces will not be coplanar.' [The reader should make sure he or she sees which faces are involved in this discussion.] Looking down from the top, the pyramids appear as in Figure 15.3.

Figure 15.3: The two pyramids, seen looking downward from above them.

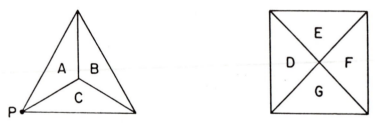

Suppose face B is glued to face D. The question, then, is this: Will face C and face G lie in the same plane, or not? (Similarly for face A and face E.) P is the point where the student in our study said the 'faces [A and C] come together.'

4. But tetrahedra *do* exist in other positions. In particular, some restaurants serve individual cream containers that are cardboard tetrahedra. One sometimes sees these piled up in disorderly arrays.

5. Without reproducing Young's complete analysis, here is his key alternative representation [The reader needs to try to see these perspective sketches as if they are really three dimensional]:

We have two *parallel* horizontal lines (shown in perspective in Figure 15.4).

Figure 15.4: To construct Young's representation, one can think of a pair of parallel lines, both lying in the same horizontal plane. They are shown here in perspective, viewed from above but not directly above.

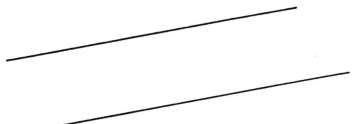

Draw perpendicular segments so as to produce a row of squares (as in Figure 15.5), which we think of as lying in a horizontal plane.

Figure 15.5: A row of squares, which we think of as lying in a horizontal plane. As shown here, we are viewing them obliquely from above.

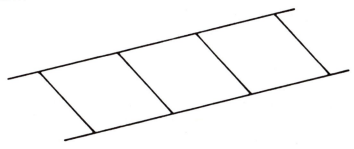

Each square is of length L along each edge (and, as before, every line segment we use will be of this same length L).

Locate the midpoint of each square, as in Figure 15.6, and at this midpoint a vertical 'tent pole' is erected (this 'tent pole' is the only exception to our requirement that each segment be of length L).

Using segments of length L, we now erect a row of 'pup tents', each square being the base of one tent, as shown in Figure 15.7.

Figure 15.6: Locate the center of each square.

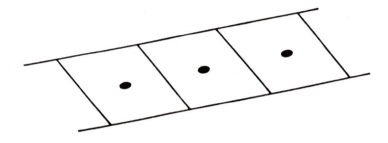

Figure 15.7: A row of 'pup tents' erected over the squares. All edges have the same length.

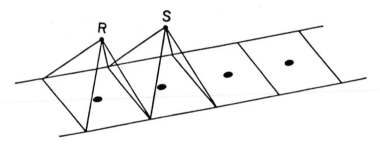

R and S are the tops of two tents. Connect R and S. The segment RS obviously has length L (note that each end is directly over the center of one of the two square bases). But this piece we have just filled in is precisely the tetrahedron in question, as one sees immediately by noting that it has the correct number of faces (namely, four), and every edge is of length L!

Now, in this representation, is there any doubt that the two triangular faces in question — face A and face E — lie in the same plane? Of course not! Face A was *constructed* to lie in the same plane as face E! It *has* to! [Cf. Figure 15.8.]

Figure 15.8: Face E and Face A MUST lie in the same plane — they were constructed that way! [See Young, 1982.]

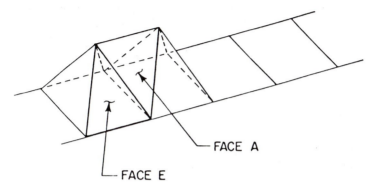

What Young has accomplished is to prove that there does exist a representation for this problem situation in which the correct answer is *immediately* obvious. This representation might be called the 'pup tents in a row' representation.

Notice that:

(i) this representation is simple enough that it can be constructed 'in your head', without requiring the use of paper;

(ii) it is based upon pre-mathematical paradigms (which can be stated in terms of 'tent poles', 'pup tents', 'single-serving cream containers', etc.).

(iii) it leads immediately to a correct solution (and, if necessary, shows us how to make a proof).

Young (1982) presents an analysis of this situation, from which we quote:

If we posit that the most likely means of attempting to solve the problem consists of an effort to mentally visualize the two solids joined in the configuration specified, it becomes evident that this procedure is not very effective. The solution is immediate when actual physical models are used, yet even after the solution has been presented verbally, few subjects can visualize it to their satisfaction. I suggest that instead of a full-blown image, it is much more likely that we create a sort of shorthand summary or mental outline of those features we see as being essential to defining the solid in question, and then mentally check to 'see' if there are any likely harmonious relationships between these salient features. In the case at hand, I propose the following likely representations of the two solids: That they are conceived of as tent-like structures, each with a center-pole which is positioned at the center of its base, and perpendicular to the base. It is as if a simple physical construction system based on polygonal base plates, a single central spine, and connecting strings were used to define the solids. (Cf. Figure 15.9.)

Figure 15.9: A 'key feature representation' suggested by Young. [Young, 1982, p. 133.]

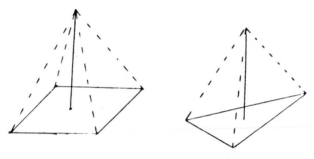

This conceptualization seems natural because it focuses on the solids as being defined by the relationship between their vertical extremes, base and apex. The idea of a spine is included as a likely feature of the abstract representation because it is the most succinct indicator of the orientation of the base, and it seems that one naturally-perceived shared quality of the two solids is that of 'pointing to the heavens'. The transformation of the tetrahedron asked in the problem requires that this orientation be changed, so it is reasonable that the new orientation be checked for creation of any interesting relationships with other features of the two solids. Again, the orientation of the spine of the tetrahedron in the joined solid yields no complementary or supplementary geometric relationships with any of the other features, including the spine of the pyramid, thus reinforcing the earlier conclusion of 'no nice fits'. (Cf. Figure 15.10.)

It is not difficult to surmise why the two solids are thought of as existing with the orientation shown in the sketches accompanying

Figure 15.10: The 'tent-pole-and-base' representation is not helpful in this problem.

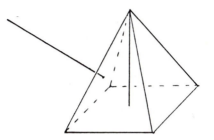

the original statement of the problem. For the pyramid, its base is distinct from the four congruent sides, so it is most easily imagined as resting on the square face; this position is also the most aesthetically pleasing, due to the symmetry it exhibits. The tetrahedron is shown in the position any physical model will necessarily assume under the influence of gravity.

The assumption that this orientation is the 'default' or 'normal' perspective from which to visualize the solids is crucial. It is necessary for all of the above discussion of possible reasons for resistance to the solution. It also reinforces the explanation of the 'base-plate and spine' representation. For those who have some experience with solid geometry, the two solids presented in the given orientation share the property of being assimilable to a sequence of solids (with the possibility of having isosceles rather than strictly equilateral triangles as faces) which lead to a cone as a limiting solid, as the sides of the polygonal base are increased to approximate a circle. (Cf. Figure 15.11.) When the tetrahedron and pyramid are (even implicitly) seen as sharing the common traits of the solids in this sequence, the importance of the quality of 'pointing in a direction', i.e., the orientation of the base as expressed through the spine, is reinforced.

In sum, such factors as simple mechanics, prior experience with sketches of three-dimensional figures, and prior experiences with relationships between geometric solids with regular bases combine to make the given orientation the inevitable starting point for thinking about this problem. With this orientation comes a predilection to select certain features of the solids as keys in the construction of a cognitive representation. The choice of features, in turn,

Figure 15.11: A sequence of solids, with the number of sides of the base increasing from three to infinity. This suggests the further power of 'key feature representations' to encompass a vast collection of specific instances.

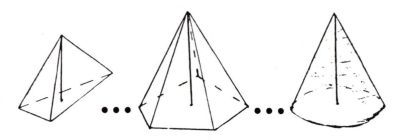

pre-determines the appropriateness of the representation as an aid in discovering the relationships whose existence constitutes the solution of the problem. It may be argued that the majority of those who failed to solve the original ETS problem did so by inadvertence, since there was no apparent reason to look for relationships which would cause faces to merge. The analysis here was not occasioned by the original students' results, but by a desire to explore the difficulty of math professionals in reconciling themselves to the known solution in the absence of physical models.

Like the algebra problem cited above, the solution becomes clear when the proper transformation of the input information is found. In this case, the geometric transformation of the tetrahedron from its 'standard' position to the position it occupies when joined to the pyramid must be accompanied by a cognitive transformation of the representation of the tetrahedron from 'base polygon with central spine' to 'space between the pyramids'. If the tetrahedron in this position is examined by itself, it takes on an entirely new aspect (cf. Figure 15.12); I have christened this avatar of the tetrahedron the 'bi-directional space wedge', due to its gravity-defying position, and the shape and orientation of the top and bottom edges.) So unusual is this position that I have found that even those with much experience in solid geometry usually fail to recognize this solid as a regular tetrahedron when initially presented as in the illustration. Once it is suggested that this is a regular tetrahedron, this fact can be verified by a variety of methods. Even though it is easy to form a chain of reasoning establishing the equivalence of the tetrahedron in

Figure 15.12: Young's 'bi-directional space wedge' does not seem, at first, to be a regular tetrahedron, but it is!

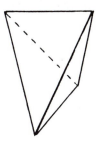

the two different positions, there persists a Gestalt-like exclusivity of the representations. Deductive and analytical equivalence cannot alone establish perceptive or cognitive equivalence, even though it is often the case that cognitive similarity leads to productive reasoning.

It seems that a cognitive prerequisite of acceptance of the solution to the original problem is the ability to 'see' the tetrahedron as a space wedge. For the above-given reasons, few subjects are well-equipped to do so. It may seem that the problem itself would provide the impetus, since it is in essence a set of instructions for placing the tetrahedron in its space-wedge position. However, the particular form these instructions take relies on the inclusion of the pyramid as essential to the construction, and it is precisely its presence that reinforces a representation of the tetrahedron (polygonal base with spine) which is least useful for conceptualizing the space wedge. The accompanying sketch (on the ETS test) also encourages abstraction of those commonalities of the two solids which are least cognitively useful for the solution. (The solids are shown positioned as in Figure 15.9, but without the 'tent-pole' vertical segments.)

A quick review of the features of the original representation of the tetrahedron which seemed to rule out any harmony with the pyramid reveals that in every instance, the space wedge suggests harmony. Note that using the same perceptual starting points (vertical extremes, i.e., 'top' and 'bottom') that gave the polygonal base and perpendicular central spine originally will yield a new, but analogous construction of the space wedge, one which contains only features giving 'nice fits' with the pyramid. Here, the 'base' and 'apex' are congruent segments lying in different horizontal planes, and oriented 90° apart (already a 'nice' property.) (Cf. Figure 15.13.)

Figure 15.13: Line segments lying in two horizontal planes.

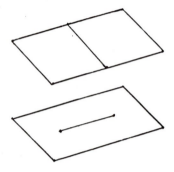

If we join them with a new spine which is perpendicular to both of them and intersects each at its midpoint, we have the skeleton shown in Figure 15.14.

Figure 15.14: The line segments are joined with a spine.

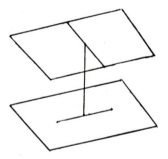

Finally, (adjusting the length of the spine as needed) we can join the tips of these two extremal segments with segments which are congruent with them, as in Figure 15.15.

Comparing the two different skeletons of the two representations, it is seen that each emphasizes a different set of features of the tetrahedron as the defining elements, and each de-emphasizes the remaining features (shown, respectively, by solid and broken

Figure 15.15: Two very different 'key-feature' representations: on the left, the bi-directional space wedge; on the right, the original 'tent pole' representation.

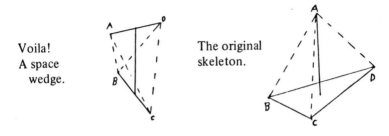

Voila!
A space
wedge.

The original
skeleton.

lines in Figure 15.15). In the original conceptualization, edge DA is not salient, yet its position in the space wedge is a key to the solution.

Using the new skeleton as our new summary of key features, everything that clashed before now fits: the new spine is parallel to that of the pyramid; the top edge of the space wedge is horizontal, thus parallel to the plane of the base of the pyramid; the horizontal cross-sections of the space wedge even turn out to be rectangles (Surprise!) of which one dimension always equals the length of the side of the corresponding square in the pyramid, and the other dimension always sums with the length of the edge of the corresponding square to total the length of one of the original congruent edges of the two solids (cf. Figure 15.16).

Figure 15.16: On the left: the two key-feature representations fit together. On the right: generating pyramids by 'spreading out' a double-thickness triangle.

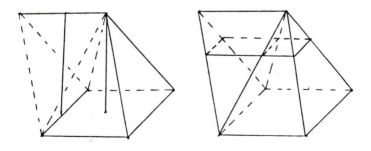

The harmony of the two solids can now be seen in a final, simple way. Both can be generated by the same pair of two-dimensional elements. Starting with a pair of co-incident equilateral triangles, with bases lying in a horizontal plane, the tetrahedron is generated by separating the apexes of the two triangles the appropriate distance, while the pyramid results from separating the bases this same distance and keeping them parallel to each other.

If such factors as prior perceptual experience and physical reality account for a tendency to perceive the solids in a manner which is hostile to an appropriate solution, what countervailing factors of this nature could help a subject to find the proper 'cognitive transform' which would lead to conceptualizing the tetrahedron in its space-wedge configuration? Again, these conjectures arise from my own experienece and discussions with colleagues, but they at least show that there exist experiences which could suggest the appropriate point of view for this problem.

My first real grasp of the solution came when I realized that the (hitherto ignored) edge AD of the tetrahedron resembled the ridge-pole extension of a Eureka brand Timberline tent (a popular back-packing tent which I own and have used extensively). These tents have an inner, self-stressed tubular A-frame from which the main body of the tent is suspended. A water-proof rainfly is provided, which is cut to fit perfectly over the outside of the aluminium skeleton. To protect the small net windows at the peaks of the face triangles shown, the rainfly is extended several feet beyond the main tent body at both ends, supported by extensions of the ridge-pole. (Cf. Figure 15.17.)

Figure 15.17: A Timberline tent with ridgepole extension.

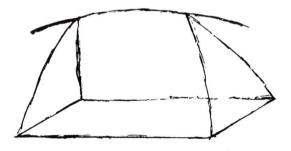

When the rainfly is draped over the entire length of this extended ridge, and secured to stakes in the ground, the face of the rainfly is stretched taut; its surface does not reveal any angular difference between the area which lies over the tent body and the area which is suspended over the void. The proportions are different, and the tent body fails to represent the pyramid of the problem due to the length of the ridgepole; nevertheless, it was the identification of the edge $\overline{AD}$ of the tetrahedron with the extension of the ridgepole that enabled me to see that just as the extension keeps the rainfly flat, the edge $\overline{AD}$ serves to align faces DAC and DAB of the tetrahedron into the planes of the adjoining faces of the pyramid. (Cf. Figure 15.18.)

Figure 15.18: The ridgepole extension, after rainfly is draped and stretched taut.

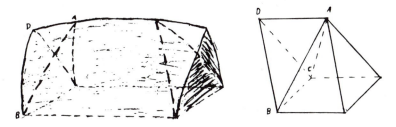

Another plausible concrete experience which could contribute to the ability to transform tetrahedra into space wedges was related by Craig Zastera, a graduate student in mathematics at the University of Illinois. He immediately recognized the space-wedge configuration I showed him as a tetrahedron, explaining that as a child, he had a set of tetrahedral hollow milk cartons at home, which his father had acquired in the course of his work as an industrial designer. Craig had often played with these cartons, fitting them together in various ways. [Young, 1982]

Young's use of introspection will undoubtedly strike some readers as methodologically unacceptable. I would urge them to reconsider. Anyone who will take the trouble to think through the pyramid problem for themselves will confirm at least part of what Young reports. In particular, they are almost certain to find that, in thinking about the tetrahedron, they are aware of *some* of its features, but *not all of them*.

The easiest way for me, myself, to think about it — up until I read Young's analysis — was (as he correctly predicts) as a horizontal triangular base, with a rigid vertical 'tent pole' altitude, the rest of the figure then being 'filled in' (as, for example, by connecting the vertices by strings and then stretching canvas faces over the strings). The 'structure' was dictated by the rigid framework. All else was 'just there'.

Now, having re-read Young's analysis many times, and having thought hard about tetrahedra, I have at least one alternative representation for the tetrahedron that I can bring to mind: the 'bi-directional wedge' representation that starts with two rigid line segments, as in Figure 15.13, and then 'fills in' with string and canvas.

In fact, I have even more alternative representations. Another has its foundation in episodic memory. I still recall when one of my students — I still remember which one, and have the illusion that I can recall the actual event (though probably I cannot, and am reconstructing it when I seem to 'remember') — presented the argument, reproduced earlier in this chapter, that the faces of the tetrahedron *could not* line up with the faces of the pyramid, because the tetrahedral faces came together in a point, whereas the pyramid's faces maintained a constant separation (which is eminently sensible if one focuses on the parallel lines where opposite triangular faces of the pyramid intersect the square base). I recall vividly what happened when, later, we tested this argument with cardboard solids, holding them as in Figure 15.19, so that $\overline{AB}$ is about to be joined to $\overline{CD}$. $\overline{CE}$ and $\overline{DF}$ are the parallel lines that indicate that faces CER and DFR (in the pyramid) 'maintain a constant separation' as one moves from right to left in Figure 15.19. By contrast, faces APQ and BPQ, in the tetrahedron, do NOT exhibit this quasi-parallel property, but instead come together in the point P.

Of course, the moment you move the two cardboard models together, a miracle occurs! Segment AB joins segment CD. The tetrahedron face AQB joins the pyramid face CRD. Point Q joins point R.

And . . . what happens to point P? What, indeed, happens to my student's 'impossibility' proof?

The Main Points in Young's Analysis

It will be worthwhile re-stating Young's main points.

(1) Even if you cannot always be sure what representation a person 'has in mind', we none the less *can* prove 'cognitive existence theorems': we can find a representation which is sufficiently 'codeable' that a person *can* hold it in his or her mind, and that

Figure 15.19: A student argued that faces CRE and DRF are in a sense 'parallel' — as one moves from left to right — because lines CE and DF are parallel in the usual sense. But faces APQ and BPQ come together at point P. Therefore it is not possible — he argued — for face AQP to line up with face CRE, and for face BQP to line up with face FDR.

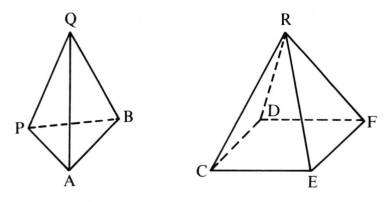

also has the further property that, using this representation, one easily solves the problem correctly.

(2) We can further require that this representation be 'learnable', in the sense that known, or probable, experiences in one's past life can be identified which would be likely to cause this particular representation to have been synthesized.

(3) We can do the same thing with representations which would lead us to *incorrect* 'solutions' of the problem.

When we have done the three things listed above, we have proved that *it is possible* that Person A has solved the problem correctly *because he or she had a useful representation in mind*, and Person B has failed to solve the problem correctly *because he or she had a possibly correct, but misleading, representation in mind*. We may not know that this is what happened, *but we do know that it could have been.*

Young's study does more than this. Besides the idea of 'cognitive existence theorems', it introduces the idea of *key feature representation*, and gives specific examples. Young postulates that a tetrahedron, or an 'Egyptian pyramid' — or, presumably most things — are *not* dealt with cognitively by a representation that directly includes *all* of their features. Instead, any single representation will include enough *key* features to specify the object (or idea) more or less adequately. Thus, for the tetrahedron, I now have in mind my original triangular-horizontal-base-and-vertical-tent-pole representation, I have the two-segments representation (as in Figure 15.13) that I learned from Young's report, and possibly some others. No single one of these representations deals well with *all* aspects of the tetrahedron. But at least either of these first two do allow for the construction – i.e. the unique specification – of the tetrahedron. These are two examples of *key feature representations*.

The mind, given no special advance preparation, does not easily move from one of these representations to another. One easily confirms this when people, knowing one representation, fail to recognize the other.

Further, *knowing* one of these representations does not easily lead people to *construct* the other representation.

Still further, there seems to be a tendency to select one representation and thereafter to base one's information processing on this single representation – leading, for example, to obstinate error in the 'two circles' problem.

The Young paper goes beyond this, however, in proposing a sequence of experiments whose outcome may be so clear that they do not need to be carried out:

By intentionally varying the form of presentation in view of the most likely experiences of the prospective audience, it would be possible to generate a range of problems, all of which contain basic information which is mathematically equivalent, but whose most likely immediate cognitive representations would be of varying utility in facilitating a solution. To illustrate this possibility for the ETS problem, one end of the spectrum would be a problem nearly identical to the pyramid-tetrahedron problem, with the addition of a second pyramid. It would ask for the number of faces on the solid created by joining the tetrahedron to the two pyramids at the triangular faces. At the other extreme would be such problems as these (try them on your colleagues):

(a) Is it possible to construct a solid that approximates a regular tetrahedron using only rectangular horizontal laminating sections? Explain.

(b) Identify the figure defined by the following analytic characteristics: On an XYZ Cartesian coordinate axis (Z vertical) every horizontal cross-section is a rectangle of fixed perimeter P units, with length parallel to the Y axis such that at height z, length equals $z\sqrt{2}$.

The key to the solution of these three problems is the same: the ability to transform the regular tetrahedron [i.e., 'the triangular-base-and-vertical-tent-pole' representation] into the space wedge [i.e., the representation of Figures 15.13 and 15.12] , and vice versa. Note that, although equivalance is formally symmetric, in cognitive practice most transformations have a preferred direction. A typical introductory algebra student is much more likely to be able to get from (a+b) (a–b) to $a^2–b^2$ than the reverse. In the ETS problem, it is probably easier to create a space wedge given a tetrahedron than to recognize a space wedge as a tetrahedron.

Summary

Several general rules are suggested by the examples considered in this chapter:

(1) A tetrahedron (or any other idea) will be represented in your mind by one or more *representations*.
(2) Each representation will be based on some, but not all, of the important attributes of the thing represented. (We have called this *key feature representation*.)
(3) Typically, in order to think about the tetrahedron (or other idea), one will retrieve or construct *one* of these representations.
(4) While good problem solvers may be skillful in rejecting one representation and seeking an alternative representation, this process is *not* easy in general, and will often be difficult or impossible.
(5) A specific problem will be easy for you to solve if you have in mind a representation which is appropriate for that specific problem, and if you bring to mind other necessary information in the form of representations appropriate for that problem. Otherwise, the problem can be difficult or impossible.

Research Strategies

Young (1982) has proposed two important research strategies:

Cognitive Existence Theorems. To explain successful (or unsuccessful) performance in solving some specific problem, one can sometimes prove a 'cognitive existence theorem' by exhibiting a representation for the problem that would have three properties:

(1) it would account for successful (or unsuccessful) performance of the problem;
(2) it can in fact be held in mind;
(3) it is believably learnable from plausible (or known) experiences in the person's past.

Representation-specific Tasks. To gain information as to whether a person does, or does not, have in mind some specific representation, one can sometimes pose questions that are easily answered if some specific representation is employed, but become very difficult if 'logically-identical' information is represented in some other way.[5]

Notes

1. Our discussion of S.'s mapping may be so brief as to make matters seem more difficult than they really are. A reader who will take paper, and write out the structure of the 'M' and 'N' problems, can easily see how one maps cognitively into the other, very much in the way that Gentner (1982) describes.

$$N \equiv 1 \ (\mathrm{mod}\ 2) \Longleftrightarrow N \equiv {}^-1 \ (\mathrm{mod}\ 2) \longleftrightarrow M \equiv 1 \ (\mathrm{mod}\ 2)$$
$$N \equiv 2 \ (\mathrm{mod}\ 3) \Longleftrightarrow N \equiv {}^-1 \ (\mathrm{mod}\ 3) \longleftrightarrow M \equiv 1 \ (\mathrm{mod}\ 3)$$
$$N \equiv 3 \ (\mathrm{mod}\ 4) \Longleftrightarrow N \equiv {}^-1 \ (\mathrm{mod}\ 4) \longleftrightarrow M \equiv 1 \ (\mathrm{mod}\ 4)$$
$$\text{and so on.}$$

This is the kind of thing that good mathematics students often 'see' in their minds. They may not (unfortunately!) know how it occurred to them, but once they 'see' it they are able to describe what they see.

2. The Exemplar/Judgement Hypothesis is partly a postulate proposed by researchers at the Curriculum Laboratory, to account for observations made there, and partly the result of our reading of Minsky's famous 'framework' paper, including Scott Fahlman's memo on 'Frame Verification'. See, e.g., Minsky (1975), pp. 264-7.

3. In fact, this applies if you recognize that testing of a proposed definition by any one student would at first be limited *both* to those examples

of *sequences* that the student has thought of, and *also* to those examples of possible *limits* he has thought of.

4. At the present time an important discussion is underway in the Soviet Union concerning the balance between 'formal' and 'intuitive' methods in pre-college mathematics. The participants in the discussion include some of the greatest mathematicians alive today – for example, Kolmogorov, Pontrjagin, Tichonov and Vinogradov. For details, see the extremely valuable analysis by Christine Keitel (1982).

5. After the first draft of this book was completed, we discovered Bertram Raphael, *The Thinking Computer: Mind Inside Matter* (Freeman, San Francisco, 1976), an extremely clear exposition of recent work in artificial intelligence. Raphael has the advantage of dealing with computer work, where precise algorithms can be fully known because they are man-made, whereas our interest is in human thought, which clearly is *not* fully known, and has complexities not seen in typical computer programs. None the less, Raphael's position on nearly every major matter is very close to our own. In particular, the Exemplar/Judgement Hypothesis is used also by Raphael (obviously, not under that name). (See Raphael (1976), pp. 50-1.) Raphael, for example, poses the problem:

Tell me which common four-letter English word ends with the sequence of letters 'ENY'.

Most people, he assumes (as we would), approach this problem by:
1. Generating examples (probably first by 'free association', getting words like 'penny' – which, of course doesn't work – and words like 'many' which is acoustically promising but loses on spelling; then, when free association fails, one perhaps resorts to going through the alphabet systematically).
2. Testing each example to see if it has the desired property (i.e. is a legitimate word).

Raphael reports:

Surprisingly enough, many find this problem extremely difficult, and some . . . even deny that a solution exists. [Raphael, 1965, p. 51]

16 SEARCHING

It is usually considered that searching one's memory for the right formula, or for the right transformation, or for the right first step, can be an important part of mathematical thought. It is even more prominent in computer work, where, of course, it is much more explicit and much more systematic. In either case, whether in humans or in computers, the search must be organized, and one common way of describing this organization is by means of a *tree*.

In computers, one typically identifies explicitly an appropriate *search space*, and then constructs a *search tree* to explore the search space in a systematic way. To illustrate what this means, consider the following puzzle:

$$
\begin{array}{r}
\text{SEND} \\
\text{MORE} \\
\hline
\text{MONEY}
\end{array}
$$

This is, in fact, an addition problem in integer arithmetic, different from usual elementary school problems only in that a one-to-one correspondence has been made between the eight digits that appeared in the original problem, and the eight letters S, E, N, D, M, O, R and Y, after which each digit was replaced by the (unique) letter corresponding to it. We are asked to recover the original problem, and also to prove that we have done so.

In other words, we are asked to find a one-to-one mapping of the digits into the eight letters, and to prove that there is no *other* mapping that would be consistent with the addition problem shown.

Could we do this by 'blind' search? The answer is an emphatic 'No!'. How many correspondences are there? If we are searching 'blindly', there are ten digits that could correspond to M, then for each of these choices, there are nine that could correspond to $\overline{\text{O}}$, then eight to N, and so on, so that there are

$$10 \times 9 \times 8 \times 7 \times 6 \times 5 \times 4 \times 3$$

different correspondences. Multiplying out, we get 1,814,400. No sane person would wish to check out almost two million possible correspondences. We MUST find a better way — and, fortunately, we can.

Part of what makes this problem difficult is the matter of *carries* —

238

we do not know, *a priori*, whether

D + E = Y

or whether

D + E = Y + 10 .

For the next column, the situation is even worse; and we could have

N + R = E

or

N + R = E + 10

or

N + R + 1 = E

or even

N + R + 1 = E + 10 .

If we are not to lose our way, we must employ some system for keeping track of our work. A search tree can do that for us. We start at the highest node, and branch downwards, indicating choices that need to be made. Suppose we identify the 'carries' as C_2, C_3 and C_4:

```
C₄ C₃ C₂
 S  E  N  D
 M  O  R  E
────────────
M  O  N  E  Y
```

Each carry is either 0 or 1.

We have not used an unknown C_5, because we can deduce the carry into the fifth (or left-most) column. M is the same as C_5. M cannot be zero, or we would not have written it down in that position. But the largest possible value of MONEY is 9999 + 9999 = 19,998, so the largest possible value of M is 1.[1] Since M cannot be zero, it must therefore be 1.

By similar reasoning, we can easily show that C_2, C_3 and C_4 must each be either 0 or 1. Since we do not know which value each has, we need to explore all of the possibilities. To keep track of the eight possibilities, we can begin a *search tree* representation, as in Figure 16.1.

We shall leave this search tree incomplete at this stage, completing it later as we get more insight into this problem.

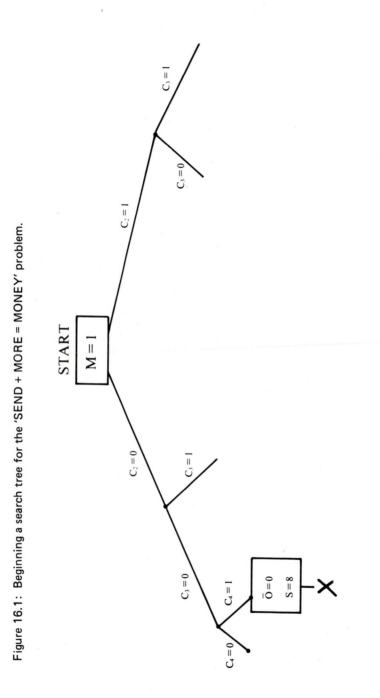

Figure 16.1: Beginning a search tree for the 'SEND + MORE = MONEY' problem.

Note: *You may wish to complete the solution of this problem yourself, right now, before you read on.*

Suppose, to get started, we carry the search tree as far as the portion
shown in Figure 16.1. Let us try to follow the tree down the '$C_2 = 0$'
branch, then the '$C_3 = 0$' branch, then the '$C_4 = 1$' branch.

At this point we can write in the values of C_1, C_2 and C_3. [Remem-
ber, we are just exploring possibilities; we do NOT know which values
of C_1, C_2 and C_3 will turn out to be correct!] For this branch in the
search tree, we have this problem:

$$\begin{array}{ccccc}
 & 1 & 0 & 0 & \\
 & S & E & N & D \\
 & 1 & \bar{O} & R & E \\
\hline
1 & \bar{O} & N & E & Y
\end{array}$$

This gives us these equations:

$$D + E = Y$$
$$N + R = E$$
$$E + \bar{O} = N + 10$$
$$1 + S + 1 = \bar{O} + 10 \ .$$

The last equation above is the most valuable; it implies

$$S + 2 = \bar{O} + 10$$
$$S = \bar{O} + 8 \qquad .$$

This should make us suspicious that we are getting near to pay dirt.
After all, S and $\bar{O}$ must both be digits, and there are not many digits to
which you can add 8 and get an answer which is itself a single digit.
Indeed, there are only two:

$$0 + 8 = 8$$
$$1 + 8 = 9 \ .$$

If you try any digit larger than 1, when you add 8 you do not get a
single-digit answer. Therefore, $\bar{O}$ must be either 0 or 1, and S must be
either 8 or 9. Since M = 1, $\bar{O}$ cannot be 1, and therefore $\bar{O}$ must be
zero. But that means that S must be 8. We have indicated this result in
Figure 16.1. Our addition problem then looks like this:

```
1 0 0
8 E N D
1 0 R E
```
───────────
```
1 0 N E Y  ,
```

and we see at once a contradiction; the third column gives us

$$E + 0 = N,$$

or $E = N$, which would contradict the requirement that the correspondence is one-to-one — that is to say, two different letters cannot both represent the same digit. Hence this branch of the search tree *cannot lead to any solutions*. We have indicated this in Figure 16.1 by terminating this branch by an 'X'.

Rather than continue this exploration of the search tree, we turn now to some actual data. B., a mathematics teacher, worked through this problem in an interview setting, and we present his work in the next section.

B.'s Solution

B. started much as we have done, by proving that M must be 1. He then produced the beginnings of a search tree, as in Figure 16.2. Working on the branch $C_4 = 0$, B. proved that S must be 9 and $\overline{O}$ must be zero. This is straightforward; the addition problem is:

```
  0
S E N D
1 O̅ R E
```
───────────
```
1 O̅ N E Y
```

This gives us

$$S + 1 = \overline{O} + 10,$$

or

$$S = \overline{O} + 9,$$

and the only digit to which you can add 9 and get a single-digit answer is, of course 'zero'; consequently, we must have

$$\overline{O} = 0$$
$$S = 9 \quad .$$

The addition problem now becomes

```
0 C₃
9 E N D
1 O R E
─────────
1 O N E Y  .
```

Figure 16.2: B. began by drawing this search tree.

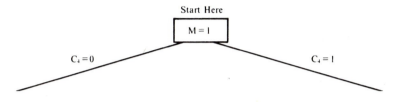

Continuing, we have

$$E + 0 + C_3 = N,$$

so that C_3 cannot be zero (otherwise $E = N$, and the one-to-one property is lost). Therefore, $C_3 = 1$. B. extended his search tree as in Figure 16.3.

Figure 16.3: B. extended his search tree.

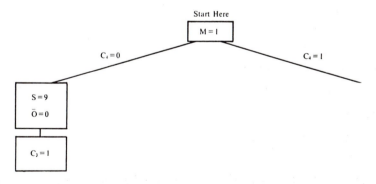

B. next turned his attention to C_2. Since this could be either 0 or 1, he constructed two branches, as in Figure 16.4. He considered next the

Figure 16.4: At this point in his work, B. realized C_2 could be either 0 or 1.

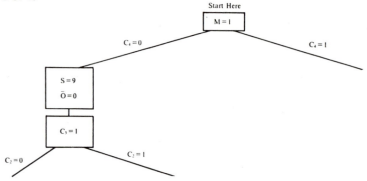

left-hand branch, $C_2 = 0$. In this case, the addition problem becomes

```
0  1  0
9  E  N  D
1  O  R  E
```
$$1\ O\ N\ E\ Y\ ,$$

B. easily obtained these equations:

$$D + E = Y$$
$$N + R = E + 10$$
$$E + 1 = N$$

From the last two, he obtained

$$E + 1 + R = E + 10$$

whence

$$R + 1 = 10$$
$$R = 9$$

and we have a contradiction, because the value 9 has already been given to the letter S. Hence this branch cannot lead to a solution. B. marked it with an X (as in Figure 16.5).

B. now turned his attention to the next branch, moving towards the right. Here, $C_2 = 1$ and B. wrote these equations:

Figure 16.5: When he found that $C_2 = 0$ led to a contradiction, B. showed this on his search tree by marking an X.

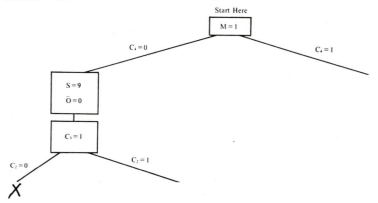

$$D + E = Y + 10$$
$$N + R + 1 = E + 10$$
$$E + 1 = N,$$

and from the last two equations above, he obtained

$$E + 1 + R + 1 = E + 10$$
$$R + 2 = 10$$
$$R = 8$$

He added this information to his search tree, as in Figure 16.6.

The addition problem now looks like this:

```
  0  1  1
  9  E  N  D
  1  0  8  E
 _____
 1  0  N  E  Y  .
```

B. now wrote:

$$N + 9 = E + 10$$
$$N = E + 1$$

$$3 \leqslant N \leqslant 7$$
$$2 \leqslant E \leqslant 6 .$$

Figure 16.6: When he found a path leading to the conclusion that R must be 8, he indicated that on the search tree.

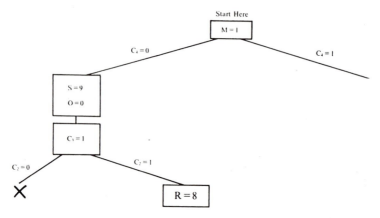

The last two inequalities above were obtained by observing that 0, 1, 8 and 9 have already been assigned (to $\bar{O}$, M, R and S, respectively). Therefore E and N must both satisfy

$$2 \leqslant E \leqslant 7 \tag{3}$$
$$2 \leqslant N \leqslant 7 \; . \tag{4}$$

However, since there is also the requirement that

$$N = E + 1,$$

we can improve (3) and (4), to get inequalities (1) and (2). At this point, B. extended his search tree, as in Figure 16.7, and prepared to deal with the five cases of possible values for E, as shown in Figure 16.7.

B. wrote:

$$D + E = Y + 10$$
$$D + E \geqslant 12 \text{ (since Y must be at least 2)}$$

that is,

$$E \geqslant 12 - D. \tag{5}$$

Now, we don't yet know the value of D, and therefore we don't know the value of the right-hand side in inequality (5). But $D \leqslant 7$, so we have

$$E \geqslant 12 - 7$$

Figure 16.7: At this point in the tree, there were five possible values for E.

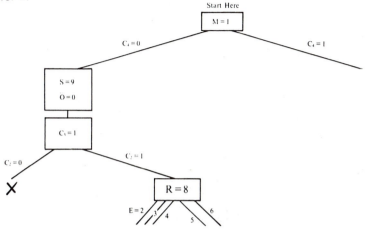

or

$E \geqslant 5$.

B. now improved inequality (2) to read

$$5 \leqslant E \leqslant 6 \tag{6},$$

and incorporated this information in the search tree, by crossing out three alternatives for values of E (Figure 16.8).

B. continued working through the search tree systematically, from left to right, so that he next dealt with the case where E = 5. The addition problem is now

```
0  1  1
9  5  6  D
1  0  8  5
```
───────────
```
1  0  6  5  Y ,
```

and only D and Y remain unknown. B. wrote

$$D + 5 = Y + 10$$
$$D = Y + 5 \ , \tag{7}$$

Figure 16.8: Three of these values led to contradictions.

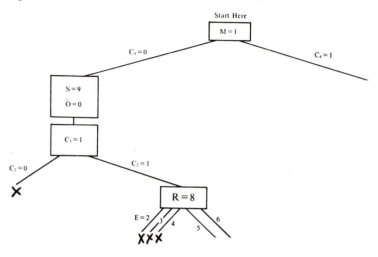

and he wrote out the digits in order,

0 1 2 3 4 5 6 7 8 9 ,

crossing off those already matched up with letters

0̸ 1̸ 2 3 4 5̸ 6̸ 7 8̸ 9̸ .

B. explained that he visualized equation (7) as a kind of 'bridge', a solid object with two feet (he thought of a device used in billiards as in Figure 16.9), that had to be placed on numbers *not yet crossed off*. This could be placed in one position only: with the feet resting on '2' and '7'. Hence, Y must be 2, and D must be 7. B. added this to his search tree (Figure 16.10). He realized that he had not completed the solution of the puzzle; it was also necessary to prove that no other one-to-one correspondence could exist that would also match the conditions of the addition problem.

B. intended to continue exploring the search tree systematically, from left to right, so that the case he should have considered next would be:

$$C_4 = 0$$
$$C_2 = 1$$
$$E = 6 \quad .$$

Figure 16.9: A 'bridge' — a device sometimes used in billiards. B. visualized it, not on a billiard table, but on a number line. When the left leg was on 1, the right leg was on 6. But if one moved the left leg to 2, the right leg would be on 7.

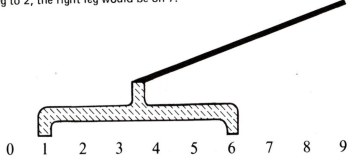

0 1 2 3 4 5 6 7 8 9

Figure 16.10: B. had found a solution! (But, of course, the task was not finished. One had to prove that this solution was unique.)

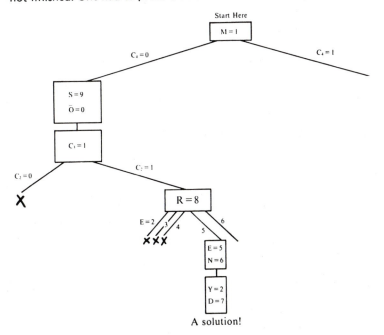

Although his search tree, written on paper, showed this is the next case, B.'s attention wandered, and the case he turned to next was $C_4 = 1$. The addition problem was then

$$
\begin{array}{cccc}
1 & C_3 & C_2 & \\
S & E & N & D \\
1 & \overline{O} & R & E \\
\hline
1 & \overline{O} & N & E & Y
\end{array}
$$

He wrote:

$$S + 2 = \overline{O} + 10$$
$$S = \overline{O} + 8 \qquad\qquad (8)$$

Now, equation (8) implies that $\overline{O}$ must be either zero or one, or else S will not be a single digit. But 1 has already been assigned to M; therefore, $\overline{O} = 0$. Hence S must be 8. But, if $\overline{O} = 0$, then C_3 cannot be zero (or else E and N would correspond to the same digit, which is forbidden); consequently, $C_3 = 1$, and the addition problem becomes

$$
\begin{array}{ccccc}
1 & 1 & & & \\
8 & E & N & D & \\
1 & 0 & R & E & \\
\hline
1 & 0 & N & E & Y
\end{array} \quad .
$$

B. added this information to his search tree, getting the result shown in Figure 16.11. Since he did not know the value of C_2, he provided for the two possibilities, $C_2 = 0$ or $C_2 = 1$.

B. now followed the branch for $C_2 = 0$, and wrote:

$$D + E = Y$$
$$N + R = E + 10$$
$$E + 1 = N \quad . \qquad\qquad (9)$$

Equation (9) is, in this case, actually a mistake, because we are on the branch where C_4 is presumed to be 1. B. did not immediately notice this error, and went on to conclude that $R = 9$, getting the search tree as shown in Figure 16.12. B. updated the addition problem as

$$
\begin{array}{ccccc}
1 & 1 & 0 & & \\
8 & E & N & D & \\
1 & 0 & 9 & E & \\
\hline
1 & 0 & N & E & Y
\end{array} \quad ,
$$

Figure 16.11: Searching for other possible solutions, in a way that is guaranteed to exhaust all possibilities.

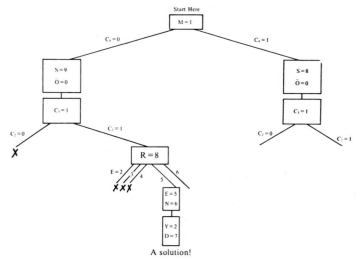

A solution!

still not noticing the error, and obtained the equations and inequalities

$$D + E = Y$$
$$E + 1 = N$$
$$D + E \leqslant 7$$
$$D \leqslant 7 - E$$
$$E \leqslant 2$$
$$\therefore \quad D \leqslant 5$$
$$2 \leqslant D \leqslant 5$$
$$2 \leqslant E \leqslant 5$$
$$3 \leqslant N \leqslant 6$$

and at this point he noticed his error. He corrected $E + 1 = N$ to read, as it should,

$$E + 1 = N + 10 \quad,$$

and went back and crossed out the 'R = 9' box in the search tree (Figure 16.13).

Figure 16.12: B. has made an error, but has not yet noticed it.

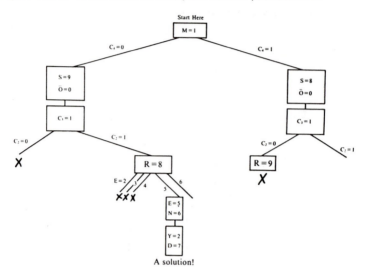

Figure 16.13: Noticing his error, B. corrects it by crossing out the 'R = 9' box on the branch $C_4 = 1$, $C_2 = 0$.

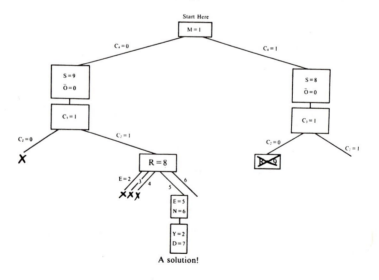

With the correct equations for this case

$$D + E = Y$$
$$N + R = E + 10 = (E + 1) + 9$$
$$E + 1 = N + 10,$$

B. obtained

$$N + R = (N + 10) + 9$$
$$N + R = N + 19$$
$$R = 19$$

which, of course, is impossible, since R must be a single digit.

Thus, the branch $C_4 = 1$, $C_2 = 0$ cannot lead to any solutions. B. marked it with an 'X'.

B. next proved that the branch $C_4 = 1$, $C_2 = 1$, implies that $R = 18$, so this branch, also, can lead to no solution.

Finally, he returned to the case $C_4 = 0$, $C_2 = 1$, $E = 6$, which he had inadvertently overlooked. $E = 6$ implies (in this case) $N = 7$, and the addition problem becomes

```
    0 1 1
    9 6 7 D
    1 0 R 6
  ─────────
  1 0 7 6 Y  ,
```

leading to the equations

$$7 + R = 6 + 10,$$

whence $R = 9$, an impossibility since the digit 9 has already been paired with the letter S. B.'s final search tree, then, looked like Figure 16.14.

The *search tree*, then, has at least three roles to play:

(1) If a person uses it, as B. did, to help guide his work, it can be of considerable value. B. made two errors in working on this problem, but was able to recover from each of them. (He used $C_4 = 0$ when he was supposed to be using $C_4 = 1$, and he bypassed the case $C_4 = 0$, $C_2 = 1$, $E = 6$.) In both cases, the search tree representation was probably helpful, if not crucial. Without it, both errors might have passed unnoticed. (B. corrected both errors himself, without outside intervention.)

(2) Even if a student (or an expert) does *not* use a search tree, it can be a valuable tool in *analyzing* their work. B.'s search tree not only

Figure 16.14: B.'s final search tree. Every path except one leads to an X. Consequently, his solution is unique.

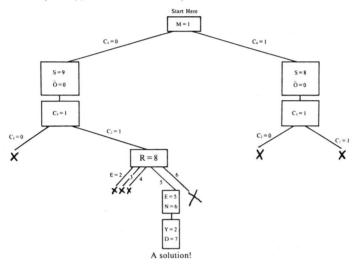

helped *him* to keep track of his work as he was doing it, it also helped *us* to analyze his work after he had finished.

(3) Had this been a computer program, and not a human performance, the tree would have been essential to guide the computer's work. There is a difference here, however: a search tree for a computer will typically be more precise and more complete than the trees made by humans usually are.[2]

Tidying Up

This was not the end of B.'s work on this problem. After completing the search tree shown in Figure 16.14, B. had the feeling that a more efficient solution was possible. It seemed to him that he had been proving the same lemmas over and over in working out Figure 16.14. He thought some of these could probably be 'moved up front' and dealt with once and for all at the outset. In order to check this out, since he already knew that one could establish $M = 1$ at the beginning, he tried to prove next that $\bar{O} = 0$. The addition problem was now

$$\begin{array}{rrrrr} & C_4 & & & \\ & S & E & N & D \\ & 1 & \bar{O} & R & E \\ \hline 1 & \bar{O} & N & E & Y \end{array}$$

and B. wrote:

$$C_4 + S + 1 = \bar{O} + 10$$
$$C_4 + S = \bar{O} + 9$$
$$S = \bar{O} + 9 - C_4$$
$$S \geqslant \bar{O} + 8 \tag{10}$$

since $\bar{O}$ cannot be 1 (because M is), inequality (10) implies that $\bar{O}$ must be zero.

B. sought next to prove that $C_4 \neq 1$. The addition problem in this case is

$$\begin{array}{rrrrr} & 1 & C_3 & C_2 & \\ & S & E & N & D \\ & I & 0 & R & E \\ \hline 1 & 0 & N & E & Y \end{array},$$

whence

$$E + C_3 = N + 10$$
$$E = N + 10 - C_3$$
$$E \geqslant N + 9 \tag{11}$$

but we also have

$$N \geqslant 2 \tag{12}$$

(since 0 and 1 are already assigned); but inequalities (11) and (12) lead to E not being a single digit, an impossibility. Therefore $C_4 \neq 1$.

B. next suspected that he could prove $C_3 = 1$, and easily did so (otherwise E = N, an impossibility).

This second time through the problem, B.'s work was far more efficient. The search tree for this second version begins as in Figure 16.15.

Figure 16.15: Solving the problem a second time, B. was able to be more efficient.

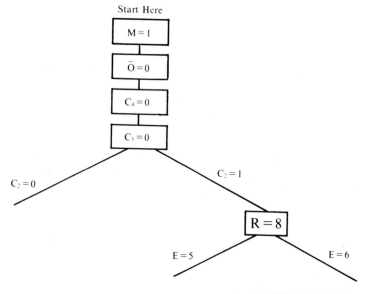

Methods of Searching

It should be clear that the use of a search tree while carrying out what ought to be a systematic search can be beneficial. Without the written tree to refer to, it is unlikely that B. would have realized that he had omitted the case $E = 6$, nor could he easily have seen that he was using $C_4 = 0$ when he was supposed to be working on the case $C_4 = 1$.

Yet, obviously, the explicit use of search trees by people trying to carry out systematic searches is probably very uncommon, for the reason that relatively few people have learned to use such trees.

Two other uses of search trees are more realistic expectations:

(i) when the search is in fact being done by a computer, not by a human;

(ii) when the tree is being used to help in the *analysis* of some search performance recorded, perhaps, during a task-based interview.

With all three uses in mind, we make a few remarks about the use of search trees:

1. It is sometimes assumed that the search space is complete. This

may be the case within a computer program, but the Long Term Study found it *not* to be the case with most humans. [Interestingly, here again those rare students who 'always make math look easy' were the same students who *did* construct complete search spaces, and did search through them systematically. We cannot begin to explain why it is always the same small group of students who turn in the strongest performances, *by almost any criterion for measuring 'strength'*.]

2. For machines, especially — perhaps sometimes for humans — the task of carrying out an *efficient* tree search is a matter of major importance. In searching a tree, especially any very large tree, you are in a position similar to a spelunker exploring a very large cave, with many alternative tunnelings in different directions. If you knew there was pirate gold down *some* labyrinth, you might be highly motivated — but in a vast array of alternatives leading to alternatives leading to alternatives, you might easily become hopelessly lost. And, of course, in many problems you do *not* know definitely that there is gold to be found.

How far will you explore each path before you give up on it, and try some other path?

The question of making a halfway reasonable plan can be subdivided into two parts: one part that depends only upon the *general nature* of caves (or trees), and a second part that makes use of specific knowledge of the problem at hand.

The main *general* decision is whether to pursue a *depth-first strategy*, or a *width-first strategy*. In a depth-first strategy you go very far down one path — perhaps even to its end — before you give up on it (or, happily, find the gold), and, if still necessary, you then move on to the next path. In a width-first strategy you go a short distance down each path — or at least down many of them — before you decide to go a little deeper (or farther) down one of them; then you go a little farther down each of them (or many of them) in turn. The advantages and disadvantages of each should be clear.

However, such pure 'tree-theoretic' choices are usually brought quickly in contact with special aspects unique to the specific problem at hand. In the 'SEND + MORE = MONEY' problem, one quickly found a few points to focus on; indeed, on B.'s second time through the problem, he constructed a far more efficient search procedure, building on things he had observed the first time through. An excellent discussion of tree searches is presented in Raphael (1976).

3. As B.'s two attempts made clear, the design of a search tree is often NOT unique. There may be many possibilities. To be sure, if we

are searching out possible sequences of moves in chess, we may feel that the first decision is unavoidably the first move, the second decision is unavoidably the second move, and so on. In 'SEND + MORE = MONEY' this is clearly not the case; the whole problem lies before our eyes, and we can choose to begin wherever we think best. Some choices will work far better than others.

But even in chess, the decisions need not be entirely decisions about *moves*. Some decisions could be decisions about *strategy* or about a *tactical line of action*. One could decide whether to keep up a relentless attack on the opponent, or pause to give better protection to your own king. Hence — because we can *choose* to face a different set of alternatives — we can end up constructing very different trees.

But, however we construct them, trees can often be helpful in guaranteeing a systematic search procedure, or a systematic analysis of someone else's search behavior.

Notes

1. Actually, because of the one-to-one correspondence, S and E could not *both* represent 9. Using this criterion repeatedly, we see that we can improve the estimate of 19,998. Surely, the largest possible value of MONEY cannot exceed

$$
\begin{array}{r}
9\ 7\ 5\ 3 \\
8\ 6\ 4\ 2 \\
\hline
1\ 8,3\ 9\ 5
\end{array}\ .
$$

The reader may see that even this estimate can easily be improved — but for our immediate purpose that is not necessary. We merely want, at this stage, to prove that M must be one, and we have accomplished that.

2. An exceptionally lucid and complete discussion of search trees used for computers is presented in Raphael (1976).

17 THE REAL-TIME CONSTRUCTION OF REPRESENTATIONS

We have referred so frequently to 'retrieval' of procedures or of frames or of data that a reader could imagine that everything we may ever need is stored somewhere in our memory, our only job being to recall it. Clearly this is false. For one thing, there is that learning which produces new knowledge representation structures to add to our permanent collection. But there is an even more dramatic sense in which what we need may not be retrievable from memory. Surely the diversity of geometric diagrams goes far beyond what we can have stored in memory. Undoubtedly the possible plots of novels, plays or movies can involve combinations and juxtapositions that are new to us, different from any plot we have ever met before.

To deal with such matters we must be able to create new knowledge representation structures right there at the moment when we need them. (For this reason they are called 'real-time' constructions; they are made as and when they are needed, the way a short-order cook prepares fried eggs and bacon. They are *not* prepared beforehand and kept ready for use, as an apple pie might be.)

Amongst the protocols from the Long Term Study, there are a number that let us see a student (or a teacher) confronted with a new situation. No adequate representation for this situation is available in memory, so one must be constructed – right now!

It does not occur instantly, as one can see by studying the protocols.

In pursuing this question, the Long Term Study used various mathematical problems in order to observe (as far as one can) how students and experts created mental representations, but the study also stepped outside of mathematics, and made use of puzzles, music and the problem of finding your way around in an unfamiliar environment. In this chapter we shall look at one example from mathematics, and one from music. The mathematical example involves some details, but we think both studies repay the effort it takes to understand them. In both of these – *and in virtually every other problem episode that we have analyzed* – we see a two-part process: as the musical theme is built up, it is simultaneously being analyzed by harmonic criteria: is the structure that is being built a reasonable one? If not, try something else! In this sense, the work is both 'top-down' and 'bottom-up' – *simultaneously*.

In the first example we consider, a teacher was trying to prove a theorem posed in Elcock (1977). One is given a triangle ABC; point M is the mid-point of segment BC. The line segment BD is drawn perpendicular to segment AM. Cf. the line (extended) through A and M; let point E lie on this line, in such a position that segment EC is perpendicular to line AM.

A diagram looks like Figure 17.1. *We are asked to prove that segment BD = segment CE.*

Figure 17.1: You are told that M is the mid-point of segment BC, that BD⊥AE, and that EC⊥AE. You are asked to prove that segment BD is congruent to segment CE. Protocol analysis indicates that solvers do NOT immediately take in all the information in the problem statement. On the contrary, a mental representation must be constructed; in order to do this, the solver admits only a small amount of information at a time.

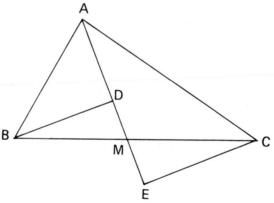

(1) 'Gating' Input Information.[1] One thing we see at once is that F., the teacher, does not take in all of the information at the outset. On the contrary, he reports that, first, he asked himself 'what are we supposed to prove?' (a) Not knowing the answer, he looked again at the problem in order to obtain the answer to this specific question: 'We are supposed to prove that segment BD = segment CE.' (b) Not knowing where things were in the diagram, he looked at the diagram and located segments BD and CE. At this point he said that, in terms of his awareness, the diagram looked essentially like Figure 17.2. (c) Because he always focused on *how things are defined* or *why they are required*

Figure 17.2: F. reported that, at an early point in constructing a mental representation of the problem, he was aware of only some of the information, with the result that he saw the diagram essentially as shown here.

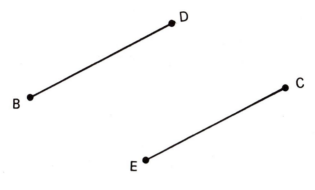

to have certain properties – or, perhaps, 'what keeps EC (say) from being a million miles long?' – he tried to look at the diagrams as if the ray $\overrightarrow{AE}$ were hinged at A. He tried visually swinging it back and forth. At first he could not see what constrained $\overrightarrow{AE}$ to lie where it did. [The answer, of course, is that if you swing ray $\overrightarrow{AE}$ into any other position, point M will no longer be the mid-point of BC – but F. had not taken in all of the available information as yet.] Somewhat dissatisfied with the inconclusive outcome of the 'what *constrains* the diagram' inquiry, F. turned to other matters. (d) F. asked himself how he could prove two segments congruent, and answered that if he could show that they were corresponding parts of congruent triangles, he would have the job done. (e) Unfortunately, when F. looked again at the diagram (Figure 17.1), he saw a great many triangles, and indeed triangle AEC struck him most forcefully. He persevered on this triangle for some time, which held up progress temporarily. (f) Ultimately, F. noticed the triangles BDM and CEM. At this point, the picture looked to him like Figure 17.3. [Notice that two processes are occurring: (i) certain key features are coming to stand out more clearly, and with a more complete delineation of their features; (ii) certain other parts of the diagram are receding into a kind of 'background noise' – or 'background greyness' – so that they are less vivid, less distinct, less attention-getting.] (g) F. noticed that the 'vertical angle theorem' implied that angle BMD

Figure 17.3: At a later point in the process of building a mental representation of the problem, F. had taken in more information, and the diagram looked to him like this.

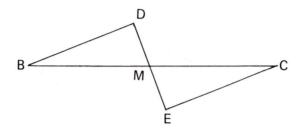

is congruent to angle CME. (h) Re-examining the problem, F. found that M was the mid-point of segment BC, so that segment BM was congruent to segment CM. (i) It took a few moments more of hunting for informational needles in an obscurantist haystack, but F. finally observed that the triangles were both right triangles. The result now followed easily.

So — we have observed that *F. did NOT take in all of the information immediately at the outset.* Had you taken away the problem statement immediately after he had 'read' it for the first time, F. would not have been able to re-state the entire problem correctly.

Instead of taking in all of the information, he first oriented himself in general, then began searching the problem statement, and the diagram, for the answers to specific questions.

(2) Representations In Your Mind. Notice that there is some reason to say that F. is building a representation *in his mind.* The only diagram on paper corresponds to Figure 17.1, and F. has not marked on this in any way. [Figures 17.2 and 17.3 come from a 'de-briefing' analysis *after* F. had solved the problem.] Yet he now sees it very differently. Indeed, once one can *see* essentially Figure 17.3, the rest is easy. F. was not able to move immediately from Figure 17.1 to 17.3, but when he did, this was an event that took place inside himself. The actual figure on paper was unchanged — but F. reported that Minsky and Papert's phrase was apt: it was as if triangles BDM and CEM were suddenly printed in a different color, so sharply did they stand out from the rest of the diagram.[2]

Analysis

The 'How-to-Solve-Math-Problems' Frame

F.'s solution of this geometric problem has more to teach us. One can imagine that F., an experienced mathematics teacher (who felt that geometry was one of his weaker areas), presumably possessed a powerful frame that might be labeled the 'How-to-Solve-Math-Problems' frame. This is presumably a rather general frame that actually embodies a number of heuristic principles. It has variables that allow one to input a description of the problem to be solved. As one of its outputs — perhaps its most important output — it will supervise the creation of an *ad hoc* representation structure for this particular problem. In order to do this, it will make use of representations retrieved from memory, and one of its tasks is to guide the process of locating these items in memory.

This 'How-to-Solve-Math-Problems' frame (call it 'Frame 1') directed F. to search in the problem statement in order to find *what we were being asked to prove*. F. did so, and this slot in the frame was filled.

Frame 1 now supervised the construction of a representation diagram *in the mind* (recall that F. used paper only *after* he had solved the problem), which caused F. to see the written diagram *so that it appeared to him to look like Figure 17.2*.

But Frame 1 has also the responsibility for assembling a procedure for solving the problem. Apparently Frame 1 resorts to the 'backward-chaining heuristic', and hence asks:

How could you prove two segments congruent?

The planning meta-language is adequate to dealing with this.

Answer: by proving that they are corresponding parts of congruent figures.
Q: What figures?
Answer: Try triangles. (This is probably the common default evaluation in this situation — and, in addition, Figure 17.1 is displaying a sizeable collection of triangles that F. can see.)

So we have two processes converging: first, the heuristic problem analysis sequence says 'get congruent figures', 'get congruent triangles', and so on. Simultaneously, we are building up a cognitive representation of the geometrical diagram itself, which ultimately comes to look like Figure 17.3.

As a construction of 'something new', Figure 17.3 is perhaps disappointing. It is clearly based on familiar results about vertical angles and right triangles. Yet it is not unexciting — indeed, F. reported that it was precisely when this *recognizable* representation was achieved that he felt that he 'understood what this problem was really all about'.

In general, we postulate that, *after retrieval of one or more frames has been accomplished, after instantiation is complete, after a representation has been made from recognizable frame components assembled in a recognizable way, we see the 'meaning' of the problem* or situation. This is the point where, in Papert and Minsky's phrase, *the key line segments, angles, etc. stand out as if they had suddenly become a different color.*

Postscript

The following year F. was asked about this same geometry problem. Although he believed he had forgotten it, the moment he saw Figure 17.1 it looked to him like Figure 17.3, so that the entire solution seemed immediately obvious. He could hardly believe that it had required considerable thought a year earlier.

Wunderbar

Our second example comes, not from mathematics, but from music. A middle-aged man, J., was a not very good amateur musician. Originally a cellist, in recent years he had given up the cello for the recorder and the piano. Whenever J. heard a new piece of music, he always heard it as a sequence of integers. He realized that, in some vague sense, these were cello fingerings. This surprised him, because it had been years since he had played the cello, and many of the pieces had been written since then, so J. could not possibly ever have played them on the cello. On the other hand, he *did* play recorder and piano — but fingerings for these instruments did not run through his mind with the tenacity of cello fingerings.

J. had never been a proficient singer, and in that sense depended upon guidance from the instruments to help him get intervals — sixths, fifths, fourths, sevenths, etc. — correct. J. did not deliberately seek these numerical sequences — they came to him automatically whenever he heard a piece of music.

J. could not imagine *why* these numerical sequences occurred to him — what purpose did they serve?

After carefully analyzing the sequences in a few cases, we would argue that they represent conscious portions of the real-time synthesis of a knowledge representation structure for the music in question. Just as our geometric structure drew upon other structures, retrieved from memory, and used as component parts — for example, the 'x' configuration of the vertical angle theorem — so, too, did this musical representation. It built upon *small intervals*, such as seconds, thirds and fourths, and upon the potential organizing ability of cello fingering, which ultimately puts major thirds, minor thirds, major sixths, minor sixths, all in the proper relationship to the diatonic scale.

While watching a movie, J. had happened to hear *Wunderbar* as part of the score. This immediately appeared to him as the numerical sequence

4 44   4 44   111   20   44

in which rhythm and pitch are combined. If we eliminate rhythm, the pitch (or fingering) sequence would be

4 4 4 4 4 4 1 1 1 2 0 4 4

J. realized that he in fact had a three-part representation:

rhythm:

fingerings: 4   44   4   44   111   20   44

direction of pitch change: 444 ↗ 444 ↘ 111 ↗ 2 ↗ 0 ↘ 44

Some excerpts from J.'s notes:

A moment ago, lying in bed, I thought this first step up was an octave — I actually considered it to be

— and I couldn't understand why the clear contradiction of the 4's both places (which just about *had* to be wrong) wasn't being corrected.

Then I decided maybe the error wasn't being eliminated because there was the possibility of some weird fingering[3] (like playing G with the fourth finger in the second position on the C string, instead of using the open G string).

But just now it occurred to me that the interval is NOT an octave, but rather a *sixth*. So maybe there exists a weighting function, that tells the 'confidence', and maybe the 'octave' was getting a low *confidence rating*, hence was not taken as producing a clear-cut logical contradiction.

Analysis of J.'s notes revealed several interesting aspects.

(1) Short Phrases Were Dealt With Independently. In fact, the whole *Wunderbar* theme was decomposed into *short sections of notes that formed local patterns.* These short sections were, at the beginning of the construction, dealt with almost independently. Separate pieces were often in different keys, and the intervals connecting the last note of one short section with the first note of the next short section were extremely vague — essentially left as 'unsolved' for the time being. One short sequence, for example, was

which did not fit in correctly with some of the other short fragments.

(2) Lack of Input Data. As J. re-examined his written notes, he realized that there were certain intervals that he had not 'heard' carefully at all. Apparently, as in the earlier mathematical examples, the operative frame *posed questions* and caused J. to listen for certain answers. But at some points in the melody reconstruction, no sharp question had been posed, and so no answer had been sought or obtained. One such example occurred at this point in the melody

Where did the notes marked 'A' belong, in relation to the preceding notes? The interval marked with a question mark seemed entirely mysterious.

(3) 'Computing' Pitch. J. noted that, after he realized the existence of the gap just mentioned, he deliberately tried to 'connect up' notes on each side of the gap, to determine their correct relation. To do this, he used a method he often used: namely, he sang the intervening portion of a scale, to see where he ended up with a note that seemed to sound correct. [*Up until this point, J. had used no auditory feedback whatsoever, neither singing, nor striking notes on a piano, etc. All of this had been done 'in his head', mostly on an involuntary basis, which the reader may also have experienced when a tune 'just keeps running through your head'.*]

So at this moment, for the first time, J. sang and listened. What he sang was:

The notes enclosed in parenthesis were deliberately interpolated in trying to get down to the correct note, which J. recognized as the note marked 'B'. This use of singing part of a scale seemed to J. to be analogous to computing or calculating in arithmetic. In any event, it caused J. to locate the note at 'B' as a minor third below the first note of the theme.

(4) 'Welding'. At first, J. had not noticed that the interval leading to 'B' was a descending octave, and the note at 'B' was defined only in

relation to the first note of the theme. Once J. did notice this octave, however, he was amazed that he had failed to see it earlier. Furthermore, the octave – an interval J. could sing reliably – had the effect of connecting the first two fragments securely together, and establishing their relationship to one another. The two short fragments had become 'welded' together to form one longer fragment.

(5) The Memory for Sensation. What J. did, in singing a scale fragment to locate the note at 'B' (and thus to establish the correct relation between the first two fragments), is interesting in itself. We have argued earlier that, for most mathematical information processing, once input data has been represented as an instantiated frame, and once the instantiation has been judged and pronounced satisfactory, then nearly all subsequent processing uses the instantiated frame as a kind of 'proxy' for the original input, and *usually ignores the input itself.*

But, if J. could recognize the note at 'B', for which he had NOT yet made a correct representation, *this must have been a case where the original 'primitive' sensory input was in some way represented in memory.* Otherwise there would have been nothing for J. to 'recognize'.

(6) Two Converging Processes. In the earlier geometric example, we saw construction proceeding along two simultaneous lines that gradually converged. Along one path we saw the geometric 'picture' itself being built up (or, as it turned out in that case, being pared down), from Figure 17.1 to 17.2 to 17.3. Simultaneously, an inquiry was pursuing questions such as: 'How can we prove that two segments are congruent?' 'Which triangles should we consider?'

The same phenomenon – of two converging processes – occurred also in the Wunderbar construction. Thus far we have looked mainly at the theme itself, as it begins to appear, written out in the bass clef (J. himself really represented it as hand positions and fingerings to play the passage on a cello, but this could hardly work as a notation here, and it is a small distortion to write it out as notes on a bass clef.)

But, simultaneously, there was the 'line of inquiry' going on. This inquiry caused J. to realize that the two fragments could not be connected as long as he did not know the interval between the last note of the first fragment, and the first note of the second fragment. Presumably, also, this inquiry led him to the strategy of interpolating a portion of a scale in order, as it were, to 'measure' how far down the note at 'B' actually was.

But, just as there is a large and powerful collection of theorems and heuristics to guide the inquiry in geometry, there is something equally powerful in music: tonality and harmonic sequence. Nearly all Western music is based on a very small collection of chords, most often on the tonic, dominant and sub-dominant chords (also known, respectively, as I, V and IV). In the key of C major, these are the chords of C, G and F. The arrangements of these chords are incredibly few in number, and all of the magnificent diversity of Western music has been created within severely tight constraints. Most of Beethoven is based on a I-V-I sequence — yet within this tiny space, within this very small apparent freedom, Beethoven found a variety of spaciousness that seems vast beyond belief — infinity, as it were, within the confines of the tiniest of thimbles.

For Beethoven this was apparently an irresistible challenge. For the task of constructing the representation of a theme, it is an extremely valuable aid. The first note is most likely to be the tonic or the dominant; the first chord is likely to be the I chord. The first cadence is likely to be a V chord, and if not that, then a IV chord. The final chord is almost certain to be a I chord. Thus, if the first notes are C, A, A (as, at that point in J.'s notes, they were), then the key is almost certainly either A minor or F major, probably the latter. Then the second fragment is probably

or something of the sort, giving an harmonic sequence I-IV-I, which is entirely possible. (Later in his notes, J. used the appearance of a dominant seventh chord just before the end of the phrase as confirmation of the correctness of a B flat-E natural sequence.)

The two converging processes — building the theme up (much as the geometric diagram was built up), and checking the harmonic sequence (much as F. had used theorems and heuristics) — finally led J. to a version of the theme which was readily recognizable as *Wunderbar*; as he had imagined, his version was set in the key of F major.

(7) Subsequent Recall. The geometric and musical examples have another point of similarity: after an interval of time, both F. and J.

believed they had forgotten their earlier construction – and, indeed, they had, for when they tried to recall it, they could not. J.'s first 'recalled' version of *Wunderbar* [two months later] was again filled with errors; but very shortly he repaired all of the errors, without requring any acoustic feedback. So both J. and F. had learned *something* – not a perfect representation, available for immediate recall, but rather an imperfect representation, readily capable of being perfected.

(8) The Next Stage. After creating the initial representation, 'forgetting' it, and subsequently re-constructing it (easily!), both F. and J. reported that they felt they had a clearer idea of the subject. In the case of *Wunderbar*, J. found that he no longer thought of it in terms of a numerical sequence, but rather in terms of muscular/tactile sensations – hand location (position) and finger position – even though he had not played a cello in years. In the geometric example, F. finally found that the proposition was entirely obvious, and he could scarcely believe that it had ever required thought.

Notes

1. The word 'gat-ing' is supposed to suggest a 'gate' that admits information at a controlled rate, as a turnstile or other gate might admit people at a controlled rate, or as the starting gate at a horse race controls the time when horses may enter the actual race.

2. F.'s phrase refers to a remark in Minsky and Papert (1972) that one may look at a chessboard and see, at first glance, merely an array of pieces, with no clear pattern. But then, suddenly, an important pattern emerges – three pieces, perhaps, locked in a 'pin' configuration. At this moment the relevant pieces seem to stand out from all the others, proclaiming the special configuration. 'It is almost as if the pieces involved had suddenly changed color.'

We interpret this as a sensation that accompanies completion of frame retrieval, mapping of input data into frame slots, and successful testing of how well it all fits. At this point, 'the pieces seem to change color'; what had been a jungle of pieces now displays a very clear pattern. At this point one might say that the configuration has acquired *meaning*.

3. Cello fingerings call the little finger 4 (whereas piano fingerings call it 5). The index finger is called 1, and the thumb is called Q. These numbers say *which* finger is determining string length, and hence pitch,

but there is no one-to-one correspondence between fingerings and pitch, because the hand may be moved back and forth along the neck of the instrument. The location of the hand is described by *positions*, which normally include 'half position', 'first position', 'second position', 'third position', 'fourth position', and a large range of 'thumb positions'. Beyond this, in most positions the fingers may stretch or not, and if they stretch, they may do so by the little finger reaching for a note a half-tone higher, or by the index finger reaching for a note a half-tone lower.

All of this would be totally confusing except that the cellist is ordinarily reading notes on a staff (usually bass clef), which provides an unambiguous definition of the intended pitch.

Apparently the very perfection of the staff notation — totally unambiguous in every regard — precludes J. from using it as his immediate response to hearing a musical phrase. Fingerings have two advantages: they are closer to actual muscular/tactile experiences in the past, and they are somewhat vague and flexible. In particular, they allow short segments to be considered independently of one another, even when the relations between the various segments are unknown. (One merely imagines that the cellist's hand moved to a different position, or to a different string.) J. had originally believed that the fingering sequences that occurred to him spontaneously whenever he heard a musical theme were in fact accurate, but when he undertook to make detailed notes for this study, he was surprised to find that, in their initial versions, they were filled with errors, which were gradually corrected over time.

18 RETRIEVAL, CONSTRUCTION AND MAPPING

Clearly, the theoretical difficulties in explaining how we match up input data with an appropriate assimilation pattern — or *idea* — are so perplexing that they seem nearly to constitute a conundrum. At least three difficulties appear in many theoretical formulations:

(1) *finding* the correct piece (or pieces) in the 'vast storage warehouse' of the mind;
(2) determining the *units* in the input data;
(3) finding the *correct mapping* of input 'units' into frame slots after the frame has been selected.

Finding genuine illustrations could involve us in considerable detail, but a much simpler suggestive example might be the equation

$$6 \sin^4 x - 5 \sin^2 x + 1 = 0. \tag{1}$$

Presumably a person attempting to solve this equation would already be familiar with quadratic equations. To keep the discussion simple, we represent this person's knowledge of quadratic equations in the form of knowing that the equation

$$ax^2 + bx + c = 0 \tag{2}$$

has the solutions

$$x = \frac{-b \pm \sqrt{b^2 - 4ac}}{2a} \tag{3}$$

[To be sure, the person may use other forms of knowledge, such as factoring, but this would not alter our discussion fundamentally. We are really concerned with *cognitive* variables, not *mathematical* variables, but the written discussion will be simpler if we use mathematical variables as a proxy for cognitive variables.[1]]

The Selection/Retrieval Question

The selection problem, of course, is this: looking at equation (1), will we be led to think of equation (2) [we really mean: the cognitive representation corresponding to equation (2)]? Will we see (1) and think 'Aha! A quadratic equation!'

This is the 'top-down' vs. 'bottom-up' processing question: if I had retrieved the quadratic equation frame, I would be doing 'top-down' processing, and the frame itself would help guide my study of equation (1). The problem is: *what would have caused me to retrieve that particular frame*? As it stands, equation (1) is NOT a quadratic equation.

A successful frame retrieval in a case of this sort is, metaphorically, a kind of stone arch, such as Figure 18.1. One side stands on the original input data, the other side stands on one or more frames retrieved from memory. If everything works out properly, the two sides come together at the keystone at the top of the arch. The input data is successfully mated to the retrieved (or constructed) frame.

If you had never seen a stone arch, how could you start at one end and build towards some expected complete structure? If you start with input data, you have no frame − no conceptual goal − to guide you. You have no target to aim towards. Suppose, indeed, you imagine that you start with the frame, and work back towards the input data. This is feasible, since the frame will guide you in what to expect, what to look for. But there is a problem: how, in this case, was the frame selected? How did you know which frame to use?

Determining the 'Units'

A more subtle problem, but a very real one, is the need to determine the *units* or *basic entities*. We have some kind of input data representation, and (when we retrieve it or construct it) some kind of frame representation. We must make a mapping from one to the other. *But it is NOT always obvious what the 'units' or 'basic entities' are*. In the case of our equation (1), above, if we assume that one basic entity in the input is the 'unknown' x, then we may try to map this into the basic entity 'unknown x' in equation (2). Such an attempt would fail! Why? Because, putting matters in these terms, x is not the basic 'unknown' unit that we should select. Then what is? The answer, of course, is that the 'basic unknown' unit in equation (1) should be chosen to be $\sin^2 x$. If we let $\sin^2 x$ in (1) map into x in (2), things work out very nicely.

Experienced mathematicians become so proficient in making a suitable identification of the 'basic entities' that they may forget the fundamental difficulty of the task. How it is done is often a considerable mystery. Consider Figure 18.2. For reference identification, we have labeled four circles in Figure 18.3, but the visual effect itself is

Figure 18.1: How can anyone build an arch? Once it is constructed, it holds together. But how can the pieces be assembled?

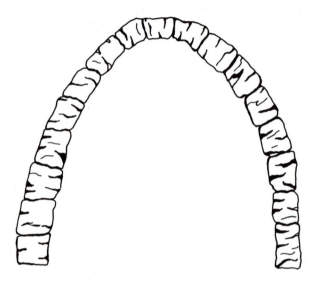

clearer when you look at Figure 18.2. The circle labeled '3' is seen by most people as belonging to the diagonal sequence. What causes this to happen? Circle 3 is actually nearer to circle 2, and even to circle 4, than it is to any of the other circles in the diagonal sequence. Somehow the 'top-down' *pattern*, rather than proximity, is able to claim circle 3 more effectively. So most people easily see two 'units' in this array: one is a vertical sequence, the other a diagonal sequence of circles.

Selecting the Mapping

Suppose a frame has been selected. Suppose, also, that units have been identified.

There still remains a problem: the units in the input data must be mapped into the variable slots in the frame. *A correct mapping must be selected.*

In the SEND + MORE = MONEY puzzle, we saw that there were nearly two million different mappings of eight digits (to be chosen from ten possible candidates) into the eight letters S, E, N, D, M, O, R, Y. Exactly one of these satisfied the constraints of the problem, and our task was to find that one. (And, of course, to prove that none of the other mappings did satisfy the constraints.)

Figure 18.2: What 'wholes' or 'parts' do you see in this configuration? (Most people see two lines of circles, each consisting of six circles.)

Figure 18.3: The circle labeled '3' is usually perceived as part of the slanted row of circles, yet it is actually nearer to circle '2'. Why is it not seen as belonging to the pattern of circles 1, 2 and 4?

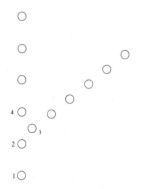

Presumably cognitive mapping could face similar multiplicities, and similar selection choices.

An Equation

You will find it helpful to solve this equation BEFORE READING THE REMAINDER OF THE CHAPTER:

$$\frac{x^2}{2{,}500} + (\log x)^2 + \log x^{19} = \frac{1}{25} \log x^x + \frac{19x}{50} - 34.$$

(The logarithms are to base ten; only integer values of x are desired.)

The real goal, of course, is to see what you can learn by closely observing your own method for solving this equation. It is not the mathematics that you should focus on, but rather on how you think about the problem, what strategy you use in attacking it.

Theory

We can think about these dilemmas of frame selection, unit identification and mapping, or we can collect and analyze some data. In this chapter we shall do both.

First, we theorize.

Retrieval

At least six possible mechanisms have been suggested that might simplify the task of frame selection. Notice that they are by no means mutually exclusive.

Bootstrapping. Perhaps processing starts with modest goals: 'I see an unknown.' 'I see a sine.' 'I see a squared term.' 'I see a pattern of three terms added together.' Each of these leads to certain associations — that is, frames that involve such things. From here, the search continues.

Not Knowing Too Much. Probably most of the quadratic-equation solving in the world is done by students who are learning to solve quadratic equations. To a considerable extent they are protected by their own ignorance — how many methods do they know that *could* be used? (Probably only two, for most students.)

The implications of this are worth reflecting on when designing school curricula.

Focus on Some Key Cue. One could — perhaps without being consciously aware of it — focus on a very small number of cues whose presence would be taken as evidence for the retrieval of some specific frame.

Using Context. One could use the context to influence the choice. Many computer programs, such as de Jong's FRUMP (de Jong, 1979) do this. So, obviously, do many students; if the section in the textbook deals with separating variables, then solve the problems by separating variables.

Using Systematic Search. A student can try to learn things in a systematic way, to develop systematic procedures for searching his or her memory. Clearly, some students take the trouble to do this. (Equally clearly, many others do not.)

Parameter-adjusting or Spreading Activation. There are obvious difficulties when we try to decide what to do first. But perhaps we need not decide. One can imagine a considerable array of 'assimilation' candidates: the unknown x, a linear combination of terms, the presence of two unknowns (x and y, say), the presence of exponents, the presence of the specific exponent 2, a sum of three terms set equal to zero, the fact that some expression is the square of some other expression, the presence of the exponent 3, the presence of a common factor, a recognizably-factorable left-hand side set equal to zero, and so on. Whenever one of these is satisfied, its 'expectation value' is increased. Certain combinations can raise some 'expectation values' quite substantially; for example, if we find *both* a sum of three terms set equal to zero, *and also* one expression that is the square of some other expression, then the odds are greatly improved that we are dealing with a quadratic equation. Hence, seeing this, we raise the 'expectation value' of 'QUADRATIC EQUATION' by a sizeable increment.

The next step, of course, is that as certain frames or assimilation patterns acquire large expectation values, they 'become active' or 'assume control'.

'Parameter-adjusting' theories such as this seem to lack the crisp definiteness of those all-or-nothing theories that make a definite selection of frames, load them into the active part of memory, and allow them — and only them — to assume control. But they have at least the virtue of avoiding problems of 'what do you do first?' Many parameters are always being readjusted simultaneously. The phenomenon of some definite plan being 'in control' is only a kind of secondary phenomenon, resulting from that plan which, at the moment, has the highest expectation value. Like Presidents, plans come and go, changing with elections, and the most important issues in the long run are the guaranteed continuity, and the responsiveness to electoral voting. Errors get corrected, sooner or later.

Units and Mappings

The same possibilities exist for identifying units, and for selecting mappings.

So much for theorizing. We turn now to some data.

P.G.'s Work on the Equation

The equation

$$\frac{x^2}{2,500} + (\log x)^2 + \log x^{19} = \frac{1}{25} \log x^X + \frac{19x}{50} - 34 \quad (1)$$

was presented to P., a university sophomore taking a course in calculus (and also to 18 other students, and to two adult experts). P.G. is a very interesting subject, because — no matter what he is doing — he is inclined to talk about it as he does it. Driving a car: 'I didn't get a good look to the left — that bush was in the way — I wanted to be sure everything was clear before I pulled out.' Trying to remember something: 'It's there in my head somewhere. I *know* it is. I just can't seem to find it.'

Obviously P.G.'s introspective remarks are presumably fallible, just as some of his perceptions are. But he does produce an ongoing verbal explanation of almost anything he does — which can be very helpful for task-based interviews. Here is a transcription of an audio-taped session where P.G. was presented with equation (1) for the first time. It resembled nothing that he had worked on in recent weeks.

1. P.G.   [reads the equation; starts work immediately]
2. P.G.: I can get all the logs on one side.
[He wrote:

$$(\log x)(\log x) + \log x^{19} - \frac{1}{25} \log x^X = \frac{19x}{50} - 34 - \frac{x^2}{2,500}] \quad (2)$$

3. Interviewer: Why did you decide to do that?
4. P.G.: Just trying to get like terms. . . [He leaves the sentence unfinished; goes on to explain further:] It's one of the things you do.

Analysis: Whatever internal cognitive mechanism you postulate, P.G.'s behavior here is clear enough. He looked quickly at the equation, immediately started writing (and talking) and, retrieving from memory 'one of the things you do', he began doing it.

5. P.G. [continuing to talk] : . . .also, I'm thinking, in one part of my head, about things I know about logs. . .if I can remember them. . .

6. P.G.: O.K. . . .Ah. . ., you can take that nineteen down in front of the log, can't you, so the log of x to the nineteenth is nineteen log x. . . [His tone of voice indicates that he's pretty sure of himself; this isn't really a question.]

7. Interviewer: . . .Sure. . .

8. P.G.: . . .and. . .ah. . .you can take that x down also. . . [referring to the last term on the left-hand side of the equation] . . . O.K. I'm going to take a log out of the whole thing [factoring the L.H. side].

9. P.G. [writes] :

$$(\log x)(\log x + 19 - \frac{x}{25}) = \qquad\qquad (3)$$

(but does not write any right-hand side] .

10. P.G.: [Looking at R.H. side of equation (2)] . . .those. . .something. . . still left with an x and an x squared. . . [very thoughtful tone] . . .quadratic? . . .still, I need those two equal zero in order to use that. . .

Analysis: Clearly by whatever mechanism, P.G. has by now retrieved the QUADRATIC EQUATION frame, and is checking how well the input data fit this pattern. Note that he is looking at, and talking about, only the R.H. side of equation (2) — which, of course, is *not* set equal to zero.

11. Long silence.

12. P.G. [excitedly] : I've got a quadratic on both sides! No, I don't. . . Yes, I do! I've got a quadratic on both sides, don't I?[2] [quite excitedly]

13. Interviewer: . . .yeah. . .that's true. . . [Actually, it isn't. The interviewer was mistaken.]

14. P.G. [continuing; it probably wouldn't have mattered much what the interviewer said] : . . .'cause I mean, I've got a log x squared [i.e. $(\log x)^2$], and a log x to the nineteenth. . . [P.G. is now looking at the L.H. side of equation (2)] . . . so. . .then

this is a log of something different [referring to the log x^{19} term in equation (2)]...so it doesn't work. This isn't the same log as that...

Analysis: Note that, in switching his attention back to equation (2), P.G. has lost sight of the helpful transformations that he previously used — on his own initiative — in obtaining the L.H. side of equation (3).[3]

15. Interviewer: You're forgetting a step you took yourself a minute ago. [pause; no reaction from P.G.] You said that log of x to the nineteenth [i.e. $\log x^{19}$] really *is* a term in the log of x [i.e. $19 \log x$].

16. P.G.: Oh... [thoughtfully, pulling on leashes[4]] You're right! [excitedly] Yes, that is! So that is. I've got log x, and log x squared [i.e. $(\log x)^2$]. But that still leaves me with a log x to the x [i.e. $\log x^x$],...which is x log x, which I don't want...

Analysis: Note that P.G. has just discarded what might have been the most valuable clue: once one has terms in $(\log x)^2$ and in x^2, the presence of a term in x log x strongly suggests the possibility of something like

$$(A \log x + B x)^2 ,$$

after which other clues fall in place and suggest correct values for A and B.

Why did P.G. throw away so valuable clue? He was in a different processing mode; having built a certain portion of the representation for this problem, he was trying to map input data into his representation. The x log x term did not fit, and so he discarded it. A better use would have been to *accept* the importance of the x log x term, and use it as a clue to building the representation (or to rejecting whatever excluded x log x).

Cumulative Analysis. Let's look at what P.G. has done thus far, and match his observed behavior with postulated information processing mechanisms.

1. First, P.G. tries to collect 'like terms' together. This would appear to be frame retrieval caused by some specific cue, or by the general 'equation solving' context.

2. Second, P.G. decided to carry out two tactical transformations:

$$\log x^{19} \rightarrow 19 \log x$$
$$\log x^{x} \rightarrow x \log x$$

This was almost certainly NOT based on any vision of what the later solution methods would be, and in that sense was mainly 'bottom-up' processing. As with most 'bottom-up' processing, it may turn out later on that this transformation did *not* advance the strategic goals (i.e. did not facilitate the application of the main final solution methods). As it happens, of course, this step *is* helpful in the long run, but surely P.G. did not know that when he decided to take this step.

3. Next, P.G. factored out log x. Again, a 'bottom-up' tactical step — and in this case one that is *not* helpful in the long run. However, while this does not produce an *equation* that is nearer to one we can work with, the thrashing about does toss up onto the beach some *ideas* or *expressions* that may be very helpful, specifically

$$\frac{\log x}{19}$$

and

$$\frac{x}{25} \ .$$

Particularly for a 'spreading activation' or 'parameter-adjusting' theory, if log x, $\frac{x}{50}$, 19, 34, 2 and 17 become things that one is thinking seriously about, then finding the key that unlocks this problem becomes much easier. The parametric values attached to some of these expressions have, presumably, been raised because the expressions are recognizable within the input data. If any prospective assimilation patterns, retrieved from memory, also attach importance to some of these expressions, their parametric values will be raised much more, beginning to point the way towards a matching-up between the input data and some (hopefully) appropriate assimilation patterns or frames.

4. In Utterance 10, P.G. sees a quadratic polynomial hiding within the R.H. side of equation (2). This cues the retrieval of the QUADRATIC EQUATION frame. Now we observe some *top-down* processing: the QUADRATIC EQUATION frame directs P.G. to check that the *other* side of the equation is zero. P.G. checks and finds that, unfortunately, it isn't.

5. In Utterance 12, P.G. recognizes that he *also* has a quadratic

expression on the L.H. side of equation (2). As a matter of fact, the input data does not match perfectly the quadratic form, but what is far more important for us is that P.G., with little apparent difficulty, has made a partially correct identification of the *unit* — the 'log x' in the input data may be the basic entity that will correspond to the 'x' in the quadratic formula

$$ax^2 + bx + c = 0 \quad .$$

[P.G. may well be thinking in terms of polynomials, here, instead of equations.]

6. In Utterance 14 we see something of great cognitive interest. First of all, we see *top-down* processing. Whatever QUADRATIC frame P.G. has retrieved takes control, and directs the operation of checking the mapping of input data into the frame slots. So P.G. checks. *But the checking procedure concludes that the mapping has failed*! Why? Because what is in **A**

$$\underline{\quad} \; (\underset{\underset{A}{\uparrow}}{\quad})^2 + \underline{\quad} \; (\underset{\underset{B}{\uparrow}}{\quad}) + \underline{\quad} = 0$$

is not the same as what is in **B**. One is 'log x' and the other is 'log x^{19}'. In a sense the check has operated correctly — but a transformation that P.G. thought of spontaneously, and used, just moments earlier is being overlooked! (That is, $\log x^{19} \rightarrow 19 \log x$.)

How come? Is this because P.G.'s available 'cognitive work space' has become filled up, and this has been deleted? Why is it not now retrieved and applied? No space left into which it can be loaded?

7. After the Interviewer's assistance, in Utterance 15, we see P.G. getting it all together in Utterance 16. He continues the process of checking the mapping of input data into the slots in the QUAD-RATIC frame, and again decides that the mapping has failed. ['. . .which I don't want. . .']. Some experts consider this term in x log x to be one of the most valuable clues in the equation, but P.G. appears to see it only as an obstacle, not as a possible guide to action.

17. P.G.: I want just a constant down there. [Gesture indicates the third term on the L.H. side of equation (2).]

Analysis: Again some top-down processing. The QUADRATIC frame dictates a constant term:

$$ax^2 + bx + c \quad .$$
$$\uparrow$$

18. Interviewer [who was wondering what P.G. would do if he *did* have the equality of two quadratic polynomials $P_1(x) = P_2(x)$] : well, if you had just a quadratic expression equal to some other quadratic expression, that might or might not help you much. . .

19. P.G. [agreeing] : I don't get a zero. . . It's not a real quadratic. . .

Analysis: This would seem to confirm that P.G. has retrieved a QUADRATIC EQUATION frame, and *not* a QUADRATIC POLYNOMIAL frame.

20. [pause]

21. P.G.: . . .'cause the only ways I can see of simplifying that [equation] depend on getting similar terms in each of those things ['things' seems to mean 'terms' — it appears that P.G. has in mind 'combining like terms', really by applying the distributive law]. . . 'cause you can't combine thirty-four with nineteen x over fifty. . .[pause]. . .and fifty is. . .ah!. . .fifty times fifty is. . .is. . . [P.G. is checking his mental calculation to be sure he is right] . . .two thousand five hundred. . .so that's x over 50 squared [$(\frac{x}{50})^2$]. [P.G. is excited about his new discovery.]

Analysis: Notice how much support this might give to a 'parameter-adjusting' or 'spreading activation' theory; P.G. *pronounced* the word 'fifty', and obviously read it. . . and '50' became more prominent in his thinking! So it became involved in more processing, and the ' $\frac{x^2}{2,500}$ ' term received increments; the checking of 50 against 2,500 became appropriate, and was in fact performed. Now, with the 'square' relationship confirmed, the parametric value of ' $\frac{x}{50}$ ' is increased considerably more. It's beginning to look important!

22. Interviewer [responding to P.G.'s enthusiasm] : . . .so that maybe gives you an idea. . .

23. P.G. [interpreting Utterance 22, following his usual practice of putting nearly everything into words] : You indicate that that should suggest something to me. . . .Obviously, it did, or I wouldn't have mentioned it, but what it suggests is. . .

[pause] ...[musing] very vague things... [pause]... I mean, I can multiply above and below by fifty over here [he indicates the R.H. side of the equation]

Analysis: P.G. seems to be reaching for rather small *possible* steps, suggesting mainly BOTTOM-UP processing.

24. P.G. [continuing]: ...and get a like term... [*Analysis*: So there is *some* use of TOP-DOWN processing, as there would have to be, since he must be looking for things he can 'recognize', but the processing seems to be *mostly* BOTTOM-UP in the sense that P.G. is looking for rather 'small' items, rather than global or strategic methods.] ...or I can say this is... [At this point, P.G. interrupts himself.] But since these aren't the same, I can't call these one, the other squared.

 [His gestures indicate that he is talking about the *unit* that ought to appear inside both pairs of parentheses in the form

$$\underline{\quad}\ (\quad\quad)^2 + \underline{\quad}\ (\quad\quad) + \underline{\quad} = 0.]$$

25. P.G. [continuing]: ...'cause they're not the same. We're missing a nineteen.
26. Interviewer: Well...but you're sort of confusing some things now. One time you're talking about 'combining like terms', and the other time you're talking about getting a quadratic equation.
27. P.G. [Responding to the words 'quadratic equation']: You just said I didn't want one, because I couldn't get a zero! [The interviewer, of course, has said no such thing. But those words that have been uttered have been interpreted by each participant in relation to their own personal mental representations.]
28. Interviewer: ...[Pause – he isn't sure how to respond...] Well, but the sort of *nice* quadratic appearance of that is *suggestive*... [He wants to undo any suggestion that quadratic equations are *verboten*, while at the same time not steering P.G. in any specific direction – a very difficult line to walk.]
29. P.G.: O.K. Well, I *got* the terms...the whole thing would *be* x, then, and *a* would be one. [Note his clear reference to

$$ax^2 + bx + c = 0.]$$

Because I got the whole thing squared, here, the top *and* the bottom. . .[referring to $\frac{x}{50}$ and $\frac{x^2}{50^2}$]

30. Interviewer: Yeah. . .so why don't you *write* some of that, to take advantage of that, so you can see what you've got. . . [P.G., as his habit, is doing most of the work in his head, and writing very little. If P.G.'s difficulties involve too small a work space in memory, writing more down on paper would seem likely to be helpful. On the other hand, a 'spreading activation' theory might suggest that the relevant parameters can be readjusted more quickly if you do do the work in your head.]

31. Interviewer [continuing] : . . .you really have an x over fifty. . .

32. P.G. [writes, without speaking, the R.H. side of the equation]

$$= (\frac{x}{50})^2 + \frac{19x}{50} - 34$$

[Detail: P.G. had long had a habit of writing in an unusual sequential order, and *not* in left-right order. In writing the R.H. side of this equation, he wrote the 19x in this order: first the 9, then the x (yielding 9x), and finally the one (resulting in 19x). In Utterance 33, he commented on this.]

33. P.G.: I'm still writing funny. I did that from the middle to the right and [then to] the left.

34. Interviewer: That has much more appearance, now, of a quadratic equation.

35. P.G.: Right. That [the R.H. side of the equation] doesn't have the problem this one [the L.H. side] did, which was an x where I couldn't. . .where I didn't want it. . .but the point is I still don't get a zero.

36. Interviewer: That's certainly true. That [intonation and gestures indicate 'what you have just written'] doesn't *solve* it [the whole problem] , but you know. . .at this stage one is looking for any clues as to what you ought to do.

37. [Background information: from the interviewer's notes, we know that at this point in the interview, the interviewer has in mind these three things:

(i) he interpreted P.G.'s phrase 'an x where I couldn't [in Utterance 35] to mean 'there is an x so placed that I cannot map this input data correctly into the assimilation paradigm which I have selected';

(ii) the interviewer said 'doesn't *solve* it', with a stress on the word 'solve', because he feared that P.G. was looking (as students often are) for a *one-step solution*. The interviewer knew that in this problem, as in most problems, one needs to carry out a planned, sustained strategy, involving more than one single step;

(iii) finally, the interviewer realized that they were running out of time for finishing this interview, because some external time constraints were about to require ending the session.]

38. P.G.: Throw up my hands and throw a beer in the audience? [P.G. is referring to a well-publicized act by a rock performer that had taken place on the previous evening.]

39. Interviewer: [P.G. and the interviewer are looking carefully at the L.H. side of the equation.] . . .but if you want to play *that* scenario out [referring to the strategy P.G. has been pursuing], to some extent your factoring out the log x. . .

40. P.G. [interrupting; he has independently had the same idea — the L.H. side cannot, *as written*, match the quadratic formula]: Yeah, it doesn't help! . . .but the point is that, with it in. . . [very definite and emphatic; but then P.G. stops dead in his tracks and is silent for some time] . . .

41. Interviewer: Well. . .if you want *that* [the L.H. side of the equation] to look *sort of* like that [the R.H. side] . . .

42. [again interrupting] 'Cause you see, with it *in*, I don't *have* a quadratic, because the same term is in everything! [P.G. is referring to his written notation

$$\log x \left(\log x + 19 - \frac{x}{25}\right) = \qquad ,$$

which is the L.H. side of equation (3) (cf. Utterance 9). He is, of course, discussing the obstacles to making the L.H. side of (3) match the L.H. side of the quadratic formula:

$$ax^2 + bx + c = 0 .$$

P.G. would like to see

$$\underline{\qquad} (\log x)^2 + \underline{\qquad} (\log x) + \underline{\qquad} = 0 .]$$

I don't have any terms *without* it. [P.G. sounds almost angry. He is arguing that he has no input to match the constant term c in the L.H. side of the quadratic equation.[5]]

43. P.G. [continuing]: . . .and so it's *not* a quadratic! I don't *have* a constant! [His inflection indicates: 'and I would certainly

need one.' But, of course, he is wrong. It would be entirely possible for *c* to be zero!]

44. P.G. [continuing]: Is this one you know you can solve? [very demanding tone].

45. Interviewer: Unless I made a mistake, it is.

46. P.G.: [continuing; P.G. has maintained control of the discussion for some time now.] ...because that's a basic problem here. I mean, no matter what you say, with this *out* of here [i.e. with the 'log x' term factored out], I no longer have a quadratic...because I don't have a squared, and then a [P.G. is at a loss for words; he probably does not recall the phrase 'linear term', although he has heard it in class. Notice that he uses the adjective 'squared' as a noun, meaning 'squared term' or 'quadratic term']...

    Without this, it's not a quadratic, and then *with* this, it's *also* not a quadratic.
    [That is, neither

    $$(\log x) \ [\log x + 19 - \frac{x}{25}]$$

    nor

    $$(\log x)^2 + 19 (\log x) - \frac{x}{25} (\log x)$$

    can be made to match the form

    $$ax^2 + bx + c \quad .]$$

47. Interviewer: ...and as we said a few minutes ago, even if it *were* a quadratic, there'd still be a question of what to do next.

48. P.G.: Yeah, because both sides would have a value. [P.G. means that he would not have a *zero* on one side of the equals sign, as the form

    $$ax^2 + bx + c = 0$$

    does.]

49. [*Analysis*: In fact, P.G. knows that he can *add* the same thing to both sides of an equation, or subtract the same thing from each side. So, surely, he can *make* one side become zero. Has he forgotten this? No, as we see from his next few remarks, instead he is *rejecting* that possibility because he believes it

will disturb the correct pattern recognition that he has already (almost) carried out.

The *fact*, of course, is that no correct pattern match can be made until after one *does* shift some items from one side of the equals sign to the other. Hence we see P.G. stubbornly clinging to a frame retrieval and *partial* match, despite his 'inability' to *complete* the mapping of the input data into the retrieved frame.

Not only is he clinging to his choice of frame, *he is also reluctant to modify the partial mapping that he has worked out*. It would seem, then, that not only is a frame selection reluctantly modified, but when a mapping of input data into chosen frame is partially complete, this partial map is *also* vigorously defended.

One could analyze this, alternately, as an instance of premature tree-pruning. Presumably the desire to preserve work already completed sets larger inhibitory parameters on 'disruptive' branches in the tree of possible actions, so P.G. rejects as 'unpromising' the very steps that he really needs to take.]

50. P.G.   [continuing] . . .This side would have to be zero. [pause] . . .Which ain't gonna work, because that's *squared* $[(\frac{x}{50})^2]$ $-$ . . .umm. . . well. . .

I'm a little bit stymied. . . .cause I mean, I can start adding and subtracting terms from side to side, here . . .but as far as I can see, that ain't gonna simplify it. . . [The premature tree-pruning occurs at this point!] . . .I don't *have* any logs over here. . .

51. Interviewer: . . .Well. . .you've got really one clue. [The pressure of time is forcing the interviewer to intervene too much at this point.]

. . .if you had a quadratic expression here, just in x [indicating the R.H. side of the equation], and *here* [indicating the L.H. side]. . .

. . .as you said. . .you came *close* to having a quadratic expression, but one of the ways it *fails* − as you said − is in having a term in *both x and log x* . . .

Now, I think that might suggest something to you. . .if you think about what happens when you *square* expressions . . .namely, if I square A plus B [that is, compute $(A + B)^2$], I get not only an A^2 term and a B^2 term, but also a term 'two AB' [i.e. the term 2AB in the expression $A^2 + 2AB + B^2$] ...so, what does that suggest, when you get a term that seems to have. . .

52. P.G.   [interrupting] : Try and factor it?

53. Interviewer: Well, it seems to me to suggest that separating the logs from the x's is *not* a good idea, because the presence of this term here [the x log x term] seems to suggest that you had something like log x plus three x [(log x + 3x)], or something, which got squared [he means something like (log x + $3x)^2$]. And if you'd had a log x plus three x which got squared, you'd have a term in log x squared [i.e. $(\log x)^2$] − which you do − but you'd also have a term in x log x. . .

54. [long silence]

55. P.G.: Yeah, but I still don't see how that works, 'cause to have to have that, you'd have to have one term that does not have A in it. [P.G. is clearly matching against $(A + B)^2 = A^2 + 2AB + B^2$, and the meta-criterion he is using in evaluating possible mappings is in fact correct. Why is it leading him astray? Because, by accident, the terms have become arranged so that a (log x) term from the *linear* term is being grouped with two pieces of the quadratic term. P.G.'s analysis is focusing *only* on the quadratic term, and overlooking possible intermingling with parts of the linear term. That is in

$$r (A + B)^2 + s (A + B) + t = 0 \ ,$$

there will be terms in A or in B that don't come from the quadratic expression at all; what P.G. is dealing with might be called $r A^2 + 2r AB + s A$. He is *incorrectly interpreting* the very cues that *should* tell him to consider shifting some terms across the equals sign.]

56. P.G.   [continuing] : . . .and one term that does not have B in it, for that to be true.

   You can't *have* A in all three terms! You can't *have* B in all three terms! It doesn't work!

57. Interviewer [concerned that P.G. is still looking for a one-step solution] : Well, except that it might have been multiplied by an A or a B or something. . . [He is being deliberately vague, because he does not want to suggest the correct line of strategy.]

58. P.G.: Yeah, but at that point you've got to have. . .you've got to have, in fact, an A squared, at a minimum.

59. Interviewer: Right.
60. [*Analysis*: In later analysis of this interview, we've come to be very much impressed by the meta-analysis that P.G. carries on, in order to shape a correct mapping of the input data into the quadratic formula. He does a large *amount* of meta-analysis, and his criteria are excellent. None the less, the correct mapping in this problem continues to elude him.

    It is also noteworthy that as he becomes drawn more deeply into a thoughtful analysis of the problem, his language becomes more mature, and he switches to correct standard English. Evidently, his usual ungrammatical language is a pose, a facade that slips away when he becomes more deeply involved.]

61. P.G.: ...and you might have more... But you see, if I put *this* in... [We have been unable to determine the referent of 'this' — P.G. was writing nothing at this point, so he must have been referring to something he had in mind. There seems to be no way to determine what it was. (At the time, the interviewer could have asked, but unfortunately he did not do so.)]

62. Interviewer: Well, I didn't mean to mislead you.
    It's hard to say...
    In the first place, a term which isn't there, isn't something that you necessarily want to be surprised at right away...

63. P.G. [interrupting] : ...because you could always drop it in...

64. Interviewer: ...it *could* have cancelled out... It could have appeared in *two* places in the equation, and it might have cancelled out.

65. [silence]

66. P.G.: Look, what you're saying... It seems to me you're saying you should factor it... [pause] ...and get an A plus B term...

67. Interviewer [who felt that P.G. was tied too tightly to the idea of $(A + B)^2$] : Well, it seems to me that it says that you probably *shouldn't* separate the x and log x terms. Putting the logs on one side and the x's on the other really doesn't work, because you've got something [he means the x log x term] that suggest that they really should be together...

68. P.G.: Yeah, but you understand that for me to look at either of these two up there as independent — to look to factor that — looking at this side first [gesture indicates L.H. side] — I've got a *log* twice — which wouldn't be bad, 'cause one time

you'd have **AB** and the other time you'd have an **A** — but I don't find x^2 over 2,500, which I'd assume would then be x over 50, in either of *these* terms. [Note the TOP-DOWN processing — P.G. has a clear $(A + B)^2$ pattern in mind — and the excellent meta-analysis!]

69. Interviewer: ...but you *did* find another x over 50.
70. P.G. [interrupting emphatically] Over there! [as if this confirms his diagnosis].
71. Interviewer: over here [The R.H. side] ; the interviewer is *agreeing* with P.G., as his gestures indicate. Despite their choice of different words — 'here' and 'there' — they *are* agreeing on the *facts*. What P.G. wants to argue about is the *interpretation* of the facts. Do the facts imply that the two sides of the equation, as presently written, should be kept separate, or that they should be merged?

    Note that, at two earlier points in this interview, P.G. has referred to the general idea of 'putting like terms together' — and, by implication, 'keeping unlike terms apart'. Of course, the frame that deals with such matters has little use in the present problem, but it may be present, and may be impeding P.G.'s progress. Note also that 'spreading activation' or 'parameter adjusting' theories could deal with this phenomenon easily; the 'collecting like terms' idea has acquired somewhat elevated parameter values, and is marginally influential in P.G.'s thinking. If, as parameter-adjusting theories usually do, one assumes lateral inhibition [cf. Minsky, 1980], so that the activity of 'collecting like terms' inhibits alternatives, then the insistent stability of P.G.'s clinging to an incorrect interpretation becomes very unsurprising.]

72. P.G.: Over there! [argumentative tone of voice — but note that the argument is over what this should *mean*.]
73. Interviewer: ...well, nothing stops you from bringing that over [to the L.H. side].
74. P.G.: ...well, then again, I'm using that over *there* [on the R.H. side].
75. [*Analysis*: The reason for P.G.'s reluctance to disassemble that part of the mapping which he has already worked out now becomes clear: he believes that his partial mappings on each side of the equation, separately, are so valuable that he does not want to disrupt them. To help improve the mapping on

the L.H. side, he would be sacrificing the mapping on the R.H. side! Of course, both matches are imperfect, and cannot be separately improved. In fact, P.G. has hit a dead end, and *must* backtrack if he is to make any further progress.]

76. P.G.: ...at which point [said slowly and thoughtfully] ... [pause]... Here the change-over wrecks *this* quadratic... [i.e. improving the L.H. side of the equation damages the R.H. side, from P.G.'s pattern-matching perspective.]

77. Interviewer: You have already taken what I had thought would be the two hardest steps — namely rewriting $\log x^{19}$ as $19 \log x$, and rewriting $\log x^x$ as $x \log x$.

78. P.G.: I've also got nineteen $\log x$... I've got two 'nineteens'! [very excitedly!] That tells you something! [P.G. is referring to the terms $\frac{19x}{50}$ and $19 \log x$.] O-Kay! Let's get *those* together!

79. [*The rest of the story*: Left to his own devices, P.G. continued for a while in this same vein, but was unable to make substantial progress. That P.G.'s thinking *had* made gains was revealed just before the end of the interview. The interviewer suggested considering the form

$$\underline{\quad} (\quad)^2 + \underline{\quad} (\quad) + \underline{\quad} = 0 ,$$

and P.G. *instantly* identified the correct 'unit' as $(\log x - \frac{x}{50})$, after which he easily solved the problem.]

An Expert's Attempt at Solution

It is interesting to compare P.G.'s work with the effort of an adult expert, who started with one advantage that he immediately acknowledged: he suspected that the problem had been made up in a systematic way, and could be solved by 'untangling' some deliberate convolutions. He saw almost immediately the 'clue' term x log x, and hence wrote

$$(\log x)^2 + \frac{x^2}{2,500} - \frac{1}{25} x \log x + 19 \left(\log x - \frac{x}{50}\right) = {}^-34,$$

from which he easily completed the solution. Afterwards, he volunteered the suggestion that he had had a very large amount of experience with linear 'scale change and translation' changes of variables, as in

$$x_{new} = a\ x_{old} + b$$

$$y_{new} = c\ y_{old} + d\ ,$$

so that he was quite prepared for

$$(\log x - \frac{x}{50})^2\ .$$

Meta-analysis

In Chapter 17 we saw that a *representation* of *Wunderbar* was being built up — the 'building' was one process — at the same time that a second activity was taking place: the partially-completed representation was being subjected to the process of meta-analysis in terms of likely harmonic sequences (and perhaps other criteria). The same pair of processes was seen in the geometry example — a representation being constructed, while at the same time a meta-analysis was being carried out.

P.G.'s work on the equation, in the present chapter, showed this same duality. A mapping of the input data was being created — actually, *two* mappings were being created, one for each side of the equation (which turned out to be a poor strategy) — while at the same time P.G. was very actively carrying out a meta-analysis to guide his search. At one point, for example, he wanted to get a zero on one side of the equation. At various times he decided this could not be achieved. He wanted to 'collect like terms', but found obstacles. He sought 'constant terms', analogous to c in the quadratic formula, terms that 'did not contain A' or 'did not contain B'. He debated the damage that he might do to one side of the equation if he shifted terms to get a better mapping on the other side. He became aware of terms — e.g. '$\frac{x}{50}$', or '19', or 'log x' — that seemed to play special roles.

While the adult expert was less talkative, he was aware of noticing the term in 'x log x' and using it as a valuable clue to shape his strategy.

But an even more striking demonstration of meta-analysis is possible, thanks to Douglas Hofstadter and Michael Battista, as we see in the next section.

The MIU System

Hofstadter (1979) presents a mathematical system, too small to be useful in designing aircraft or anything like that, that none the less has great value as an object of study, because in many essential features it offers a precise parallel to the major mathematical systems. The system contains *one axiom*, which is a short string of symbols, only two symbols long. It may not look to you like the sort of thing that you expect an axiom to be, but here it is:

MI .

The system has four *rules of inference*, namely:

(1) From any string that ends in I, you may (if you wish) create a new string by attaching U to the end of the string. [E.g. from the axiom MI you could create the new string MIU, or from the string MIIII you could create the new string MIIIIU.]

(2) From any string of the form Mx, where x is a substring, you can form the new string Mxx. [E.g. from the string MIU you can produce the new string MIUIU.]

(3) If III occurs in a string, a new string can be formed by replacing the III by U. [Example: From MIIII one can create MUI, or, alternatively, MIU.]

(4) If UU occurs in a string, a new string can be formed by deleting it. [E.g. from MUUUII, one could create the new string MUII.]

Any reader who has not already read either Hofstadter's book, or Battista (1982), may be amazed at the form of this mathematical system. Every 'theorem' will be a string of symbols, in which every symbol will be either 'M' or 'I' or 'U'.

For illustration, we present the derivation of the theorem MUIIU. Here it is:

Statement	Reason
MI	Axiom
MII	Rule 2
MIIII	Rule 2
MUI	Rule 3
MUIU	Rule 1
MUIUUIU	Rule 2
MUIIU	Rule 4

Thus, the formal steps 'within the system' must follow the four explicit rules. The process of 'construction' we see unfolding before our eyes in the left-hand column: MI became MII, which became MIIII, which became MUI, and so on.

But we can also see the second process, the meta-analysis, at work. Consider this question: Is the string UI a 'theorem' in this system? That is to say, can we build the symbol string.

UI

by starting with MI (the only axiom we have!), and building by using the four 'inference' rules?

Clearly we cannot, because the desired string contains no 'M', we *must* start with a string that contains M (namely, the string 'MI'), and none of the four rules will ever result in the deletion of an M.

Now this line of argument does NOT lie *within* the system, and hence it is a meta-analysis in the sense that we use the term.

Is MU a theorem? No, as both Hofstadter and Battista prove; suppose we call the 'I-count' of any string the number of Is in the string. We must start with MI, which has I-count one. The proposed theorem has I-count zero. Now, using Rule 1 or Rule 4 will never change the I-count of a symbol string. Rule 3 reduces the I-count by exactly 3; hence, the use of Rule 3 could produce a string of I-count 0 only if one started with an I-count that was a multiple of 3.

Now Rule 2 can only *double* the I-count of a string. It cannot produce a string with an I-count of zero unless it starts with one. In the same way, it cannot produce a string with an I-count that is a multiple of 3 unless it starts with a string whose I-count (N, say) is a multiple of 3 (that is, if N is not a multiple of 3, then $2^k . N$ is not a multiple of 3).

Hence *no* string with an I-count of zero can be a theorem – and, in particular, MU cannot be.

As Battista remarks (p. 217), 'one interesting and useful fact about working with the MIU system is that it is . . . [easy to tell whether] one is mechanically deriving theorems within the system, . . . [or whether] one is deriving truths. . .about the system.'

'Deriving truths about the system' is included within what we are calling *meta-analysis*. But our category is broader than Hofstadter's, because we include *any* attempted analysis of this type whether correct or incorrect, whether 'logical' or 'heuristic' or 'common-sensical' or merely based upon a (possibly incorrect) evaluation of the possibilities. Thus, we include P.G.'s analysis that he cannot get a zero on one side of the equation, because this is how he *did* analyze the task, even though, of course, he was mistaken.

We shall see further examples in the next chapter.

Notes

1. The distinction between 'mathematical' variables and 'cognitive' variables deserves some further discussion. If one sees

$$(\text{some expression})^2 - 5 \ (\text{some expression}) + 6 = 0 \ ,$$

one might check that the expressions in both parentheses were the same, and if so pronounce this to be a quadratic equation. If one did this *without* assigning any special variable name to the expression, we would call this a *cognitive variable*. If, instead, one thought (or wrote) an equation giving the expression the name 'x' (or any other standard variable name), we would say we were dealing with a *mathematical variable*. Cognitive variables involve only recognition of familiarity — we realize we are seeing the same expression for a second or third time. This is often clear in the language of both students and experts, who may use phrases such as 'and over here I have the same thing squared'. In mathematics it is usually easy to *explain* a cognitive variable to an interviewer (or a reader) *as if it were a mathematical variable* — but in truth we suspect this is often a disguise, an easy means of achieving communication. What the person *thought* (and may have *said*) was 'I have this big mess here' . . . Consider, for example:

$$(\sinh^{-1} \sqrt{x^2 + a^2}) \, (\text{erf } x^2) - (\text{erf } x^2) \, (\sinh^{-1} \sqrt{x^2 + a^2}) = 0 \ .$$

Shifting cognitive variables around is probably very similar to shifting wooden blocks around when you are young, and may make use of some of the same information processing mechanisms.

2. P.G.'s use of the English language may require some explanation. He is a voracious reader, and hence has a large vocabulary, much of which he uses. He also has a determined disdain for the constraints of grammatical usage, and does not allow himself to be deflected from personal (or peer) preferences in linguistic matters.

3. One analyst, in working with this transcript (and with the audio-tape) said that he felt that P.G. had a small 'working space' in memory (*active* part of memory), and that things might get loaded, then used, then over-written by something else. The analyst proposed the metaphor of a man living in a tiny cabin and owning a very large number

of dogs, most of whom lived out-of-doors on long leashes. When P.G. needed to re-use an idea, he had to pull on the correct leash to get it back inside active memory — and sometimes the leashes got mixed up.

4. To use the language of the preceding note.

5. If P.G. had a meta-vocabulary for analyzing situations such as this — words like 'linear term', 'quadratic term', 'terms of degree n', etc., he might be able to deal with this pattern better. But these *words* would only be useful if they were strongly connected to a deeper knowledge of factoring, pattern-matching, and so on.

19 'RECOGNITION' PROBLEMS

There is one class of problems that deserves special attention, although it seems not to have been recognized in the problem-solving literature. This is the class of problems which no ordinary student can possibly solve except by *recognizing* the problem. For most school problems, one can 'work the problem out' if one is skillful enough and sufficiently determined. But for the present class of problems this is simply not the case. Unless you are Euler or von Neumann, you cannot 'work the problem out'. Your only hope is to recognize it.

The Derivative of the Log Function

As one instance, suppose that you know the following limit:

$$\lim_{h \to o} (1 + h)^{1/h} = e \doteq 2.718 \quad .$$

You can see the plausibility of this by checking with a hand-held calculator, and you can read the result in a book — but if you are truly an 'ordinary' student, you would not have been able to work this through for yourself. [Indeed, most 'ordinary' students consider it obvious that the limit

$$\lim_{h \to o} (1 + h)^{1/h}$$

must be one. This, of course, is quite false.]

Suppose, however, that we *do* know this limit, and suppose we are asked to find the derivative, $\frac{dy}{dx}$, if

$$y = \log x$$

We can get started by the ordinary sort of 'working our way through the problem':

$$\frac{dy}{dx} = \lim_{h \to o} \frac{f(x+h) - f(x)}{h}$$

$$= \lim_{h \to o} \frac{\log (x + h) - \log x}{h}$$

$$= \lim_{h \to o} \frac{1}{h} \ [\log \frac{x + h}{x}\ ]$$

$$= \lim_{h \to o} \frac{1}{h} \ \log (1 + \frac{h}{x})$$

$$= \lim_{h \to o} \log (1 + \frac{h}{x})^{1/h}$$

At this point we can go no further unless we recognize a similarity between

$$\lim_{h \to o} \log (1 + \frac{h}{x})^{1/h} \tag{1}$$

and

$$\lim_{h \to o} (1 + h)^{1/h} \tag{2}$$

But, of course, mere 'similarity' is not enough. If we are lucky enough to see the relevance of (2), and to retrieve it from memory, we still have the task of devising a precise mapping of the input data (1) into the assimilation paradigm (or 'frame') that we retrieved from memory and that is represented by (2).

Watching students attempt to create this mapping is instructive.

Nearly always students attempt to map the 'h' of (1) into the 'h' of (2). Of course! After all, the simplest mapping is a kind of identity mapping: map 1 into 1, '(' into '(', '+' into '+', and so on. But if you start out by mapping the 'h' of (1) into the 'h' of (2), then you need to do *something* about the 'x' in (1), and — as P.G. did in the preceding chapter — you run into a dead end. No suitable solution exists.

The value of good meta-language descriptors in this task is very clear. *If* we can look at (2) and see that we have[1] 'one plus something tiny' with a large exponent, and that the large exponent must be the *reciprocal* of the 'something tiny', then the task of constructing the mapping becomes easy. Looking, now, at (1), we see:

    (i) Something tiny added to one? Yes! (We assume $x > 0$.)
    (ii) Large exponent? Yes!
    (iii) Is exponent the reciprocal of the 'something tiny'? No!

So. . .our task is to cause (iii) to earn the answer 'Yes'. We can do this easily — for example, by using one of my favourite heuristics:

What would you *like* to see there? Well, then, *put* it there! (And, of course, you must then make it legal!)

So we take (1)

$$\lim_{h \to o} \log (1 + \frac{h}{x})^{1/h} \tag{1}$$

rewrite it as

$$\lim_{h \to o} \log (1 + \frac{h}{x})^{x/h} \tag{1'}$$

(which is NOT equal to (1)), then *make* it equal to (1) by rewriting it as

$$\lim_{h \to o} \frac{1}{x} \log (1 + \frac{h}{x})^{x/h} \quad, \tag{1''}$$

use continuity to rewrite it as

$$\frac{1}{x} \log [\lim_{h \to o} (1 + \frac{h}{x})^{x/h}] \quad, \tag{1'''}$$

and *now* we can map the troublesome part of (1''') into (2) by mapping the '$\frac{h}{x}$' of (1''') into the 'h' of (2).

A Limit Problem

Another 'recognition' problem is the following (from Anton, 1980, p. 571):

Find

$$\lim_{n \to \infty} a_n, \text{ if}$$

$$a_n = \sum_{k=0}^{n-1} \frac{1}{1+\dfrac{k}{n}} \cdot \frac{1}{n} . \tag{3}$$

Again, our only real hope is to recognize this problem. Have we ever seen anything like it?

The factor $\dfrac{1}{n}$ is a clue. This *could* be the base of each rectangle in an inscribed or circumscribed rectangular approximation to an area — that is, an upper or lower sum in the definition of the Riemann integral.

Can we concoct a function $f(x)$ such that (3) will be

$$\sum_{k=0}^{n-1} f(x_k) \cdot \triangle x \quad ,$$

and where

$$x_k = x_0 + k(\triangle x) \quad ?$$

Well, a good bet is to begin by taking $\triangle x = \dfrac{1}{n}$, not at all an uncommon choice. Then $x_0 = 1$, $x_k = 1 + (k/n)$, and if we choose $f(x)$ to be

$$f(x) = \frac{1}{x} \quad ,$$

we can put this all together and see if we have successfully mapped our present problem into some known piece of knowledge:

$$f(x_k) = \frac{1}{1+\dfrac{k}{n}}$$

$$f(x_k)\triangle x = \frac{1}{1+\dfrac{k}{n}} \cdot \frac{1}{n}$$

$$\sum_{k=0}^{n-1} \frac{1}{1+\dfrac{k}{n}} \cdot \frac{1}{n}$$

is the area of the circumscribed rectangular approximation shown schematically in Figure 19.1. This is an upper sum for

$$\int_1^2 \frac{dx}{x} \quad ,$$

so that

$$\lim_{n \to \infty} \sum_{k=0}^{n-1} \frac{1}{1 + \frac{k}{n}} \cdot \frac{1}{n} = \int_1^2 \frac{dx}{x} = \ln 2 \quad .$$

Figure 19.1: The problem in question can be recognized as an upper sum in the definition of a definite integral. The curve is

$$y = \frac{1}{x} \quad .$$

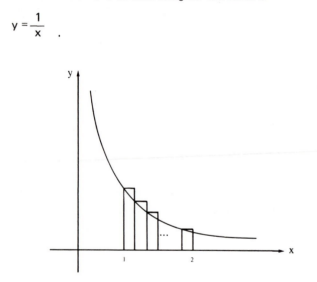

An Infinite Series

Here is yet another 'recognition' problem:
  Determine whether the infinite series

$$\sum_{k=1}^{\infty} k^2 \sin^2 \left(\frac{1}{k} \right) \tag{4}$$

converges or diverges.

Students often think of this first as being similar to

$$\sum_{k=1}^{\infty} k^2 \quad ,$$

except that the sine function may weight the terms of the sum in some weird way. This line of analysis is usually unproductive.

Think, instead, that we have the sin σ, where σ is a small number. Does *that* suggest anything?

If you are fortunate, this clue may lead you to retrieve

$$\lim_{\sigma \to 0} \frac{\sin \sigma}{\sigma} \quad , \tag{5}$$

which means dealing with a sine function, *divided* by its input. [Note the role of meta-language descriptors!]

Do we, in fact, *have* a sine function divided by its input? At first casual glance it may not seem so; but *multiplying*, after all, is really the same as dividing (i.e. multiplying by ½ is the same as dividing by 2, and so on). Hence we can rewrite (4) as:

$$\sum_{k=1}^{\infty} \frac{\sin^2 (\frac{1}{k})}{(\frac{1}{k})^2} \tag{4'}$$

The similarity between (4') and (5) is immediately apparent, and so the nth term in (4') is

$$a_n = \frac{\sin^2 (\frac{1}{n})}{(\frac{1}{n})^2} \quad , \tag{6}$$

and we are interested in

$$\lim_{n \to \infty} \frac{\sin^2 (\frac{1}{n})}{(\frac{1}{n})^2} = 1$$

which is after all, is really

$$\lim_{\sigma \to 0} \frac{\sin^2 \sigma}{\sigma^2} = [\lim_{\sigma \to 0} \frac{\sin \sigma}{\sigma}]^2 = 1 \quad .$$

Thus we have an infinite series $\Sigma\ a_n$ where $a_n \to 1$. Since the a_n do NOT go to zero, the series must diverge.

'Recognition' Problems

Are 'recognition' problems truly a different *kind* of problem? No, of course not. It is really a matter of degree. Any problem is impossible if you are unable to recognize its key terms. In that sense, *every* problem is a 'recognition' problem. But we have used the designation 'recognition problem' to call attention to certain problems where the student who knows the usual facts and techniques — such as arithmetic, the process for finding the derivative of a polynomial, the ability to solve quadratic equations, etc. — may run into difficulty because none of his most familiar tools may suffice to allow him to 'work through' the problem.

Recognition problems are interesting in the way that all *extremes* tend to be interesting: *in a recognition problem, nearly all of the effort must go into retrieving a correct 'assimilation paradigm', and devising a correct mapping into it.* Aside from this, the usual 'calculations' play only a minor role.

Note

1. In this analysis we focus on the 'mapping of h' problem. There is, to be sure, another question: the continuity of log x, which allows us to replace

$$\lim_{z \to z_0} \log z$$

by

$$\log (\lim_{z \to z_0} z) = \log z_0 \quad ,$$

but we do not discuss this in the present analysis.

20 WHAT *IS* 'PROBLEM SOLVING'?

In recent years attention has shifted away from rote learning, and focused instead on so-called 'problem solving'. In many ways this is a welcome development, because nearly every important use of mathematics does, indeed, involve problem solving.

But when one reads research on 'problem solving', one is often left at a loss to say *what* it is that is being studied.

We would argue that this uncertainty arises because few researchers have postulated any *explicit* model of the information processing that is presumed to be involved in the activity of 'problem solving'. In short, they do not tell us what they are studying! Once again, it is as if we had chemists working with orange powders and colorless liquids and no theory within which the substances, and their interactions, could be described.

In this chapter we postulate one model to describe what takes place during problem solving.

Two Simultaneous Processes

We postulate two large processes, essentially simultaneous. One focuses on the building of representations, and is highly specific and detailed. [In the example of proving theorems in Hofstadter's MIU system, this corresponds to the detailed two-column proofs used in Chapter 18.]

The second large process is a meta-analysis, employing meta-language descriptors, etc. [In the MIU example, this was used in proving that UI is not a theorem, nor is MU. In P.G.'s work, this meta-analysis was used when P.G. decided that he did not want to disturb his partial mapping of the right-hand side into the quadratic equation, and so on.]

Let us now look at each process separately.

Building Representations

In the first of the two processes, the representation building process, we postulate seven steps, as follows:

(1) Examining the problem (i.e. the 'input data') for cues or clues to guide retrieval.

(2) Retrieving from memory some knowledge representation structure ('KRS') that seems likely to be helpful.

(3) Gradually *building up a representation* for the problem (i.e. for the input data).

(4) Building up a representation for a matching piece of 'knowledge'.

(5) Making two mappings, the first of which maps (at least some of) the input data into *its* representation, and the second of which maps the problem representation into the 'knowledge' representation.

(6) Evaluating the adequacy of the constructions, retrievals and mappings, and accepting or rejecting portions of this work.

(7) Cycling back through steps 1 through 6, as often as necessary.

In Chapter 18, P.G., confronted with the equation

$$\frac{x^2}{2,500} + (\log x)^2 + \log x^{19} = \frac{1}{25} \log x^x + \frac{19x}{50} - 34,$$

saw some cue or clue that caused him to retrieve:

(i) the idea of grouping 'like terms' together;

(ii) the possibility of rewriting

$$\log x^{19}$$

as

$$19 \log x;$$

(iii) the possibility of rewriting

$$\log x^x$$

as

$$x \log x ;$$

and so on;

'Scales' or 'Grain Size'

Notice that these processes operate on several levels, just as computers typically do. At a 'large grain size' one may deal with *computing weekly earnings of workers.* At a more minute grain size, this will involve going through the list of hourly employees, retrieving their time-clock records, computing earnings, withholding taxes, etc. At what might be considered a yet finer grain size, this will involve various table look-ups, additions, multiplications, etc. At a still finer grain size, this involves binary code, 'borrows' and 'carries', finding addresses in the computer's memory, transfers from one register to another, and so on.

In rather a similar fashion, P.G.'s use of Steps 1 and 2 could be analyzed at a finer 'grain size', and involved a rapid use of all seven steps at this finer level of detail. But just as the human computer user may order the machine to compute the week's payroll, without thinking in terms of the binary code inside the hardware, we will try to stay with one grain size in analyzing P.G.'s — or anyone's — behavior. Sometimes this is impossible. Also, it is sometimes hard to be confident *which* grain size or 'level' one is using. None the less, to the extent that one can analyze performance by staying on a single level, this method offers a valuable simplicity.

In a first cycle through, the representations are typically incomplete, as we have seen in examples from geometry, music, algebra and calculus. In subsequent cycles through the steps, the representations are further elaborated.

Meta-analysis

Simultaneously with the actual construction of representations, another set of processes are taking place, the *meta-analyses* of the construction work, as when, in Chapter 18, P.G. decided 'I need a zero there', or 'I need a constant term there' [Lit.: 'a term without A' and 'a term without B'], or 'I must not destroy the partial mapping of the right-hand side of the equation by transferring terms across the equals sign in order to improve the mapping on the left-hand side'.

A frequent ingredient in this meta-analysis involves assessing your progress, or lack of progress, in carrying out a tree search. The analysis and planning may involve avoiding one branch because you would encounter problems that you do not know how to deal with, or delaying the exploration of some tree branch that involves very uncongenial computations. One adult of our acquaintance monitors his own tree-searching performance, and tries (usually unsuccessfully) to resist his usual tendency towards premature pruning away of some tree branches. As he says, 'I am a poor chess player because I see — "oh, if I play there, I'll lose the queen!" — and so, of course, I don't explore *that* branch any further. I don't look two or three steps further, and see that I could win by checkmating my opponent. As soon as I see trouble down some path, I retreat and avoid that path in the future.'

This is virtually a second (higher) level of meta-analysis; it is almost a meta-analysis of the (lower level) meta-analysis.

How Problem-solving Fails

Given this model, we can analyze instances of actual behavior to see where the process fails. Consider the common error of beginning students, in rewriting

$$\sqrt{x^2 + 2^2}$$

as

$$x + 2 \ .$$

This is clearly wrong. But where, precisely, did the process fail? (In fact, it may have had more merit than one first acknowledges!)

The operative cues are clearly the square root and the exponents.

At the meta-analysis level, these are considered, and seen to match in a useful way. 'Squaring and taking the square root are inverse processes.' Hence one 'cancels out' the squaring and root-taking operations, and writes

$$x + 2 \ .$$

Where the process has failed is in omitting those steps dealing with the construction of representations, the construction of mappings and the evaluation of what has been done.

If we take the 'inverse process' idea, we can represent this as

$$\sqrt{A^2} = A \ ,$$

provided $A > 0$. So here we have our *representation of relevant knowledge* (Step 4).

Now we must map the input data representation, which could be

$$\sqrt{x^2 + 2^2} \ , \tag{2}$$

into (1). If we are careful, we find that this cannot be done — so we avoid the error of writing

$$x + 2 \ .$$

Beginning students are not likely to be careful with (1), they may use an unsatisfactory representation for the problem – perhaps just

'it's some things you square, then you take the square root'

– which omits the essential structure of the problem, and they are likely to be equally vague in dealing with the essential mappings.

But compare this with a successful calculus student, asked to integrate

$$\int \frac{dx}{\sqrt{x^2 + 1}} , \tag{3}$$

who uses the 'what you *like* to see there' heuristic. Well, since I have to take a square root, what I'd like to see there would be a square. All right, then let's *put* a square there! How can I turn a *sum* of squares into a square? Do I know anything that does that?

Of course I do! The identity

$$\tan^2 \sigma + 1 = \sec^2 \sigma \tag{4}$$

does exactly that.

All right. I must match

$$x^2 + 1 \tag{5}$$

with the left-hand side of (4), which is easily done; let

$$x = \tan \sigma .$$

The next part of the activity is routine:

$$dx = \sec^2 \sigma \, d \sigma$$
$$x^2 + 1 = \tan^2 \sigma + 1 = \sec^2 \sigma$$
$$\frac{\sec^2 \sigma}{\sec \sigma} \, d \sigma = \int \sec\sigma \, d \sigma$$
$$= \ln | \sec \sigma + \tan \sigma | + C$$

(because of a nifty trick that we shall not discuss here), and so, finally (using another good trick)

$$\int \frac{dx}{\sqrt{x^2 + 1}} = \ln | \sqrt{x^2 + 1} + x | + c$$

This elegant bit of problem solving has more than a little in common with the beginner's error

$$\sqrt{x^2 + 2^2} = x + 2.$$

But, of course there are also some very important differences, including:

   (i)   the expert's better heuristics;

  (ii)   the expert's greater knowledge (including the identity
       $\tan^2 \sigma + 1 = \sec^2 \sigma$);

 (iii)   the expert's careful construction of detailed representations;

 (iv)   the expert's careful construction of legal mappings.

Comparisons

We would not be satisfied with the knowledge that Person A solved one — or many — problems more quickly, or more successfully than Person B did. Such knowledge strikes us as incomplete. We would want to know how, in terms of our postulated model (or of some other model), their performances were different.

21 THE 'PARADIGM' TEACHING STRATEGY

If one were to believe popular accounts, one might conclude that something known as 'the new mathematics' was created in the late 1950s and early 1960s, that it was tried in US schools, and that it failed disastrously.

This is all quite wrong.

In the 1950s and 1960s, *many* different school curricula were created – by Caleb Gattegno, by David Page, by Zoltan Dienes, by William Johntz, by Leonard Sealey, by UICSM, by the Madison Project, by Robert Karplus, by UMMaP, by SMSG, by ESS, by Patrick Suppes, by Layman Allen, by USMES, by Burt Kaufman, and by other groups and individuals. These programs were not all similar – some were mainly abstract, some used mainly concrete learning experiences; some stayed close to traditional content, some explored very different content; some dealt only with mathematics, some combined mathematics and science, some approached mathematics mainly *through* science; some assumed considerable rote learning, others assumed very little; some emphasized 'discovery learning', others used it little or not at all; some undertook extensive teacher education programs, some took an opposite route and sought to prepare so-called 'teacher-proof' material. Some focused on tiny pieces of knowledge, others emphasized learning more sizeable pieces of knowledge by having students undertake 'projects' of significant size (rather like PhD theses scaled down to be appropriate for fifth-graders). Some accelerated student progress, so as to fit at least two years of calculus into secondary schools, while other curricula retained the usual pace of American school mathematics. Some focused on academically-oriented students, some on the weaker students, and others on the full range of students.

How could so great a diversity of innovations have been lumped together and seen as a single new program?

Furthermore, the claim that these new curricula were widely implemented in US schools was equally misleading. Most schools experienced little or no change. Indeed, so small were the modifications of older curricula that scholarly reports speak of 'nullification by partial assimilation'.

Finally, did the new curricula fail? In those few schools where they were extensively and carefully implemented, the best of the new

311

curricula produced very pronounced *gains* in student performance. The fact is that they did *not* fail; on the contrary, they were markedly successful (cf. Hopkins, 1965; Dilworth, 1973).

Our concern here, however, is not primarily historical. Rather, we want to look closely at one innovative feature of some of these curricula, the so-called 'paradigm teaching strategy', which was not fully appreciated when it first appeared. Before defining this phrase, we give an example.

Introducing Negative Numbers

In a curriculum that is responsive to student initiatives, it is necessary to introduce negative numbers, perhaps as early as grade 2, and certainly by grade 4 or grade 5, in order to deal with student questions about 'What's over there?' [on the left of zero on the number line, or in the 2nd, 3rd and 4th quadrants in Cartesian co-ordinates], or what happens to $(\Box \times \Box) - (5 \times \Box) + 6$ when you put 2 into each $\Box$, thereby coming face to face with

$$4 - 10 = \underline{\hspace{1cm}} \quad .$$

A method for dealing with '4 - 10', devised by the Madison Project for use in Accra, Ghana, was subsequently extended for use everywhere, and is even the basis for some recent computer-delivered CAI lessons. The 'assimilation paradigm' in question uses a bag, partially filled with pebbles, and a pile of pebbles on the table. To mark a reference point, some student — Kwami, let's say, since this was first used in Accra — claps his hands. We put, say, 4 pebbles into the bag (getting them, of course, from the pile on the table).[1] To keep track, we write on the chalkboard

$$4 \quad .$$

Now we *remove* from the bag 10 pebbles, and write

$$4 - 10 \quad .$$

The questions, now, are these:
1. Are there *more* pebbles in the bag than there were when Kwami clapped his hands, or *less*?
     Answer: Less.[2]
2. How many less?
     Answer: 6 less.

We consequently write

$$4 - 10 = {}^-6 \quad ,$$

and read this as 'four minus ten is negative six'. The 'negative' tells us that there were fewer pebbles in the bag.

This activity – presented to a class essentially as we have described it here – was called the 'Pebbles-in-the-Bag' activity, and is an example of an *assimilation paradigm*. Using such activities was called the *paradigm teaching strategy*.

Before going on, it may be well for the reader to pause and ask what else could have been done, instead, as a means of introducing the idea

$$4 - 10 = {}^-6 \quad ?$$

Of course, one once used the ammeter on an automobile's instrument panel, labeled from $^-20$ to $^+20$ – but these ammeters largely disappeared from the dashboard around 1940 or so. Or one sometimes uses temperatures above and below zero (Fahrenheit, say) – but Accra, Ghana is on the equator. Or one sometimes uses double-entry bookkeeping, or the upwards and downwards movements of the prices of various stocks – but neither seemed appropriate for young children, whether in Africa or in Connecticut.

One could construct a set of ordered pairs

$$\big\{ (4, 10), (5, 11), (6, 12), (1, 7), (2, 8), \ldots \big\}$$

and give it the name $^-6$. But do children really know more about 'sets' and 'ordered pairs' and abstract definitions than they do about pebbles and bags of pebbles and piles of pebbles and 'putting' and 'taking'?

Here, of course, is the point. Abstract definitions are quite properly seen as a glory of modern mathematics, but they are NOT useful for the instruction of beginners, where one *must* build on things that the students already understand.

It is worth mentioning that the 'paradigm teaching strategy' was devised by *teachers*, and came from their feeling of the best way to communicate with children at the deepest possible level.[3] In 1960 the idea of creating 'assimilation paradigms' was not well received in many circles. Given the studies of recent years, however, it has become clearer that learning is primarily *metaphoric* – we build representations for new ideas by taking representations of familiar ideas and modifying them as necessary, and the ideas we start with often come from the earliest years of our lives (which is why Papert's 'turtle geometry' is so valuable in the early study of geometry). Hence, what was once an 'intuitive' choice by teachers could now be defended on more theoretical grounds. Children have extensive experience with, and therefore powerful representations for, such actions and situations as taller, shorter, distance, move, interchange (put block A where block B was, and block B where block A used to be), counting, before, after, put, take, give, inside (a bag or box or room or automobile, etc.), share, share equally, divide up, split up (as when some children go for ice cream and others do not), half, straight, level (horizontal), tilted (or 'not level'), perpendicular (although they may not know the *word*, they know the idea, as the drawings of even young children show clearly[4]), heavy, light, lift, carry . . . and so on.

In trials with thousands of children on three different continents and in many different cultures, the 'Pebbles-in-the-Bag' activity has proved a reliable way to introduce negative numbers to young children.

The Paradigm Teaching Strategy

What properties of the 'Pebbles-in-the-Bag' activity qualify it as an 'assimilation paradigm'?

First, *it involves ideas for which virtually all students have powerful representations*. For example, nearly every student knows that if you have a bag that is partially filled with pebbles, and if you then put two pebbles into it, it will have *more* pebbles in it than it had before you did that.

Second, *it is a reliably accurate 'isomorphic image'* for all operations of the form

$$A + B$$

or

$$A - B   ,$$

where A and B are positive integers (or 'counting numbers').

Third, as a result of the two preceding properties, it *tells a student how to deal with problems* such as $4 - 10 = {}^-6$. You do not need to remember how to deal with $4 - 10 = \underline{}$; the 'story' itself guides you to a solution. (We have seen some unsuccessful attempts at constructing assimilation paradigms where ambiguities, arbitrariness or randomness destroyed the value of the story as a clear and correct guide to action.)

Finally, *it is simple*. (We have also seen attempts that failed because the 'paradigm' was *more* complicated than the mathematical operations it was supposed to guide.)

The theory of representations presented in this book gives a clear explanation for the value of the 'paradigm teaching strategy'. The teacher is leading the student to use available representational devices to create a representation of the problem situation, and a representation of corresponding 'knowledge'. Because the latter *is* strong, the student knows how to proceed. He uses his knowledge of pebbles and bags and putting-things-into-bags in order to solve the mathematical problem. From the point of view of mental representations, there is very little mystery as to why the paradigm teaching strategy works so well.

When 'Abstract' Mathematics Isn't

Notice that nothing said in this chapter, or in this book, precludes the possibility of learning *abstract* mathematics at some later point in the student's life. After all, if students have extensive *experience* with mathematics, many matters that might seem 'abstract' to outsiders may seem comfortably *experience-based* to these particular students. Precisely this constitutes one of the main goals of the Madison Project curriculum. All important mathematics 'makes sense' — but more often than not one must have an appropriate experiential background in order to understand the challenge that is being faced, and the nature of an effective response. Education must provide the experience, not assume it.

Notes

1. A film, entitled 'A Lesson With Second Graders', shows how this so-called *Pebbles-in-the-Bag* activity is presented to elementary school children. The film can be obtained from the Study Group for Mathematical Behavior, P.O. Box 2095 — Station A, Champaign, Ill. 61820.
2. I concede that one school of thought would prefer to say 'fewer'. The underlying situation is that the older parts of the English language were created before one had a modern view of mathematics. To a mathematician, *all* numbers should, where feasible, be considered the same kind of thing. Mathematicians do not use '=' to denote equality of integers, and some other symbol to denote equality of rational

numbers, nor '+' for the addition of integers, and some other symbol for the addition of rational numbers. In counting, one finds irregularities from 1 to 20, but by the time they reached 20 most cultures saw the virtues of minimizing deviations (such as undeviginti). I think that, had a modern mathematical view prevailed, one would not have developed special language for different kinds of numbers. If ½ is less than ¾, then 3 is less than 4, and 3 pebbles are less than 4 pebbles. It is well known that the older parts of a language are the most irregular — witness 'I am', 'you are', 'he or she is'. Only later do people come to appreciate an abstract view that deals with many situations in a systematic and regular way, with the fewest possible exceptions, irregularities, deviations or special cases. Witness the modern introduction of the word *sibling*, and the urgent present need for something better than 'he or she' or '(s)he'. To a mathematician a straight line is a curve, though a curve with zero curvature, since it is clearly undesirable to single out zero (or lines) as special cases except in those instances where this happens to be appropriate. Hence I favor a single name for one quantity being smaller than some other, whatever the context or numbers involved.

3. Cf., for example, Robert B. Davis, *Discovery in Mathematics: A Text for Teachers*, Cuisenaire Company of America, New Rochelle, NY, 1980.

4. Cf., e.g., Brearley and Hitchfield, 1969, p. 81 and elsewhere.

22 SOME CLASSICAL ERRORS

Some student errors occur so commonly that they deserve to be called 'classical'. In this chapter we consider a few of these, and how they can be explained by cognitive theory.

Errors Considered Earlier

Binary Reversions

We have seen, in Chapter 7, examples such as

$$4 \times 4 \rightarrow 8.$$

(The arrow is used here to indicate a claimed equivalent or 'answer'. Use of an equals sign, =, would seem unjustified. We usually prefer to reserve the 'equals' sign for its proper mathematical meaning. Very often the arrow indicates an attempted re-writing according to some rule or procedure, as in $x(y + z) \rightarrow xy + z$, an example we shall consider below.)

Another example of a similar nature is

$$2^3 \rightarrow 6 \ .$$

These were explained as *binary reversions*. A well-established frame, learned earlier, is ordinarily elicited by a visually-similar cue. Since the eliciting cues are not sharply distinguished, following Feigenbaum's Law of Minimal Necessary Discrimination, confusion results, and the well-established frame is preferred to a tentative new one.

Language-induced Errors

Inaccuracies or ambiguities in natural language descriptions can lead to errors. Beginning students who read

$$2x - x$$

as 'two x, take away x', often write the answer as 2:

$$2x - x \rightarrow 2.$$

The language can surely be heard to suggest this (Chapter 14). The claim that the sequence

$$1, 1, 1, \ \ldots$$

diverges 'because the terms are not getting closer to anything' (Chapter

15) is another example of beginners being led astray by their use of natural language.

Frame-retrieval Errors

Errors such as

$$
\begin{array}{r}
131 \\
+ \ 26 \\
\hline
357
\end{array}
$$

(Jamesine Friend; see Chapter 8), or the Clement/Rosnick error

$$6S = P$$

(also Chapter 8), have been analyzed as the retrieval of an incorrectly-chosen frame, where the chosen frame functions in a useful way in other situations, but should *not* have been used in the present context, or as the retrieval of a frame that does not quite fit the present task at hand (as, for instance, the way the most basic binary operation frame *demands* two inputs), perhaps confounded by the Brown-Matz-Van Lehn Law that the higher level goals MUST be achieved if at all possible, so that constraints may be relaxed in order to satisfy these high level goals (Chapter 8).

Representation Errors

Representations are not usually perfect, and usually are not meant to be. After all, the power of abstraction comes from discarding some intellectual baggage that was, hopefully, not entirely essential. But working with imperfect representations necessarily involves hazards. When a rolling wheel is represented as if it were rolling along a line, but in fact it is rolling around the outside of a circle, important error can easily result, as we saw in Chapter 15. And if an abbreviated 'key feature representation' – which necessarily omits *some* features of the thing which it represents – turns out to omit one or more features that are crucial for the present task at hand, the process of reconstructing a fuller representation may not include these features either, with the result, as Young has shown in his analysis of the 'pyramids' problem, that the task cannot be carried out successfully (Chapter 15).

Other Errors

Of course, *any* step in the postulated mechanisms is a potential candidate for malfunctioning, so that in principle a very large variety of errors are possible, in addition to those we have considered explicitly. The goal in any case is to match up any observed error with some failure in mental information processing that would have caused such an error. This appears to be possible in a very large number of cases, and the results reveal a very great orderliness to errors – even, in many cases, a kind of 'reasonableness' to them, just as it is 'reasonable' to expect that a beam will fail when it is severely overloaded. This does not mean that the failure is to be ignored – a wrong outcome is unequivocally wrong – but one can often see why, under the circumstances, it *had* to happen.

Incomplete or Inadequate Frames

In Davis[5], we report three interview/observation sessions with Peter, a college sophomore studying the use of convergence tests for infinite series. In this work, one commonly encounters expressions such as

$$E(k) = \frac{2^k (k + 1)}{k!} \quad , \tag{1}$$

or

$$G(k) = \frac{k^k (k + 1)!}{(k + 1)^{k + 1} k!} \quad , \tag{2}$$

and so on.

Where do these terms come from? Unfortunately, there are several possibilities, and one needs to be careful to separate them in one's mind. $E(k)$, or $G(k)$, or other expressions of this type may be:

   (i)   the kth term of the series;
  (ii) the ratio needed for the ratio test;
 (iii) the kth root needed for the root test;

or any of several other possibilities. How one deals with $E(k)$ or $G(k)$ depends upon which of these it is. One may want to take the limits as k increases towards infinity, or perhaps not. If a limit r exists, one may want to compare it with 1 (i.e. is $r = 1$, $r > 1$ or $r < 1$?), one may want to accept any non-zero finite value, or one may need only to know that the limit is 0.

A student who had learned this topic well would have built up in his or her mind a sizeable knowledge representation structure, or frame, to deal with such questions. If we cannot actually describe this frame, we can at least suggest it via the following 'questionnaire' metaphor: once activated, the frame will seek inputs for certain key frame variables. In reality, a typical student will obtain these inputs by glancing at what he or she has written on the paper, or perhaps by running over the problem in memory. But to make this process more graphic, *imagine* that input values are obtained by sending out a written questionnaire. What kinds of questions would appear on this questionnaire? For our well-prepared student it would look something like this:

k^{th} term of series: _____

series, in sigma notation: _____

series, written without sigma notation: _____

n^{th} partial sum: _____

sequence of nth partial sums: _____

Is it obvious that this series converges or diverges?   Yes   No

    Which? _____

    How do you know? _____

Clues that suggest which test to apply: _____

_____

_____

_____

Test chosen for trial: _____

Fill in the following where appropriate:

    ratio $\dfrac{U_{k+1}}{U_k} =$ _____

    $\lim\limits_{k \to \infty} \dfrac{U_{k+1}}{U_k} =$ _____

Series chosen for comparison: _____

    Does this comparison series converge? _____ diverge? _____

$\dfrac{U_k}{a_k} =$ _____

k^{th} root $\sqrt[k]{U_k} =$ _____

and so on.

While this 'written questionnaire' is purely imaginary, it *does* contain the *kind* of information that a good student will want to know. Notice that we can get reasonable estimates of the input data that a student is seeking, if we observe what that student writes, what he asks, and so on.

Now Peter, who was having great difficulty with this chapter in the book, clearly had no such structure or representation in mind. His representation for the topic of 'convergence of infinite series' was extremely fragmentary, and – to continue with our 'questionnaire' metaphor – his input search corresponded to a questionnaire that looked more like this:

Expression: _____

Ratio of f (k + 1) to f(k): _____

Other expression: _____

And one more expression, if any: _____

But this, of course, meant that Peter never really knew whether he wanted

$$E(k)$$

or

$$\lim_{k \to \infty} E(k) \quad .$$

Whichever it was, he didn't know whether he needed to compare it with 1, or with 0, or do something else with it. We would say that Peter had never synthesized an adequate knowledge representation structure, in his mind, for the topic of convergence of infinite series.

Part of Peter's difficulty apparently stemmed from his erroneous assumptions about how one studies mathematics. In English courses, and in a course on the anthropological study of American Indians, Peter needed only to read a novel, or a chapter, in order to have its contents stored clearly in his memory and readily available for retrieval. He believed he could deal with mathematics in this same way, but in fact he could not. The result of this approach was a failure to create adequate mental representations of key topics in mathematics. Peter's frames tended to be sketchy and incomplete. (For details, see Davis, note 5.)

Rules That Make Rules

Matz (1980) introduces the idea of 'rules that make rules', and uses this conceptualization to explain an interesting phenomenon.

Students, usually at the ninth-grade level (though younger in our study), who are beginning to learn how to solve quadratic equations by the method of factoring, are taught that when zero is obtained as the result of a multiplication

$$A \cdot B = 0 \quad ,$$

we have a very special situation: *we actually know the value of one of the factors A and B.* Specifically, one of them *must be zero.* (This is sometimes called the *Zero Product Principle.*) No similar result holds for any other value of the product. Thus, if

$$A \cdot B = 32 \quad ,$$

perhaps $A = 16$ and $B = 2$, or perhaps $B = 64$ and $A = \frac{1}{2}$, or perhaps $A = {}^-32$ and $B = {}^-1$, and so on. We know neither the value of A nor the value of B. But if

$$A \cdot B = 0 \quad ,$$

the situation is entirely different; either $A = 0$ or $B = 0$ (or, possibly, both are zero).

Our beginning students may seem to understand all of this, quite well. On this basis they learn to solve

$$(x - 2)(x - 3) = 0$$

by saying:

'Either $x - 2 = 0$, in which case $x = 2$, or else $x - 3 = 0$, in which case $x = 3$.'

Unfortunately, with dismal regularity, a large proportion of our beginning students also solve

$$x^2 - 5x + 6 = 2$$

by saying:

'By factoring, we get $(x - 3)(x - 2) = 2$. Therefore, either $x - 3 = 2$, in which case $x = 5$, or else $x - 2 = 2$, in which case $x = 4$.'

What is perhaps most remarkable about this error is that it recurs again and again. A student may make it, may be shown the error, may correct it . . . but then, quite soon, he or she goes back to making this same error. Why is this mistake so hard to eradicate?

Because, Matz says, *it is continually being recreated*. If we speak of axioms and theorems at the level of the 'Zero Product Principle' as *surface-level rules*, then Matz postulates a 'deeper' level of rules that function to *create* 'surface-level rules'. Clearly, in order for anyone to learn arithmetic, there must be a deeper-level rule that says 'the specific numbers don't count — you could use other numbers'. Without such a rule, a person who was taught how to add

$$\begin{array}{r} 53 \\ + 21 \\ \hline \end{array}$$

would be unable to add

$$\begin{array}{r} 54 \\ + 22 \\ \hline \end{array} \quad ,$$

or

$$\begin{array}{r} 71 \\ + 14 \\ \hline \end{array} \quad ,$$

or *any* sum other than $53 + 21$. Clearly, it does not work like that — people *can* learn how to add, even if the numbers are some they have never seen before. Have *you* ever seen the number 63,971 before? Probably not — but you could cope with it in an addition problem!

Indeed, when a student is taught to solve

$$(x - 2)(x - 3) = 0 \quad ,$$

the teacher surely expects that the student *will* be able to solve

$$(x - 7)(x - 5) = 0 \quad .$$

Hence, in

$$(x - a)(x - b) = c \quad ,$$

it really does NOT matter what the integer value of *a* is, nor of *b*. But *c* does matter!

This is probably the first important case the students have met where the specific identity of a number played such an obvious, crucial role.

Now, it is the common pattern of any rule to *over-generalize* at first. Only with experience and refinements are appropriate constraints brought into play.

So — what *should* we expect?

The rule that 'the specific identity of the numbers doesn't matter' is surely there.

It should be expected to over-generalize.

Hence, it not only goes from

$$[(x - 2)(x - 3) = 0] \Rightarrow (x - 2 = 0) \lor (x - 3 = 0)$$

to the desired generalization

'For all *a* and all *b*,
$$[(x - a)(x - b) = 0] \Rightarrow (x - a = 0) \lor (x - b = 0)'$$

but goes *beyond* this, to the incorrect generalization

'For all *a*, all *b*, and all *c*,
$$[(x - a)(x - b) = c] \Rightarrow (x - a = c) \lor (x - b = c)',$$

the error *should* be a persistent one, and it is!

It is evidence in support of Matz's interpretation that students make the error of writing

$$x^2 - 10x + 21 = 12$$
$$(x - 7)(x - 3) = 12$$

Either

$$x - 7 = 12$$

or else

$$x - 3 = 12,$$

whereas they do NOT make the error of factoring the 12, and obtaining answers such as

Either

$$x - 7 = 6$$

or

$$x - 3 = 2.$$

Marcia's Subtraction

Davis and McKnight (1980) report a sequence of interviews with a third-grade girl named Marcia. At the first interview it becomes clear that Marcia has learned the usual subtraction algorithm very well, and uses it reliably, with one exception: if a problem involves 'borrowing across zeros', Marcia gets it wrong *in a very systematic way*:

$$
\begin{array}{r}
7{,}002 \\
-25 \\
\hline
\end{array}
$$

$$
\begin{array}{r}
{}^{6}\!\cancel{7}{,}00\overset{1}{\cancel{2}} \\
-25 \\
\hline
\end{array}
$$

$$
\begin{array}{r}
{}^{6}\!\cancel{7}{,}00\overset{1}{\cancel{2}} \\
-25 \\
\hline
7
\end{array}
$$

$$
\begin{array}{r}
{}^{5}\!\overset{6}{\cancel{\cancel{7}}}{,}\overset{1}{\cancel{0}}\overset{1}{\cancel{0}}\overset{1}{\cancel{2}} \\
-25 \\
\hline
7
\end{array}
$$

$$
\begin{array}{r}
{}^{5}\!\overset{6}{\cancel{\cancel{7}}}{,}\overset{1}{\cancel{0}}\overset{1}{\cancel{0}}\overset{1}{\cancel{2}} \\
-25 \\
\hline
87
\end{array}
$$

$$
\begin{array}{r}
{}^{5}\!\overset{6}{\cancel{\cancel{7}}}{,}\overset{1}{\cancel{0}}\overset{1}{\cancel{0}}\overset{1}{\cancel{2}} \\
-25 \\
\hline
5{,}087
\end{array}
$$

In short, her version of the subtraction algorithm might be described as: 'when necessary, borrow from the nearest non-zero term on the left; decrement it by one, and add 10 in the column where you are working'.

This algorithm is wrong *only* in the inclusion of the restriction

'non-zero'.

Of course, if the problem does not involve zeros, there is no difference between Marcia's algorithm and the correct algorithm.

Note that we do *not* say that Marcia would herself give this description of her algorithm. This description comes from adult observers who studied what, exactly, Marcia did. Marcia herself had no articulate explicit description of her algorithm — she merely *used* it, and used it consistently.

That was what Marcia *did*.

Now. . .how would one describe this in cognitive terms?

There is one description that does not presuppose much theory. From observation, it is clear that someone can behave in a certain way *because they have memorized a rule which they are following* — or, alternatively, they can behave in a certain way because they know from experience that this is an effective or appropriate way to behave. The first mode of behavior is usually called *rote*, the second is usually considered *meaningful* or *experience-based*.

Marcia, it turned out, was familiar with Dienes MAB blocks (cf. Chapter 2), and could represent a numeral — 2,375, say — as an array of MAB blocks [the correct representaation would be 2 blocks, 3 flats, 7 longs and 5 units]. However, she did *not* relate these representations to subtraction. On the contrary, 'subtraction', for Marcia, was the following of a rote rule. In the Madison Project curriculum, students deal *first* with actual arrays of blocks, and carry out addition and subtraction with the actual peices of wood. They later learn to keep a written record of these transactions, this written record is gradually refined, and it ultimately becomes the usual subtraction algorithm.

In Marcia's school, although students learned about MAB blocks, the algorithms themselves continued to be taught as rote rules.

Does it make any difference?

Definitely! Had Marcia learned the 'record-keeping' approach, she would have realized that the 'borrowing'

$$\overset{\scriptstyle 6}{\cancel{7}},00\overset{\scriptstyle 1}{\cancel{2}}$$

makes no sense at all in terms of the blocks. You have traded one large BLOCK (actually consisting of 1,000 units) for ten tiny UNITS. This would *look* wrong and *feel* wrong, because the MAB blocks are arranged so that, in a fair trade, volume is conserved and mass is conserved.

But, of course, in using a rote rule one has only the rule itself as a guide. The only question is: have I followed the rule carefully? But, as we have seen, minor changes in the way a rule is stated — changes so seemingly unimportant that they can pass unnoticed by most students — can in fact alter the outcome in a major way.

Marcia clearly believed she had followed the rule correctly. (The transcript of the interview — presented in its entirety in Davis and McKnight, 1980 — makes Marcia's confidence quite evident.) Since no *meaning* was being applied, she had no other criterion to apply.

From a deeper cognitive point of view, one can relate her behavior to the postulated division of memory into an 'abstract' or 'token' memory, and a 'whole-text' memory (cf. Chapter 5). The postulated distinction was this: a fairly complete and detailed memory record for a procedure or an experience (or for anything else) may be stored in the *whole-text* portion of memory. Because available cognitive work space is limited, loading whole-text representations can be undesirable — they occupy too much of the *work-space* memory, excluding (or erasing!) other needed information. One way to deal with this is to match important items in whole-text memory with drastically-abbreviated representations for this same item, and to store these short 'summary' forms in the 'abstract' section of memory. Connections between the two are, of course, maintained, so that whenever a 'summary' needs to be expanded, its whole-text version is available and can easily be retrieved.

If Marcia had learned the subtraction algorithm as a record-keeping device to record transactions with the actual MAB blocks, the algorithm itself would be a kind of 'summary' version, *attached to a whole-text version*.[1] The interviewer could have activated this association, Marcia could have retrieved the 'whole-text' record of experiences with MAB blocks, and the silliness of trading one large BLOCK for ten tiny UNITS would have been apparent.

The remedy would also have been apparent. One large BLOCK should be traded for ten FLATS — this would *look* fair and it would *feel* fair (and it would *be* fair — each flat contains 100 units):

$$\overset{6}{\overset{|}{\cancel{7}},}002 \qquad .$$

Now, that having been done, *one* FLAT could be traded for ten LONGS:

$$\overset{9}{\overset{6}{\overset{|}{\cancel{7}},}}\cancel{0}02 \qquad .$$

Finally, one of these newly-acquired LONGS could be traded for ten more UNITS:

$$\overset{99}{\overset{6}{\overset{|||}{\cancel{7}},}}\cancel{00}2 \qquad .$$

The subtraction problem is now easily completed:

$$\begin{array}{r} 6,977 \end{array}$$

A Later Interview With Marcia

The fact of Marcia's errors in subtracting when zeros were involved (as in the example above) was communicated to Marcia's teacher, who sought to provide remediation. The remediation, however, was on a rote or abstract level. Specifically, Marcia was told that, when she had a '700', as in

$$7,002 \quad ,$$

it was better to deal with the 700 as a single number, and decrement *it* by one:

$$700 - 1 = 699,$$

so:

$$\begin{array}{r} 7,002 \\ - \quad 25 \\ \hline \end{array}$$

becomes

$$\begin{array}{r} 699\,_1 \\ 7,00\!\!\!/2 \\ - \quad 25 \\ \hline \end{array}$$

after which the rest is easy.

In fact, this did not work. When asked to subtract

$$\begin{array}{r} 7,002 \\ - \quad 28 \\ \hline \end{array} \quad ,$$

Marcia used the 'treat 700 as a single unit' approach, and thus got the correct answer.

However, Marcia didn't believe it! Later in the interview it was revealed that Marcia thought her *original* (erroneous) method was correct, and believed that the new $700 - 1 = 699$ approach was some kind of fraudulent (but diplomatic) concession to adult authority and inexplicable adult idiosyncrasy. After Marcia had calculated

$$
\begin{array}{r}
699 \\
\cancel{7,00}\,1\!2 \\
- \quad 28 \\
\hline
6,974
\end{array}
$$

she was told that some children solved this problem incorrectly, by writing

$$
\begin{array}{r}
5 \\
6 \quad 11 \\
\cancel{7,00}\,2 \\
- \quad 28 \\
\hline
5,084
\end{array}
$$

Marcia was asked how she could help these children to get the correct answer. For an interval, Marcia maintained a thoughtful silence, then quietly said, 'They aren't really wrong. You shouldn't change the way they are doing it.'[2]

This phenomenon, of trying to change the knowledge representation structures in someone's mind by *telling* them something, appears time and time again in school mathematics. The knowledge representation structures usually remain unchanged (although there may be a *temporary* modification of *superficial behavior,* not unlike Galileo's alleged 'conversion' to an earth-centered astronomy).

The Epistemological Aspect of Marcia's Belief

Had Marcia been able to relate her subtraction algorithm to the physical, tangible, experiential reality of transactions with MAB blocks, she would have seen her error, and would have seen how to correct it. The proper trade for one BLOCK is clear, if one has the wooden pieces in mind (or even in one's hands).

The school curriculum, however, did not build on *meaning* and *experience.* It did not treat mathematical symbols as mere symbols, and asked students to be mindful of the actual *things* which the symbols denote.

Hence Marcia was left with only a rote rule to follow. In this situation, Marcia was further handicapped by her notion of what actually constitutes a *single, self-consistent rule.* This is a confusion that many students face. For example, having learned the *definitions* that

$$
\begin{aligned}
2! &= 2 \cdot 1 \\
3! &= 3 \cdot 2 \cdot 1 \\
4! &= 4 \cdot 3 \cdot 2 \cdot 1 \quad,
\end{aligned}
$$

they believe they now know *one complete, self-consistent rule*. That 6! is defined as

$$6! = 6 \cdot 5 \cdot 4 \cdot 3 \cdot 2 \cdot 1$$

seems consistent with this rule, and they accept it. Even the definition of 1! as

$$1! = 1$$

seems to fit.

When, however, they are told that the definition of 0! is

$$0! = 1 \quad ,$$

students object. This is NOT consistent with the pattern!

But it *is* consistent with the definition; more precisely, n! for an integer $n \geqslant 0$, is really defined like this:

$$1! = 1$$
$$\text{For } n > 1, \quad n! = n \; [(n - 1)!]$$
$$0! = 1.$$

This, taken together, is *one* single, self-consistent definition — but many students at first find this hard to accept. It does not match their idea of *one* definition.

The same problem arises with a function $y = f(x)$ defined as:

For $\quad |x| < \dfrac{\pi}{2}$, $\quad y = \dfrac{2}{\pi} x$.

For $\quad |x| \geqslant \dfrac{\pi}{2}$, $\quad y = \sin x$.

This is *one* function; it is, in mathematically-meaningful terms, one single 'rule'. But beginning students do not see it this way.

The fact is, if I define $f(n)$ for $n = 1, 2, 3, \ldots$, I have NOT defined $f(n)$ for $n = 0$, and — since no previous definition has been given — I am *logically* free to define $f(n)$ any way I like. How I *ought* to define it, to make $f(n)$ maximally useful, depends upon the underlying structure of the relevant mathematics. The beginning students err in thinking that one builds mathematics by reflecting transparent superficial 'patterns'. This is wrong. One builds mathematics by identifying and revealing fundamental 'patterns' that often, like mineral riches and petroleum, lie hidden deep beneath the surface.

The Distributive-law Error

Finally, one of the most common errors in mathematics. Asked to rewrite x (y + z), many beginning students write

$$x (y + z) \rightarrow xy + z \quad .$$

This is, of course, wrong, the correct re-writing being

$$x (y + z) \rightarrow xy + xz \quad .$$

Even after being 'corrected', students often continue to make this error.

Matz (1980) has conjectured that, for some students, this may be a *control* error. They may just lose track of the algorithm they are trying to use. A metaphor may make this clearer.

Control Errors

A person making *Coquilles Saint Jacques*, an elegant French way to serve deep-sea scallops, may be cooking mushrooms in butter, grating cheese, separating eggs, parboiling or steaming scallops, melting butter and mixing in flour, scalding some cream with onions, clove and bay leaves, then adding the scalded cream to the butter and flour, removing this from the heat and adding egg yolks, adding wine, stirring this mixture over a hot flame, adding the grated cheese, adding the scallops, adding the mushrooms, filling shells with this mixture, topping with bread crumbs and cheese, and briefly putting the filled shells under a broiler.

I have left out one or two subtleties, in the interest of greater simplicity.

While each of these operations is being performed, many of them simultaneously, the person doing the cooking must somehow keep track of all of these 'sub-assemblies'. To lose track may mean finding yourself needing to add cheese which should have been grated, but wasn't, or needing to add cream that should have been scalded, but wasn't. If you didn't get the onions sliced before you needed them, that may mean a delay, and the scallops may get overcooked, or may get cold. And if, when you remove the shells from the broiler, you still have the egg yolks left over, this is not a bonus, it is a mistake.

Keeping track of all of these sub-assemblies is an example of a *control* task. The same sort of thing must be done, internally, by a computer as it carries out some complex task that involves many sub-assemblies (and computer tasks often get down to sub-sub-sub-. . .-sub-assemblies for a *very* large number of 'subs').

Analysis of the information-processing tasks that the human mind performs shows that the mind, too, must have internal mechanisms for 'keeping track of where we are', for making sure that we do not 'lose our place' as we work through a complex task.

As Matz (1980) points out, 'control' errors may show up in mistakes such as

$$x(y + z) \rightarrow xy + z$$

(where we are using the arrow to indicate an attempted rewriting – in this case, a rewriting that intended to make use of the distributive law, but did so incorrectly). Two sub-assemblies were required, xy and (separately) xz, after which they should have been combined in a final assembly.

$$(xy) + (xz) \quad .$$

But in fact there are sub-sub-assemblies, so that the actions, at a finer level of detail, would look more like this:

observe parentheses and other structural features
recognize the task and lay out a plan
locate x, see that it is to be multiplied by something
find the something (Danger Spot **A**)
multiply
find the next operation (Danger Spot **B**)
carry it out
continue finding the next operation, and carrying it out, until there
    aren't any more operations that need to be performed.

The internal information processing in a student's mind is not entirely unlike our busy chef; many steps must be taken, various partial results must be stored until some larger assembly is ready to make use of them, *where* they are stored must be recorded in some fashion, the next step must be identified and executed, and so on. The internal processor may, like the chef, lose track of some step or some ingredient.

But there are reasons for suspecting that the incorrect writing

$$x(y + z) \rightarrow xy + z$$

may not be best conceptualized as a control error in general terms. It is not usually seen as a result of cognitive overloading, but instead is mainly an error made by beginners. General control errors are usually a part of behavior – such as distractability – when the priorities in our information processing are under stress. But our present error is more often seen as one made by beginners. In the next section we consider an alternative explanation of this distributive-law error.

A Defective Frame

Suppose, instead, that the learner has not yet synthesized an adequate mental representation for this piece of knowledge. Consider the sub-sub-assemblies listed in the preceding section. The third and fourth sub-assemblies involve noticing that x is 'to be multiplied by something', and *finding* that 'something'. We know that, in general, *beginners work with very sketchy descriptions of cognitive processing steps and cognitive entities*. If one is working with a vague specification of that 'something', when one looks at the symbol string

   $x (y + z)$

one finds

   x

then

   $x ($

(and thinks: 'Ah, yes! A parenthesis! In algebra that means multiply!') and then finds

   $x (y$,

so that, evidently, x is to be multiplied by y. So one writes

   xy .

Now, what is to be done next? Looking one finds

   $x (y +$,

so that, evidently, something is to be *added*. What? Looking at the symbol string, one finds that z is to be added. Therefore, one writes

   $xy + z$.

Now, what is to be done? Looking at the symbol string, one sees that there is nothing else to be done. Therefore, stop.

The preceding analysis follows the general pattern of language learning suggested by Selfridge (1982), Baker and McCarthy (1981), Berwick (1977), and others.

There is an alternative to interpreting a symbol string sequentially, one entry at a time. This alternative is to pattern-match the entire string against a known pattern stored in memory. (This parallels, among many other things, the distinction between 'phonics' and 'sight recognition' in reading English words and sentences. Do you 'sound it out', or do you 'just know'?)

But, for a student to be able to deal with $x(y + z) = xy + xz$ by pattern-matching, *there has to be a memorized pattern that this input can match*. For a beginner, there may not be.

In the next section we see a method devised by Young to help beginning students synthesise an appropriate memorized frame, so that pattern-matching becomes possible.

Young's Vector Approach

Young (1981a) hypothesized that the distributive law itself, by its nature, is difficult for beginners to assimilate. It is a poor foundation on which to build a mental representation.

Could there be a better foundation?

Young decided that a 'concrete' or 'experiential' introduction might be easier to design for the concept of *vectors* than for the distributive law itself, because the distributive law has all kinds of non-symmetries, whereas symmetry or parallel processing is the very essence of vectors. If, say, I have a vector

$$\vec{i} + \vec{3j}$$

and I want to double it, I must treat *each component exactly the same* — namely, double it, getting

$$\vec{2i} + \vec{6j} \quad .$$

This is easily seen from graphical representations. Alternatively, following a suggestion of W.W. Sawyer, one can use price or demand vectors. If one violin student requires \$2.50 worth of sheet music, \$1.50 worth of rosin and a \$15.00 music stand, one has a vector

$$\begin{pmatrix} 2.50 \\ 1.50 \\ 15.00 \end{pmatrix} \quad .$$

For two students, one has

$$2 \times \begin{pmatrix} 2.50 \\ 1.50 \\ 15.00 \end{pmatrix} = \begin{pmatrix} 5.00 \\ 3.00 \\ 30.00 \end{pmatrix} \quad .$$

The 'parallel' or similar treatment of each component is clear. Young arranged a seventh-grade course sequence so that students *first* learned about vectors, and *then* went on to learn about the distributive law.

The error

$$x(y + z) \rightarrow xy + z$$

virtually disappeared (cf. Young, 1981a).[3]

Changing Horses in Mid-stream

We do not attempt to include here *all* of the error types reported in Davis, Jockusch and McKnight (1978), nor should the list there be considered complete. There are many types of errors, and a complete list may not even be practical. We do, however, mention one further error that occurs quite frequently: losing your sense of direction, reversing yourself and undoing what had previously been accomplished. Thus, in adding the fractions

$$\frac{x - 2}{x + 1} + \frac{x - 1}{x + 2}$$

one needs a common denominator, and may write

$$\frac{x - 2}{x + 1} + \frac{x - 1}{x + 2} = \frac{(x - 2)(x + 2)}{(x + 1)(x + 2)} + \frac{(x - 1)(x + 1)}{(x + 2)(x + 1)} \quad .$$

In studying the written work of 50 beginning algebra students, Elizabeth Jockusch found frequent instances where, having proceeded as above, the student saw the possibility of canceling some common factors, and did so:

$$\frac{x - 2}{x + 1} + \frac{x - 1}{x + 2} = \frac{(x - 2)(x + 2)}{(x + 1)(x + 2)} + \frac{(x - 1)(x + 1)}{(x + 2)(x + 1)}$$

$$= \frac{(x - 2)\cancel{(x + 2)}}{(x + 1)\cancel{(x + 2)}} + \frac{(x - 1)\cancel{(x + 1)}}{(x + 2)\cancel{(x + 1)}}$$

$$= \frac{x - 2}{x + 1} + \frac{x - 1}{x + 2} \quad .$$

An even more common example occurs when a beginning calculus student attempts to evaluate

$$\int e^x \sin x \, dx$$

by integrating by parts. Using integration by parts *once,* one obtains

$$\int e^x \sin x \, dx = e^x \sin^x - \int e^x \cos x \, dx \quad .$$

This seems to have accomplished nothing; one impossible integral has been replaced by another. Anyone subject to the error of premature tree-pruning might well decide there was no good result to be obtained by exploring that branch any further, and might therefore drop it from further consideration.

That student, of course, would be wrong. If we use integration by parts *one more time*, we get the desired result — *but only if we continue in the same direction that our work has been taking*.

But how can we describe that direction, and be sure to stay the course?

Well, we have been *differentiating the trig function*, and *integrating the exponential*. Let's do that once more:

$$\int e^x \sin x \, dx = e^x \sin x - \int e^x \cos x \, dx$$
$$= e^x \sin x - e^x \cos x - \int e^x \sin x \, dx \quad .$$

But, if we have

$$\int e^x \sin x \, dx = e^x \sin x - e^x \cos x - \int e^x \sin x \, dx \quad ,$$

we can *add* this unknown integral to each side of the equation above, getting

$$2 \int e^x \sin x \, dx = e^x \sin x - e^x \cos x \quad ,$$

whence (inserting a constant of integration) we have

$$\int e^x \sin x \, dx = \frac{e^x \sin x - e^x \cos x}{2} + C \quad .$$

Suppose we had *reversed* ourselves, and gone backwards instead of forwards? That is to say, suppose that on the second use of integration by parts, we had *differentiated the exponential and integrated the trig function*? Then we would get

$$\int e^x \sin x \, dx = e^x \sin x - \int e^x \cos x \, dx$$
$$= e^x \sin x - e^x \sin x + \int e^x \sin x \, dx \quad ,$$

or

$$\int e^x \sin x \, dx = \int e^x \sin x \, dx \quad ,$$

which, while true, is not at all helpful.

There are at least two *cognitively* relevant aspects to this error. In the first place, if the student does not recover from the error, and go back and try the opposite choices for *u* and *dv*, one is seeing a *premature tree-pruning error* — the discarding or overlooking of an important possibility.

Second, the beginning student probably could not be expected to foresee what would happen when he used integration by parts a second time, beyond realizing that the exponential would remain unchanged, and the trig function would cycle back to become a sine. So we are talking about prodigious foresight. But after one has had the experience of working through this problem, and *thinking deeply about it afterwards*, one has hopefully created a sturdy *knowledge representation structure* that encompasses all of the key aspects of the problem. In the future, this KRS, or 'frame', will provide appropriate prompts so that one will *notice* the 'directionality' implicit in what one is doing, keep track of it and avoid 'reversing' and undoing one's previous work.

When 'Critics' Fail to Fire

As we mentioned earlier, Simon, Matz and others use the term *critic* to refer to a procedure in your mind that ought to recognize certain evidences of error. Thus, when Marcia wrote

$$
\begin{array}{r}
7,002 \\
-\quad 25 \\
\hline
5,087 \quad ,
\end{array}
$$

a 'size' critic should have fired: 'If I had about seven thousand dollars, and I spent twenty five, and then had about five thousand left. . .
. . .*something would be wrong*!'
Such a critic should have fired,[4] but in Marcia's case it did not.

Of course, the non-firing of critics does not *cause* errors in the first place, but it allows an error to survive when it ought to have been detected and corrected. Possessing an abundance of critics is one of the attributes that distinguishes experts from novices (cf. Matz, 1980). This observation matches everyday knowledge – an expert is more likely to 'sense' when something is wrong. One (or many) of the expert's critics will fire.

Notes

1. Admittedly, when one has long experience using 'summary' or 'abstract' versions of some piece of knowledge, the connections to early 'meaningful' experiential origins can become weak. However, if strong connections to the whole-text records of experiences with MAB blocks

had existed in Marcia's mind, the interviewers (or the teacher) could have mobilized them. As the full interview protocols show, this was impossible.

2. This quotation renders Marcia's meaning exactly, but is not *verbatim*. For the *verbatim* transcription, carefully taken from a tape recording of the interview, see Davis and McKnight, 1980, p. 61. We justify our restatement on the grounds that posture, inflection and actual choice of words all contribute to the meaning of a spoken communication. The choice of words is often the least important of these. Consider, for example, what was actually communicated between two people if one of them said 'Oh, yeah' — or if one of them said 'I needed that'.

3. Of course, from a 'constructivist' point of view (cf. Thompson, 1982), one is not so much interested in how many errors were made, nor in how many students made them, as one is in the question: how did the students *think about* these problems (a) in the case of students in the traditional sequence; and, (b) in the case of Young's 'vectors-first' sequence.

4. Recall that 'fire', as used here, means 'to become active'. This usage is an adaptation from language used in studies of neurons.

5. The details of Peter's work on convergence tests for infinite series are presented in Davis, Robert B. (1982) 'Frame-Based Knowledge of Mathematics: Infinite Series', *Journal of Mathematical Behavior,* vol. 3, no. 2 (Summer), pp. 99-120.

23 DEFICIENCIES IN TYPICAL SCHOOL CURRICULA

Clearly there are variations from one school to another, but none the less certain weaknesses in school mathematics curricula are so widespread that they can be considered typical, though not universal. In this chapter we consider four of these.

The Problem of Non-accumulating Bits

One decision that must be made in shaping a curriculum and its presentation to students might be called 'the size of the bits and pieces' that the student is asked to deal with.

At one extreme, one can have very small 'bite-sized chunks' — no task is ever very novel, nor very complex, nor very challenging, nothing more than a simple answer to a simple question. At the opposite extreme, one can present larger tasks, such as 'Find the height of the flagpole in the school yard', and leave it as a task for the students to decompose this into smaller sub-tasks. There are effective intermediate choices that fall between these two extremes. (For example, one can prepare beforehand for the 'flagpole' task by making scale drawings and by measuring angles.[1])

Various 'chunk sizes' are defensible, *provided that ultimately the ideas come through*.

Unfortunately, in far too many school curricula, the 'big ideas' do not come through to most students.

Dealing with small pieces, and never fitting them together, is so common an intellectual problem that there is even a phrase reserved to describe it: 'not seeing the forest for the trees'. Yet many educators seem not to have noticed the danger — at least, many curricula do not successfully avoid this hazard.

In most areas of knowledge, including mathematics, it is usually the forest that is important, yet all too often students see only a few trees, whose interrelationships are never appreciated. To emphasize the importance of the forest — that is to say, of knowledge integrated into larger wholes — we reproduce two quotations. In the first, two world famous mathematicians and a brilliant young student are discussing

339

what it means to think about mathematics:

> Bers:[2] I think the thing which makes mathematics a pleasant occupation are those few minutes when *suddenly something falls into place and you understand*. Now a great mathematician may have such moments very often. Gauss, as his diaries show, had days when he had two or three important insights in the same day. Ordinary mortals have it very seldom . . .But the quality of this experience − those who have it know it − is really joy comparable to no other joy. . .So − this has been observed by many people − the work consists in preparing yourself for this moment of understanding, which comes as a result of an unconscious process.
>
> Puckette:[3] Most of my mathematical experience has been rigged, so far. I have been taught. . . Most of the experience given to me has been moments of joy, simply because it is in fact possible to bring them to me. You stare at a problem on a competition or exam for 30 minutes or so and suddenly the whole thing flies together. The attraction. . .is that it's great fun.
>
> Sullivan:[4] There are always rare moments of understanding that are very nice. . . I remember one experience. I was already a graduate student and I was trying to learn some of Milnor's work. . . I remember going back and trying to think it through one more time. *Suddenly I got the picture that he was actually trying to present in his whole book* a sort of geometrical picture that involved this idea of transversality. . . From that, the whole book just sort of fell away. That was the point from which I reproduced the whole book, even though before it was all in my head as a big complicated thing. The whole thing just fell away and for the first time I realized that I really could understand some nontrivial mathematics. Before that I never really felt the master of something; . . .This was sort of a geometrical idea that was very strong. It was a very vivid experience.
>
> . . .It's not easy, mathematics. The idea that it is possible to really understand something *very well and in a very simple way* was a kind of thought process that I just didn't know. Before [this experience] everything [in mathematics] had been like history; I mean, how do you 'understand' history? You know it, talk about it, go on and on and on; but you can't just suddenly see it coming out of a point. There, to me, was a big step. And the idea that you can have ideas like this, new ideas, not just understanding other people's ideas − that was really getting somewhere. [This conversation was audio-taped by Allen Hammond and is reproduced in his essay 'Mathematics

– Our Invisible Culture' (Hammond, 1980). In the portion presented here, we have added italics and modified some punctuation, in an attempt to compensate for missing inflections and other signals.]

For our second quotation on the value of the 'forest', we repeat a remark of David Page, the creator of one of the best of the 'new mathematics' curriculum revision projects of the 1950s and 1960s. Page reported visiting Cape Cod as a guest of friends who were devoted sailors, and who persuaded Page to go as crew on a sail. Page found it intolerably dull – nothing but tying knots and pulling on ropes and coiling ropes and ducking your head. His friends found it fascinating and exciting and pleasurable – but, says Page, 'I was tying knots – they were *sailing*.' *That*, of course, is the difference between the forest and the trees.

To return to the remarks of Dennis Sullivan, what is this sudden reorganization of knowledge that took place inside his head? We would construe that he is talking about the synthesis of a better *representation* – a representation so powerful that it was capable of generating an almost instantaneous restructuring of an entire book, and a very elaborate and complex book at that! Characteristically for this phenomenon, Sullivan cannot really tell us what it is. The representation is so powerful that we sense Sullivan's excitement about it – but there is no way that Sullivan can reach out and build the same representation within *our* heads – only we can do that, and only after years of hard work.

So the danger is two-sided. A curriculum that consists only of tiny bite-sized pieces may fail to produce this synthesis of the 'big ideas'. But if we try an opposite extreme, we can let Sullivan make up some sentences to describe his synthesis, and we can learn those sentences and repeat them – but we will still *not* have synthesized Sullivan's internal representation for this very large body of very complex information.

Another way to look at the matter is to relate it to 'abbreviated' representations vs. 'full-text' representations (cf. Chapter 5). Sullivan's new ease of thinking may be due in part to the synthesis of appropriate 'abbreviated' representations, perhaps in the sense of Young's *key-feature representations* (Chapter 15). But for Sullivan, either these representations are so adroitly concocted that they embody *all* the most important features, or else they get strength from their connections with the 'whole-text' representations which Sullivan has in his mind, but which we do not have in ours.

Pedagogical Aspects

Some of the weakness of school curricula in such matters is probably due to the common school assumption that knowledge is coded in the form of verbal statements, and that therefore when we tell someone these statements we convey thereby the corresponding knowledge. Since a large part of mathematical knowledge is *not* coded in statements, but rather in some deeper non-verbal form, this 'telling' process does not usually succeed.

One Pedagogical Solution

One pedagogical approach that seems often to avoid the 'two-small-pieces' error at one extreme, or the equally dangerous errors lurking at the opposite extreme, is to require that the curriculum and instruction be so arranged that the student sees every new idea or new technique as a *tool* for accomplishing a sensible goal. Finding the height of the flagpole can be used in this way, so that working with similar triangles becomes a tool for solving this problem. Studying the position, velocity and acceleration of a free-falling body can provide a task context for the computation of rates of change, differentiation and anti-differentiation. (For this general approach, cf. Davis, 1967.)

Stein and Crabill (1972) employ the task of maximizing the volume of a tray made from a given square of material as the goal task which involves uses of arithmetic, algebra, graphing functions and determining slopes. Thus, all of these smaller tasks are learned in a context where they must be seen as *tools*, not as isolated examples of 'things one might do – but *why*?'

The Problem of Superficial Verbal Approaches

In the preceding discussion of 'fitting the pieces of the puzzle together so that you can see the whole picture' (as it were), it was necessary to touch upon a second important weakness of typical school curricula: *putting too much faith in 'telling' students knowledge in the form of simple statements.* Even if we repeat Dennis Sullivan's words, we do not have – and do not acquire – his internal mental representation of Milnor's work. Sullivan *understands*, and we do not.

But this issue of over-reliance on superficial verbal exchanges deserves comment in its own right. Bertrand Russell has remarked on the great human ability to produce seemingly meaningful language that has in fact become separated from whatever meaning it may once have had. If I say 'perhaps we're getting crossover in the gamma spectrum', you can pause, nod your head sagely and solemnly thoughtfully agree — 'crossover in the gamma spectrum' — without knowing what, if anything, the words mean, nor even what discipline might meaningfully make such a pronouncement. A great deal of schooling operates on precisely this level.

Rote Imitation of Procedures

I might observe carefully the actions of a priest, and later go through those same actions myself. Not only does this not make me a priest, it does not guarantee that I know why the acts are performed, or what they are supposed to mean. Far too much mathematics is taught on precisely this basis, and the results are usually unsatisfactory. Why? The extensive representation machinery, the meta-language descriptors, the structure of goals and sub-goals are not being built up. Without them one has an action which may (or may not) be remembered, but there is no diagnostic apparatus to tell the student *when* to use the action, and none of the meta-structure that could provide adjustments to changed circumstances that may be encountered at some time in the future.

The Too-slow Pace

In studying schools across the United States, we once observed a teacher spending a 45-minute class period writing on the chalkboard

$$x^a \cdot x^b = \qquad ,$$

for different positive integer values of a and b, and going around the class in order, calling on one student at a time to recite the answer. For example:

$$x^2 \cdot x^3 =$$

would elicit the student response 'x to the fifth'. These were good students, and every student answered correctly every time they were called on.

It turned out that this was the second day in a row that the teacher had done precisely this — with an academically-strong college-preparatory group of students, for whom this pace was far too slow. The students learned little or no mathematics from these sessions, although they may have been learning patience.

The pace in many classrooms is far too slow, in precisely this fashion. Is this a cognitive problem? Do students really benefit from progressing this slowly?

All of the evidence says 'no'. Why, then, is this slow pace so common, if students don't benefit? The answer seems to be that *schools* do benefit — for example, if a class moves ahead at a reasonable pace, what happens if a student is absent? There are few resources usually available to help the student catch up when he returns to school. The faster the curriculum moves, the more severe this problem will be. But with a slowly-moving class, as with a slowly-moving soap opera, one can miss a day here and there with no noticeable loss of comprehension. For students this is not a benefit, but for schools it is.

Of course ease of catching up by students who have missed a few days of class is not the only reason for the persistence of the much-too-slow curriculum. I leave to the reader the task of identifying some additional reasons. One thing, however, is certain: the slow pace is NOT required because of student cognitive limitations. For at least 25 years far too many experimental curricula have demonstrated that students can learn mathematics at a much more rapid pace — there really can be no doubt about students' ability to move ahead faster. The explanations for the 'too-slow pace' do not lie within children's cognitive capabilities.[5] They must lie within the sociology or intellectual culture of schools and communities.

Notes

1. There is a Madison Project film that shows just such a lesson. The students invent a variety of different methods, some sighting and using protractors to measure the angle of elevation, some using shadows, and some using the artist's method of sighting so that a pencil held in the hand is seen to be the same length as the more distant flagpole. Craig Fisher, for NBC News, produced a TV special which also shows how this lesson can go, in a school in San Diego County, California.

2. Lipman Bers, a giant of twentieth-century mathematics, was born in Latvia, and is now a professor at Columbia University. With Abe Gelbart, Bers created the theory of pseudo-analytic functions, extending work of Riemann, Euler, Cauchy and Weierstrass — which, in turn, was an extension of Isaac Newton's calculus.

3. Miller Puckette was, at the time this interview was taped, an outstanding mathematics student at MIT. While still in high school he was twice a member of the United States team that competed in the International Mathematics Olympiad.

4. Dennis Sullivan, a topologist, is a professor at the Institute des Hautes Etudes Scientifiques in Bures-sur-Yvette, France.

5. Among 'curriculum revision' projects that have demonstrated that children can learn far more mathematics, moving forwards at a considerably faster pace, one could mention David Page's 'Arithmetic Project', William Johntz's 'Project SEED', Burt Kaufman's project at Nova High School and at CEMREL, Layman Allen's work with logic, and the Madison Project. Students at University High School in Urbana can complete at least two years of calculus, with a deeper-than-usual level of understanding, by the time they are 17 or 18 years old. Many go far beyond this, adding university courses in mathematics, chemistry and computer science. Some idea of the possibilities can be obtained by looking carefully at student work published in the *Journal of Children's Mathematical Behavior*, vol. 2, no. 2 (Spring 1979).

24 WHERE DO WE STAND TODAY?

Informed opinion agrees that the United States faces a crisis in educating its young people in the areas of mathematics and science. This is no exaggeration, as several studies have demonstrated. Unfortunately, while there is broad agreement on the *general* nature of the 'crisis', as one attempts to become more precise the consensus grows shakier. However, a group of recent studies of great importance – the so-called 'disaster studies' – may help to build a consensus. In this chapter we take a partisan view of the problem, which may at least serve as a starting point.

Two Basic Problems

We would argue that, as one looks carefully at school mathematics classes, one finds two *major* problems: *first, the pace is dangerously uneven.* In grades 1 through 9, the pace (as discussed in Chapter 23) is very leisurely. The days pass by, and little progress is made. Ninth-grade algebra takes an entire school year to get to the solution of quadratic equations. Such a pace is far more leisurely than the cognitive capabilities of the students would dictate. The students pay a hurtful price for this when they arrive at college, especially if they enroll in a college of engineering. Now the pace becomes frantic. Within a short two years the students are expected to devour Anton's *Calculus* (or some equivalent text), to learn chemistry at least as far as problems like these:

> 'Water gas' is 50% hydrogen and 50% carbon monoxide. How much heat is liberated when 22.4 litres (at STP) of water gas are burned? Repeat for 22.4 litres (STP) of methane. Which is the better fuel?

> What angle would you expect to be formed by the C, O, and H nuclei in an alcohol molecule?

and to learn physics as far as problems like these:

> A cube 10 cm on an edge contains argon. What is the separation in energy between the lowest two energy levels? How does this compare with the thermal energy of the argon atoms at 300K?

346

How does the structure of the periodic table support the need for a fourth quantum number?

If the electron did not spin, how would the chemical properties of helium be different?

Why is a population inversion necessary between two atom levels for laser action to occur?

A rocket ship moving away from the earth at a speed 12/13 of the speed of light reports back by sending waves of frequency 100 MHz as measured in the frame of reference of the rocket ship itself. At what frequency are these signals received on earth?

(Of course, physics, chemistry and calculus are not the only subjects these students are studying.)

A reader who does not understand our concern over the slow pace for nine years, and the hectic pace in college, should: (a) observe some classes in grades 2 through 9; (b) try to solve the college problems posed above (remember that, for a rocket ship traveling 12/13 of the speed of light, Newtonian mechanics and universally-invariant time are inappropriate assumptions — one must use relativistic transformations to get from the reference frame of the ship to the reference frame of the earth); (c) talk with some freshmen and sophomores majoring in engineering, and see how well they understand what they are doing.

The Wrong Orientation

The too slow-pace for nine or more years, followed by a frantic mad rush for the next few years, is not the only weakness in present-day programs. *It is also the case that mathematics is presented from a wrong point of view*: it is presented as a matter of learning dead 'facts' and 'techniques', and *not* in terms of its true nature, which involves processes that demand thought and creativity: confronting vague situations and refining them to a sharper conceptualization; building complex knowledge representation structures in your own mind; criticizing these structures, revising them and extending them; analysing problems, employing heuristics, setting sub-goals and conducting searches in unlikely (but shrewdly-chosen) corners of your memory.

Correcting These Deficiencies

Although one might not know it from most popular reports in the press, the fact is that, in the thirty years from the 1950s to the 1980s a few successful 'new mathematics' programs have demonstrated, beyond any doubt, that both of these deficiencies can be corrected. Academically-inclined students can complete two years of calculus in high school (and many students can do more!), with a good level of understanding. Mathematics can be experienced as creative problem analysis and resourceful problem solving at every grade level from first grade through to senior year in high school.[1]

The question, then, is this: *why are these solutions not implemented in typical schools*? This question is surprisingly difficult to answer.

Not Because of Cognitive Limitations in Students

In the first place, the non-proliferation of these curricula is *not* due to any cognitive inability of most students. The trials of the 1950s and 1960s demonstrated that students are well able, cognitively or intellectually, to move ahead far faster in mathematics and to deal with a 'problem-analysis' and a 'heuristic' approach to mathematics. So the most obvious possible reason is not, in fact, the actual reason.

Not Because of Time Limitations

Well, then, is the non-implementation of these curricula due to a shortage of time in the school day? Surely a reasonable conjecture – but studies such as Hopkins (1965) have demonstrated that, when part of the usual time devoted to rote arithmetic is used, instead, for a 'problem analysis' approach to algebra and geometry, *performance in arithmetic itself improves*! This, then, turns out to be one further instance where 'less is more'.

Consequently, the failure of schools to adopt a curriculum that allows students to move ahead faster, and with deeper understanding, cannot be blamed on an actual shortage of class time. What would be needed would be the reallocation of existing time devoted to rote arithmetic.

Reasons

We have seen two non-reasons. What, then, *are* the real reasons? Probably at least these:

(1) Teacher Education. The new curricula depend upon teacher education programs that are not usually available. (Cf, e.g., the report of the Conference Board of the Mathematical Sciences, 1975.)

(2) Expectations. Teachers and parents do not believe that students *can* or *should* learn mathematics as a challenging, creative subject.

(3) Disagreement Among Innovators. The various innovative curricula of the 1950s and 1960s agreed only on the undesirability of the 'traditional' curriculum – they disagreed completely on the design of a better curriculum (although several of the innovations were able to demonstrate their value, compared to the 'traditional' curriculum).

(4) Goal Conflicts. The new curricula involved a rejection of many traditional goals. As Jack Easley has pointed out, many parents and teachers believe that it is morally good for students to learn a subject which they do not understand, but must learn precisely and obey completely. (Two slogans that are intended to characterize this approach were proclaimed by a dissenting British educator: 'It doesn't matter what you teach the child, so long as he doesn't understand it!' and 'It doesn't matter what you teach the child, so long as he doesn't like it!') As Easley says, the new curricula in science and mathematics challenged this traditional view of the moral value of uncomprehending obedience – but it was a view that parents and teachers were unwilling to abandon.

(5) Ideas. Finally (another reason suggested by Easley), the new curricula focused on *how students analyzed problems*, upon how students *thought* – that is to say, they focused on *ideas* in the minds of students. This was too radical an innovation to be accepted easily, and it challenged too many taboos.

The 'Disaster' Studies

A series of recent studies are leading to a deeper understanding of the problem, and may thus point towards real improvement. The studies – by Erlwanger, Lochhead, Clement, Rosnick, di Sessa, Green and others – show in detail how many students, believed to be successful when one judges by typical tests, are revealed as seriously confused when one looks more closely at how they think about the subject.

From these studies there emerge two aspects of learning mathematics and science: on the one hand, one has the learning of abstract formal systems, including verbally-stated definitions, the imitation of procedures that have been demonstrated, and so on. On the other hand one has the knowledge representation structures that have been built up in students' minds. Typical tests deal only with the first of these, and it is in dealing with the second – the internal representation structures – that these studies broke new ground.

In one task used by di Sessa (1982), a 'dynaturtle' – think of it as a rocket-powered space ship – is in the lower-left corner of the CRT computer screen, and is to travel to a target destination in the upper-right corner. The space ship is pointed vertically upwards – call this the positive direction of the y-axis, and pretend that the origin (0, 0) is at the lower-left corner of the screen, with the upper-right corner being, say, (10, 10). A student can press K, R or L on the keyset. Pressing K fires the rocket, and adds a *vector* increment to the ship's velocity – the increment vector points in the direction the ship is pointing at the moment when the rocket is fired (i.e. when K is pressed). Pressing R causes the ship to rotate 30° clockwise, and L causes a similar rotation counterclockwise; as long as the rocket is not fired, the orientation of the ship has no effect on the motion – unlike automobiles, rocket ships travel just as comfortably sideways or backwards as they do forwards.

Di Sessa's subjects included eight students in grade 6 from a local elementary school, and an engineering student who had studied a year

Figure 24.1: Initial appearance of the computer screen at the beginning of di Sessa's task.

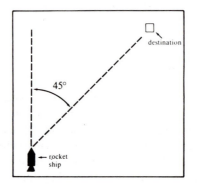

of physics in high school, plus the relevant parts of physics coursework at the engineering school.

If we are contrasting the abstract formalisms taught in school vs. the 'intuitive' knowledge representation structures built up inside the subjects' minds (mostly by outside-of-school experiences), how can we tell them apart? Broadly speaking, the formalisms of school deal with *Newtonian physics* (we neglect corrections of quantum mechanics or relativity) — the state of a body is summarized completely by its velocity vector, its position and its orientation or 'attitude'. The effect of a 'push' or a 'kick' is to contribute a vector increment to the vector velocity (see Figure 24.2). The increment will be in the same direction as the kick itself, but the subsequent velocity usually will not be.

Figure 24.2: According to Newtonian mechanics, a 'push' or kick gives a vector increment to the velocity vector. The increment is in the same direction as the push, but the final velocity usually will not be.

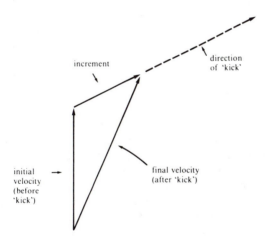

By contrast, the dynamics of everyday life has the appearance of being Aristotelian: things move because they are pushed, and they move in the direction of the push.

For the purposes of modern technology, Aristotelian physics is wrong and Newtonian physics is correct. To be sure, a chair, pushed around the room, seems to obey the Aristotelian Laws: push it and it moves; do not push it, and it remains in place. When you do push it, it moves in the direction towards which you pushed it.

This appearance is, of course, the result of an incomplete analysis of the situation. There are at least four forces on the chair: gravity pulls it downwards; the normal component of the force exerted by the floor is upwards, and just balances the pull of gravity, so that the chair neither rises like a helium-filled balloon, nor descends through the floor like a bomb fragment dropped from a great height.

So much for the vertical forces. Your push constitutes a horizontal force; the friction force from the floor opposes this, making the chair harder to move, and causing the chair to stop the moment you stop pushing it.

Because he ignored most of these forces (among other errors), Aristotle arrived at his description of motion. He could not satisfactorily explain (though he tried) the flight of an arrow, which continues to move even after it leaves the bow, although nothing is really pushing it any longer. The motion of the moon, or of a space ship, shows this phenomenon clearly. They move even when nothing 'pushes' them. In short, they obey Newton's Laws, not Aristotle's.

The curriculum goal is, then, for students to learn Newton's Laws, both in the formalisms of vector addition, the solution of differential equations of motion, etc., and also in the sense of possessing a collection of knowledge representation structures that also embody Newtonian principles.

Di Sessa's evidence is that half of this goal is being achieved. Students *do* learn the Newtonian formalisms that are embodied in their homework problems and examination questions. However, their mental representation structures are still largely Aristotelian. For the elementary school students in di Sessa's study, such a situation is unsurprising and undisturbing. But di Sessa found the same phenomenon in the one engineering student whom he studied, and other studies (with more subjects) at the University of Massachusetts and at Johns Hopkins University have found the same result. At this level, the result is surprising and is disturbing.

Consider the first student responses in di Sessa's study. Nearly all students try first to point the not-yet-moving rocket ship towards the target, then fire the rocket by pressing K. This cannot be done; the spaceship would need to rotate clockwise 45°, which cannot be achieved by the 30° increments that are available. It is important to notice that all subjects immediately accept this impossibility, and move on to other strategies.

What most subjects do next is to press K, thereby causing the space-ship to acquire a constant vertical component of velocity. (The ship begins to move upwards, and continues to move in this direction with a constant speed.) The ship is rotated 90° clockwise (by three presses of R), which by itself has no effect on the upwards motion (remember that this is a rocket ship, not an automobile!), and the subject waits until the y-coordinate of the ship equals the y-coordinate of the target, before pressing K. At this point, the ship skids diagonally off the top of the screen, as in Figure 24.3.

Figure 24.3: Subjects are surprised, and disappointed, to see the rocket ship skid off the top of the screen, moving diagonally up and to the right after the horizontal component of velocity is added. (Of course, the upwards velocity component is still present.)

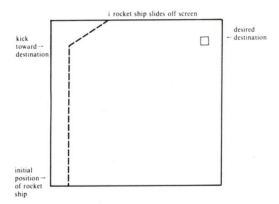

Student response to this disappointment stands in sharp contrast to their response to the impossibility of turning 45°. Whereas the 45°-turn strategy was immediately abandoned, and a search started for other approaches, in this case of sliding-off-the-top-of-the-screen, the method is *not* immediately abandoned. Students persevere for a long time, and complain that the machine isn't working correctly. Clearly, we have come up against one of those stable, persistently-defended ideas that students (and all of us) have. The situation is strikingly similar to the

$$6S = P$$

error found by Rosnick and Clement, and to Marcia's insistent belief in her (incorrect) algorithm for subtraction. We have come up against a well-established knowledge representation structure.

The rocket ship, behaving unlike a chair, refuses to move in the direction of our push. Of course it is our Aristotelian frame that is wrong, not the performance of the computer. Since no downwards push has canceled the upwards velocity, the ship *must* run off the top of the screen.

Di Sessa follows his students through a sequence of ingenious strategies, all built up by the 'assembling' and modifying of experientially-acquired knowledge representation structures. For details (which are fascinating!) see di Sessa (1982).

The point relevant to our present discussion is that students who are *successfully* completing formal studies are, in fact, learning how to pass tests on the formal definitions and algorithms — but in many cases their internal knowledge representation structures are *not* consistent with this formal knowledge. In a conflict situation, the formalities are often abandoned, and the unmodified (i.e. 'wrong') internalized frames are used in attempts to solve a problem.

The di Sessa, Clement-Rosnick, Green *et al.* and Erlwanger studies are grouped together as the 'disaster studies' in the sense that, in all of them, *students who are thought to be successful in learning elaborate formal systems are suddenly revealed to harbor wrong basic ideas at the most fundamental level.* They have no idea how large numbers are (Erlwanger, as in the conversion $\frac{2}{10} \to 2.10$), they do not know what a numerical variable is (Clement and Rosnick, $6S = P$), and they do not know Newton's three fundamental laws of motion. Yet they have been working — supposedly correctly — with these ideas for months or even for years. *They have been misunderstanding much of the material they were supposed to be learning.*

Experienced teachers have long realized that some students 'study the night before the test', can use their imitative capabilities to produce seemingly correct answers to test questions, and can fail to learn the subject, while none the less passing the test. A constructionist would say that these students have failed to synthesize correct knowledge representation structures within their own minds. The 'disaster studies' are showing more precisely just how these student failures occur, and by so doing they may help towards the design of future curricula that will avoid this kind of student failure to understand what was supposed to be learned.

Note

1. None of this claim is exaggerated, nor unsubstantiated. Madison Project films show actual classroom lessons in grades 2 through 10; Page's Arithmetic Project also has films; the Dilworth-Warren evaluation of California programs supports this claim (Dilworth, 1973); Papert's work with LOGO environments supports it; Kaufman's work at Nova High School in Florida, and subsequently at CEMREL, supports it; the judgement of the Cambridge Conference on School Mathematics supports it. Unfortunately, while these results are genuine and well-documented, appropriate reports are not easily available. One can start with Howson, Keitel and Kilpatrick (1981), Hayden (1982), Cambridge Conference (1963, 1967), Steiner (1971) and Braunfeld and Deskins (1975) — but diligent search is required to uncover most of the evidence. The remarkable fact is that the very important work of the curriculum improvement projects of those thirty years has hardly been studied! The *Journal of Children's Mathematical Behavior*, vol. 2, no. 2 (1979) and the *Journal of Mathematical Behavior*, vol. 3, no. 1 (1980) have samples of student work. *JCMB*, vol. 2, no. 1 (1978) has some evaluative data.

25 THE COGNITIVE SCIENCE APPROACH TO MATHEMATICS EDUCATION

In this book we have presented an approach to the study of mathematical thought that seems to have promise. When we look at physics or chemistry or medicine, we find that their accumulation of knowledge is built on the foundation of a *postulated* collection of basic concepts. None of these fields could have prospered if they had dealt only with 'observable' data, such as the readings on voltmeters and accelerometers and pH meters and thermometers. Instead, they have postulated the atom, the gene, the virus, the atomic nucleons, layers of orbital electrons, the neutrino, the ether, the photon, alpha rays, beta rays, displacement current, the Lorentz contraction, the s-flavored quark, the antistrange antiquark and the gluon, to mention only a very few. They have taken from the geometers the postulation of a flat three-dimensional space, and implicitly assumed a universally-invariant time.

Not everything postulated in physical science has survived unchanged as more data has accumulated. On the contrary, most postulated entities have been greatly changed with the passage of time and the gathering of evidence. But that is more a strength than a weakness — once a generally adequate conceptual framework was created by *postulation*, modifications, extensions and even rejection gradually became possible, if not inevitable.

It has been a weakness of educational theory that it has attempted to avoid the postulation of fundamental constructs. This avoidance has led to an impoverishment of theoretical discussions, and it is the building of theory that is the deepest trademark of science.

Probably nothing postulated in this book is stated in an absolutely correct form. Indeed, uncertainties are clearly present, nowhere more evidently than in the nature of large information representation structures, whether 'chunks' (George Miller), or 'frames' (Minsky), or 'scripts' (Schank), or 'models' (Papert), or 'powerful ideas' (again, Papert), or 'schemas' (Piaget) or 'assimilation paradigms' (Davis). But the true business of mathematics instruction is to help the student to construct, in his or her own mind, a large collection of knowledge representation structures that provide powerful forms of all of the key ideas of mathematics: points, infinite sets, lines, real numbers, the limit of an infinite sequence — or, for that matter, what the fraction

356

$$\frac{13}{7}$$

means, or the decimal 2.10, or the statement

$$^{-}1 \text{ x } ^{-}1 = {}^{+}1,$$

or the fact that $y = \frac{1}{x}$ is continuous at x_0 if $x_0 > 0$. If our goal involves the representations of key ideas in the student's mind, we must be willing to try to talk about such matters. Many good teachers always have been. If research in the mid-twentieth century usually avoided such questions, considering them hopelessly 'unscientific', the *alternate paradigm* of recent years is less reticent, and is making a determined effort to talk about *ideas* in a rational and appropriate way. Among its various advantages, the alternate paradigm may make it possible for teachers and researchers once again to talk with one another so that each understands the other.

The Postulated Structure

We review here the broad outlines of the mechanisms and structures postulated in this volume.

Non-verbal Knowledge

While some mathematical knowledge may be coded and processed in the form of natural-language statements, a very large part of it is not.[1] For this non-verbal knowledge, we have drawn a distinction between something you know that is essentially sequential, vs. something you know that can be dealt with in nearly any order. Your knowledge of the alphabet is probably largely sequential. If I ask you what letter comes seven letters before M, you probably aren't immediately able to answer. But if I ask you about the rooms in your home — which rooms, say, face north — you probably know without the need to work through a pre-determined sequence. Your knowledge of the rooms is coded and stored in such a way that you can start anywhere, and process information in any direction. You have what computer terminology calls 'random access'. For the alphabet your experience has been more rigidly sequential, and so the most available representations are also sequential.

Sequential Representations

Among sequential representations, we have distinguished *visually-moderated sequences* (which require inputs to be assembled), vs. *integrated sequences* (which do not).

Non-sequential Representations

We have considered primarily the 'chunks', 'frames' or 'scripts' that have been postulated by various investigators to provide for organized structures capable of representing complex knowledge.

The Process of 'Assembly', Using Metaphors

We have postulated that new knowledge representation structures are ordinarily created by combining, modifying and extending previously-created structures. But these earlier structures were themselves created in this same way. One can trace this backwards, and find that in many cases — probably *most* cases, but we know no reliable way to count — a sophisticated idea can be seen as built from the very simple ideas learned in early childhood, ideas such as heavy, near, far, tall, short, immovable, next, up, down, before, after, and so on. This process of 'assembling' has, of course, gone on within a person's mind for years. *In cases where it has not, a student has only a very unsatisfactory kind of 'superficial verbal' knowledge, unrelated to actual experience.* We all have met people who could 'say the words', but did not know what the words meant.

From such analyses, we see explanations of the effectiveness of the *paradigm teaching strategy*, and the value of so-called *experiential learning*.

Alternatives to Statements

Besides whatever knowledge may be coded in the form of natural language statements, we have postulated two main alternatives. First, the (primarily non-verbal) representation structures of the 'procedure' or 'frame' types; and, second (a postulate used by Scott Fahlman, Marvin Minsky and Edwina Rissland), the Exemplar/Judgement hypothesis: the mind possesses the capability of constructing examples (or possibly hypothetical examples) to meet certain specifications, and of making judgements about these examples. Can there be an even prime? Can there be a function that is discontinuous at every point? Could a three-legged animal walk into this room? Can someone be his own uncle? In how many different ways can an infinite sequence diverge? Can there be a statement whose truth value cannot be determined? Can it snow on July 4th? Can you face directly south, turn to your right 90°, and *then* be facing directly south? If ϵ is a positive number, can there be a positive number *smaller than ϵ*?

One easily deals with questions of this general type, although some specific instances may be difficult. (E.g., can there be an integer n such that $n > 2$, and $x^n + y^n = z^n$ has positive integer solutions for x, y and z?) Hence this capability provides another mechanism by which information can be coded and stored in the mind. The existence of such a mechanism has profound implications for what is, and is not, possible in human thought.

Many school programs fail because they assume, perhaps tacitly, that all knowledge exists, is stored in memory and is processed, in the form of natural-language statements. Successful advertising does not make this error. If we show a chauffeur carrying Brand X whisky from the Rolls to the mansion door, we have given the viewer an exemplar that will 'come to mind' and will influence behavior, in a way that could never be accomplished by an explicit statement.

A Complete Memory Search Is Not Possible

Naïvely one sometimes assumes that if you 'know' something, then you know it, and that is all there is to it. If you have some information stored in your mind, you can retrieve it. Well, maybe. But then again, maybe not. If you try to write down every male first name that you know, you will quickly find that this is an impossible task. From time to time you will inevitably think of others that you *did* know, but did *not* write down on the list. You can only find things in memory when some kind of search mechanism or strategy or accident leads you to them. Juries distrust the witness who says he did not think of something that he surely knew — but the truth is that we all do this every day.

Concise, Abbreviated Representations

Effective processing requires that each important piece of knowledge be represented in at least two forms, a 'whole-text' form of representation that includes details, and a concise, abbreviated representation (a 'summary' or 'abstract') that does not. Even two forms may not be enough; more likely some entries require at least three forms: (i) a very concise 'executive summary' that can be used in planning; (ii) a brief form that may suffice for use in many cases, without using up too much memory in the severely limited 'active work-space' area; (iii) a far more extended form that can be called upon if necessary — at the price of allocating much of the work-space memory to this single item.

'Work-Space' Memory

The preceding section reminds us of another postulate: memory is divided into at least two parts, a small active 'workbench' part, which is where all active processing occurs, and a vast 'warehouse' part, where very large amounts of information are stored. For processing to occur, items must first be located (somehow) in memory, then copied (by non-destructive read-out) into the work-space area, and then processed. The work-space memory is uncomfortably small and confining, as we all know when we try to 'keep too many ideas in mind' at the same time. When new items are entered into work-space memory, some older items there may be erased. The small size of work-space memory is one of the reasons that short versions of knowledge representations are needed, so that at least a few items can be thought about simultaneously. If an entry in work-space memory is erased, the knowledge is not lost (because a warehouse record still exists) but the knowledge temporarily becomes unavailable for active processing.

The Need to Generalize

The limited work space, however, is not the only reason why shorter forms are required. There is also the need to generalize. A 'whole-text' representation would be too specific, since it contains too many details. Generalization can be achieved in at least two ways: by the creation of abbreviated 'summary' versions of knowledge items, or, alternatively, by creating an isomorphism between two items. In the first case, one could consider the whole-text version of *Romeo and Juliet*, and from it prepare a brief summary. This summary, if it omitted the right details, might then also describe *West Side Story*, so that a 'generalization' has been arrived at.

The second mechanism would create a generalization in a quite different fashion: a mapping (or 'isomorphism') could be created between *West Side Story* and *Romeo and Juliet*, in the way described by Gentner for the creation of an isomorphism between the solar system and an atom. The more familiar representation would then be a *metaphor* for the newer idea. ('Maria' would map into 'Juliet', just as the atomic nucleus maps into the sun.) *But this isomorphism is itself an item of knowledge*, on a more abstract level.

Some mechanism of one of these types, or perhaps of some other type, must make possible the metamorphosis of an item from Brewer's *personal memory* (where items include extensive specific detail) into an item in *generic memory* (where items omit detail and are cast in more abstract form).

Meta-language

In the mathematical task of finding anti-derivatives (or 'indefinite integrals'), it is valuable to remember that 'a sine squared is almost a cosine squared', but 'a sine is *not* almost a cosine'. Thus,

$$\int \sin^3 x \, dx$$

is easily evaluated, because (after we separate off the sinx dx that we need in order to have du) we have

$$\int \sin^2 x \, \sin x \, dx \quad,$$

which is

$$\int (1 - \cos^2 x) \sin x \, dx \quad,$$

for which immediate evaluation is possible.

Similarly, in finding

$$\lim_{h \to 0} \ln \left(1 + \frac{h}{x}\right)^{\frac{1}{h}} \tag{1}$$

one uses the known limit

$$\lim_{h \to 0} \ln (1 + h)^{\frac{1}{h}} \quad. \tag{2}$$

The key step is that expression (1) must be mapped correctly into expression (2). An error at this step is easily made — one can attempt an 'identity' mapping, by mapping the 'h' in (1) into the 'h' in (2), and so on.

This attempt will fail. But a re-analysis of (1) and (2) easily leads to a correct mapping: in each case, one has 'something small' that is added to 1, and the exponent in (2) *must be the reciprocal of this 'something small'*. Hence the exponent in (1) must be

$$\frac{x}{h} \quad,$$

and, following the heuristic that if you need some entry in an expression, you should put it where you need it (and then see if there is a legal way to justify this alteration), we re-write (1) in the illegal form

$$\lim_{h \to 0} \ln (1 + \frac{h}{x})^{\frac{x}{h}} ,$$ (1')

and then make a *legal* re-writing as

$$\lim_{h \to 0} \frac{1}{x} \ln (1 + \frac{h}{x})^{\frac{x}{h}} .$$ (1'')

It is now clear that the term

$$\frac{h}{x}$$

in (1'') must be mapped into the 'h' of expression (2).

In both of these examples we have used *meta-language* or *meta-analysis* — in short, we have developed language (and concepts) to allow us to describe *attributes* and *processes* that are applicable to lower-level entities for which we already had mental representations.

'Key-feature' Representations

Probably all mental representations omit something. One hopes that a representation will include the most important aspects of the reality which it represents. Young (1982) has proposed a particularly elegant form of mental representation, called 'key-feature' representation, whereby certain features — hopefully the main ones — are explicitly present in the representation, and other features must be inferred. Young has used his postulated mechanism to explain a problem on a recent ETS examination, and why its correct answer eluded the experts. Young also established some measure of plausibility for his various proposed representations by showing how each could have been learned from previous experience.

The 'O'Hare Airport' Solution

Suppose our present task involves a problem — call it Problem A — that is in fact similar in a few respects to some other problem — Problem B, say — that we have solved some time in the past. How can this similarity be discovered and used? Clearly, one cannot search vast areas of memory, seeking 'possibly similar problems'. Schanck and Kolodner (1979) have proposed a possible mechanism, variously called 'The O'Hare Airport' solution or the 'library book' solution. Suppose that the similarity between Problems A and B lies in the fact that both make use of some common sub-routine (i.e. 'frame' or 'procedure'), say item C.

When the new Problem, A, is analyzed to the point where the need to use item C becomes apparent, one retrieves item C and finds that, along with item C, there comes a record of previous problems that have made use of C. One is thus led to Problem B, and may be able to extend the match beyond item C, using other parts of Problem B to help solve Problem A.

Orderliness

Once such postulates are made, and examples of human behavior are analyzed in terms of these postulates, a very great regularity or orderliness becomes apparent. We consider here three instances, from among the numerous examples seen in earlier chapters.

Feigenbaum's Law of Minimal Necessary Discrimination asserts that frames and procedures will evolve so as to make discriminations where these have been necessary, but probably *not* beyond that point. Hence the early frame for subtraction does *not* pay attention to the order of the inputs. If the operation is subtraction, and the inputs are 5 and 7, the desired output must be 2. Inasmuch as $7 - 5 = 2$ is the *only* form initially considered, this frame makes only those discriminations which have been important.

When, later, the student encounters

$$5 - 7,$$

this frame will be retrieved (presumably by the 'subtraction' cue); it will, of course, produce the answer '2', *and this is what one actually observes.*

The antidote to this error is to establish a new assimilation paradigm for subtraction, and the 'Pebbles-in-the-Bag' learning experience does this, providing, in effect, a powerful new metaphor.

As a second example, if learning is based upon a metaphoric use of previous knowledge, and especially of 'early-childhood' ideas, then '$12 \div 4$' can be dealt with easily by, for example, visualizing 12 cookies arranged in 4 rows, with 3 cookies in each row. Thus $12 \div 4$ should be easy *conceptually*, and it is.

On the other hand, $12.56 \div 3.29$ should be very difficult *conceptually* — and observation shows that it is! (We are speaking, not of *computation*, but of possessing a good mental representation of the problem.) One *cannot* visualize 12.56 cookies arranged in 3.29 rows. If no other simple *assimilation paradigm* can be built in the child's mind, then 12.56 ÷ 3.29 will remain conceptually elusive.[2] (Of course, other powerful assimilation paradigms are available, and one can help a student to learn them; but if this is *not* done, 12.56 ÷ 3.29 will continue to pose difficulties, as it in fact does.)

For a third example, Jamesine Friend's discovery that

$$\begin{array}{r} 128 \\ + \ 71 \\ \hline \end{array}$$

is usually error-prone, with

$$\begin{array}{r} 128 \\ + \ 71 \\ \hline 99 \end{array}$$

and

$$\begin{array}{r} 128 \\ + \ 71 \\ \hline 899 \end{array}$$

being especially common wrong answers, reveals a phenomenon that is actually the inevitable consequence of: (i) the existence of a primary-grade addition frame that demands two inputs; (ii) the Brown-Matz-Van Lehn Law that high-level goals MUST be met, with constraints being relaxed if necessary to do this; and (iii) the fact that one possible default procedure consists of ignoring operations that cannot be carried out.

Thus, when the multi-column addition procedure calls upon the single-digit addition frame for the units column, all is well:

$$\begin{array}{r} 128 \\ + \ 71 \\ \hline 9 \ , \end{array}$$

using 8 + 1 $\longrightarrow$ 9. Similarily, when the multi-digit procedure calls upon the single-digit addition frame for the tens column: 2 + 7 $\longrightarrow$ 9, hence

$$\begin{array}{r} 128 \\ + \ 71 \\ \hline 99 \end{array}$$

But now, in the hundreds column, the multi-digit procedure calls upon the single-digit addition frame to 'add 1', and this frame, requiring two inputs, refuses to function.

At this point, a 'repair' occurs in the sense of Matz, Brown, Burton and Van Lehn: since the single-digit adder refuses to perform, one 'repair' is to forget about it, and go on without it. This produces the answer '99'. Another repair is to relax the constraint of looking in the *same* column (i.e. the hundreds column) for the second input; instead, shift to a different definition of 'left-hand column' to mean 'left-most column'. Hence, pick up the '7', and get the answer:

```
 128
+ 71
 899
```

One has to be impressed by the great orderliness and regularity in human mathematical behavior. Very little seems to be arbitrary, random or capricious.

Problem Solving

It could well be argued that 'problem solving' is the central, and most important, activity in mathematics. Suppose you are a parcel delivery service. You want to guarantee to deliver a package, provided that it is not too large. How can you define 'too large'? You don't want to base the definition on *volume*, or else you may find yourself called upon to deliver the world's longest piece of uncooked spaghetti, which may have a small *volume* despite its great length (not to mention fragility). Devising a way to measure the size of a parcel that will be appropriate for your shipping service is then a *problem*, and you need to solve it.[3]

Here is another problem: Let p, q, r and s be positive real numbers. Prove that

$$\frac{(1 + p^2)(1 + q^2)(1 + r^2)(1 + s^2)}{pqrs} \geq 16 \quad .$$

[Used by Schoenfeld and by Pedersen in problem-solving studies.]

Here is a third problem, suggested by McShane, which we state in its entirety:

A pile of coal catches on fire.

Here is a fourth problem: Evaluate the integral

$$\int_1^\infty \frac{1}{x}\sqrt{1 + \frac{1}{x^4}} \quad dx \quad .$$

(This integral arises in computing the surface area of a trumpet-shaped paint can that *can* be filled with paint (its volume is finite), but whose inside surface *cannot* be completely painted (its area is infinite).)

Here is a fifth problem: explain the meaning of the paradoxical situation mentioned in the fourth problem.

Here is a sixth problem: If N is a non-negative integer, for what real values of t will the system of two simultaneous equations

$$\begin{cases} (x - t)^2 + y^2 = 1 \\ \quad x^2 - y^2 = 0 \end{cases}$$

have exactly N solutions?

Finally, here is a seventh problem: interpret the symbols in the following computer program so that the procedure will determine the *greatest common divisor* (GCD) of the positive integers x and y, and prove that the procedure must actually succeed:

```
TO:   GCD /x/ /y/
10    Compute max(b) ∃ x = by + r, r ⩾ 0
20    If r = 0, return /y/
30    GCD /y/ /r/
END
```

Of course, if you want to determine whether it is economically preferable to install aluminium siding on your house, that is a problem. If you want to estimate the cost of moving your household possessions to Cleveland, that is a problem. If you want to measure the surface area, or the center of mass, of a two-year-old child, those are problems. The problems that appear on exams or placement tests or College Board tests or Putnam contests are problems. Creating an appropriate notation to allow you to write down what you need to write down is a problem. Breaking an adversary's code is a problem. Choosing an appropriate definition is a problem.

Of course problem solving is central to all of mathematics, both pure and applied.

But what is 'problem solving'?

A Skeleton Outline of Typical Steps

We have argued that *problem solving* consists of essentially ten steps, with repetitions or omissions occurring in various specific cases:

(1) Looking for cues or clues within the problem that can guide an initial retrieval from memory.

(2) Making this retrieval (which may involve searching decision trees).
(3) Gradually building up a *mental representation* for the problem. (Although we say 'mental representation', some notations on paper or on a chalkboard may also be used.)
(4) Building up a mental representation of a corresponding piece of knowledge. (Again, paper, chalkboard or reference books may also be used.)
(5) Making mappings of input data into the problem representation.
(6) Making mappings between the problem representation and the knowledge representation.
(7) Evaluating the adequacy of these retrievals and these mappings.
(8) If necessary, using heuristics, or setting subgoals, in order to create some revised representations.
(9) Cycling back as often as necessary.
(10) Using some 'stopping rule' to know when to quit.

An Example

These ten steps are employed flexibly, with some variation in sequential order. Consider the task of evaluating the integral

$$I = \int_1^\infty \frac{1}{x} \sqrt{1 + \frac{1}{x^4}} \quad dx \quad .$$

Many lines of attack are possible; we present two:

First Method. One heuristic says: identify some aspect of the problem that you don't like, and see if you can eliminate it, or diminish it. If, reasonably enough, we decide to eliminate (as far as possible) the use of *fractions*, we can make a change of variable:

$$t = \frac{1}{x},$$

whence we get

$$dt = \frac{-1}{x^2} \quad dx$$

$$I = -\frac{1}{2} \int_1^0 \frac{1}{t^2} \sqrt{1 + t^4} \quad (2t\,dt) \quad .$$

Using the same 'eliminate the difficulties' heuristic, we can try to eliminate the square root. Using the 'what would you *like* to see' heuristic, we want $1 + t^4$ to be a perfect square. But can a *sum of squares* become a square? Yes, because of the identity

$$\tan^2 \theta + 1 = \sec^2 \theta.$$

If $1 + t^4$ is to match $\tan^2 \theta + 1$, then we must have

$$t^2 = \tan \theta,$$

whence

$$2tdt = \sec^2 \theta \, d\theta,$$

$$\sqrt{1 + t^4} = \sec \theta,$$

and the integral becomes

$$I = -\frac{1}{2} \int_{\pi/4}^{0} \frac{\sec^3 \theta \, d\theta}{\tan \theta} \tag{3}$$

There are many cues suggested by (3), and the problem is to reject those that are least promising. Suppose we decide to change all trig functions to sines and cosines. We get

$$I = -\frac{1}{2} \int_{\pi/4}^{0} \frac{1}{\sin \theta \cos^2 \theta} \, d\theta. \tag{4}$$

How shall we deal with (4)? One method — the cognitive analysis of this step is left as a challenge to the reader! — is to re-write the '1' in the numerator as

$$\sin^2 \theta + \cos^2 \theta,$$

which leads to

$$I = \frac{1}{2} \int_{\pi/4}^{0} \frac{-\sin \theta \, d\theta}{\cos^2 \theta} - \frac{1}{2} \int_{\pi/4}^{0} \frac{d\theta}{\sin \theta},$$

from which (multiplying the fraction in the second integral by

$$(\csc \theta + \cot \theta) \, / \, (\csc \theta + \cot \theta),$$

a very interesting idea!) we get

$$I = \frac{1}{2} \left[\frac{1}{\cos\theta} - \ln \left| 1 + \cos\theta \right| + \ln \left| \sin\theta \right| \right]_0^{\pi/4},$$

which diverges to positive infinity.

Second Method. In the original integral,

$$I = \int_1^\infty \frac{1}{x} \sqrt{1 + \frac{1}{x^4}} \ dx,$$

$1 \leqslant x$, so we have

$$\sqrt{1 + \frac{1}{x^4}} \geqslant 1,$$

and

$$I \geqslant \int_1^\infty \frac{1}{x} \ dx,$$

and this new integral clearly diverges to positive infinity.

Any interested reader can run through this problem and see how the various steps are used in the process of solving. One or two steps involve thought processes that are especially difficult to explain, and therefore especially interesting on that account.

Problem-solving and Meta-language

We have emphasized that, in typical solving, two activities take place in parallel. One is *constructive* — building representations, building mappings, etc. — and the other is *analytical* (using meta-language to guide the construction processes). This same duality could be seen, for example, in the process of creating a mental representation for a piece of music: ambiguities in the construction process were sometimes resolved by the application of harmonic or stylistic criteria, which constituted a meta-language for that task.

'Arithmetic' May be Too Narrow

In terms of mathematical content, we have looked at arithmetic, algebra, geometry, calculus, applied mathematics and computer programming. This may seem like an unusually broad range that makes extreme demands on the reader. Our justification is that arithmetic, alone, may give a distorted view of the kind of information processing that is required in 'thinking about mathematical problems'. In much arithmetic the decision trees are so simple as to be unimportant. Memory searches, also, are uncharacteristically uncomplicated. Hence one comes close to dealing with straight recall. Many fundamental processes — for example, the need to recognize and resolve ambiguities — are hardly present in simple arithmetic thought. By using a broader range of mathematical topics, one improves the odds of getting a reasonably representative picture of the kind of mental information processing that mathematics requires.

The 'Disaster Studies'

Of special importance are the so-called 'disaster studies', by Lochhead, Clement, Rosnick, di Sessa, Green, Erlwanger, Alderman, Johnson and others. These studies show how, in quite precise ways, many students who are thought to be 'successful' have in fact failed to learn even the essential rudimentary aspects of the subjects. 'Successful' arithmetic students may have no idea of the *size* of the numbers they deal with, and may use many incorrect algorithms (Erlwanger, 1973, 1974). 'Successful' engineering students may have quite wrong ideas about the very fundamental concept of *variable*, and may adhere to these wrong ideas with remarkable tenacity (Rosnick and Clement, 1980). 'Successful' physics students may insistently violate Newton's Laws, on which all of their formal work has been based (di Sessa, 1982, McCloskey, *et al.*, 1980).

In all of these cases we see students who have used the human ability to imitate, and to use new language, in order to learn a form of knowledge which has allowed them to pass tests on the formal apparatus of mathematics and physics, without acquiring the 'assembled' experiential metaphors that would give meaning to this work.

In our view, a strong instructional program operates both at the formal level[4] (i.e. with algorithms, definitions, notations, etc.), and also at the *experiential* level, taking pains to make contact with the student's existing representation structures, and helping the student to build, revise and extend these structures by the process of 'assembly' (including the process of 'educating your intuition'). The 'disaster studies' reveal that present-day programs often fail to achieve this; instead, they develop the formalisms, but neglect the building of powerful representations, created on an experiential foundation.

The 1950s Paradigm

A few decades ago — roughly, in the 1950s — the usual research paradigm in mathematics education was to compare two 'treatments' — perhaps two different algorithms for subtraction, or two different instructional strategies — and to see which seemed more successful. 'Success' was typically determined by the use of a multiple-choice test.

This paradigm led to very little real progress. Why not? Many answers can be given; we cite seven weaknesses of this '1950s paradigm':

(1) The important question of *how to design effective learning experiences* was usually neglected. It was as if we were to use elaborate psychometrics to determine whether people preferred Beethoven or Clementi, without showing any interest in the rules of harmony, counterpoint, orchestration and composition that distinguished Clementi from Beethoven.

(2) The multiple-choice tests did not reveal what the students had actually learned. (Cf., e.g., the 'disaster studies'. Krutetskii (1976) deals with this matter at some length.)

(3) In fact, one *cannot* compare, say, 'discovery teaching' with 'non-discovery teaching'. You could prove that it is impossible to play the violin, by observing my efforts to play the violin. This is not, however, a fair test, because I cannot play the violin. But other people can. Similarly, one can only compare *some specific attempts to do 'discovery' teaching,* vs. *some specific attempts to do 'non-discovery' teaching.* One or both may be done very well, or moderately well, or badly, or even very badly. Hence the outcome *cannot* be said to compare the results that *other* attempts might have obtained. One has NOT compared 'discovery' and 'non-discovery' teaching *in general. But that is the way the results are invariably interpreted.*

(4) By omitting a concern for actual thought processes, the 1950s paradigm omitted the essential characteristic of mathematical 'knowledge' — a good mathematician is good at thinking about certain kinds of problems in certain ways.

(5) Further, by omitting the postulation of a *theory* (or *conceptualization*) of human information processing, the 1950s paradigm attempted what has never really succeeded: an empirical science without a postulated conceptual foundation.

(6) Studies in the traditional paradigm were typically of very short duration, perhaps only two weeks long. Important developments in a person's mathematical knowledge usually take far longer. (But, unfortunately, certain superficial developments can occur very quickly.) By contrast, the studies on which this book is based involved following the same students for five consecutive years, and sometimes longer.

(7) The 1950s paradigm did not address deeper issues, such as the desirability of teaching arithmetic, algebra and geometry simultaneously in grades 1 through 6, or the creation of an alternative geometry course such as Papert's 'turtle geometry', or the use of an instructional program with a well-designed experiential developmental sequence paralleling the development of abstract formalisms.

Reasons For Optimism Today

Although mathematical instruction around the world is often unsatisfactory in many ways, at present there are reasons for cautious optimism, including:

(1) The 'alternative paradigm', with its emphasis on task-based interviews and on a postulated theory, is already demonstrating a great regularity and orderliness in human mathematical behavior. One need not settle for a student's choice in a multiple-choice test, but can go quite far down the road of identifying the analysis which led the student to make that choice. Indeed, one can even go quite far towards determining why the student carried out that particular analysis, and not some other.

(2) The 'disaster studies' are showing, with valuable precision, how students are often surviving abstract coursework (and passing the attendant tests), without an adequate problem-representation

capability, or adequate heuristics – without developing an intuitive 'gut feeling' for the subject. This should point towards improvement in overly-abstract, overly-formalistic curricula.

(3) Our understanding of human thought processes has never really been data-poor. We observe countless instances every day. The big problem is that our attempts to think about thinking have been *metaphor-poor*. The process of 'assembly' – of building up new ideas by using pieces of previously-built ideas – is just as essential in thinking about thinking as it is in thinking about mathematical questions. But in thinking about thinking we have lacked appropriate metaphors. Freud looked towards fluid flow – hardly suitable in the long run. Kurt Lewin looked towards topology and vector analysis, a shrewd choice in many ways, but also unsuitable for substantial progress. Nowadays far better metaphors are becoming available, primarily from the field of artificial intelligence. This is unsurprising; workers in AI are trying to program computers to learn from experience, to play winning chess, to interpret photographs, to control robots, to perform symbolic manipulations in mathematics, to translate from one language to another and even to understand natural language and human speech. These are tasks that resemble mathematics far more closely than fluid flow does.

(4) Over the past several decades some excellent methods for improving the teaching and learning of mathematics have been developed, by Moore (cf., e.g., Lucille Whyburn, 'Student Oriented Teaching – The Moore Method', *Amer. Math. Monthly* (1970)), Polya (1954, 1957, 1965), Page (1964), Papert (1980), Walter (1970) and others.[5]

(5) The past ten or twelve years have seen the emergence of significant *international* co-operation in mathematics education, as in the case of ICME-IV at Berkeley, California, and the European BACOMET group under the direction of Otte (Germany), Christiansen (Denmark) and Howson (UK). This is important because within a single nation mathematics education has usually been too small a venture to achieve critical mass, and also because new points of view have been contributed by different countries (cf., e.g., Davis, Romberg, Rachlin and Kantowski, 1979).

(6) A troublesome question has been where to locate mathematics education within the departmental structure of universities. Some progress is being made towards solving this problem, and at a number of universities top-level administrators are aware of the need, thanks partly to efforts by the National Academy of Science and

the National Academy of Engineering, and to professional groups such as the Illinois Council of Teachers of Mathematics. The SESAME group at UC Berkeley, and the Division for Study and Research in Education at MIT have suggested new possibilities, but these excellent institutions are regrettably unstable.

(7) Within the National Science Foundation, the National Institute of Education, and the US Department of Education there has been intelligent support and excellent judgement. This support has been drastically reduced in recent years, and many enlightened scientist-administrators have left government service, but something still remains, and a process of rebuilding may soon begin, as awareness of our national need becomes more widespread.

This all adds up to some justification for cautious optimism — and some very compelling reasons for energetic activity as soon as possible.

Notes

1. There exist nowadays some computer programs that can, in a limited sense, 'read' ordinary English sentences and paragraphs, at least within restricted domains of knowledge. Virtually all of these begin by 'translating' from natural language into some representation that represents *concepts* and not *words*. See, for example, De Jong (1979).

2. Judah Schwartz, of MIT, has proposed this problem: 'If a hen and a half can lay an egg and a half in a day and a half, how many eggs does one hen lay in one day?'

Think about it. (Schwartz does, in fact, have a simple conceptual scheme for dealing with such problems.)

3. An interesting problem in the 'parcel shipping' context is the following. A shipping service will accept parcels whose longest dimension does not exceed 1 meter. You want to ship a very thin, rigid steel tube 1.6 meters long, which must not be bent. You *can* do it. How?

4. Note that we do NOT mean 'formal level' in the sense of Piaget. Rather, we mean 'formal' in the sense of being able to use the mathematical formalisms of vector analysis, solution of differential equations, etc. — while perhaps still not knowing 'intuitively' (that is, *experientially*) what kinds of motions to expect an object to display (as in the work of di Sessa and of the Johns Hopkins group (McCloskey, *et al.*, 1980)).

5. A more complete list should also include at least these names: John Trivett, Edith Biggs, Beryl S. Cochran, Layman Allen, Leonard Sealey, Caleb Gattegno, Katherine Pedersen, William Johntz, Gertrude Hendrix, Emily Richards, Donald Cohen, Lauren Woodby, Gerald Glynn, Sharon Dugdale, Bonnie Anderson Seiler, Katie Reynolds Hannibal, Katharyn Kharas, Elizabeth Herbert and Sue Monell. Their work has often been presented at NCTM (the National Council of Teachers of Mathematics) meetings, and in teacher-education workshops, but has been inadequately recorded in professional journals, and insufficiently analyzed. See, however, Hayden (1982) and Howson *et al.* (1981).

BIBLIOGRAPHY

Abelson, Harold and di Sessa, Andrea (1981) *Turtle Geometry* (MIT Press, Cambridge, Mass.)

Alderman, Donald L., Swinton, Spencer, S. and Braswell, James S. (1979) 'Assessing Basic Arithmetic Skills and Understanding Across Curricula: Computer-Assisted Instruction and Compensatory Education', *Journal of Children's Mathematical Behavior*, vol. 2, no. 2 (Spring), pp. 3-28

Anderson, John R. and Bower, Gordon H. (1980) *Human Associative Memory: A Brief Edition* (Lawrence Erlbaum Associates, Hillsdale, NJ)

Anderson, Richard D., Garon, Jack W. and Gremillion, Joseph G. (1973) *School Mathematics Geometry* (Houghton Mifflin, Boston, Mass.)

Andert, Kay, Davis, Robert B., Kumar, Derek and McKnight, Curtis C. (1981) 'Assessing Student knowledge by Task-Based Interviews and Other Methods' (unpublished research report, Curriculum Laboratory, University of Illinois, Urbana, Ill.)

Arpaia, Pasquale J. (1974) 'Discoveries in Mathematics: How Are They Made?', *Mathematics Teacher*, vol. 67, no. 5 (May), pp. 447-9

Baars, Bernard J. and Kramer, Diane N. (1982) 'Conscious and Unconscious Components of Intentional Control' (paper presented at the Fourth Annual Conference of the Cognitive Science Society, Ann Arbor, Michigan, 4-6 August)

Baker, C.L. and McCarthy, J.J. (1981) *The Logical Problem of Language Acquisition* (MIT Press, Cambridge, Mass.)

Battista, Michael, T. (1982) 'Formal Axiomatic Systems and Computer-Generated Theorems', *Mathematics Teacher*, vol. 75, no. 3 (March), pp. 215-20, 252

Berwick, R.C. (1977) 'Learning Structural Descriptions of Grammar Rules from Examples', *Proc. of the 5th International Joint Conference on Artificial Intelligence* (The Artificial Intelligence Laboratory Publications Dept, Cambridge, Mass.)

Block, Ned (ed.) (1981) *Imagery* (MIT Press, Cambridge, Mass.)

Bobrow, Daniel G. and Collins, Allan (eds.) (1975) *Representation and Understanding* (Academic Press, New York, NY)

Boule, Pierre (1975) *The Test* (Vanguard Press, New York, NY)

Boylls, C.C. (1976) 'A Theory of Cerebellar Function with Applications to Locomotion. II. The Relation of Anterior Lobe Climbing Fiber Function to Locomotor Behavior in the Cat' in COINS Technical Report 76-1, Department of Computer and Information Sciences, University of Massachusetts, Amherst, Mass.

— (1982) 'Internal Directional Reference Frames for Motor Coordination', *Proceedings of the Fourth Annual Conference of the Cognitive Science Society*, pp. 22-3

Bransford, John D. and Johnson, Marcia K. (1972) 'Contextual Prerequisites for Understanding: Some Investigations of Comprehension and Recall', *Journal of Verbal Learning and Verbal Behavior*, vol. 11, pp. 717-26

Braunfeld, Peter and Deskins, W.E. (eds.) (1975) *The Teaching of Algebra at the Pre-College Level* (CEMREL, St Louis, Mo.)

Brearley, Molly and Hitchfield, Elizabeth (1969) *A Guide to Reading Piaget* (Schocken Books, New York, NY)

Brewer, William F. (1982) 'Personal Memory, Generic Memory, and Skill: A Re-Analysis of the Episodic-Semantic Distinction', *Proceedings of the Fourth Annual Conference of the Cognitive Science Society*, pp. 112-13

Britton, Bruce K. and Tesser, Abraham (in press) 'Effects of Prior Knowledge on Use of Cognitive Capacity in Three Complex Cognitive Tasks'

Brown, John Seely and Burton, Richard R. (1978) 'Diagnostic Models for Procedural Bugs in Basic Mathematical Skills', *Cognitive Science*, vol. 2, no. 2 (April-June), pp. 155-92

Brown, John Seely and Van Lehn, Kurt (1980) 'Repair Theory: A Generative Theory of "Bugs"' (unpublished research report) (Xerox Palo Alto Science Center, Palo Alto, Calif.)

Bulkeley, William M. (1982) 'First Intelligent Mobile Robots Soon May Serve as Plant Sentries', *Wall Street Journal* (Monday, August 16), p. 15

Bundy, Alan and Welham, Bob (1981) 'Using Meta-level Inference for Selective Application of Multiple Rewrite Rule Sets in Algebraic Manipulation', *Artificial Intelligence*, vol. 16, no. 2 (May), pp. 189-211

Cambridge Conference on School Mathematics (1963) *Goals for School Mathematics* (Houghton Mifflin, Boston, Mass.)

Cambridge Conference on Teacher Training (1967) *Goals for Mathematical Education of Elementary School Teachers* (Houghton Mifflin, Boston, Mass.)

Charniak, Eugene (1981) 'A Common Representation for Problem-Solving and Language-Comprehension Information', *Artificial Intelligence*, vol. 16, no. 3 (July), pp. 225-55

Clement, John (1982) 'Analogical Reasoning Patterns in Expert Problem Solving', *Proceedings of the Fourth Annual Conference of the Cognitive Science Society*, pp. 79-81

Clement, John, Lochhead, Jack and Monk, George S. (1981) 'Translation Difficulties in Learning Mathematics', *American Mathematical Monthly*, vol. 88, no. 4 (April), pp. 286-90

Cochran, Beryl, Barson, Alan and Davis, Robert B. (1970) 'Child-Created Mathematics', *Arithmetic Teacher*, vol. 17, no. 3 (March), pp. 211-15

Collins, A.M. and Quillian, M.R. (1969) 'Retrieval Time from Semantic Memory', *Journal of Verbal Learning and Verbal Behavior*, vol. 8, pp. 240-7

— (1972) 'Experiments on Semantic Memory and Language Comprehension' in Gregg, L.W. (ed.), *Cognition in Learning and Memory* (Wiley, New York, NY)

Conant, James, B. (1950) *The Overthrow of the Phlogiston Theory: The Chemical Revolution of 1775-1789* ('Harvard Case Histories in Experimental Science', Harvard University, Cambridge, Mass.)

Conference Board of the Mathematical Sciences. National Advisory Committee on Mathematical Education (1975) *Overview and Analysis of School Mathematics, Grades K-12* (Conference Board of the Mathematical Sciences, Washington, DC)

Cremin, Lawrence (1961) *The Transformation of the School* (Vintage Books, New York, NY)

Davis, Robert B. (1967a) 'Mathematics Teaching – With Special Reference to Epistemological Problems', Monograph No. 1, *Journal of Research and Development in Education* (Fall)

— (1967b) *Explorations in Mathematics. A Text for Teachers* (Addison-Wesley, Palo Alto, Calif.)

— (1971/2) 'The Structure of Mathematics and the Structure of Cognitive Development', *Journal of Children's Mathematical Behavior*, vol. 1, no. 1 (Winter), pp. 71-99

— (1976a) 'An Economically-Feasible Approach to Mathematics for Gifted Children', *Journal of Children's Mathematical Behavior*, Supplement Number 1 (Summer), pp. 103-58

— (1976b) 'Mathematics for Gifted Children – the Ninth-Grade Program', *Journal of Children's Mathematical Behavior*, Supplement No. 1 (Summer), pp. 176-215

— (1980a) *Discovery in Mathematics: A Text for Teachers* (Cuisenaire Company of America, New Rochelle, NY)

— (1980b) 'The Postulation of Certain Specific, Explicit, Commonly-Shared Frames', *Journal of Mathematical Behavior*, vol. 3, no. 1 (Autumn), pp. 167-201

— (1982) 'Complex Mathematical Cognition' in Ginsburg, Herbert P. (ed.), *The Development of Mathematical Thinking* (Academic Press, New York, NY), pp. 253-90

Davis, Robert B. and Greenstein, Rhonda (1969) 'Jennifer', *New York State Mathematics Teachers Journal*, vol. 19, pp. 94-103. Reprinted in Crosswhite, F. Joe, Higgins, Jon, Osborne, Alan and Shumway, Richard (eds.) (1973), *Teaching Mathematics: Psychological Foundations* (Charles A. Jones Publishing Company, Worthington, Ohio), pp. 74-82

Davis, Robert B. and Douglas, Jodie (1976) 'Environment, Habit, Self-Concept, and Approach Pathology', *Journal of Children's Mathematical Behavior*, Supplement No. 1 (Summer), pp. 229-65

Davis, Robert B., Jockusch, Elizabeth and McKnight, Curtis C. (1978) 'Cognitive Processes in Algebra', *Journal of Children's Mathematical Behavior*, vol. 2, no. 1 (Spring), pp. 10-320

Davis, Robert B. and McKnight, Curtis C. (1979) 'Modeling the Processes of Mathematical Thinking', *Journal of Children's Mathematical Behavior*, vol. 2, no. 2 (Spring), pp. 91-113
(1980) 'The Influence of Semantic Content on Algorithmic Behavior', *Journal of Mathematical Behavior*, vol. 3, no. 1 (Autumn), pp. 39-87

Davis, Robert B., McKnight, Curtis C., Parker, Philip and Elrick, Douglas (1979) 'Analysis of Student Answers to Signed Number Arithmetic Problems', *Journal of Children's Mathematical Behavior*, vol. 2, no. 2 (Spring), pp. 114-30

Davis, Robert B., Romberg, Thomas A., Rachlin, Sidney and Kantowski, Mary Grace (1979) *An Analysis of Mathematics Education in the Union of Soviet Socialist Republics* (ERIC Clearinghouse for Science, Mathematics, and Environmental Education, Ohio State University, Columbus, Ohio)

Davis, Robert B., Young, Stephen and McLoughlin, Patrick (1982) *The Role of 'Understanding' in Mathematical Thinking* (final report NSF SED 79-12740, University of Illinois, Urbana, Ill.)

de Groot, Adriaan D. (1975) 'Perception and Memory vs. Thought: Some Old Ideas and Recent Findings' in Kleinmuntz, Benjamin (ed.), *Problem Solving: Research, Method, and Theory* (Robert Krieger, Huntington, NY)

de Heinzelin, Jean (1962) 'Ishango', *Scientific American* (June), pp. 105-16

De Jong, Gerald (1979) 'Prediction and Substantiation: A New Approach to Natural Language Processing', *Cognitive Science*, vol. 3, no. 3 (July-September), pp. 251-73

DeVault, M. Vere (1981) 'Computers' in Fennema, Elizabeth (ed.), *Mathematics Education Research: Implications for the 80's* (Association for Supervision and Curriculum Development, Alexandria, Va.), pp. 131-49

Dickens, Charles (1931) *Hard Times* (J.M. Dent and Sons, London)

Dilworth, Robert P. (1973) 'The Changing Face of Mathematics Education' (Final report of the Specialized Teacher Project, 1971-72, California State Department of Education, Sacramento, California)

di Sessa, Andrea A. (1982) 'Unlearning Aristotelian Physics: A Study of Knowledge-Based Learning', *Cognitive Science*, vol. 6, no. 1 (January-March), pp. 37-75

Ebbinghaus, H. (1964) *Memory* (Dover, New York, NY)

Elcock, E.W. (1977) 'Representation of Knowledge in a Geometry Machine' in Elcock, E.W. and Michie, Donald (eds.), *Machine Intelligence 8* (John Wiley & Sons, New York, NY), pp. 11-29

Erlwanger, Stanley H. (1973) 'Benny's Conception of Rules and Answers in IPI Mathematics', *Journal of Children's Mathematical Behavior*, vol. 1, no. 2 (Autumn) pp. 7-26

— (1976) 'Case Studies of Children's Conceptions of Mathematics' (unpublished PhD thesis, University of Illinois, Urbana, Ill.)

Ernest, John (1976) 'Mathematics and Sex', *American Mathematical Monthly*, vol. 82, no. 8 (October), pp. 595-614

Fahlman, S.E. (1979) *NETL: A System for Representing Real-World Knowledge* (MIT Press, Cambridge, Mass.)

Feigenbaum, Edward A. (1963) 'The Simulation of Verbal Learning Behavior' in Feigenbaum, Edward A. and Feldman, Julian (eds.), *Computers and Thought* (McGraw-Hill, New York, NY)

Friend, Jamesine E. (1979) 'Column Addition Skills', *Journal of Children's Mathematical Behavior*, vol. 2, no. 2 (Spring), pp. 29-57

Geertz, Clifford (1980) 'Blurred Genres: The Refiguration of Social Thought', *American Scholar*, vol. 49, no. 2 (Spring), pp. 165-79

Gentner, Dedre (1980a) 'Metaphor as Structure-mapping' (paper presented at the meeting of the American Psychological Association, Montreal, Canada)

— (1980b) 'The Structure of Analogical Models in Science', *BBN Report No. 4451* (Bolt, Beranek, and Newman, Inc., Cambridge, Mass.)

— (1982) 'Structure-Mapping: A Theoretical Framework for Analogy and Similarity', *Proceedings of the Fourth Annual Conference of the Cognitive Science Society*, pp. 181-4

Ginsburg, Herbert (1977) *Children's Arithmetic: The Learning Process* (Van Nostrand, New York, NY)

Goldberg, Julius G. (1978) 'Psychology Research into Mathematics Learning and Teaching in the USSR and Eastern Europe' in Swetz, F.J. (ed.), *Socialist Mathematics Education* (Burgundy Press, Southampton, Pa.)

Golding, William (1955) *Lord of the Flies* (Capricorn Books, New York, NY)

Golomb, Solomon W. (1965) *Polyominoes* (Scribner's, New York, NY)

Greene, Peter H. (1982) 'Why Is It Easy to Control Your Arms?' (paper presented at the Fourth Annual Conference of the Cognitive Science Society, Ann Arbor Michigan, 4-6 August)

Greeno, J.G. (1980) 'Psychology of Learning, 1960-1980: One Participant's Observation', *American Psychologist*, vol. 35, no. 8, pp. 713-28

Groen, G.J. and Parkman, J.M. (1972) 'A Chronometric Analysis of Simple Addition', *Psychological Review*, vol. 79, pp. 329-43

Groen, G.J. and Poll, M. (1973) 'Subtraction and the Solution of Open-Sentence Problems', *Journal of Experimental Child Psychology*, vol. 16, pp. 292-302

Groen, Guy and Resnick, Lauren B. (1977) 'Can Preschool Children Invent Addition Algorithms?', *Journal of Educational Psychology*, vol. 69, pp. 645-52

Halmos, P.R. (1975) 'The Teaching of Problem Solving', *American Mathematical Monthly*, vol. 82, no. 5 (May), pp. 466-70

Hammond, Allen L. (1980) 'Mathematics — Our Invisible Culture' in Steen, Lynn Arthur (ed.), *Mathematics Today* (Vintage Books, New York, NY)

Hannibal, Katie Reynolds (1976) 'Observer Report on the Madison Project's Seventh Grade Class', *Journal of Children's Mathematical Behavior*, Supplement No. 1 (Summer), pp. 159-75

Hawkins, David (1966) 'Learning the Unteachable' in Shulman, Lee S. and Keislar, Evan R. (eds.), *Learning by Discovery: A Critical Appraisal* (Rand McNally, Chicago, Ill.), pp. 3-12

Hayden, Robert W. (1981) 'A History of the "New Math" Movement in the United States' (unpublished PhD thesis, Iowa State University, Ames, Iowa)

Herndon, James (1965) *The Way It Spozed To Be* (Bantam Books, New York, NY)

— (1971) *How to Survive in Your Native Land* (Simon and Schuster, New York, NY)

Hinsley, Dan, Hayes, John and Simon, Herbert (1977) 'From Words to Equations: Meaning and Representation in Algebra Word Problems' in Just, Marcel and Carpenter, Patricia (eds.), *Cognitive Processes in Comprehension* (Lawrence Erlbaum Associates, Hillsdale, NJ), pp. 89-106

Hinton, Geoffrey (1979) 'Some Demonstrations of the Effects of Structural Descriptions in Mental Imagery', *Cognitive Science*, vol. 3, no. 3 (July-September), pp. 231-50

Hofstadter, Douglas R. (1979) *Gödel, Escher, Bach: An Eternal Golden Braid* (Basic Books, New York, NY)

— (1982) ' "Default Assumptions" and Their Effects on Writing and Thinking', *Scientific American*, vol. 247, no. 5 (November), pp. 18-36

Holyoak, Keith J. (1982) 'Mental Representations', *Science*, vol. 217, no. 4557 (23 July), pp. 348-9

Hooper, Kristina (1981), 'Multiple Representations Within the Mathematical Domain' (unpublished research report, University of California at Santa Cruz)

— (1982) 'The Use of Computer Graphics in the Development of Mathematical Imagery' (paper presented at the Annual Meeting of the AERA, New York, NY, March)

Hopkins, Charles D. (1965) 'An Experiment on Use of Arithmetic Time in the Fifth Grade' (unpublished doctoral dissertation, School of Education, Indiana University, Terre Haute, Indiana, June)

Howson, Geoffrey, Keitel, Christine and Kilpatrick, Jeremy (1981) *Curriculum Development in Mathematics* (Cambridge University Press, Cambridge)

Johnson, Paul E. and Thompson, William B. (1981) 'Strolling Down the Garden Path: Detection and Recovery from Error in Expert Problem Solving' (unpublished research report, Psychology Department, University of Minnesota, Minneapolis, Minn.)

Kaput, James J. and Clement, John (1979) Letter to the Editor, *Journal of Children's Mathematical Behavior*, vol. 2, no. 2 (Spring), p. 208

Karplus, Robert, Pulos, Steven and Stage, Elizabeth K. (1980) 'Early Adolescents' Structure of Proportional Reasoning', *Proceedings of the Fourth International Conference for the Psychology of Mathematics Education* (Lawrence Hall of Science, University of California, Berkeley, Calif.), pp. 136-42

Keitel, Christine (1981) 'Educational Reforms in the USA — A Wasted Chance?' (University of Bielefeld, Bielefeld, Germany)

— (1982) 'Mathematics Education and Educational Research in the USA and USSR: Two Comparisons Compared', *Journal of Curriculum Studies*, vol. 14, no. 2, pp. 109-26

Kieran, C. (1980) 'The Interpretation of the Equal Sign: Symbol for an Equivalent Relation vs. an Operator Symbol', *Proceedings of the Fourth International Conference for the Psychology of Mathematics Education* (Lawrence Hall of Science, University of California, Berkeley, Calif.), pp. 163-9

Kieran, Tom, Nelson, Doyal and Smith, Grant (to appear) 'Graphical Algorithms in Partitioning Tasks'

Krutetskii, V.A. (1976) *The Psychology of Mathematical Abilities in School-children* (Kilpatrick, J. and Wirszup, I. (eds.), trans. by Joan Teller), (University of Chicago Press, Chicago, Ill.)

Kuhn, Thomas S. (1970) *The Structure of Scientific Revolutions* (2nd edn) (University of Chicago Press, Chicago, Ill.)

— (1977) *The Essential Tension: Selected Studies in Scientific Tradition and Change* (University of Chicago Press, Chicago, Ill.)

Lakoff, George (1982) 'Metaphor and the Construction of Reality', *Proceedings of the Fourth Annual Conference of the Cognitive Science Society*

Lakoff, George and Johnson, Mark (1980) 'The Metaphorical Structure of the Human Conceptual System', *Cognitive Science*, vol. 4, no. 2 (April-June), pp. 195-208

Larkin, Jill, McDermott, J., Simon, D. and Simon, H.A. (1980) 'Expert and Novice Performance in Solving Physics Problems', *Science*, vol. 208 (June), pp. 1335-42

Lave, Jean (1982) 'Arithmetic Procedures in Everyday Situations' (paper presented at the Fourth Annual Conference of the Cognitive Science Society, Ann Arbor, Michigan, 4-6 August)

Lave, Jean, Murtaugh, Michael and de la Rocha, Olivia (in press) 'Recounting the Whole Enchilada: The Dialectical Constitution of Arithmetic Practice' in Rogoff, B. and Lave, J. (eds.), *Everyday Cognition: Its Development in Social Context* (Harvard University Press, Cambridge, Mass.)

Lawler, Robert W. (1977) 'Order Free Adding', *LOGO Working Paper no. 59* (Artificial Intelligence Laboratory, MIT, Cambridge, Mass.)

— (1981) 'The Progressive Construction of Mind', *Cognitive Science*, vol. 5, no. 1, pp. 1-30

— (1982) 'Extending a Powerful Idea', *Journal of Mathematical Behavior*, vol. 3, no. 2 (Summer), pp. 81-98

Lindsay, Peter H. and Norman, Donald A. (1977) *Human Information Processing* (Academic Press, New York, NY)

Lochhead, Jack (1980) 'Faculty Interpretations of Simple Algebraic Statements: The Professor's Side of the Equation', *Journal of Mathematical Behavior*, vol. 3, no. 1 (Autumn), (1973), pp. 29-37

Lundberg, A. and Phillips, C.G. (1973) 'T. Graham Brown's Film on Locomotion in the Decerebrate Cat', *Journal of Physiology* (London), vol. 231, pp. 90-1

McCloskey, Michael, Caramazza, Alfonso and Green, Bert (1980) 'Curvilinear Motion in the Absence of External Forces. Naive Beliefs About the Motion of Objects', *Science*, vol. 210 (5 December), pp. 1139-41

McNeill, David (1982) 'Metaphoric Gestures', *Proceedings of the Fourth Annual Conference of the Cognitive Science Society*, pp. 18-19

Marshall, John C. (1982) 'Models of Reading and Writing: Evidence From Acquired Disorders of Visible Language' (paper presented at the Fourth Annual Conference of the Cognitive Science Society, Ann Arbor, Michigan, 4-6 August)

Marshall, John C. and Newcombe, Freda (1966) 'Syntactic and Semantic Errors in Paralexia', *Neuropsychologia*, vol. 4, pp. 169-76

Matz, Marilyn (1980) 'Towards a Computational Theory of Algebraic Competence', *Journal of Mathematical Behavior*, vol. 3, no. 1 (Autumn), pp. 93-166

Miller, George (1956) 'The Magic Number 7 ± 2', *Psychological Review*, vol. 63, pp. 81-97

Minsky, Marvin (1975) 'A Framework for Representing Knowledge' in Winston, P. (ed.), *The Psychology of Computer Vision* (McGraw-Hill, New York, NY)

— (1980) 'K-lines: A Theory of Memory', *Cognitive Science*, vol. 4, no. 2 (April-June), pp. 117-33

Newcombe, Freda and Marshall, John C. (1980) 'Transcoding and Lexical Stabilization in Deep Dyslexia' in Coltheart, Max, Patterson, Karalyn and Marshall, John C. (eds.), *Deep Dyslexia* (Routledge and Kegan Paul, London), pp. 176-88

Ortony, Andrew (1976) 'SAPIENS: Spreading Activation Processing of Information Enclosed in Associative Network Structures' (unpublished)

Page, David A. (1964) *Number Lines, Functions, and Fundamental Topics* (Macmillan, New York, NY)

Papert, Seymour (1980) *Mindstorms: Children, Computers, and Powerful Ideas* (Basic Books, New York, NY)

Papert, Seymour and Minsky, Marvin (1972) 'Artificial Intelligence Memo No. 252' (unpublished research report) (Artificial Intelligence Laboratory, MIT, Cambridge, Mass.)

Peuser, G. (1978) *Aphasie* (Wilhelm Fink Verlag, Munich)

Pimm, D. (1980) 'Metaphor and Analogy in Mathematics', *Proceedings of the Fourth International Conference for the Psychology of Mathematics Education* (Lawrence Hall of Science, University of California, Berkeley, Calif.), pp. 157-62

Pollack, Jordan and Waltz, David (1982) 'Natural Language Processing Using Spreading Activation and Lateral Inhibition', *Proceedings of the Fourth Annual Conference of the Cognitive Science Society*, pp. 50-3

Polya, George (1954) *Mathematics and Plausible Reasoning*. Vol. I: *Induction and Analogy in Mathematics*. Vol. II: *Patterns of Plausible Inference* (Princeton University Press, Princeton, NJ)

— (1957) *How to Solve It -- A New Aspect of Mathematical Method* (Doubleday Anchor, Garden City, NY)

— (1962/5) *Mathematical Discovery – On Understanding, Learning, and Teaching Problem Solving*, Vol. I (1962); Vol. II (1965) (Wiley, New York, NY)

Quinn, Naomi (1982) 'Metaphors for Marriage in Our Culture' (paper presented at the Fourth Annual Conference of the Cognitive Science Society, Ann Arbor, Michigan, 4-6 August)

Raphael, Bertram (1976) *The Thinking Computer: Mind Inside Matter* (W.H. Freeman, San Francisco, Calif.)

Resnick, L.B. (1976) 'Task Analysis in Instructional Design: Some Cases from Mathematics' in Klahr, David (ed.), *Cognition and Instruction* (Lawrence Erlbaum Associates, Hillsdale, NJ)

Rissland, Edwina L. (1978) 'The Structure of Mathematical Knowledge', *Technical Report No. 472* (Artificial Intelligence Laboratory, MIT, Cambridge Mass.)

— (1980) 'Example Generation', *Proceedings of the Third National Conference of the Canadian Society for Computational Studies of Intelligence* (Victoria, BC, May)

— (1981) 'Constrained Example Generation', *Technical Report 81-24* (Dept. of Computer and Information Science, University of Massachusetts, Amherst, Mass.)

Rosnick, Peter (1981) 'Some Misconceptions Concerning the Concept of Variable', *Mathematics Teacher*, vol. 74, no. 6 (September), pp. 418-50

Rosnick, Peter and Clement, John (1980) 'Learning Without Understanding: The Effect of Tutoring Strategies on Algebra Misconceptions', *Journal of Mathematical Behavior*, vol. 3, no. 1 (Autumn), pp. 3-27

Rumelhart, David E. and Ortony, Andrew (1977) 'The Representation of Knowledge in Memory' in Anderson, Richard C., Spiro, Rand and Montague, William (eds.), *Schooling and the Acquisition of Knowledge* (Lawrence Erlbaum Associates, Hillsdale, NJ)

Russell, Bertrand (1958) *The ABC of Relativity* (New American Library, New York, NY)

Saffran, E.M., Schwartz, M.F. and Marin, O.S.M. (1976) 'Semantic Mechanisms in Paralexia', *Brain and Language*, vol. 3, pp. 255-65

Schank, Roger C. (1975) 'The Structure of Episodes in Memory' in Bobrow, D.G. and Collins, Allen (eds.), *Representation and Understanding* (Academic Press, New York, NY)

— (1977) 'Representation and Understanding of Text' in Elcock, E.W. and Michie, Donald (eds.), *Machine Intelligence 8: Machine Representations of Knowledge* (John Wiley, New York, NY)

Schank, Roger C. and Kolodner, Janet (1979) 'Retrieving Information from an Episodic Memory, or Why Computers' Memories Should Be More Like People's', *Research Report No. 159* (Department of Computer Science, Yale University, New Haven, Conn.)

Schoenfeld, Alan H. (1978) 'Presenting a Strategy for Indefinite Integration', *American Mathematical Monthly*, vol. 85, no. 8 (October), pp. 673-8

— (1979) 'Explicit Heuristic Training as a Variable in Problem Solving Performance', *Journal of Research in Mathematics Education,* vol. 10, no. 3 (May), pp. 173-187

Selfridge, Mallory (1982) 'How Do Children Learn to Judge Grammaticality?', *Proceedings of the Fourth Annual Conference of the Cognitive Science Society*, pp. 27-9

Simon, Herbert A. (1979) *Models of Thought* (Yale University Press, New Haven, Conn.)

Smith, Stanley and Sherwood, Bruce Arne (1976) 'Educational Uses of the PLATO Computer System', *Science*, vol. 192, pp. 344-52

Stefik, Mark (1981a) 'Planning with Constraints (MOLGEN: Part 1)', *Artificial Intelligence*, vol. 16, no. 2 (May), pp. 111-39

— (1981b) 'Planning and Meta-Planning (MOLGEN: Part 2)', *Artificial Intelligence*, vol. 16, no. 2 (May), pp. 141-69

Stein, Sherman K. and Crabill, Calvin D. (1972) *Elementary Algebra – A Guided Inquiry* (Houghton Mifflin, Boston, Mass.)

Steiner, Hans-Georg (ed.) (1971) *The Teaching of Geometry at the Pre-College Level* (D. Reidel Publishing Company, Dordrecht, Holland)

Suppes, P. and Groen, G.J. (1967) 'Some Counting Models for First Grade Performances on Simple Addition Facts' in *Research in Mathematics Education* (National Council of Teachers of Mathematics, Washington, DC)

Sussman, Gerald (1982) 'Mechanistic Models of Semantic Memory: From NETL to the Connection Machine' (paper presented at the Fourth Annual Conference of the Cognitive Science Society, Ann Arbor, Michigan, 4-6 August)

Thomas, George B., Jr. and Finney, Ross L. (1979) *Calculus and Analytic Geometry* (5th edn) (Addison-Wesley, Reading, Mass.)

Thompson, Patrick W. (1982) 'Were Lions to Speak, We Wouldn't Understand', *Journal of Mathematical Behavior*, vol. 3, no. 2 (Summer), pp. 147-65

Time (1981) 'High-I.Q. Battle for the Gold', vol. 118, no. 4 (27 July), p. 67

Tulving, E. (1972) 'Episodic and Semantic Memory' in Tulving, E. and Donaldson, W. (eds.), *Organization of Memory* (Academic Press, New York, NY)

Turner, Joseph (1971) *Making New Schools*, (McKay, New York, NY)

Van Lehn, Kurt (1982) 'Bugs are Not Enough: Empirical Studies of Bugs, Impasses and Repairs in Procedural Skills', *Journal of Mathematical Behavior*, vol. 3, no. 2 (Summer), pp. 3-71

Walter, Marion I. (1970) *Boxes, Squares and Other Things (A Teacher's Guide for a Unit in Geometry)* (National Council of Teachers of Mathematics, Washington, DC)

— (1979) 'Frame Geometry. Problem Posing and Solving in Informal Geometry', *Oregon Mathematics Teacher* (September), pp 19-22

Whitney, Hassler (1981) 'Letting Research Come Naturally' (mimeographed, Institute for Advanced Study, Princeton, NJ)

Whyburn, Lucille S. (1970) 'Student Oriented Teaching – the Moore Method', *American Mathematical Monthly*, vol. 77, no. 4 (April), pp. 351-9

Winograd, Terry (1971) 'Procedures as a Representation for Data in a Computer Program for Understanding Natural Language' (unpublished PhD thesis, MIT, Cambridge, Mass.)

Winston, P.H. (ed.) (1975) *The Psychology of Computer Vision* (McGraw-Hill, New York, NY)

Woods, S.S., Resnick, L.B. and Groen, G.J. (1975) 'An Experimental Test of Five Process Models for Subtraction', *Journal of Educational Psychology*, vol. 67, pp. 17-21

Young, Stephen (1981a) 'Notes on Errors in Fractions, Addition, and Multiplication' (unpublished notes, Curriculum Laboratory, University of Illinois, Urbana, Ill.)

— (1981b) 'The Role of Fractions in Beginning Algebra' (unpublished research report, Curriculum Laboratory, University of Illinois, Urbana, Ill.)

— (1982) 'The Mental Representation of Geometrical Knowledge', *Journal of Mathematical Behavior*, vol. 3, no. 2 (Summer), pp. 123-44

INDEX

ABAMPAMP 83
abbreviated representations *see*
   representations
absence of experiential frames *see*
   frames
accommodation 65
ACT theory 109, 132n1
activation *see* memory, spreading
   activation models
adding 16-17
'adding numbers of unlike sign' 201
addition 113-14; arithmetic addition
   vs. algebraic addition 165-70
Alderman, Donald L. 370
Alex 154-6
algorithm for addition 9
'All elephants are gray.' 209-10
Allen, Layman 311, 345n5, 375n5
alternate paradigm 87-96, 357, 372
alternatives to statements 358; *see
   also* Exemplar/Judgement Hypothesis
analysis of student answers 91
Anderson, J.R. 109
Anderson's Law of Non-deletion 109,
   112, 125
Andert, Kay 96n4
appropriateness *see* judging appropriateness of retrieval and instantiation
Archimedean postulate 63
Archimedes 2-3
Aristotelian dynamics 350-4
Arithmetic Project 345n5; *see also*
   Page, David
arithmetical performance in everyday
   settings 159-60
art *see* young children's art
artificial intelligence 28
assembly 154-179, 358; *see also* pre-
   mathematical frames, representations
assimilation 65
assimilation paradigms 103, 304, 313,
   356-7, 363; *see also* assembly,
   assimilation schemas, chunks,
   frames, metaphors, representations
assimilation schemas 125; *see also*
   assembly, assimilation paradigms,

chunks, frames, metaphors, representations, schemas
associations 40-3

'back to basics' vii
BACOMET 373
Battista, Michael 293, 294-6
Benny 97-9, 133n6
Bers, Lipman 340, 344n2
big ideas 339
Biggs, Edith 375n5
binary reversions 100-4, 317
Bobrow, Daniel G. 193
Booker T. Washington Elementary
   School vii, 95n2
bottom-up processing *see* top-down
   vs. bottom-up processing
Boylls, C.C. 153n1
brain damage 194-8
brain lesions *see* brain damage
branching 41; *see also* control
Braunfeld, Pater 355n1
Brewer, William 79, 82, 360-1
Brown, Graham 152n1
Brown, John Seely viii, 43, 104, 109,
   364-5
Brown-Matz-Van Lehn Law 109-10,
   318
bugs 43-4
building representations *see* representations
Burton, Richard R. 365

Cambridge Conference on School
   Mathematics 355n1
Cantor, Nathaniel ix
cats, high decerebrate 152n1
cello fingerings 264-70
CEMREL 345n5, 355n1
'changing horses in mid-stream' 335-7
characteristics of frames *see* frames
Charniak, Eugene 133n8
Christiansen, Bent 373
chunks 41, 78, 154, 356-7; *see also*
   assembly, assimilation paradigms,
   defective frames, frame retrieval
   errors, frames, instantiation of
   frame variables, memory, metaphors, reliance on instantiated